FREE JOAN LITTLE

Justice, Power, and Politics

Coeditors

Heather Ann Thompson
Rhonda Y. Williams

Editorial Advisory Board

Peniel E. Joseph
Daryl Maeda
Barbara Ransby
Vicki L. Ruiz
Marc Stein

The Justice, Power, and Politics series publishes new works in history that explore the myriad struggles for justice, battles for power, and shifts in politics that have shaped the United States over time. Through the lenses of justice, power, and politics, the series seeks to broaden scholarly debates about America's past as well as to inform public discussions about its future.

More information on the series, including a complete list of books published, is available at http://justicepowerandpolitics.com/.

FREE JOAN LITTLE

THE POLITICS OF RACE,
SEXUAL VIOLENCE,
AND IMPRISONMENT

Christina Greene

The University of North Carolina Press

Chapel Hill

*This book was published with the assistance of the
Z. Smith Reynolds Fund of the University of North Carolina Press.*

© 2022 The University of North Carolina Press

All rights reserved

Set in Scala, Burnaby Stencil, and News Gothic
by codeMantra

Manufactured in the United States of America

Cover silhouette inspired by an image in *Triple Jeopardy*,
the newspaper of the Third World Women's Alliance.

Author's note on language: Throughout this book, I have kept self-naming terms such as "negro" or "colored" that were used at the time by African Americans. The N-word, in its entirety, also appears a few times when quoting creative works by Black writers and when referencing or quoting hateful language used by some white people against African Americans in order to demean them. While encountering these words is difficult, I feel it's important not to silence the writers or to erase the anti-Black language in the historical record, so I have quoted them verbatim.

LIBRARY OF CONGRESS CATALOGING-IN-PUBLICATION DATA
Names: Greene, Christina, 1951– author.
Title: Free Joan Little : the politics of race, sexual violence,
and imprisonment / Christina Greene.
Other titles: Justice, power, and politics.
Description: Chapel Hill : The University of North Carolina Press, [2022] |
Series: Justice, power, and politics | Includes bibliographical references and index.
Identifiers: LCCN 2022022448 | ISBN 9781469671307 (cloth) |
ISBN 9781469671314 (paperback) | ISBN 9781469671321 (ebook)
Subjects: LCSH: Little, Joan—Trials, litigation, etc. | Trials (Murder)—
North Carolina. | Justifiable homicide—North Carolina. | Sexual
abuse victims—North Carolina. | African American women—Legal
status, laws, etc. | Prisoners—Civil rights—North Carolina. | Anti-rape
movement—United States. | African American feminists—History.
Classification: LCC KF224.L52 G74 2022 | DDC 345.73/02523—dc23/eng/20220801
LC record available at https://lccn.loc.gov/2022022448

For

BONNIE JOHNSON

dear friend and

participant-historian in the

1970s Black Women's Retreat

CONTENTS

List of Illustrations x

Introduction: They Had No Plans to Capture Her, but to Kill Her 1

PART I   Jim Crow Justice and the Civil Rights Trial of the 1970s

   1   She Won't No Joan of Arc: Hardscrabble
Life in Eastern North Carolina 9

   2   We Had an Instinctive Love for the Negro Race:
Liberals, Conservatives, and the Politics of Crime 23

   3   Power to the Ice Pick: Building a Defense,
Mounting a Campaign 32

   4   Joanne Is You . . . Joanne Is Me! Everywoman and
the Construction of Black Womanhood 44

   5   Joanne Little Acted for Us All: Black Power,
Gender, and the Defense of "Sister Joan" 53

   6   Joan Little Is Like Rosa Parks! The Trial
Testimony of Joan Little 63

PART II   **This Army of the Wronged: Forgotten Women and Prison Organizing in the Civil Rights–Black Power Era**

7   Child, Why Are They Bringing You to Trial? The Prison Movement and the Joan Little Case   *79*

8   The Police Would Follow Our Van as We Picked Up Kids: Black Power, State Repression, and Carceral Politics   *89*

9   Slaves of the State: The Sisters Behind the Brothers and the North Carolina Prisoners' Labor Union   *96*

10   There Must Not Be Another Attica: Action for Forgotten Women and the Prisoner Strike at the North Carolina Correctional Center for Women   *107*

11   We Will Savor the Sweetness of Freedom: Prisoner Intellectuals and the Power of the Word   *123*

12   So Now I Take My Stand: The Prison Writings of Joan Little   *139*

PART III   **Who Will Revere the Black Woman? . . . To Whom Will She Cry Rape? Carceral Politics and Organizing Against Sexual Violence**

13   Bringing This to the Attention of the Nation and the Movement: Third World Women, Sexual Assault, and Lethal Self-Defense   *153*

14   The Kind of History That Really Does Get Lost: Black Feminism, Multi-issue Organizing, and the Whitewashing of Women's Liberation   *173*

15   That Space for Black Feminism to Grow and Flourish: The Washington, D.C., Rape Crisis Center   *183*

16   A Way to Free Themselves: Black Feminists and the National Black Women's Health Project   *193*

17 What Chou Mean *We*, White Girl? White Women, Antiracism, and Sexual Violence   207

18 The State Is in No Way Our Ally: Race, Sexual Violence, and the Dangers of Carceral Solutions   219

Epilogue: The 1994 Crime Bill and the Violence Against Women Act: Searching for Safety in the Carceral State   231

Postscript   245

Acknowledgments   249

Notes   253

Bibliography   309

Index   331

ILLUSTRATIONS

Figures

Joan Little *xiv*

Women protesters, Wake County Courthouse *37*

Protesters with signs, "Free Joanne Little" and "Justice for Joanne" *40*

Woman with flyer in "Free Joanne Little" and "Power to the Ice Pick" T-shirt *41*

Joan Little and attorney Jerry Paul *48*

Jerry Paul with reporters, Karen Galloway in rear *50*

Demonstrator with sign, "Defend Black Womanhood" *54*

March in support of Joan Little *61*

Joan Little and Karen Galloway *71*

Demonstrator with banner, "Stop Slave Labor in N.C. Prisons" *103*

Women protesters outside Raleigh Women's Prison fence *111*

Raleigh Women's Prison strikers in yard   113

Break de Chains of Legalized U.$. Slavery—cover   129

Prison guard sketch   131

Armed women sketch   136

Joan Little sketch   142

Yvonne Wanrow   157

Inez García and Joan Little Benefit   164

Black Women's Liberation   176

Nkenge Touré   185

Loretta Ross   186

Byllye Avery   194

Maps

Map of North Carolina   8

ABBREVIATIONS

AAWO	Alliance Against Women's Oppression
AFFW	Action for Forgotten Women
CWJ	Concerned Women for Justice
DOC	Department of Correction
HBCU	historically Black colleges and universities
LEAA	Law Enforcement Assistance Act / Law Enforcement Assistance Administration
NABF	National Alliance of Black Feminists
NBFO	National Black Feminist Organization
NBWHP	National Black Women's Health Project
NCCCW	North Carolina Correctional Center for Women (Women's Prison)
NCPLU	North Carolina Prisoners' Labor Union
NOI	Nation of Islam
NOW	National Organization for Women
RCC	rape crisis center
VAWA	Violence Against Women Act

FREE JOAN LITTLE

Joan Little, 1975.
Courtesy of the North Carolina State Archives
and the *Raleigh News and Observer*.

INTRODUCTION

They Had No Plans to Capture Her, but to Kill Her

In the early hours of August 27, 1974, prison officials found the jailer, Clarence Alligood, slumped on a bunk in the woman's section of the Beaufort County Jail in eastern North Carolina. His lifeless body bore eleven stab wounds, including seven in his chest and one that pierced his heart. Naked from the waist down, except for his brown socks, Alligood clutched his trousers in one hand; an ice pick dangled loosely from the other. A trail of dried semen trickled down his left thigh. His shoes were in the narrow hallway outside the jail cell; a negligee and bra hung on the cell door. The prisoner, Joan Little, was nowhere in sight. She was five feet three inches tall, twenty years old, poor, Black, and in trouble.[1] He was white, sixty-two years old, and, at 200 pounds, nearly twice her size. On these facts, both sides would agree.[2]

Those who believed Joan Little was guilty saw a "hardened criminal with the instincts of a black widow spider," a Jezebel who lured the unsuspecting Alligood into her cell with promises of sex.[3] In the moment of his climax, the wanton young woman ruthlessly stabbed and killed the poor, defenseless man. On the other side, feminists of all kinds, Black Power activists, prison abolitionists, Black working-class church ladies, and traditional civil rights leaders saw a victim of sexual violence and racism, a vulnerable Black woman who had valiantly defended herself against one of the age-old and unforgivable crimes of white supremacy. Although they would differ among themselves about whether sexism, racism, or poverty was most salient, her defenders all discerned a young woman, destitute, alone, and terrified at her predicament, who did what any trapped victim would do—defended herself and then fled in a panic.

Darting around hedges, hiding behind buildings, and eluding police in what Southern Christian Leadership Conference (SCLC) leader Golden Frinks called "the pattern of the old Underground Railroad," Little remained on the lam for less than a week. Officials invoked a Reconstruction-era fugitive law that allowed anyone to shoot and kill the young woman on sight. While in hiding she learned that Alligood was dead and knew her life was in danger, now more than ever. "If they had apprehended me, . . . then my side would never be told," Little recalled. "I didn't know about the fugitive law," she said. "All I knew was I had to get to somebody."4 With the assistance of local attorney Jerry Paul, some subterfuge involving a wig, mistaken identities, and a nerve-wracking trip in the dead of night, Little made her way to Chapel Hill about two hours away. Meanwhile, Paul had notified Durham activist Celine Chenier and other likely supporters in the Durham–Chapel Hill area, where a multiracial group of about a dozen women and men anxiously awaited Little's arrival.5

When Joan walked into Chenier's Durham apartment on September 2, 1974, the Black women rushed to greet her. Hugging and kissing the young fugitive, they were relieved to see her alive. "We knew that they were after her with rifles and guns, that they had no plans to capture her, but to kill her," Chenier recalled. "That first night I saw Joan Little as myself, as did most of the black women who were there." Joan's presence evoked "four hundred years of being raped by white men. . . . Joan Little is me, could be me, and I remember saying at the meeting that I would have done what Joan did," Chenier acknowledged. "We all felt that she had done what she had to do. She had defended herself! She had defended her womanhood!"6

Joan appeared overwhelmed by the affection and support. As the group, about half women, gently pressed her for details, she tried to answer their questions, often uttering only a word or two in response. But when she began to describe the struggle with Alligood over the ice pick, she broke down. Jerry Paul hurried her into to a back room so she could regain her composure, and they left soon afterward. From that gathering, the Free Joan Little campaign was born. The next day, Little, surrounded by her attorneys and supporters, turned herself in to authorities in Raleigh. It took no time for a Beaufort County grand jury to indict her for first-degree murder. If convicted, Joan would face a mandatory death sentence in North Carolina's gas chamber.7

The Free Joan Little campaign raised an enormous defense fund for the young defendant, attracted the support of a broad swath of activist groups, and generated widespread media attention, making the case a national and even international cause célèbre. Joan remained in the North Carolina Correctional Center for Women (NCCCW or "Women's Prison"), while her supporters raised the $115,000 bail and her lawyers secured a change of venue to Raleigh, which boasted its first Black mayor. The judge claimed he granted the request to move the trial to the state capital because the extensive publicity had made a fair trial in Beaufort County impossible. But Little's legal team also had conducted a survey of potential jurors in Beaufort County and surrounding counties that revealed entrenched white racial prejudice and a dearth of women and African Americans on juries. Halfway through the Raleigh murder trial, her attorneys' skills and the prosecution's lack of evidence led Judge Hamilton Hobgood to reduce the first-degree murder indictment to second-degree murder. After a five-week trial in August 1975, a majority-female jury, composed equally of Blacks and whites, found Joan Little not guilty.[8]

Joan Little's troubles, however, did not end with her acquittal on the murder charge. Several months later, she lost her appeal on the 1974 felony theft convictions that had landed her in the Beaufort County Jail in the first place. The triumphant defendant in the rape-murder trial returned to Women's Prison in Raleigh to serve a seven-to-ten-year and possible fourteen-to-twenty-year sentence. Media coverage of the rape-murder trial had made Joan Little easily the best-known inmate at NCCCW; and both Little and her supporters believed that her acquittal for killing a jailer made her highly vulnerable to harm, not only from the guards but also from some of the inmates. "I'm as good as dead in North Carolina," Little said. Good behavior earned her work-release privileges in a nearby dentist office. But the office reportedly received death threats, and despite positive reports from prison supervisors, altercations with fellow prisoners halted her work-release privileges. Denied parole several times, she was "depressed," "desperate," and sure she was being "railroaded." So, one day in October 1977, Joan scaled the ten-foot fence at Women's Prison and headed north. As Joan tells it, climbing the fence was fairly simple: a new male guard was "too busy" watching the "legs and hips" of the women inmates.[9]

Two months later, a former boyfriend tipped off the New York Police Department concerning Joan's whereabouts. A high-speed chase through the streets of Brooklyn by "New York's finest" ensued, and Joan and a male friend were apprehended. She was sent to Rikers Island, the city's notorious jail, to await a hearing on her extradition to North Carolina. At Rikers, she presumably met Black Liberation Army member Assata Shakur (Joanne Chesimard), who had written a public appeal in support of Little's 1974–75 murder case. According to Joan, the political prisoner helped her endure life behind bars, this time in a northern cell. Shakur would soon become one of America's best-known political fugitives after she managed her own escape from a federal prison and fled to Cuba, where she remains in exile to this day.[10]

Many of the supporters who had backed her during the 1974–75 Free Joan Little campaign rallied behind the young woman once again. Radical attorney William Kunstler, who had been ejected by the North Carolina judge during Little's murder trial, took up her extradition case. Rev. Herbert Daughtry, a Brooklyn, New York, pastor and founder of the National Black United Front who had had his own brushes with the law, reached out to Black activist ministers. Others launched a petition drive demanding that New York governor Hugh Carey deny the "brutal and unusual request" to return the young woman to North Carolina. Black feminist attorney Florence "Flo" Kennedy from the Coalition Against Racism and Sexism echoed Little's fears. In a friend-of-the-court brief, Kennedy argued that sending Little back to North Carolina would "expose her to irreparable and inconsionable [sic] injury." The National Council of Churches thought so too and urged Governor Carey to allow Joan to serve out her sentence in New York. But the governor remained unmoved by the appeals and protests. When a Brooklyn judge upheld Carey's extradition order, Kunstler was incensed: "To order Miss Little's extradition . . . was an act not only of sheer racism but of political cowardice as well," he said. A Queens, New York, minister compared the governor to Pontius Pilate. "Joan is being crucified," he said. Crying and screaming when she heard the news, Joan had to be carried out of the crowded courtroom by court officers. By June 1978, she was on her way to Women's Prison, handcuffed and shackled with waist chains for the trip back to North Carolina.[11]

Little received an additional six months to two years' prison time for the escape, was paroled in 1979, and was forced to leave the state. Forty years later, she recalled her hasty departure: without notice she was ferried out of Women's Prison in the middle of the night, put on a plane heading north, and ordered not to return to North Carolina. Over the next four decades, Little stayed out of the limelight and tried as best she could to rebuild her life.

The Joan Little case, a story of race, sexual violence, and criminal punishment in the South, a tale so hauntingly familiar it resonates across 400 years of American history. Before it was over, most whites in

North Carolina just wanted to be rid of the trial that had cast such a negative light on their state. It was after all, said one local white resident, "a case about nothing." They of course, were mistaken; for, as another observer remarked, "It was a case about everything in their history." But this was not simply a southern tale. It reverberated across the Mason-Dixon line with national implications that were every bit as important.[12]

As in most sexual assault and murder cases where there were no witnesses, we may never know the "truth" about what precisely happened between a white jailer and his Black female prisoner that August night in 1974. Yet Joan Little's guilt or innocence is less significant than the historical and political undertones of the case. Little never wanted to become a cause célèbre, although she was far more politically astute than either her advocates or critics acknowledged. She drew national attention because activists understood that her murder-rape trial reflected the complex cross-currents surrounding racial and sexual politics in the 1970s. Perhaps most important, the case was a commentary on the historic sexual abuse of Black women. That Joan was a woman in captivity evoked the bitter truth about slavery: an enslaved woman's body was never her own. But in the mid-1970s, it was also a case study of a woman's right to defend herself, even to kill her assailant, when threatened with sexual assault. The trial had other racial and sexual ramifications, as well, shining a spotlight on a criminal legal system that imprisoned disproportionate numbers of impoverished African Americans and that posed special dangers of sexual vulnerability for Black women. The Little case also drew attention to the narrow legal definition of rape and to the underrepresentation of women and Black men on juries; and it became a testimonial against the racially discriminatory use of the death penalty.[13]

For nearly a half century, the Joan Little rape-murder trial has continued to invite scholarly attention and inspire social justice activism. The case and Little herself have assumed iconic stature. However, the image of Joan Little as a symbol of the "after-life of slavery" or a timeless victim-survivor-warrior outside of history obscures critical aspects of her case. Competing discourses surrounding Black womanhood, respectability politics, and the contradictions that came with mounting a legal defense along with a political campaign designed to attract broad public support and save the life of a young Black woman all call for greater scrutiny. Just as Rosa Parks's life story has too often been reduced to a single-day on a Montgomery bus, treatments of Joan Little typically focus solely on her rape-murder trial, allowing her detractors to dismiss her as simply a lawless young woman. Even sympathetic activists and scholars have done little to challenge or complicate this view, although most also point to her limited opportunities shaped by racism and poverty as explanations for her run-ins with law enforcement. After all, Little confessed to the 1974 felony theft charges that landed her in the Beaufort County Jail and led to her fateful encounter with jailer Clarence Alligood. Her guilt, at least in the felony theft case, *seemingly* requires no further investigation. And yet there is much more to the story. By looking *backward* to Little's encounters with local police and the legal system in the years before her rape-murder trial, and *forward* to the years following the case, we may arrive at a fuller understanding of the politics of race, sexual violence, and incarceration in the 1960s, 1970s, and 1980s.

Finally, centering African American women in historical narratives about prison organizing and antirape activism in the 1970s and 1980s suggests a more expansive definition of political prisoners and political engagement. Black women's activism, including Black feminism, also calls for a more nuanced understanding of the various streams of women's liberation. Rooted in the long arc of African American women's protest traditions, Black women, from the 1960s to the 1980s, were a both *a part of* and *apart from* the more visible, women's liberation movements of those years. Far from the declension narrative that until recently has shaped most histories of "second wave" feminism—which frequently concentrated on white, middle-class women outside the South—or the popular notion that Black women remained absent from the women's antirape movement, African American women and other women of color found new outlets for their struggles against sexual violence. Similarly, accounts of prison organizing during these years have highlighted uprisings in men's prisons and the headline-grabbing news of radical Black men. Too often, incarcerated women have either been ignored or dismissed as largely apolitical and unorganized. Yet women too fought their own carceral battles on both sides of the prison walls; and they were also instrumental in providing assistance to men's prison protests.

This then is not a biography of Joan Little. Rather, it is an account of how the racial and gender politics of the 1970s and 1980s, collided with a young, Black woman in eastern North Carolina in the last quarter of the 20th century. In crafting a more inclusive history of this period that centers the experiences and organizing efforts of African American women in particular, we may find lessons for the ongoing struggles against racialized sexual violence and imprisonment in our own century.

PART ONE

JIM CROW JUSTICE AND THE CIVIL RIGHTS TRIAL OF THE 1970S

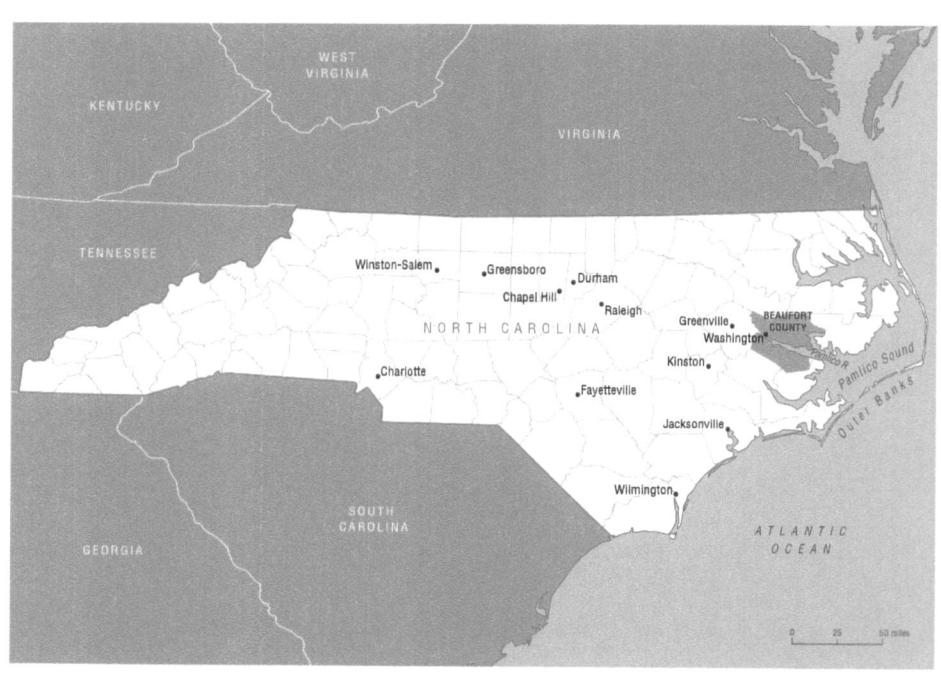

Map of North Carolina.
Produced by the University of Wisconsin Cartography Lab.

1

She Won't No Joan of Arc

Hardscrabble Life in Eastern North Carolina

Joan Little was born and raised in Beaufort County in eastern North Carolina. Shielded from the Atlantic Ocean by a thin strip of islands known as the Outer Banks, the county wraps around the Pamlico River, which in turn empties into the Pamlico Sound. Largely rural, poor, and with a long history of entrenched racism that belied the state's more progressive image, the area has often been compared to the Deep South.

Before it was the South, before its life was structured around the ongoing struggle between the descendants of enslaved Africans and their enslavers, it was other people's homeland. In 1550, prior to the arrival of Europeans, over thirty different Indigenous groups lived throughout present-day North Carolina, with an estimated population of over 100,000. By 1800 that number had dropped to about 20,000. The Algonkian- (or Algonquian-) speaking Indigenous peoples inhabited the coastal region of North Carolina, with the Secotan Confederation in the far eastern part and some areas south of the Pamlico River in present-day Beaufort County; the Pamouik Nation claimed the western part of the county. In 1712, the area was named after the British Duke of Beaufort, becoming Beaufort Precinct and renamed Beaufort County in 1729. By the 1790s, the county had nearly 5,500 whites and over 1,600 enslaved Africans but no recorded Indians.[1]

ittle's hometown of Washington, "Little Washington" as North Carolinians call it, is the county seat. Founded in 1776 at the base of the Pamlico River, it was reportedly the first town named after George Washington, and its port later became a part of the Underground Railroad. On the eve of the Civil War in 1860, the population of Little Washington numbered 1,600. Beaufort County recorded close to 14,700 inhabitants. The nearly 6,000 enslaved people comprised 40 percent of the county population; slightly over 700 were listed as "free colored," possibly Indians and/or mixed-race persons. When Union troops arrived in North Carolina in 1862, enslaved African Americans escaped to the eastern part of the state along the coast, including Beaufort County. The following year, armed Black residents and fugitives joined with the Union Army during the unsuccessful siege of Little Washington by the Confederates.[2]

Lumbering, commercial fishing, and shipbuilding once thrived in Beaufort County; but silt filled the river bottom, closing the docks in Little Washington and flattening the area's economic base until light manufacturing jobs came to the county in the mid-1960s. At that time, the region saw a huge Ku Klux Klan (KKK) revival, attracting thousands of new members and even larger crowds to mass rallies. Little Washington had its own Klavern; and nightriders terrorized Black activists in the northern part of the county, often in response to school desegregation efforts by the National Association for the Advancement of Colored People (NAACP). During the 1960s, the county lost 10 percent of its Black population while Little Washington lost 15 percent of its Black population as locals left for better opportunities elsewhere. By 1970, African Americans totaled 4,746, 52 percent of Little Washington's population of 8,960. "Some people stay in Washington," Joan Little remarked during a 1977 interview. "But most of my friends have gone. Young people don't hang around there nowadays. Only place they can work is the garment factory, Hamilton Beach or this yarn place, and they seldom hire a lot of young people. . . . there's no real jobs for them there." The town's African American population continued to shrink as poverty persisted.[3]

In the 1970s, a white journalist and attorney from Little Washington offered his own harsh assessment of the town: "a county seat with a past but no future. . . . Washington stagnated, its period of expansion and vitality at an end, its racially segregated neighborhoods standing side by side, separate and unequal, two towns within one." Jim Crow laws and customs had relegated most African Americans to "a jumbled collection of hutches and shanties." Although the civil rights movement brought some improvements, including the election of an African American city councilman, the town retained many of its old ways.[4]

When Joan Little's murder trial opened, news outlets from near and far brought unprecedented attention to the area. Sheriff Otis "Red" Davis and many local whites resented the media's depiction of the town and county as racist backwaters. Some were certain that "hit and run" reporters deliberately sought out "idiosyncrasies to confirm their own simplistic, clichéd caricatures of the Old South." Others saw it as an "orchestrated slander campaign to pin the national rap for racism on Beaufort County." The locals had somewhat of a point, for the rest of the country was hardly immune from widespread racial segregation or racist policies and practices that left northern de jure discrimination much closer to southern de facto discrimination than most northern whites liked to admit.[5] To counter these perceived slights, Sheriff Davis complained that African Americans received preferential treatment in the criminal justice system at the expense of whites. He also boasted that he had received the vast majority of the Black vote. But the sheriff conveniently ignored the voting rights lawsuits that Black residents filed, well into the 1990s. Beaufort County remained under the preclearance section of the 1965 Voting Rights Act until the legislation was gutted by the U.S. Supreme Court in 2013.[6]

Jerry Paul, Joan Little's white, thirty-three-year-old Durham attorney, saw things a bit differently from the Beaufort County sheriff. Like Little, Paul was born and raised in Little Washington. A former East Carolina University football player, Paul took a job with the American Civil Liberties Union (ACLU) in Greenville and started a local ACLU chapter there after earning his law degree at the University of North Carolina at Chapel Hill. He also was well-known for defending African Americans and civil rights activists in North Carolina, often pro bono. "People wanted to believe after Watergate that the system worked. The system didn't work," he said. Journalist Mark Pinsky, who reported on racial justice and civil rights issues in the South, shared Paul's skepticism. Beaufort County "was dragging its feet" regarding "voting rights, jury service, public accommodations, school desegregation . . . and police brutality," he claimed.[7]

This was Joan's Little Washington. The eldest of nine children in a struggling family, Little's hardscrabble life was not unlike scores of other poor, African American women who would find themselves behind bars across the nation. She was born May 8, 1954, just days before the U.S. Supreme Court unanimously ruled that segregated public schools were unconstitutional;

but it would take another decade or more, scores of lawsuits, and a well-organized Black freedom movement before Beaufort County and most of the South abided even piecemeal by the landmark ruling. Joan recalled attending the segregated "colored" school in Little Washington, where Black students received the discarded textbooks from the white schools. "We were the last to get the books," she said. Her mother, Jessie Williams, found a house several miles outside of town in Chocowinity, but it was too far to walk, so the school bus picked up Joan and her siblings. "I was a B student. It wasn't that I didn't like school. . . . I had a lot of issues at home."[8]

As in many small southern towns, nearly every aspect of public and private life in Little Washington was segregated, with the railroad tracks serving as the dividing line between Black and white neighborhoods. "Most of the black streets are dirt streets," Joan noted. In myriad ways, both small and large, African Americans were reminded of their second-class status. Even the road to the whites-only Butcher Beach was paved, while the Griffin Beach road for Black residents remained unpaved. A local café refused to serve Black customers if they entered the "white" side, which was air-conditioned. The movie theater was segregated too. "That's just the way we were treated in that town. . . . Blacks go upstairs, in the balcony. You didn't go in the front door, you came in the back door," Joan explained. Whether for religious reasons or perhaps in an effort to shield her daughter from some of the stings of segregation, Joan's mother forbade her to go to the local theater. But the curious youngster did not always mind her mother. "The one time I ever went to the movies was to see *Gypsy Rose Lee* and when I came out it was dark and I thought, 'Oh no my momma's gonna get the switch, she's gonna get me now!'" Joan tried to sneak into the house, "and as I get ready to slide in the window, my mother's standing there. . . . I got my head in, she knock me right out back the window . . . locked me [out and I had to] sleep on the porch."[9]

Of course, the humiliation of Jim Crow laws and customs did not wholly define Black life in Little Washington, even for restless youth like Joan. Although the streets emptied out in the white part of town by 9 p.m., young Black Washingtonians could find relief in several small clubs. "On the corner of Fourth . . . that's were all the blacks hang out," Joan remarked. A game of pool, a drink, and some music were welcome relief, especially on hot summer nights.[10]

Joan's parents, Jessie Ruth Little and Willis Williams (who was married to another woman), split up when Joan was a child and her father followed scores of other African Americans looking for a chance and a new start in the urban North. But Willis returned frequently to Little Washington, and Jessie bore several more children with him. In 1961, Jessie married Arthur Williams (no relation to Willis) and had four more children with her new husband for a total of nine. Joan was just six at the time of the marriage, but she didn't approve. "I resented that for a long time," she recalled. "You ain't my father and you can't tell me what to do," was her attitude toward her new stepfather. Jessie Williams worked as a domestic, minding white women's children, and Joan's grandmother, who was illiterate, often looked after Joan and her siblings. Money was tight and the house was crowded, forcing Joan to share a bed with two of her sisters. But her mother had an upholstery machine and used her skills to pretty-up the house. "It was real nice in there," Joan recalled. Jessie's husband, Arthur, worked for a logging trucker and took other seasonal work. "Sometimes he didn't have a job, but being in the country we could survive," Joan explained. The family had a garden and her brothers fed the pigs, while Joan did the dishes. "That's why I never wanted a job working in a restaurant." Still, feeding the large family put a strain on the household budget, so the younger kids ate first. "You gotta try here with twenty-four biscuits, but by the time it reaches you, there's one left," Joan recalled.[11]

Although Little maintained that he was a good provider, Arthur Williams reportedly had a drinking problem, and Joan never cared much for him. "We avoided each other. . . . When he was in the house, I stayed on one side. . . . He's there, I don't want to be there." Joan claimed that her stepfather favored his own biological children and disciplined the other children more harshly but left her alone. After he supposedly held one of her brothers by the feet and beat him, Joan threatened him: "I tell him if you don't put my brother down, . . . what I'm gonna do." But "when he tells my mother, she's gonna take his side." Arthur reproached his wife, Jessie, for Joan's defiance. "Joan is disrespectful. It's cause you let her get away with it," he complained. By the time Joan was a teenager, Jessie had secured a job at the Hamilton Beach Appliance factory on the night shift. So Joan took to sneaking out, running with "brothers that . . . live in the hood. . . . They protect you," she explained. Reminiscing about her early life decades later, she had a different perspective. "A lot of things you don't see as a child," she said. "You want your mother to be in the house. You don't understand she gotta work to make ends meet. I wasn't grounded enough to just stay focused. . . . My whole thing was to get away from it."[12]

Making her way through an array of low-wage, dead-end jobs, starting when she was still in high school, first picking tobacco and then waiting tables in a local café, Joan increasingly chafed under the problems at home and the constraints of small-town life. Restless, smart—a social worker noted Joan's intelligence—and with not much to engage her in Little Washington, the rebellious teen soon earned a rough reputation among some of the locals. But youthful pranks and minor mischief comprised the bulk of her misdeeds. As Joan tells it, she was more "wild" than "bad." "Most of the time I'm not even doing anything," she insisted. One evening, she and one of her brothers went joyriding in their mother's car. Spotting a flatbed truck in front of them, Joan decided to ride on the hood of the car and hurl herself onto the back of the truck. She missed the truck but fell sideways and rolled off the road, escaping unscathed. Hoping to elude her devout and strict mother, Joan sometimes arranged to meet a local boy at a friend's house. When she was fifteen, she went to stay with her aunt who lived nearby, but the aunt was even stricter than her mother. Joan took to sneaking out and meeting her boyfriend, who was eighteen and, according to her mother, too old for Joan. Unable to control her teenage daughter's behavior, Jessie convinced a Beaufort County judge in 1968 to send Joan to the Dobbs Training School for delinquent girls in Kinston, about an hour away. The Black press, however, later reported that Joan was sentenced to the training school before her mother understood what was happening—not an uncommon practice—and that Jessie Williams approached attorney Jerry Paul to obtain her daughter's release. Years later Joan mused about her upbringing: "If I had somebody that could show me, tell me. My mother wasn't an educated person, but she knew what was right and what was wrong. . . . I think she did the best [she could]. . . . [But] a lot of things could have turned out differently."[13]

North Carolina ranked first in the nation in the number of youth per capita sentenced to juvenile training schools, the euphemism for youth jails. In separate studies, the Duke University Center on Law and Poverty and the North Carolina Bar Association reported that race determined placement in these institutions, in spite of official prohibitions against racial discrimination. Both reports found deplorable conditions in the state's training schools, declared them a "total failure," and recommended closing them in favor of community-based services for troubled youth.[14]

A 1967 presidential commission similarly recommended the creation of extensive community programs as alternatives to juvenile training schools, which were failing to rehabilitate youthful offenders. Despite some of the gains that civil rights activists had made throughout the state and the nation, Joan was not waiting around for reforms that likely would never happen at the Dobbs Training School. Indeed, by 1974, North Carolina was still one of six states without any state-funded community programs for juvenile offenders.[15]

Although Joan claimed that Dobbs "wasn't that bad," she rebelled after being disciplined for "talking loud in the lounge." Her punishment was to buff the floors all night on her hands and knees "with an army blanket to make it really shine." But "I wasn't going for it. So I stepped," she said. Joan headed north, where she stayed with relatives and attended schools in Newark, New Jersey, and in Philadelphia. A thyroid condition brought her back to North Carolina in 1970 within weeks of graduating from Simon Gratz High School in Philadelphia. She went north again briefly, getting a manufacturing job in New Jersey; but transportation difficulties and low wages led her home once again. By the time she was eighteen, Little was on her own and had rented a small house in Little Washington. Hanging out in poolrooms, she drifted in and out of a series of low-wage, dead-end jobs before taking up with Julius Rogers, a hard-drinking man nearly twice her age. Rogers ran a local juke joint "where music was loud and cheap whiskey" could be had at inflated prices. The older man taught her to hang drywall, and they picked up odd jobs throughout the Piedmont and eastern North Carolina where she reportedly earned good money.[16]

Between 1973 and 1974, Joan Little was picked up several times for shoplifting. In one instance, a friend of Joan's was arrested and gave police Little's name, but the charges were dropped. Another run-in with law enforcement occurred when police discovered a sawed-off shotgun in a car Joan was driving. She claimed the gun wasn't hers and that she hadn't even known it was there. All the charges, except for a minor shoplifting charge, were dismissed. On one occasion, the arresting officer admitted he had never actually seen her with any stolen merchandise. Joan pleaded guilty to one of the shoplifting charges, acknowledging decades later that she had stolen earrings from a Woolworth's store, and she received a six-month suspended sentence. Later, police officer Sherwood Sawyer testified that Black residents complained about Joan and her boyfriend Julius Rogers running a theft ring, sending thieves to commit robberies and then selling the stolen property. Sawyer also claimed that Joan had allowed her brother's fourteen-year-old girlfriend, Melinda Moore, to take the rap for one of the petty theft charges. "That's just about the reputation that she has," the policeman asserted. In a recent conversation Joan denied the allegations, pointing out that neither she, Rogers, nor Moore were ever arrested on any of these charges.[17]

Joan Little's more serious legal troubles began when she and her brother, Jerome Little, were arrested in January 1974. They were charged with three felony counts for breaking into Black-owned trailer homes and stealing property valued at $1,300. Both pleaded not guilty. The trial was fraught with problems and inconsistencies. The most egregious was Jerome's sudden about-face confession, in which he pleaded guilty to the misdemeanor charge of possession of stolen merchandise and agreed to testify against Joan. According to Jerome, Joan and Julius Rogers were the thieves. Jerome testified that he discovered the goods in his own trailer and also in Rogers's club but had no idea how they got there. Initially intending either to return the stolen property to the owner or bring them to the sheriff's office, Jerome placed the items in Rogers's car and set out with his teenage girlfriend, Melinda Moore. However, Moore became frightened and before they could reach a decision about what to do, the local sheriff pulled them over. One of the theft victims, Roland Rhodes, was with the sheriff and recognized some of his personal belongings in the car. The sheriff ordered Jerome to drive to the precinct; however, the police car overheated and Jerome gave him the slip. Jerome and Melinda were sure the sheriff had seen the stolen property, so they decided to ditch the items in the woods before proceeding to the police station nearly ninety minutes later. After an interrogation, Jerome then led the sheriff to the pilfered property in the woods and was booked on theft.[18]

During the trial, Roland Rhodes testified that he heard Joan tell Melinda Moore to plead guilty because she was a minor and nothing would happen to her. But in Joan's account, she had asked Rhodes not to file a complaint against Melinda since she was only fifteen. "I tried to settle it out of court," Joan testified. Rhodes acknowledged that both Julius and Joan had tried to convince him not to involve law enforcement after he saw some of his stolen property in Rogers's place. They promised to return the items or to pay for them; but before a deal could be reached, Rhodes filed a police complaint. Rhodes also testified that Moore told him the break-in was Joan's idea. Rhodes's girlfriend, Patricia Mills, confirmed Rhodes's account, testifying that she was present during the conversation and saw Melinda wearing her stolen blouse and jewelry. But Joan denied Rhodes's allegation and insisted that she had simply urged Melinda to return the blouse and other stolen items to the owners so that no charges would be filed.[19]

After the jury reached its guilty verdict against Joan, but before sentencing, she decided to confess, possibly hoping to reduce her prison time. Joan admitted that she, Jerome, Melinda Moore, and her brother Wilbur Moore had all burglarized the trailers. "If you don't have money you're gonna stay in jail," Joan explained years later. "Most people get tired of being in there and they're gonna take a plea bargain." She also felt that as the older sister, she should take the blame. Some thought her confession was a desperate attempt to protect her boyfriend, Julius Rogers. However, Rogers was never charged. Jerome was acquitted of the felony charges, found guilty of a misdemeanor, and placed on probation. Joan, however, received two seven-to-ten-year prison terms.[20] "Anyway I tell my story is implicating him. Anyway he tell his story is implicating me," Joan said. "It came down to me and Jerome in the end . . . they offered him a lesser sentence cause it was me they were after."[21]

Judge Robert Martin suspended Joan's second seven-to-ten-year sentence, which was consecutive not concurrent, in lieu of a five-year probation. He ordered that she have no contact with Julius Rogers, unless they were married, and that she be gainfully employed. Joan also was barred from the "vicinity" of Rogers's club for five years, an ambiguous order that her attorneys noted could apply to the entire town of Little Washington. If Joan violated these terms, the court would impose the second seven-to-ten-year consecutive prison term. Efforts to control Black women's sexual behavior had a long history, but in 1974 the court's prohibition against Joan's association with Rogers, *unless they were married*, seemed especially onerous. Indeed, the potential fourteen-to-twenty year sentence for a nonviolent property offense was rather harsh for a nineteen-year-old with no prior prison time or felony convictions. Karen Galloway, Little's African American cocounsel in her rape-murder trial, concurred nearly forty years later: "The sentence was extremely stiff for a first offender."[22]

When Jerry Paul and his team of attorneys took on Joan's murder-rape case in 1974–75, they also appealed her earlier felony theft conviction, citing fourteen errors in the 1974 robbery trial. They argued that evidence and hearsay testimony were improperly admitted; that the jury was given confusing or erroneous instructions, including the judge's failure to instruct jurors that they could convict on misdemeanor rather than felony charges; and that "'a serious question of effective representation by counsel'" marred the court proceedings. According to Galloway, Joan's lawyer in the felony theft trial knew almost nothing about the case before appearing in court to represent her, and he had spoken to Jerome first. "That concerned me more than anything," Galloway remarked. Nor was the jury informed about the reasons for Jerome's surprise testimony and sudden change of plea. Instead, the court allowed Jerome to testify against Joan while giving her lawyer, Leroy Scott, little opportunity to cross-examine him. Even the state's brief rebutting the defense arguments repeatedly noted that Little's defense counsel had never objected to much of the court testimony against her, including Scott's failure to question Jerome about his change of plea after he turned state's evidence and testified against Joan.[23] Many believed that Jerome had reached a plea bargain with the prosecution, although his lawyer denied making any kind of deal. And finally, no direct physical evidence tied Joan to the stolen merchandise. Aside from Jerome's accusation and Joan's late-hour confession, the only proof of Joan's guilt came from an eyewitness who said she had seen two women and a man outside one of the trailers. One of the women wore a coat similar to one owned by Joan; but Joan claimed that Jerome's girlfriend, Melinda, often wore her clothes after Joan allowed the two to live in her place while she stayed with Rogers.[24]

Even the prosecution admitted the evidence against Joan was weak. During Joan's appeal on the felony conviction, the prosecutor maintained that they had a stronger case against Joan than Jerome. However, state prosecutor Sam Grimes later acknowledged that the state actually had more evidence against Jerome, who was arrested with the stolen items, but that "Joan was the one we were really after, and we never would have convicted her without him." The prosecution's real target may have been Joan's boyfriend, Julius Rogers, who'd had his own brushes with the law: "I might have been convicted of assault with a deadly weapon," Rogers conceded. "[But] I've never been convicted of stealing anything." Jerome had named Rogers as the mastermind behind the thefts, a view shared by both the prosecution and Joan's mother. Rogers was questioned and testified during Joan's felony theft trial but was never arrested or charged. Thus, prosecutors may have hoped that Joan might lead them to Rogers. However, no one thought that Joan was a dupe. She was "too alert, not dumb-witted by any means," Grimes said.[25]

But even assuming Joan was guilty of the theft—and she acknowledged in a recent interview that it had been her idea, although she insists she broke into one trailer, not three, and stole only food and clothing—her treatment raises important questions about race and the criminal legal system in North Carolina and the nation in the 1970s, particularly around sentencing. For example, Judge Martin failed to grant Joan "committed youth offender" (CYO) status. Youthful felons under the age of twenty-one, excluding those convicted of first-degree murder or rape, were eligible for CYO status. This meant they could be granted parole at any time during their sentence, usually for "good behavior" or "gain time" (i.e., work). Just under 50 percent of youth offenders received CYO status in North Carolina. However, the judge ruled that Joan must serve at least two years before becoming eligible for parole. According to Jerry Paul, youth were especially vulnerable in eastern North Carolina. "You've got more young people in jail than anywhere else, and I had defended many of them," he said. Even more disturbing was Paul's claim that one prosecutor in the area had put more people on death row than the combined death row population in twenty-four of the thirty-four states that had capital punishment statutes.[26]

Police officer Sherwood Sawyer's remark about Joan Little's character reflected age-old negative stereotypes about Black women and suggests that she may well have been a victim of racially biased policing, spurred as much by her reputation as a "bad" girl as by any serious criminal activity. Looking back decades later, Joan believed that she was indeed targeted by local police. In a 2013 interview, Joan remarked that Sheriff "Red" Davis had threatened her after one of her false arrests: "I'm gonna get you," he allegedly warned her. A study of juvenile training schools indicated that such placements frequently stigmatized and handicapped young people leading to "heightened police surveillance," and lending credence to Joan's claim.[27] Thus, while the portrayal of Joan as a disreputable young woman gained widespread currency during the murder-rape trial, this image seems to have haunted her much earlier and may well have made her a target of racial profiling and police harassment.

Little's alleged bad-girl reputation included rumors about her sexual behavior as well. A local attorney claimed that she'd been treated for syphilis as a teenager and supplied with birth control pills by the county health department. "Ladies of the night" supposedly sold their services at Julius Rogers's club; and police also suspected that Joan and Julius ran a prostitution ring outside Camp Lejeune, the marine base in nearby Jacksonville. But Joan denied all these claims and noted that she was never arrested on any of these charges. "I was just a teenager out there doing stupid things. I didn't know anything," she insisted. She admitted that some of the people she hung with were involved in prostitution. "It was about making money," she said. "I didn't, they did." During the murder trial, Joan was also accused of being a lesbian and of having a lover at Women's Prison in Raleigh, where she was held during the rape-murder trial. Little rebutted the gossip, claiming that she was kept apart from the other women prisoners. She also noted that one of her "boosting" (shoplifting) friends in Little Washington was a "flip" (lesbian), and the girl's mother had allowed Joan to stay with them before she got a place of her own, which may have fed the rumors about Joan's sexuality.[28]

Joan was similarly stigmatized when officials falsely inflated her age, legally making her an adult rather than an alleged juvenile offender. Sheriff Davis's warrant for Little's arrest after the August 1974 encounter with jailer Clarence Alligood and her subsequent escape from the Beaufort County Jail erroneously listed her age as twenty-five. Joan was nineteen at the time of her arrest and conviction on the felony theft charges and she turned twenty shortly before her escape. But the error continued to be misreported in the press. Exaggerating a suspect's age was one of the ways officials criminalized Black youth. Adding years to her real age and circulating rumors about Joan's presumed sexual activities cast her as immoral and sexually deviant, a conniving adult seductress fully capable of luring an innocent man into her cell and brutally stabbing him before fleeing into the night.[29]

Historically, African American girls and women who did not adhere to strict rules of propriety in both the North and the South frequently were accused of prostitution. But even "respectable" Black women were vulnerable. As historian Cheryl Hicks has shown, simply appearing in public spaces unescorted by a man could land a Black woman in jail for solicitation in the first decades of the twentieth century. Shoplifting also has historically been both gendered and racialized, viewed as "'an ancient, if not honorable, art,'" particularly for white middle-class women. Medicalized as "kleptomaniacs," such women often escaped imprisonment and retained at least some measure of respectability. As certain immigrant and working-class women attained social and cultural "whiteness," they were sometimes viewed as "fallen women" worthy and capable of rehabilitation. However, no such options were available for African American women. Marked by their race as "born thieves," Black women were criminalized and portrayed in the press as "colored amazons." The image cast aspersions on offenders and nonoffenders alike. As historian Kali Gross has noted, while the vast majority of Black women (and men) did not break the law, "the image of the Colored Amazon cast long shadows." The caricature portrayed African American women not only as unlawful but as defeminized sexual aggressors, a reconfiguring of the age-old Jezebel stereotype.[30]

In the small-town South, many of these ideas found fertile ground well into the 1970s and beyond. A textile executive in Joan's hometown remarked, "I tell you one thing, she didn't lose her honor in that cell, she'd lost that years ago at Camp Lejeune." Jerry Paul confirmed his townsmen's views: "I know what their attitude toward Joan is," he said. "They figure Alligood was just having a little fun. It's completely accepted." Forty years after the case that had brought international attention to their small town, some locals still held pejorative views of Little. "She won't no Joan of Arc," said a former law partner of one of Little's prosecutors and a former fellow law student of Paul's.[31]

Such perceptions of Joan may have been both false and unfair, but her attorneys remained concerned about her reputation, and a few even shared some of the negative views of Joan's character. "She's no angel," one said. Even Jerry Paul referred to Little's "negative side" and claimed she was neither an "honest" nor a "kind" person. But he blamed her "environment" for creating her presumed "personality flaws." Joan "couldn't stay out of jail, because her talents never were encouraged," he said.[32]

However, Karen Galloway, Paul's cocounsel, painted a more nuanced picture of the young woman. "She was cunning . . . she was a survivor. She knew the streets," Galloway conceded. "Joan Little didn't say she was a saint. She said, 'I'm a human being.'" Joan also "was probably more conservative as a young person," she said. Like Paul, Galloway also saw great potential in Joan's largely undeveloped gifts. If she'd had the opportunity, Joan could have been "brilliant," the attorney insisted. Perhaps remembering Joan's prison writings and several published poems and sketches, Galloway commented, "I was just impressed with her writing ability. Because she was so talented. . . . if she had a teacher . . . that pushed her, where would she have ended up? . . . I always wondered about that." Instead, Joan's public image "was always negative. . . . She's intelligent. That never came out."[33]

Even some of Little's supporters harbored rather harsh judgments about her, though none thought she was guilty of murder. Winston-Salem Black Panther Party leader Larry Little (no relation), who later headed the national Free Joan Little campaign, echoed her attorneys' views that she was "not a saint." Golden Frinks, the African American field secretary for North Carolina's Southern Christian Leadership Conference, claimed that Little had "the reputation of a wayward girl . . . and was a bad girl in that community." The civil rights leader raised money for Little's defense during the murder trial but was prevented from speaking on her behalf at her mother's church, presumably because the pastor didn't want crime discussed from the pulpit. "She wasn't church," Frinks said. "Because of her past life which the local people did not exactly feel was up to the general moral standard of the community, they had ostracized her." Years later, several African American women in Little Washington recalled that some in the Black community were reluctant to help Joan because of her "reputation." But Frinks also believed that Joan's older friends and "society" had led her astray. "You can't blame Joan for being Joan, but we can blame society for creatin' a Joan Little," he said. "Joan herself is not basically bad. It was her associates and the system that were bad."[34]

Karen Galloway, Jerry Paul, and Golden Frinks all attempted to restore some measure of respectability to Joan's tarnished image by implicating "society" in some of the decisions Joan made. They pointed to the ways racism and poverty had limited her opportunities, shaping her behavior and influencing her choices. At the same time, all three also understood that Black female propriety still mattered, especially in criminal defense trials.

Little was deeply disturbed by many of the public portrayals of her. "That ain't me," she insisted at the time. She acknowledged that she was no "saint," but she was hardly "the worst sinner in the world." Writing from Women's Prison after the trial, Joan presented herself as "an average, twenty-two year old woman trying to live her life." She vowed not to "go back to the old way of life." But the "way of life" she depicted was more bleak than criminal and reflected an aimless despair that was distressing coming from such a young person. Describing her pretrial life, she said, "I looked at myself as being almost a tramp on the street, someone that had no future or meaning in life. If I were to pass away I . . . felt like I was just another corpse making room for somebody else that was coming into the world that could do something meaningful."[35] Today, Joan still maintains that those who really knew her in Little Washington did not hold unfavorable views of her.

In fact, Little's Black women supporters were less likely to entertain pejorative opinions of the young woman. Christine Strudwick, a Durham civil rights activist who helped to organize Concerned Women for Justice for Joan Little, refused to judge Joan. During the murder trial, African American women at a local college also vigorously defended Little against male students who questioned Joan's innocence and believed that she "kind of got what she deserved." According to one Black woman activist, too many Black men across the state derided Little as "a nappy headed, evil, loud mouth Sapphire." Following Little's acquittal, Galloway lambasted African Americans who had shied away from the young defendant. They "should hang their heads in shame. . . . [We] worked against insurmountable odds, some of which came from black people," she chided.[36] Whatever the truth was about Little's local reputation, such sentiments suggest that despite the gains of the Black freedom and feminist movements, negative perceptions of Black womanhood were pervasive. More important, those attitudes both obscured and justified the discriminatory penal practices imposed on Black women deemed disreputable and disposable. Indeed, both her supporters and detractors understood that how Joan Little was portrayed inside and outside the courtroom could be the difference between life and death for the young woman.

2

We Had an Instinctive Love for the Negro Race

Liberals, Conservatives, and the Politics of Crime

A closer look at Judge Robert Martin's judicial record as well as his political leanings may shed some light on Joan Little's conviction and sentencing in her 1974 felony theft trial. In 1960, Martin had campaigned for gubernatorial candidate I. Beverly Lake, a hard-core segregationist. As state attorney general, Lake proposed that North Carolina fund private schools in order to skirt the U.S. Supreme Court's *Brown v. Board of Education* decision. But Martin insisted that he harbored no animosity toward African Americans. Shortly before Little's theft trial he told one reporter, "I was raised in a mainly black county. I ate with them and played with them." Blind to his own racialized paternalism, he continued, "We had an instinctive love for the Negro race. Why my secretary is black. That should show you how I feel about them."[1]

In the early 1970s, Judge Martin gained notoriety in two high-profile North Carolina trials tainted by egregious racism. The first involved the acquittal by an all-white jury of three white men (one of whom was a known KKK associate, and perhaps member) for the 1970 murder of a twenty-three-year-old Black veteran in front of scores of witnesses in Oxford, North Carolina. Two years later, Martin presided over the notorious Wilmington Ten trial, in which nine African American civil rights activists and one white female were falsely convicted on felony charges of arson and conspiracy to assault emergency personnel. Seven were under age twenty-one, but Judge Martin sentenced all the defendants, including civil rights leader Ben Chavis, to various terms of fifteen to thirty-four years. A broad-based campaign arose in support of the defendants and, as with Little's murder trial, well-known activists such as Angela Davis helped to bring national and international attention to the case. In 1976, Amnesty International took up the Wilmington Ten cause, citing human rights violations. Four years later, a federal appeals court overturned the convictions, ruling that the judge and prosecution had allowed perjured testimony, limited defense cross-examination of key prosecution witnesses, and withheld crucial evidence from the defense. In 2012, the defendants finally were "pardoned with innocence," by outgoing North Carolina governor Bev Perdue, meaning no crime had been committed.[2]

Judge Martin's harsh sentence in Little's felony theft trial was neither surprising nor unusual. North Carolina had vastly differing sentencing practices, and plea bargaining was a particular problem. With no formal sentencing guidelines and with judges actively participating in the plea bargain process, differential sentencing was widespread across the state. One legal scholar in the mid-1970s found that white middle-class defendants received much more "lenient treatment." Defendants who pleaded guilty won reduced charges and shorter sentences. Not only "character and past record" but race and class were key factors shaping "indeterminant" sentences (i.e., the broad discretion granted to judges and parole boards to determine prison sentencing). In 1979, the North Carolina legislature enacted the Fair Sentencing Act, which eliminated indeterminant sentences and prevented judges from setting both minimum and maximum prison terms. However, it was delayed until 1981 and even then judges retained wide latitude in sentencing.[3]

Prisoner rights advocates had long pressed for changing indeterminant sentencing practices and their efforts led to widespread reforms. Yet reforms did not necessarily end racial bias in sentencing and could even make a bad situation worse. For example, determinant sentencing and mandatory minimums, such as the three-strikes rule, imposed rigid rules on the courts and left almost no room for judicial discretion. Coupled with discriminatory policing, arrest, and conviction rates, this supposed reform meant that prisoners of color frequently spent more time behind bars compared to whites convicted of similar offenses.[4]

The North Carolina General Assembly Commission on Correctional Programs acknowledged that such disparities in sentencing were a major cause of prison unrest. Throughout the 1960s and 1970, the state's jails and prisons saw scores of prisoner protests. The most serious was in 1968 at the men's Central Prison in Raleigh. But women's prisons were not immune. In 1975, the North Carolina Correctional Center for Women (NCCCW, known as "Women's Prison") in Raleigh—where Little was incarcerated during and after her rape-murder trial—was the site of a sit-down strike by women inmates that erupted in violence.[5]

Along with horrendous prison conditions and discriminatory sentencing practices, North Carolina had the second-highest rates of confinement in the early 1970s for both felony *and* misdemeanor convictions. Felons had the third-longest average sentences, and even misdemeanor sentences were twice the national average. By 1980, the state had the highest incarceration rate in the country.[6] Although African Americans were 22 percent of North Carolina's population, racial disparities among prisoners, especially women, were striking. In 1972, only 3 percent of the state's prison population was female, but Black women made up two-thirds of those held at Women's Prison. (African American men were 55 percent of Central Prison's all-male population.)[7] The overrepresentation of Black women continued as the inmate population expanded in North Carolina and across the nation.[8] While it is widely assumed that a rising crime wave was responsible for the prison population explosion nationally, scholars have found little correlation between increasing crime rates and imprisonment during this period. And, according to the FBI Crime Report, North Carolina had lower crime rates in every major category compared to neighboring states.[9]

However, another more insidious factor fueled arrest, sentencing, and incarceration practices in North Carolina and throughout the country. Well before Richard Nixon's "law and order" campaign and Ronald Reagan's War on Drugs, financial incentives established in the mid-1960s played an important role in driving the growing prison population. The 1965 Law Enforcement Assistance Act (LEAA) and the 1968 Omnibus Crime Control and Safe Streets Act provided federal support to local law enforcement. While some scholars have noted earlier trends in setting the stage for the modern U.S. carceral state, Heather Thompson asserts that the 1965 and 1968 federal anticrime legislation together created "the largest crime-fighting bureaucracy the nation had ever seen."[10]

To most observers, LEAA and the Omnibus Crime Control and Safe Streets Act were clear evidence of a right-wing backlash against the civil rights movement and President Lyndon Johnson's Great Society. After all, Arkansas senator John McClellan, a notorious anticommunist and civil rights opponent, was a chief sponsor of the anticrime legislation. One pundit called the 1968 law "a piece of demagoguery devised out of malevolence and enacted in hysteria."[11] However, many liberal Democrats, including staunch civil rights supporters and those who believed poverty was a major cause of crime, were eager to prove their "tough on crime" bona fides by backing the new federal anticrime initiatives. And despite his misgivings, Johnson signed both bills. After launching a presidential crime commission in 1965, he declared before Congress, "I hope that 1965 will be regarded as the year when this country began in earnest a thorough and effective war against crime." Like other liberals, Johnson linked the fight against crime to his antipoverty program: "The war on poverty is a war against crime," he said.[12]

Ironically, not only northern Democrats but the U.S. Civil Rights Commission and the NAACP all believed federal funding for police professionalization and the overhaul of the criminal code to eliminate disparities would create a "race-neutral, fortified criminal justice system." However, political scientist Naomi Murakawa has shown that the ambiguity of such legislation effectively "buttressed carceral strength in ways especially detrimental to people of color." To be fair, civil rights proponents, and Black community leaders in particular, pressed for community control of law enforcement programs and demanded social services to curb poverty and other urban ills. Johnson and liberal Democrats enacted legislation for halfway houses, after-school programs to prevent juvenile delinquency, alternatives to prison for drug addicts, bail reform, and legal representation in federal courts for low-income defendants. However, Johnson also imbued the Black poor with the stigma of criminality. Echoing Daniel Patrick Moynihan's indictment of an alleged Black matriarchal family of domineering mothers and absent fathers, Johnson pointed to structural inequality and cultural damage as causes of Black crime while also insisting on individual responsibility.[13]

When Richard Nixon won the presidency in 1968, he became the perfect foil to Johnson's more beneficent linkage of the wars on poverty and crime. "The solution to the crime problem is not quadrupling of funds for any government war on poverty," Nixon insisted, "but more convictions." Congress jumped on board and reauthorized the crime bill in 1970 with even more money than Nixon had requested. In short order, the nation began to witness elevated arrest rates, backed-up court calendars, and crowded correctional facilities. As Murakawa notes, "Johnson's modernization to improve minority relations slipped easily into Nixon's modernization to be tough on crime." And federal largesse often made all the difference, enhancing the militarization of local police and private policing.[14]

Although concern over urban uprisings fueled support for national anticrime legislation, rural areas without race "riots" also received federal funds.

Southern lawmakers, such as North Carolina senator Sam Ervin and South Carolina's segregationist senator Strom Thurmond upheld the white South's historic commitment to states' rights and limited federal control by funneling federal funds directly to the states through block grants. The 1968 Safe Streets Act allocated federal support to states on a per capita basis for *any* purpose that could be associated with reducing crime, thus giving wide latitude to states and with few federal strings attached. According to one congressional wag, the Law Enforcement Assistance Administration (also abbreviated LEAA, it was the agency created by the act) was nothing but a "secretary and a check-writing machine." Another assessment noted that on both the federal and state levels, the Law Enforcement Assistance and Safe Streets Acts remained "subservient to entrenched and politically powerful criminal justice agencies. . . . and to the maintenance of the status quo."[15]

In North Carolina, even state oversight was minimal. Regional policy boards had nearly free reign in allocating LEAA money and were dominated by law enforcement. Moreover, few African Americans were appointed to the boards and they were totally absent in some areas of the state, despite federal requirements. As one report about LEAA's impact in North Carolina noted, "The lack of minority representation suggests that the LEAA program has served to extend discriminatory practices in the regions." But the federal dollars kept coming. Between 1969 and 1975 North Carolina received just under $50 million in LEAA funds; and over 74 percent went to policing. In 1974, the year Joan Little was denied committed youth offender status, the state's Department of Correction, which was allocated funds separately from policing, obtained $3 million, its largest LEAA grant ever. Ironically, a third of the money was directed to youth offender services.[16]

Crime control, once considered primarily a state and local matter, now had unprecedented federal support. By providing financial inducements for state and local officials to increase their arrest, conviction, and sentencing rates, liberal reformers along with conservative politicians set in motion the nation's move toward mass incarceration and the prison boom, well before the War on Drugs was launched.[17] According to Robert Perkinson, "The upswing in imprisonment began first and took hold most intensely in the South." Throughout the twentieth century, the South had imprisoned disproportionate numbers of its citizens, especially African Americans, most of whom were leased to private enterprises, then sent to chain gangs and later to state-run prison farms. But beginning in 1972, the regional imprisonment differential began to widen even more, and by 1980, the South's rate was 75 percent higher than the North's. "In aggregate terms, the South was locking up more than twice as many individuals as any other region," Perkinson noted.[18]

By 1981, when the Law Enforcement Assistance Administration had been disbanded (even its supporters were calling it a failure), the federal government had distributed nearly $10 billion to over 80,000 crime control projects, and nearly three-quarters of the funds went to policing. Despite the closure of LEAA, federal funding for local law enforcement continued through other agencies and legislation well into the 1980s and 1990s.[19]

Thus, Little's seven-to-ten-year sentence, and her potential fourteen-to-twenty-year prison term, can be better understood within the context of discriminatory "tough on crime" policies of both liberal and conservative politicians *prior to* and *apart from* the War on Drugs. By end of the 1970s, North Carolina boasted the highest per capita incarceration rate in the nation. Higher rates of imprisonment also brought higher costs, and by 1975 the state ranked second in the percentage of its budget spent on crime.[20] Beaufort County seemed to be on board with the new emphasis. In the early 1970s, the county received state and federal funds for a new courthouse and jail.[21] Despite the improved facilities, "time inside the Beaufort County jail was still close arrest," observed a local attorney. Indeed, following her conviction in the felony theft trial, Joan Little spent countless hours locked in a five-by-seven-foot cell, with a toilet, a sink and a twenty-seven-inch-wide cot. Although the Beaufort County jailers ran a rather "loose ship," permitting prisoners to leave their cells and make calls from the prison staff office, there was no opportunity for prisoner exercise or any kind of rehabilitative activities. Even worse, women had no privacy. A TV monitor allowed jailers to look directly into the women's cells. In an effort to protect themselves from the leering eyes of male guards, Joan Little and her fellow prisoners hung sheets across the bars of their cells. "Ordinarily the situation was not tense, but the potential for violence was always present," the Little Washington lawyer added ominously.[22]

Hoping to appeal her conviction but with no money for a lawyer, Little passed the summer of 1974 in the Beaufort County Jail reading romance magazines, Perry Mason mysteries, and her prison Bible. She alternated reading with solving crossword puzzles, writing letters to friends, and scrawling increasingly desperate notes about Julius Rogers in the margins of both her puzzle books and novels. When sleep eluded her, she listened to the all-night country-and-western music radio station from Greenville. And jailer Clarence Alligood frequently delivered sandwiches and cigarettes to her cell during his night shifts. Joan had few visitors that summer, mostly just her distraught mother. Occasionally, she was allowed into the jailers' office to make phone calls.[23]

As weeks turned to months, Joan grew increasingly apprehensive. Unable to come up with the $1,400 demanded by attorney Leroy Scott to appeal her three felony convictions of breaking and entering, larceny, and possession of stolen merchandise, her prospects looked bleak. As she would discover later, Scott had not only failed to submit an appeal within the eighty-day time limit imposed by the court, he also had failed to inform her of her right to a public defender based on her inability to cover attorney fees. Nearly three months passed before Joan Little's final encounter with Alligood took her on a more perilous journey through the criminal legal system. Her decision to fight back, to flee, and then to surrender to authorities would sharpen the debates about race, sexual assault, lethal self-defense, and incarceration. And it altered her life forever.[24]

Perhaps it is not surprising that Joan Little's 1974 trial and felony theft conviction have gone largely unexamined. Few have bothered to ask exactly how or why the nineteen-year-old landed in the Beaufort County Jail in 1973 and 1974 in the first place. Nor has much attention been given to her earlier experiences in the criminal legal system as a teenager in the late 1960s and early 1970s, prior to the 1974–75 murder-rape case. Instead, nearly all assessments of the young woman have proceeded on the assumption that she was simply a common street criminal. After all, she confessed to the 1974 felony theft charges, making additional scrutiny seem unwarranted.[25] A closer examination of these earlier events, however, reveals that Little's encounters with law enforcement and in the courts were riddled with racial injustice and abuse, starting with her placement in the juvenile detention center in 1968. Following her stint at the "training center" and her return to North Carolina in 1970, Little was likely a target of racial profiling, police surveillance, and false arrests. Most important, she was the victim of inadequate counsel and widespread racially discriminatory sentencing practices during her felony-theft trial.

In effect, the tendency toward triumphalist narratives with Rosa Parks–like heroines has highlighted the more celebratory aspects of the Joan Little saga at the expense of this equally compelling and far more representative story about pervasive abuses in the policing, sentencing, and imprisonment of Black women and men. The Wars on Drugs and Crime exacerbated these practices, but the roots of our contemporary carceral state can be found in harsh penal practices of the American South long before federal crime policies were enacted. The ideological basis for mass incarceration was created decades earlier in the criminalization of Blackness, and in ways that were highly gendered. In the nineteenth century, Black codes, Jim Crow laws, and convict leasing followed the abolition of slavery and the collapse of Reconstruction. When African Americans headed for the "Promised Land" of the North in the early decades of the twentieth century, northern policing tactics, devised largely to meet earlier waves of unwelcome immigrants and militant labor organizers, made recent Black migrants new targets for racialized containment and control.[26]

Ending legal discrimination and establishing formal citizenship rights for African Americans have never ensured Black freedom. After the civil rights victories of the 1960s, heightened policing of Black communities and mass incarceration replaced more overt racial discrimination as new forms of anti-Black social control. Indeed, a closer look at Joan Little's experiences within the criminal punishment system were typical of the kind of "justice" low-income African Americans were likely to find in North Carolina and across the country, despite the achievements of the civil rights movement. By the 1960s and 1970s, urban uprisings and Black Power militancy prompted both liberal Democrats and conservative Republicans to recast the age-old "condemnation of blackness" in racially coded "tough on crime" rhetoric and to promote ever-more-punitive penal policies. Little's encounters with law enforcement prior to and apart from both Richard Nixon's "law and order" policies and Ronald Reagan's "War on Drugs," suggest that her treatment may well have been fueled, at least in part, by unprecedented federal financing of local crime control, begun in the mid-1960s. Although Black and brown men were the primary targets of an increasingly harsh criminal legal system, Black women were not immune.[27] This broader interrogation of Joan Little's "criminality" thus moves us beyond simplistic assessments of her guilt or innocence; for our treatment of the guilty, not only the innocent, may well be the more accurate measure of a society that purports to guarantee equal justice under the law.

Finally, Joan Little's earliest encounters with law enforcement and the courts challenge the trope of the "strong Black woman." As historian Chana Kai Lee explains, "Too often our study and research of black female historical figures yield depictions of yet another 'strong black woman.'" Political scientist Melissa Harris-Perry notes the danger in elevating these stories of triumph: "The ideal of the strong black woman is impossible to maintain. Its insistence that black women can always make a way out of no way sets the stage for failure. . . . and that failure can be used to rationalize continuing inequality." Thus, the heroine-survivor, an identity that Little's supporters would thrust upon her during her murder-rape trial, too easily determined Black women's worth, marginalizing those who were unable to "make a way out of no way" and neglecting the systemic impediments of power, control, and exclusion that shaped individual choices and behavior.[28]

Certainly, Joan Little's experiences as a youthful "delinquent" and convicted felon are as significant as her rape-murder trial and the Free Joan Little campaign. This broader assessment of Joan Little's treatment reminds us that for every courtroom victory, there were scores of women—largely poor women of color—who did not fare so well. Little's acquittal on the murder charge should be celebrated for what it reveals about the power of organized protest; for without the massive publicity and successful fundraising efforts, she may well have been convicted and executed. But our retelling of the Free Joan Little campaign can easily become a self-congratulatory morality tale that reinscribes stereotypes regarding Black womanhood. In effect, Joan the Jezebel becomes Joan the Victim-Survivor. The triumphalist narrative of "the strong Black woman" within the context of the criminal legal system may be particularly insidious. It suggests, perhaps unwittingly, that if Joan Little, an impoverished, wayward young woman, can find justice in a southern courtroom, then Jim Crow justice may well be a remnant of the past. Of course, accounts of victory over discrimination, of perseverance in the face of adversity, are critical to a more accurate rendering of our past. But if we tell only the more celebratory, triumphant stories, we risk creating iconic heroines and heroes while obscuring the more fully realized, even flawed, human beings who did not always prevail.

Prison abolitionist Angela Davis captured the vulnerability that Joan Little faced that summer night in 1974 when Clarence Alligood entered her cell: "Had Joan Little been killed by Alligood [a] verdict of 'justifiable homicide' would have probably closed the books on such a case," she said. Little understood quite well that she was both fortunate and atypical to have survived Alligood's sexual assault and law enforcement's order to shoot her on sight after she fled from the jail. "I am only one out of 100 that lived to tell it," she noted.[29] Even more extraordinary was her acquittal by a North Carolina jury. How that remarkable outcome unfolded is the subject of the remaining chapters in part 1.

3

Power to the Ice Pick

Building a Defense, Mounting a Campaign

"New South" North Carolina had long promoted its "progressive mystique." Yet the state harbored enough "Old South" racism for Jerry Paul, Joan Little's white defense attorney, to put his home state, and eastern North Carolina in particular, on trial. An ex-football player from Little Washington who had gained a reputation among civil rights activists for defending Blacks, Paul minced no words when it came to describing local whites: "I know these people. I know what they are," he said. "They're racists in Eastern North Carolina and they know they're racists, but in 1975 it may not be a good thing to admit you're a racist."[1]

Indeed, there was enough official chicanery in the investigation of the deceased white jailer, Clarence Alligood, and the grand jury proceedings to remind observers that the criminal justice system still showed a callous disregard for Black life. The Beaufort County grand jury had quickly indicted Joan Little for first-degree murder of the jailer, which carried a mandatory death penalty. But jurors never heard that Alligood had been found without his pants inside Joan's empty cell. Nor did they hear about signs of recent sexual activity, most notably the dried semen on Alligood's leg that appeared to have been wiped off. Other crucial physical evidence also was mishandled. The jail cell was scrubbed clean before forensics could be obtained; photographs were damaged; and no one bothered to take fingerprints off the ice pick, the alleged murder weapon. The blood-stained sheet beneath Alligood's lifeless body disappeared. So did his pants, reappearing months later after repeated demands from the defense. "There was lots of confusion," Willis Peachy, the twenty-six-year-old Beaufort County deputy, offered feebly.[2]

The local paper similarly omitted these details and editorialized that Clarence Alligood was "a good man" who had given "his life in the line of duty. What more can any man give?" Louis Randolph, the sole African American on the city council of Little Washington, had his own take on the investigation, calling it a "cover-up" by local law enforcement.[3] Although the grand jury was interracial, with four Black and twelve white jurors, researchers later hired by the defense discovered that almost no African Americans and few women ever served on juries in eastern North Carolina. Their findings helped convince a judge to move the trial from Beaufort County to Raleigh, which had a Black mayor.[4]

If Clarence Alligood was hardly a "good man," Joan Little was seemingly no Rosa Parks. Little had neither Parks's aura of respectability nor her activist credentials, making Jerry Paul's comparison between the two women look like a stretch to many. Yet the two shared similarities that might have surprised the casual observer. For one thing, Little was far more politically astute than even her defenders seemed to realize. And evidence suggests that a youthful Parks may also have been subjected to a white man's unwanted sexual advances. Parks's history of organizing against racial violence and the rape of Black women by white men dated to the 1940s, prior to the Montgomery Bus Boycott; and in the 1970s she helped launch a Joan Little Defense Fund in her adopted city of Detroit.[5]

Following the grand jury indictment for first-degree murder, Joan Little quickly became a national and international cause célèbre. While highlighting the racial dimensions of the death penalty and what would soon be called the prison-industrial complex and later the carceral state, a broad array of reformers and radicals linked Little's case to their own social justice goals. Scores of civil rights, Black Power, prisoner rights, and women's groups rallied behind the young woman. Supporters of Yvonne Wanrow, an Indigenous woman in Washington State who had similarly resorted to lethal self-defense, drew comparisons between the Wanrow and Little cases. In California, Chicana activists coupled Little's trial with the Inez García case, in which a Latinx woman had defended herself by killing her rapist attacker. In Georgia, the Atlanta Lesbian Feminist Alliance (ALFA) and Black nationalists, including the Black Women's United Front, drew parallels between Joan Little and Dessie X. Woods, another Black woman on trial for killing her white male attacker.[6]

Across the Atlantic, in London, the *Economist* magazine hurled blame at the entire nation. "Rape is American as apple pie," the editors sneered. Feminists in Holland began fundraising for Little; and the International Federation of Arab Attorneys, representing nineteen Arab states, donated $1,000 to her defense. Closer to home, a Black soul station in Memphis collected over $20,000 in a monthlong plea to listeners. In response to an appeal from Representative Shirley Chisholm of Brooklyn (the first Black woman elected to Congress), even the U.S. Department of Justice took notice and sent an observer to the trial.[7]

Throughout the country, organizers mounted rallies in New York, Boston, San Francisco, Chicago, Detroit, Atlanta, and elsewhere. Former Student Nonviolent Coordinating Committee (SNCC) activist Julian Bond launched a nationwide fundraising appeal from the Southern Poverty Law Center, and later attended the trial. Prisoner newsletters including the *Midnight Special* and *No More Cages: A Bi-monthly Women's Prison Newsletter*, as well as the lesbian-feminist newspaper *off our backs* covered the case. The women's antirape newsletter, published by the Washington, D.C., Feminist Alliance Against Rape (FAAR), helped to generate feminist support nationwide. Meanwhile, the Black Panther Party named Joan Little "Woman of the Year" for 1975; the more mainstream Black weekly, the *Chicago Defender*, declared her one of four African American "Newsmakers" of 1975; and the *Washington (D.C.) Star-News* heralded the case as "the civil rights trial of the '70s."[8]

African Americans, especially women, were among Little's earliest and most ardent supporters. Angela Davis, Coretta Scott King, radical feminist attorney Florence Kennedy, Rev. Ralph Abernathy, comedian Dick Gregory, and Health and Hospital Workers Union 1199 executive Doris Turner were just some of her better-known Black supporters. Black cultural activists responded too, using their creative talents to dramatize Joan Little's predicament. Bernice Johnson Reagon, a former SNCC activist and founder of the Black female a cappella group Sweet Honey in the Rock, wrote and recorded the song "Joan Little" as a fundraiser for Little's defense. The song became a kind of anthem for the Free Joan Little campaign. Soul singer Dee Dee Warwick, sister of R&B star Dionne Warwick and cousin of future pop legend Whitney Houston, remarked that she drew inspiration from Little's case when she wrote and performed "She Was Just One Woman." Ed Bullins, former minister of culture for the Black Panthers and a leading playwright in the Black Arts Movement, wrote *Jo Anne!*, which was staged at the Riverside Church in New York City.[9]

Formed by local activists shortly after Little surrendered to authorities in early September 1974, the Free Joan Little campaign drew support from national Black feminist organizations including the Combahee River Collective, the National Black Feminist Organization (NBFO), and the Third World Women's Alliance. All had made prisoner abuse, including the rape of Black women prisoners, one of their concerns. Throughout the country, local Black feminist groups sent messages of solidarity, including Black Women Organized for Action in California and the Chicago NBFO (renamed the National Alliance of Black Feminists). Black women in scores of other women's organizations, such as Barbara Brooks, a staff member at the Cambridge, Massachusetts, YWCA, organized fundraisers and demonstrations. "Joan represents the people that are overshadowed, that never get a chance. This happens all the time—what's unusual is that we're hearing about it," Brooks remarked. In Raleigh, about 300 well-organized African American women pledged their support. Black feminists there had reportedly split from the local NOW chapter to form Raleigh Feminists Organized for Action, and the local NBFO similarly backed Joan Little.[10]

Whatever their differences with white women, Black feminists called on white feminists to promote the Free Joan Little campaign. NBFO member Afi Phoebe appealed to the predominantly white National Organization for Women (NOW) to send busloads of peaceful protesters to the courthouse in Raleigh where Little's trial was scheduled. Although NOW had not addressed rape when the organization formed in 1966, local chapters, such as the Northern Virginia chapter—which provided crucial information on sexual assault to Little's defense team—did take up the issue. But in 1971, the national organization passed a resolution urging law enforcement to treat rape and rape victims more seriously; two years later, NOW created the Rape Task Force headed by Mary Ann Largen, from the Northern Virginia chapter. The task force was mandated to investigate rape laws and propose a model rape statute; it was also charged with researching victim services, self-defense tactics, and possible coalitions with antirape groups.[11]

By 1974–75, the national NOW office saw the Joan Little case as a chance to prove its concern for poor women and women of color; the four NOW task forces on rape, minority women, criminal justice, and women in poverty were probably among Little's most fervent supporters within NOW.[12] The task forces called on the national office to make April 14, 1975 (the scheduled opening of Little's rape-murder trial), a day of national action; and they cosponsored a press conference in Washington, D.C., the following day with Congresswoman Shirley Chisholm. At the press conference, Chisholm;

NOW head Karen DeCrow, Representative Yvonne Brathwaite Burke (D-Calif.), one of the first Black women to graduate from the University of Southern California Law School (in 1956); and Senator Charles Mathias (R-Md.) highlighted not only Little's case but the "general plight of poor persons, minorities and women within the prison system." After meeting with Little's defense attorneys, Chisholm appealed to the U.S. attorney general. In her letter, Chisholm claimed that Little was unable to secure a fair trial in Beaufort County, which she believed constituted a Fourteenth Amendment violation of due process and equal protection under the law. Chisholm also put Little's predicament within the larger context of imprisoned women across the country who were vulnerable to sexual abuse; and she called on the Justice Department to "conduct a much-needed investigation" in North Carolina and throughout the country. NOW followed suit, also calling on the federal government to launch a major study of prison conditions, the sexual abuse of incarcerated women, and the quality of legal assistance available to poor people. The four NOW task forces continued their support even after Joan's acquittal. For example, Mary Ann Largen and Del Robbins, coordinators of NOW's Rape Task Force and Minority Women's Task Force, respectively, reminded members that Joan still faced an appeal for her 1974 felony theft convictions. They urged NOW members to educate the public and the judiciary on the "racist/sexist undertones" of the case and Joan's vulnerability as "a poor woman subject to the criminal justice system." The NOW Rape Task Force also helped to raise money for Jerry Paul's disbarment hearing before the North Carolina Bar Association in response to his actions during the Little trial.[13]

Together with the national office, hundreds of NOW chapters across the country initiated actions on behalf of Joan Little. New York members launched a mock trial, while Philadelphia organized a demonstration supporting women's right to self-defense, and Savanah held a teach-in on incarcerated women. But local NOW chapters were not always eager to associate themselves with the controversial case. The North Carolina NOW State Convention apparently took some urging. Marjorie Nelson, a white northern feminist whose daughter had helped the Little defense conduct a survey of white attitudes among potential jurors, was surprised to find scant interest in the case among white women after she arrived in Raleigh in 1975. Nelson decided to attend the statewide NOW conference at Meredith College to encourage feminist support for Little's upcoming trial. At the conference, she attended a workshop on Black feminism in which a group of angry women decided to demand that the NOW State Convention publicly back

Women protesters in front of Wake County Courthouse, 1975.
Both African American and white women proclaimed their
right to self-defense against sexual violence.
Courtesy of the North Carolina State Archives
and the *Raleigh News and Observer*.

Little. In response, the state organization adopted a resolution supporting both Joan Little and the prisoners at the North Carolina Correctional Center for Women in Raleigh, where Joan had been held for nearly six months before her trial.

The State Convention called on its eight NOW chapters throughout North Carolina to organize separate efforts for Little and pledged that its top legislative priority for the coming year would be to push the state legislature to reform the current "deplorable conditions" at Women's Prison. Although Laine Calloway, the newly elected NOW state coordinator, cautioned that the organization was not rendering a verdict on the Little trial, a group of more than two dozen Black and white NOW members protested at the Wake County Courthouse the next day with a sign reading "Joan Is Our Sister."[14]

Not all North Carolina NOW chapters needed directives from the State Convention. In April 1975, Greensboro NOW had cosponsored a public question-and-answer forum on the case with the local rape crisis center (RCC) and the Greensboro YWCA Public Affairs Committee, featuring Yvonne Davis, the Durham coordinator of the Joan Little Defense Fund. The NOW chapter in Fayetteville, located about sixty miles south of Raleigh and headed by Minnie Bruce Pratt, who would become a leading white lesbian-feminist, antiracist activist, also covered the Little case. Little's ordeal spurred the Fayetteville chapter's interest in prison conditions at Raleigh's Women's Prison and in jails across the state.[15]

The day before Little's trial opened at the Wake County Courthouse, Charlotte NOW held a press conference on the courthouse steps. The group not only championed a woman's right to self-defense; like the NOW State Convention, the Charlotte chapter also denounced the conditions at Women's Prison and promised that elimination of the prison's "deplorable conditions" and reform of rape laws to protect rape victims who testified in court would be their top legislative priorities for 1975. This was not Charlotte NOW's first public support for Black freedom; nor was it the chapter's first critique of the state's punitive legal measures against African Americans. In 1972, Charlotte NOW unanimously adopted a resolution calling for an end to the "legal political reprisals against minority groups" and in support of the Charlotte Three, three Black male activists given lengthy prison sentences for their civil rights activities.[16]

The most important NOW support, however, came from the head of NOW's Rape Task Force, Mary Ann Largen, who provided direct assistance to Little's defense team. According to Little's cocounsel, Karen Galloway, Largen gave her an intensive tutorial in the feminist analysis of violence against women. Rape was not about sex; it was about power, control, humiliation, and degradation; when perpetrated by men against women, rape was a pillar of male supremacy. Black women, of course, needed few lessons to understand what hundreds of years had taught them: that the rape of Black women by white men was also a pillar of white supremacy. "A rapist doesn't want sex, he wants control. For a whole year I was working on that argument," Galloway recalled. Largen also convinced Jerry Paul to let Galloway speak to the press. "She knew that there were a lot of women's organizations who would listen to a woman more than Jerry Paul," Galloway explained.[17]

On the national level, several prominent white feminist politicians responded to Little's case, including Congresswomen Bella Abzug and Elizabeth Holtzman of New York. Abzug was a founder of the National Women's Political Caucus and a former attorney in the Willie McGee case, which, like the Little case, became a cause célèbre and attracted worldwide attention. McGee was a Black man falsely convicted and executed in 1951 for the alleged rape of a white woman in Mississippi. Holtzman, at the time of the Little trial the youngest woman ever elected to Congress, had attracted national attention during the Watergate hearings; she joined twenty-seven other members of Congress demanding that the U.S. attorney general investigate the charges against Little and the alleged sexual abuse of other women in the Beaufort County Jail.[18]

The widespread support for Joan Little infuriated racists and self-defined members of the "silent majority." Many of them felt compelled to offer their impassioned anti-Black opinions to the presiding trial judge, Hamilton Hobgood, who received over 1,200 letters, postcards, and telegrams from throughout the nation and even from other countries. Hobgood also reportedly received 400 media requests to cover the trial. He assigned thirty-two spaces for news media and an adjoining courtroom with a sound system relaying the trial proceedings was set-up to accommodate the additional press. Reporters from Reuters and the Associated Press were granted seats in the trial, which enabled newspapers throughout the country, and even around the world, to follow the story.[19]

Indeed, the monthlong trial had enough spectacle and controversy to assure massive media and public attention. During pretrial motions, Southern Christian Leadership Conference (SCLC) leader Golden Frinks erected tents in Joan Little's hometown, naming it Resurrection City after Martin Luther King Jr.'s 1968 Poor People's Campaign.[20] But conflicts and accusations among Little's supporters, especially surrounding fundraising, threatened to derail defense efforts to build public support. Washington, N.C., city

"Free Joanne Little" and "Justice for Joanne" became the rallying cry among many of her supporters outside the Wake County Courthouse, 1975. Courtesy of the North Carolina State Archives and the *Raleigh News and Observer*.

councilman Louis Randolph accused Frinks of collecting money in town for the SCLC rather than for Little's defense. Later, Frinks and Joan Little's mother, Jessie Williams, brought a lawsuit against Jerry Paul, charging him with mismanaging defense funds. Jessie Williams even claimed the defense attorneys were drugging her daughter and keeping her in hiding. She also thought that Joan was feigning illness in order to delay the trial. Paul countered these accusations by accusing Frinks of sexism for questioning Karen Galloway's experience. He also announced that Joan Little had received death threats; and he hired two large male bodyguards to escort her in and out of the courthouse, lending a theatrical air to Joan's daily appearance before the media.[21]

On the eve of the trial, the Reverends Leon White and Charles Cobb of the United Church of Christ Commission for Racial Justice joined 1,000 of Little's supporters at a Raleigh prayer vigil. Nearby, plainclothes detectives stood watch as gospel music wafted across the praying crowd.[22] Others preferred a more provocative form of protest. Until a judge banned all demonstrations

Some protesters paired the "Free Joanne Little" demand with the more provocative "Power to the Ice Pick" as Joan Little's rape-murder trial opened in 1975. Courtesy of the North Carolina State Archives and the *Raleigh News and Observer*.

outside the courthouse, "Power to the Ice Pick" became the mantra chanted by Little's most militant defenders:

> One, two three,
> Joan must be set free
> Four, five six,
> Power to the Ice Pick
> Seven, eight, nine,
> Should have done it a thousand times.[23]

High drama was in full display inside the courtroom as well. During the trial, Judge Hobgood did his best to control courtroom antics that often gave the proceedings a circus-like air. On the first day of the trial, Little's lead defense attorney, Jerry Paul, called for Hobgood to recuse himself, claiming the judge was incapable of "giving Joan Little a fair trial. . . . to sit there and say like the Queen of Hearts—Off with their heads—because the law is the law—is to take us back a hundred years."[24] Paul also demanded that the assistant state attorney general be removed from the case because he had once represented Ku Klux Klan imperial wizard Robert Shelton before the House Un-American Activities Committee. The defense wanted another special prosecutor, John Wilkerson, who was hired by the Alligood family, gone as well. They argued that Wilkerson had represented Joan Little in two previous cases and was therefore biased against her.[25] Judge Hobgood declined to recuse either the prosecutors or himself. But he did charge Paul with contempt; and he evicted one of the defense attorneys, Morris Dees, and sent another, William Kunstler, to jail. Dees, a thirty-eight-year-old, independently wealthy volunteer lawyer for the Southern Poverty Law Center, allegedly had tampered with one of the prosecution's witnesses. The judge also refused to allow Kunstler, the nation's most famous radical attorney, to replace the ousted Dees. Instead, he ordered Kunstler to jail for contempt after the attorney announced to a packed courtroom, "I'm glad to see that the quality of justice in North Carolina courts has not improved."[26] Even after the trial, the spectacle continued and controversy swirled. Like Kunstler, Jerry Paul's contempt charge landed him in jail, but it also nearly cost him his law license from the North Carolina Bar Association.[27] Regardless of Paul's unconventional tactics and flamboyant courtroom style, this was no laughing matter; and Paul and Joan Little's additional five defense attorneys did their best to insure that she received a fair trial and avoided a death sentence.

Midway through the legal proceedings, Judge Hobgood cited lack of evidence in the state's case and reduced the charge against Joan Little from first- to second-degree murder. Yet the courtroom spectacle did not abate. In closing arguments, one of the prosecutors flung himself on the floor in a one-man wrestling match, hoping to convince jurors that Joan could not possibly have fought off the much-larger Alligood, as she had testified. And in his closing remarks to the jury, defense attorney Jerry Paul thundered like a revival preacher, proclaiming that Joan Little, like Rosa Parks, "was a heroic figure, chosen by God to put an end to the historic degradation of black women."[28]

Some may have questioned whether Little was just like Rosa Parks. But the defense was conjuring another image of the young woman for the jury; for key to both Joan Little's defenders and detractors were competing discourses surrounding race, rape, and the construction of Black womanhood. Thus, while Judge Hobgood's ruling removed the death penalty as a possible outcome for Joan, her fate nevertheless hung in the balance between dueling depictions of Black womanhood. For even with the reduced charge, Joan faced up to thirty years in prison if convicted.

Joanne Is You... Joanne Is Me!

Everywoman and the Construction of Black Womanhood

To the prosecution and to her detractors, Joan Little was a conniving Jezebel and a heartless murderer. To the defense and her myriad supporters, she was another Rosa Parks, a worthy, if flawed, victim-warrior.[1] One of the most striking aspects of the case was its contrast with the Montgomery Bus Boycott and the influence of respectability politics in struggles for racial justice. What had changed since Black activists in Montgomery, two decades earlier, had refused to back Claudette Colvin or Mary Louise Smith, two teens arrested on Montgomery buses for violating Jim Crow seating laws just months before the same action by Rosa Parks sparked the beginning of the modern civil rights movement? Why were the reputations and backgrounds of Colvin and Smith too tarnished to spur a mass protest movement, while Joan Little, another presumably "disreputable" young southern Black woman, was able to marshal national and even international backing?

Part of the answer lay in her supporters' ability to construct new definitions of Black womanhood, for a major dilemma facing her legal defense team and the Free Joan Little campaign was how to portray Joan Little. Building support for Joan Little entailed crafting careful public relations and political organizing strategies in which attorneys and activists walked a tightrope between sometimes competing images of Black womanhood. On what basis could supporters be attracted to the case? Issues of race, class, sexuality, region, and political ideology all figured into the equation. Her advocates could emphasize Joan Little's vulnerability as a destitute young Black woman or they could create a universal Everywoman. Each strategy had potential pitfalls. Organizing campaigns usually are built around common interests; but making Joan into a generic woman might erase the distinctive historical relationship Black women had to sexual assault, costing the defense an important base of support among African Americans. Stressing Joan Little's distinctiveness, however, could draw attention to her seemingly rough and more unflattering traits and thus alienate potential backers.[2]

Not surprisingly, stereotypes defaming Black female sexuality were rampant among Joan Little's critics. Historically, assertions of Black female lasciviousness and immorality had justified the outrageous claim that it was impossible to rape a Black woman. Such attitudes persisted well into the 1970s. After a young African American woman at East Carolina University was raped shortly before Joan Little's trial, the judge threw out the case citing lack of probable cause. "There ain't no way in the world a black woman can be raped," he reportedly remarked to Jerry Paul, who was defending the young woman. During Little's trial, a car dealer in her hometown echoed the racist stereotype. "Fucking is like saying good morning, or having a Pepsi Cola." Southerners were not alone in voicing such sentiments. In 1978, Connecticut governor Ella Grasso endorsed a call to review state Superior Court judge Walter Pickett after he dismissed a rape conspiracy charge saying, "You can't blame somebody for trying." A former Beaufort County sheriff perpetuated another myth about Black women as carriers of disease when he expressed doubt that Clarence Alligood had sexually assaulted Little: "Why would he want a woman like that, all eat up with syphilis like she was."[3] Her detractors, both Black and white, also used accusations of "deviant" sexuality to sow doubts about her innocence, the classic weapon deployed against unruly women, including "uppity" Black women. Whispers that Little was a prostitute and that she was a lesbian swirled throughout her hometown and beyond. The prosecution used both sets of rumors to cast aspersions on Joan Little's character and credibility.[4]

On the other side, both Black and white supporters constructed Joan Little as an icon of defiled womanhood. "Free Our Sisters: Free Ourselves" was the banner under which the national NOW office launched its defense of Joan Little. NOW president Karen DeCrow both acknowledged and downplayed the racial and class dimensions of Joan Little's case. Underlining the vulnerability of all women to rape, DeCrow asked, "Can a Joan Little happen in your community?"⁵ Other predominantly white feminist outlets echoed similar warnings: "As women, we're all on trial here," opined the *New Women's Times*. "Not one of us is immune from the possibility of either rape, assault, or some kind of sexual abuse." In remaking Joan Little as the quintessential Everywoman, NOW and other majority-white feminist groups made Joan Little into a political activist and erased her more unflattering traits. However, painting Joan Little as an iconic, universal woman risked obscuring how race and class shaped women's experiences of sexual violence. Moreover, when white feminists invoked the Everywoman icon, they may well have reinscribed "whiteness" as the mark of the normative Everywoman.⁶

Yet the Everywoman trope was more complex, and white women were not alone in making Little into a universal symbol. Black supporters also portrayed Joan as an iconic Everywoman. The lyrics in Sweet Honey in the Rock's anthem encouraged all women to see themselves in Joan's predicament:

Joanne Little, she's my sister
Joanne Little, she's our mama
Joanne's the woman
Who's gonna carry your child
Joanne is you and
Joanne is me . . .

Bernice Johnson Reagon, the former SNCC activist who wrote and performed the song, commented years later about the impact it had on other women: "It was like something had been unleashed in the culture," she recalled. "Women would just scream on that line: 'Joanne is you, Joanne is me.'" As a Black woman, Reagon understood that the trial was about racialized sexual violence; however, she claimed that in performing the song, she transcended the historic specificities of the case: "When it happened she was in a situation of a Black woman with a white man," Reagon remarked. "But what she [Joan Little] opened for me was any woman anywhere who is violated."⁷

Constructing a "generic woman" was undoubtedly a strategic decision of Little's defense team and her numerous supporters, regardless of race or gender. Julian Bond contrasted the Joan Little trial with another recent high-profile case centering on a Black woman, Angela Davis. Before her capture and acquittal for the murder of a judge in a California courtroom, Davis had gone underground and had become the first Black woman to appear on the FBI's Most Wanted list. "Angela Davis was a superstar. . . . Joan Little is every woman," Bond asserted. Little's cocounsel, Karen Galloway, painted a similar picture: "JoAnne Little is just Ms. Average America," she said.[8]

Little's defense attorneys drew attention to Little's commonalities with women more generally, and especially to the poor; but they also stressed that her experiences in jail, including sexual assault, were typical of female prisoners. "She is just an average prisoner," Galloway said. "The things that happened to her have happened to many prisoners, so she represents the vast majority of women prisoners, and the plight of poor people in general."[9]

The embrace of the Everywoman symbol by both Black and white activists and Little's legal team suggests that it was more malleable, a blank slate upon which each woman could write her own particular social locations and multiple identities. Still, Black activists' portrayal of Joan Little as the symbol of universal womanhood raises intriguing questions. Was this Everywoman's racial identity coded Black? Was class, a crucial factor in shaping Joan Little's life experiences, simply erased? Or was the construction of an African American Everywoman a clever shortcut to Black female respectability? In the end, making Joan Little a blank slate onto which supporters could create their own version of the young woman helped to attract a broad swath of supporters to the Free Joan Little campaign and to build a massive defense fund, both of which proved crucial to her acquittal.

Amid the cacophony of defenders and detractors, Joan Little seemed unsure how to respond. At times she rejected the multiple political movements and ideological battles swirling about her, each claiming to represent the real Joan Little and the true significance of her case. Feeling pulled in numerous directions, she sometimes lashed out at her supporters whom she felt pressured her to toe a particular political line. "I'm nobody's cause," she said. "I am on trial for my life," she reminded a *Jet* magazine reporter. Ethel Payne, known as the "First Lady of the Black Press," understood the perils of notoriety. Writing in the *Chicago Defender* after Joan Little failed to appear for a scheduled spot on NBC's *Today Show*, Payne observed, "Like many other headliners who have become cause célèbres, Joan Little seems to have been taken over body and soul by professionals who make a specialty of exploiting them.... Is it too much to ask for a moratorium on the commercialization of human misery?"[10]

At other moments, however, Little was grateful for the national effort made in her behalf. She sometimes even wrapped herself in a feminist banner and embraced the Everywoman identity: "Whichever way the trial turns out, it won't be me," she said. "It will be all women.... The question is whether a woman has the right to protect herself."[11] But Little also crafted

Shortly after fleeing from the Beaufort County Jail in August 1974, Joan Little turned herself in to the North Carolina State Bureau of Investigation. Defense attorney Jerry Paul, a native of Little Washington, accompanied her. Courtesy of the North Carolina State Archives and the *Raleigh News and Observer*.

a public persona as the historic Black female victim-crusader fighting specifically on behalf of African American women: "My case is important for all women, but it's more important for Black women. It's for the future, so this won't happen to other Black women," she insisted.[12]

During the trial, Little tried to dispel the image of the wanton seductress-killer, casting herself as a vulnerable but still kind-hearted Black woman who read her Bible and was sorry for her past misdeeds. About her escape and voluntary surrender she explained, "I only wanted to get out of Beaufort County because I knew that if the . . . police . . . had seen me on the streets that they would have shot me down and I wouldn't a had a chance to be in this courtroom now to tell what happened. . . . They had [said] I had intentionally left a man to die and had killed him and I wanted the people to know that I wasn't that type of person, to leave a person there you know, and not try to help him."[13]

In the courtroom, Little's defense team carefully transformed the young defendant into a paragon of female virtue. Aware of the importance of Joan's physical presentation, they deliberately softened her image. Gone was the large Afro, replaced by shorter, and sometimes even straightened, hair, possibly a wig. Gone too were the "thigh-length mini-skirts, the knee high boots and sexy slacks," replaced by "longer soft, silky dresses, and a quiet almost demure demeanor," observed the *Afro-American* (Baltimore). Jerry Paul's references to Rosa Parks sought to tie his client to the iconic Black activist; and he may well have hoped to remind jurors of the popular misperception that Parks was simply a soft-spoken, respectable seamstress who was just too tired to relinquish her seat to a white passenger on a Montgomery bus.[14]

Contests over the meaning of Black womanhood were in full display throughout the trial, not just in how the defense constructed Joan's image or in Jerry Paul's invocation of Rosa Parks. If we understand a murder trial, at least in part, as public drama and spectacle, then the bodily presence in a southern courtroom of the lead defense team—the white Jerry Paul and the Black Karen Galloway—offered a visual and corporeal counternarrative to the exploitative race and gender relations that characterized so much of southern history. Jerry Paul, the white man from Beaufort County, could as easily have been a good-old boy as a radical lawyer. Karen Galloway, also a native North Carolinian and one of the first African American women to graduate from Duke University Law School, knew that but for a few twists of fate, her life might have been quite similar to Joan Little's. But in their present roles, Paul and Galloway promised a repudiation of the Old South: jailer Clarence Alligood, the archetypal southern white, patriarch rapist, and Joan

Jerry Paul often shocked reporters with his provocative comments and flamboyant courtroom style, which earned him a contempt-of-court ruling, during Joan Little's rape-murder trial. Little's cocounsel, Karen Galloway, the first African American woman to graduate from the Duke University Law School, is partially visible in the left rear behind Paul. Courtesy of the North Carolina State Archives and the *Raleigh News and Observer*.

Little, the captive slave woman and victim of white male lust and violence. While Galloway was clearly the more groundbreaking figure, both she and Paul were visual markers of a New South, one in which white men and Black women stood side-by-side in defense of violated Black womanhood. Together, they challenged a sexualized racial caste system that historically had granted white men unfettered access to Black women's bodies as laborers, breeders, or objects of sexual violence.

From another perspective, the New South image that the two projected was more ambiguous and resonated with vestiges of the very legacy that Joan Little's defense team simultaneously evoked and transcended. For Karen Galloway's Black female body also was appropriated by the defense in ways that replicated both old and new relations between Black women and white men, and suggested that the New South found it difficult to leave behind the shackles of the Old South. Jerry Paul consciously and deliberately deployed Karen Galloway's physical presence in the courtroom as a surrogate for Joan Little. "Joan is a lower-class black. Karen is a middle-class black," he remarked to a journalist. Paul intentionally constructed an alternative image of Black womanhood for the jury by substituting one Black female body (Karen's) for another Black female body (Joan's): "I've got to give them an image of what Joan can be . . . and maybe is," he admitted. Karen became the flesh and blood symbol of respectable Black womanhood, the embodied counterpoint to the impoverished and presumably disreputable Joan Little. The fact that some observers often confused the two women outside the courtroom made Jerry Paul's defense strategy all the more effective. But that Jerry Paul could so easily deploy the physicality of Karen Galloway's Black female body conjured up images of the age-old master-slave relationship that left Galloway slightly uneasy and disquieted.[15]

The prosecution tried to undercut the defense strategy by appropriating Karen Galloway's respectable image themselves, hoping to contrast the attorney's decorum with the allegedly dishonorable and untrustworthy Joan Little. One of the prosecutors even referred to Galloway as a "lady," a term historically reserved exclusively for white women by southern whites. But Jerry Paul merely flipped the script of virtuous white womanhood. Reading from an anonymous Black woman's 1902 letter to the *Independent* magazine, "A Colored Woman, However Respectable, Is Lower than the White Prostitute," Paul reminded the jury of the long history of white men's sexual abuse of Black women.[16] And by invoking the iconic Rosa Parks, Paul hoped the jury would see the courage of the seasoned activist in Joan's act of lethal self-defense and riveting courtroom testimony.

Although the Joan Little case challenged the legacy of Black female respectability, Paul's reference to Rosa Parks showed that the politics of respectability still mattered. The civil rights, Black Power, and women's liberation movements all could take some credit for eroding the notion that only a "virtuous" woman was worthy of freedom from sexual assault. Yet Little's supporters as well as her detractors also understood that how Little's Black womanhood was constructed, both inside and outside the courtroom, could mean the difference between conviction and acquittal; and before Judge Hobgood reduced the charge to second-degree murder, it could easily spell the difference between life and death for the defendant.[17]

5

Joanne Little Acted for Us All

Black Power, Gender, and the Defense of "Sister Joan"

Joan Little's trial not only sparked contests over the meaning of Black womanhood inside the courtroom and between Joan Little's advocates and accusers. It also unleashed a pointed discussion among African American women and men in the civil rights and Black Power movements about race, rape, and gender. While these public utterances did not reflect the full range of Black opinion about the Little case, they nevertheless provide revealing glimpses into the attitudes of a number of prominent Black activists and Black Power groups.[1]

Little's trial offered a prime opportunity to showcase male enlightenment on the issue of rape and sexism. However, Black Power and civil rights leaders, especially men, frequently asserted a woman's right to self-defense, even to use lethal force if necessary, while also reinscribing masculinist politics in several ways. First, they often stressed a *Black* woman's right to self-defense against a *white* male attacker. By privileging the racial and at times the class-based dimensions over the gendered aspects of the case, they deftly elided the issue of intraracial violence against African American women. Second, they frequently maintained that the rape of Black women was primarily a weapon of white supremacist terror designed to emasculate Black men by reminding men of their inability to protect *their* women. Finally, they sidestepped the

The right of Black women to defend themselves against sexual violence was a central feature of the Free Joan Little campaign, both inside and outside the courtroom.
Courtesy of the North Carolina State Archives and the *Raleigh News and Observer*.

feminist analysis that understood rape as a form of male dominance and instead portrayed the Joan Little case as a *human rights*, rather than a *women's rights*, issue. These arguments had roots in a distinctive African American history of white supremacist violence against both Black men and women. Yet by framing the Little case in these ways, some Black activists failed to directly challenge male sexism and lost the chance to demand Black women's right to freedom from all sexual assault, whether interracial or intraracial.[2] Moreover, Black men's promise of protection often came at a price: male dominance and control. Some African American women, including nationalists, found the idea of Black male protection appealing, an antidote to a society that offered them neither respect nor safety.[3]

Maulauna (Ron) Karenga, leader of the Us Organization, penned an eloquent appeal for Little in the *Black Scholar* that at first glance looked as if it might have been featured in *Ms.* magazine. Calling Little a symbol "of all womanhood in resistance everywhere against rape," he declared that her case underlined "the right of women everywhere to be free from sexual abuse, oppression and exploitation."[4] Karenga was an unlikely advocate for a woman's right to protect herself against sexual violence. He had recently been released on parole after serving four years in prison for the sexual torture of two Black women (he insisted that he had been framed). Yet on closer inspection Karenga's and other Black nationalists' defense of Joan Little did not fundamentally challenge male dominance; many Black Power activists—women as well as men—perceived the Joan Little trial as an assault on the entire Black community. Little's actions in defending herself were a blow not against patriarchy and misogyny but against white supremacy.[5] Although Karenga also derided male chauvinism and called for equality between African American women and men, elsewhere he criticized "separatist moves" and "dual approaches to liberation," arguing that Black women and men must unite in a common struggle against the white oppressor. While he acknowledged that class was also a factor in Little's oppression, Karenga privileged the struggle of racism over sexism in the movement for Black liberation: The "rape of a black woman by a white male is first an expression of racism," he insisted.[6]

Despite his failure to emphasize the gendered dimensions of rape, Karenga did suggest that Little's killing of Alligood in self-defense challenged an age-old myth about Black women. The widely held fiction posited that Black women colluded with white men to oppress Black men, both in slavery and in freedom. By colluding with white men, particularly during slavery, Black women presumably received favored treatment in return, even if this meant giving themselves sexually to white men. After Emancipation, Black women were denigrated as emasculating matriarchs and loud-mouthed sapphires, selfishly promoting themselves while undermining Black men. Ironically, the stereotypes and accusations mirrored the prosecution's theory behind Joan Little's guilt: Black women were simply devious Jezebels, willing to use their wanton sexuality to gain advantage for themselves at the expense of men.[7]

Many Black nationalists, especially men, viewed rape as an assault on Black manhood. The historic control of Black women's bodies by white men—whether as laborers, breeders, or objects of sexual abuse—had functioned as a mechanism of social control meant to degrade Black men as well as women. According to Karenga, "The rape of a black woman by a white male is also a historical continuation of a personal and political terrorism directed against black women and the black community since slavery. It was designed to raise enduring doubt in the black man's mind about his manhood and ability to rise up against the oppressor given his painful inability to defend himself or *his* woman," declared Karenga.[8]

Black nationalists were not the only Little supporters making such claims. Civil rights leaders Ralph Abernathy, heir to Martin Luther King Jr.'s SCLC, and Julian Bond made similar appeals in the name of Black masculinity. In a call to African American men leading up to Joan's murder trial, Abernathy announced, "Our job is to go in the streets with demonstrations to show that we are sick and tired of abuse of black women by old white men." If a white woman had killed a Black male rapist, she "would be given a medal of honor," Abernathy insisted. "Well hell, we think as much of *our* women as white men think of *theirs*."[9] Thus on one level, Black men's pronouncements on the Joan Little case can be read as a contest between Black and white men over the control and possession of Black women's bodies.

There was a certain irony to calling on Black men to protect Black womanhood, for Joan Little had been unable to rely on any man to protect her from Alligood's sexual advances. With no female or Black guards employed at the Beaufort County Jail and Alligood the only jailer on duty that fateful summer night, Joan had been forced to defend herself. And while "the promise of protection" has been viewed as a male prerogative and an affirmation of manhood, Joan Little drew on a long legacy of Black women's armed self-defense.[10] Karenga acknowledged the limits of male protection, but not because it reinforced male dominance and female powerlessness. Rather, he thought the promise of protection handicapped women by making them dependent and vulnerable, especially since it was "impossible [for Black men] to be present all the time to protect each of our women." Thus, he saw no contradiction between men's safeguarding of women and Black women's right to self-defense.[11] Black women must be able to "act decisively to defend themselves, as well as our collective interests," he asserted. In a nod to female self-determination, Karenga suggested that "if we want to protect our women, it must be done with their conscious and committed cooperation." Perhaps not surprisingly, Us, as well as the Black Panther Party, supported weapons-training for Black women.[12]

Reverend Abernathy may not have publicly endorsed weapons training for women. But at a rally of 2,000 supporters in Joan's hometown, he praised her decision to fight back against Alligood's sexual assault, calling it an act of "constructive homicide." She put that ice pick "at the right place at the right time," he added. Some might have found such sentiments from a minister marking the anniversary of Martin Luther King Jr.'s assassination surprising. Yet as historian Tim Tyson reminds us, nonviolence and armed self-defense coexisted "in tension and in tandem" throughout the southern Black freedom movement of the 1950s to the 1970s.[13]

Bond, Abernathy, and Karenga recognized the potential of Joan Little's case to unite women across class and racial lines; but they also drew sharp distinctions between the experiences of Black and white women: "If this had been a white woman, I can't conceive that an indictment would have even been brought," Bond said.[14] Although all three Black male leaders noted the racial privilege that "whiteness" conferred upon white rape victims, they ignored the fact that there was no clear legal precedent for *any* woman to kill her rapist jailer, or any rapist for that matter. Indeed, women of all races frequently found themselves behind bars after defending themselves against sexual or physical assault.[15]

Some of Little's defenders elided the gendered dimensions of rape by calling her attack a *human* rights, rather than *women's* rights, violation. "Sis Joanne is black and poor, a victim of class and race violence and restrictions on human freedom," asserted Karenga. Little exercised not necessarily a woman's right to self-defense, he said, but a "human right of resistance against all assaults."[16] From exile in Cuba, Black Panther Party founder Huey Newton similarly painted Joan Little's courage as a battle-cry for human freedom, comparing her to enslaved women like Harriet Tubman and Sojourner Truth, "who stood against rape and human bondage [and] cried No More abuse to humankind." The Southern Poverty Law Center, which spearheaded much of the fundraising for Little's defense, combined both a gendered and human rights appeal. The group affirmed the right of women to defend themselves against sexual violence and drew attention to the sexual vulnerability of women prisoners, while also warning "HUMAN RIGHTS AT STAKE."17

Framing Little's plight as a violation of human rights drew on a rich history of African American freedom claims. In the 1940s and early 1950s the NAACP and the left-leaning National Negro Congress and Civil Rights Congress had appealed to the United Nations, providing detailed accounts of the gross abrogation of African American human rights in the United States. However, Cold War politics and the collapse of the Black Left stymied this strategy. In the 1960s, proponents of Black Power revived the call for human rights, especially after Malcolm X and the Black Panther Party drew attention to the most damning of the earlier petitions: "We Charge Genocide: The Crime of Government Against the Negro People." Submitted to the United Nations in 1951 by the Civil Rights Congress, "We Charge Genocide" was a 237-page petition outlining anti-Black violence and racist discrimination in all areas of public life. Little's male defenders' skirting of feminist analyses by invoking human rights also had an ironic twist; for feminists throughout the world would soon echo Black freedom fighters by redefining rape as a human rights violation. But even in the 1970s, some feminists portrayed the trial in a similar vein: "Quite simply, a human life and human rights are on trial," wrote the *New Women's Times*.18

Not only men but some Black women framed justice for Joan Little as a demand for Black liberation and human rights rather than women's liberation. Yet most African American women understood the gendered as well as the racialized dimensions of the case. Elaine Brown, who became head of the Black Panther Party in the wake of Huey Newton's self-imposed exile, portrayed Joan Little as a defender of the "humanity and dignity of Black, poor and oppressed humankind." "Joanne Little acted for us all," she said. However, Brown also refuted the Jezebel image that had stigmatized Black women for centuries. Reversing the racialized discourse on rape, she attributed traits to Joan Little that historically had been associated with virtuous white womanhood. Joan Little was "so delicate, so innocent, so naïve about what could possibly go on in the jail cell," Brown insisted. The Panther leader also turned the myth of the Black male rapist on its head. Little's white rapist-jailer, Alligood, was a "slovenly, low-grade and ill-bred pig—a native son of America" who had crept into Joan's cell "in hot pursuit of his fantasies of what Black women were all about," she claimed. For Brown this was not simply a murder case but a political trial that underlined everything that was wrong with America: "It has to do with whom [sic] she killed"—a white man—"and who she is"—a poor, Black woman—"and what the circumstances were."19

Following Little's acquittal, Elaine Brown underlined the significance of the case for Black women in particular. According to the Panther leader, Joan Little's killing of her rapist-jailer was a courageous act of defiance on behalf of African American women everywhere. "Joan Little made the decision that brings tears to my eyes," Brown said, "because I have a daughter, because I am a woman, and because I have a mother like all of us do. I know the rapes and heartaches we have suffered all of these many years." She thanked Little for showing the world "that we no longer have to tolerate rape in *our* community," an ambiguous phrasing that may well have included intraracial as well as interracial rape.[20]

It is difficult to read Elaine Brown's public utterances without recalling her autobiographical account, published nearly two decades later, of her narrow escape from an attempted gang-rape by a group of Black youths. And despite her leadership of the Black Panther Party, Brown would soon be the victim of physical abuse at the hands of male Panthers, including her former boyfriend, Huey Newton.[21] For African American women, raising the problem of intraracial rape was always loaded. It risked reinforcing the historic myth of the Black male rapist that had fueled false accusations of rape from white women, as well as lynchings and court-ordered death sentences of Black men for decades. Despite the fact that the overwhelming majority of all rapes were (and still are) intraracial, not interracial, public discussion of Black-on-Black sexual abuse within the African American community was, as Paula Giddings noted, "the last taboo."[22] For many Black nationalists, especially men, Joan Little represented not necessarily the right of all women everywhere to defend themselves against all rape but instead the right of a Black woman to defend herself against a white male attacker.

Elaine Brown was not the only woman to challenge sexism within the Black Power movement. Despite the hypermasculinity commonly associated with Black Power politics, African American women frequently fought for women's equality from within Black Power and Black nationalist organizations, including not only the Black Panther Party, but the Congress of African People, the National Black United Front, and even the Nation of Islam.[23] Amiri Baraka (LeRoi Jones), founder of the Congress of African People and the Committee for a Unified Newark, recalled that Black women in both groups fought the brothers "tooth and nail about [their] chauvinism." By the early 1970s, women such as Amina Baraka, wife of Amini, promoted more progressive views regarding gender equality and advocated for women's key political roles within Black nationalist and Pan-African liberation struggles. The women's efforts spurred Black nationalist leaders such as Baraka, Haki

Madhubuti, and Maulana (Ron) Karenga to repudiate male chauvinism by the mid-1970s. In 1975, women in the Congress of African People formed the Black Women's United Front, a Black nationalist group dedicated to ending the "triple oppression" of Black women; they also called for demonstrations in twenty-one cities to coincide with the opening of the Joan Little trial.[24]

Still, the Black Panther Party was more likely than many other Black Power groups to link the gendered and racialized aspects of the Little case. The Panther newspaper editorialized that Joan Little's case "will have far-reaching effects on the issues of women's right to self-defense when raped and law enforcement of rape." The editors believed that the "sexist *and* racist treatment of Black women prisoners" was also "on trial" and that the "nationwide support of JoAnne [has] sternly warned would-be rapists, police departments and district attorneys' offices across this country that we will no longer tolerate the chauvinistic and flippant attitude generally taken toward rape cases."[25]

The Panthers' new sensitivity regarding the sexual abuse of African American women was likely a consequence of Black women's growing influence in the Party. Women were a majority of Panther members by the late 1960s and increasingly held leadership positions in the Party. The government crackdown on the organization frequently targeted male Panthers, creating leadership opportunities for women. When Elaine Brown assumed the top Party leadership position following Huey Newton's exile, she brought more women into key positions. Although Panther men were usually the targets, women were not immune from police harassment and imprisonment on trumped-up charges.

The Black Panther Party had come a long way since heralding the 1968 publication of Eldridge Cleaver's prison writings in *Soul on Ice*. Praised by the *New York Times* as "brilliant and revealing," it was included in the Party's list of recommended readings. In the collection of essays, Cleaver, the Party's minister of information and a convicted rapist, deliberately taunted white supremacists by summoning the image of the Black male rapist. Black men's most revolutionary act against white men was the rape of white women, he maintained. Even more disturbing was Cleaver's admission that he had raped Black women first as "practice."[26] Cleaver supposedly renounced his earlier views about rape. However, it was an open secret that his wife, Kathleen— the first woman on the Panther's Central Committee and a pivotal leader in her own right—faced ongoing struggles against his physical abuse of her. According to political theorist Joy James, the issue of male violence against women in the Party and in its rival group Us "remains somewhat of a taboo

The Black Panther Party and a wide array of protesters
demanded "Freedom for Sister Joann Little," 1975.
Courtesy of the North Carolina State Archives
and the *Raleigh News and Observer*.

among African Americans." As historian Robyn Spencer concludes, "The Black Panther Party's record on gender is complex, filled with innovative moments of gender progressiveness as well as moments of blatant misogyny and sexism."[27]

Angela Davis was perhaps the most prominent radical Black women to highlight both the gendered and racialized implications of Joan Little's predicament. Davis had left the Black Panther Party after only a short stint, primarily because of its treatment of women, and joined the Che Lumumba Club, a local all-Black communist organization in Los Angeles. She was also cochair of the leftist National Alliance Against Racist and Political Repression, which backed the Joan Little campaign.[28] Leading up to the rape-murder trial, Davis appeared with Little at mass rallies, and she attended Little's trial for about a week. She offered an explicitly Black feminist, antiracist, and class-based analysis of Little's case in her widely read *Ms.* magazine article, which appeared shortly before the trial began. In her article, Davis linked Little's experience to the history of lynching, underlining the invisibility of Black women in a crime defined almost exclusively as a weapon against Black men. That Joan Little was indicted for murder simply because she had

Joanne Little Acted for Us All

defended herself against rape and would face a mandatory death sentence if convicted was "still too close to the lynch law of the past," Davis insisted.[29]

Like Karenga, Davis noted the historical rape and sexual abuse of Black women by white men both during and after slavery. She too understood that rape not only served to oppress Black women but also was "a means of terrorizing the entire black community." However, she echoed as well the feminist claim that all rapes constituted the "overt and flagrant treatment of women . . . as property." Rape and the fear of rape was "a form of mass terrorism" directed against all women, Davis maintained. Yet Black women's relationship to sexual assault was distinctive: cast as Jezebels, they were deemed lascivious and incapable of being raped.[30]

One of the defining features of the 1970s feminist antirape movement was its insight that sexual assault is not simply a personal tragedy or a random, isolated act by a deranged stranger but primarily a systemic weapon of male domination. For generations, African Americans had also understood rape as a racist political tool, an analysis echoed by Black nationalists. "Rape is not just a simple sexual and physical act, but a psycho-social and political one also," Karenga asserted.[31] Feminists on both sides of the color line extended this notion by insisting that rape was not an act of lust but an abusive exercise of power, control, and dominance exercised by men over women. (During this period, most antirape activists generally did not address the sexual assault of men by other men, except in prison; nor did they consider sexual harassment of men by women.)

Davis pointed out that the conviction rate for rape was the lowest of all violent crimes, regardless of the race of the victim, and that, for Black women survivors, both racism and male supremacy were "mutually reinforcive." However, the race of the alleged rapist was as important, if not more so, in determining sentencing. Ninety percent of those executed for rape between 1930 and 1967 were African American men, Davis noted. Still, despite these differences, both Elaine Brown and Angela Davis called for a broad-based coalition across racial and gender lines. Brown urged everyone, "Black and white, young and old," to unite behind Little, while Davis warned, "Our ability to achieve unity may mean the difference between life and death for Sister Joan."[32] Thus, while the Free Joan Little campaign created a basis for solidarity among African American women and men, and potentially among all women, it also evaded the more challenging matter of intraracial sexual assault. It was not a new dilemma. Equally challenging were the interracial and class-inflected divisions that would plague women's efforts to organize against sexual violence throughout the 1970s and 1980s.[33]

Joan Little Is Like Rosa Parks!

The Trial Testimony of Joan Little

This chapter includes descriptions of graphic sexual violence from the trial testimony that may be triggering for some readers. For further discussion, see the first endnote for this chapter.

While the Joan Little case and the Free Joan Little campaign drew an array of public supporters and detractors, nothing captured the public's attention or the jury's sympathy as Joan Little's own harrowing courtroom testimony.[1] Her defense team had rehearsed the young defendant for the upcoming trial; but they had deliberately refrained from asking her to describe the events of the night in question. "I was the only one she told it to and she told it to me only one time before she took the stand," said defense attorney Jerry Paul. "I wanted a raw, natural emotionalism," he explained, perhaps unwittingly reinforcing racist stereotypes about supposedly hyperemotional Black women. "In cross examination, on the other hand, I wanted her calm and creative. She should answer succinctly, without hesitation, and without leaving anything out." Paul was certain that if Joan stuck to her attorneys' instructions, the prosecution would have a hard time confusing her or accusing her of lying. Prosecutors repeatedly tried to question Joan about her prior felony theft conviction, hoping to raise doubts among the jurors about Joan's honesty. However, the resolute young woman refused to answer questions about the felony trial by asserting her Fifth Amendment rights.[2]

When Joan finally told her story before a packed courtroom, she spoke in a barely audible voice, frequently choking back tears or sobbing freely. "He said that he had been nice to me and it was time that I be nice to him," she testified. "He said I may as well do it because if I told . . . any of the others about it, the jailers, that none of them were gonna believe me anyway." During William Griffin's six-hour interrogation over several days, the prosecutor repeatedly forced her to recount the brutal and humiliating details of the sexual assault. Joan described how jailer Clarence Alligood took off her gown, felt her breasts, and put his hand between her legs. Griffin wanted to know why she succumbed to Alligood's demands and didn't fight back.[3]

GRIFFIN: You never screamed, hollered, shouted, pushed him away, struck him, or anything during this period of time?
LITTLE: I was scared. I didn't know whether to scream or what, because he could have killed me right then and there.
GRIFFIN: He didn't have a weapon did he?
LITTLE: He was bigger than me.
GRIFFIN: He had not threatened you, had he, had he said anything except make a proposition to you?
LITTLE: He said some things later.
GRIFFIN: He had not threatened you; he had not said he was gonna hurt you; all he said to you in effect was that he wanted to have sex with you, is that right?
LITTLE: Yes sir.
GRIFFIN: And you didn't holler, you didn't scream, you didn't fight him off, is that right?
LITTLE: No I did not, but if you had been a woman you wouldn't have known what to do either. You probably wouldn't have screamed either, because you wouldn't have known what he would have done to you.

Griffin was not about to let it go. "I'm asking you what you did. You didn't . . ." But she cut him off: "I answered your question, Mr. Griffin."[4]

Joan's testimony drew on her experience as a Black woman in the Jim Crow South and evoked the long history of racialized sexual terror against Black women. In fact, on the night in question, Little was the only inmate in the women's section of the jail and Alligood was the sole jailer on duty. Griffin asked why she had never told anyone about Alligood's repeated sexual advances, even though she had testified that she told only her mother. Her response illuminated the cruel history of southern racial mores. "In Washington, North Carolina, coming up as a black woman it's different in saying what you did and having your word to go against a white person's. It's not acceptable," she answered. Nearly thirty years later, Little's cocounsel, Karen Galloway, elaborated, "Joan knew that nobody was going to believe her. She's in jail. She's a black woman. He's white. He's a male. He believes he can do anything he wants to do to a black woman. He's been taught that all his life."[5]

As the hours dragged on, the prosecution's cross-examination grew increasingly bombastic and abusive. Griffin began yelling at Joan and berating her for using the word "sex" instead of "pussy."

> GRIFFIN: Say exactly what he said.
> LITTLE: He grabbed for my neck and he reached for me and told me to come over, that he wanted to have sex with me.
> GRIFFIN: Is that what you said yesterday? Did he say sex or did he use some other term?

But Joan was not so easily bullied and she resisted the prosecutor's efforts to publicly demean her.

> LITTLE: Mr. Griffin, the reason I am using the word sex is because it's still embarrassing to me.
> GRIFFIN: I want to ask you what the word was you used yesterday, and you said it yesterday, and you can say it again for us today; what was it that he said?
> PAUL: I object. She has said it once.
> COURT: Overruled, she can say it on cross-examination.
> LITTLE: He said he wanted me to give him some pussy.

Little described how Alligood forced her to her knees, holding the ice pick to her head, while he sat half-naked on the jail cot. "I was looking at the ice pick that was pointed directly at my face," she testified. But Griffin hadn't finished trying to humiliate Joan.

> GRIFFIN: What did he say?
> LITTLE: To go ahead and do it.
> GRIFFIN: Go ahead and do it; now he had said he wanted you to have traditional sex with him, and yet he pulled you down to have unnatural sex with you, is that right?
> PAUL: I object. She never said that.
> COURT: Well, sustained.
> GRIFFIN: I am trying to keep from using the word.
> PAUL: Then why does he want her to use the word?

Griffin's hypocrisy and his own clear discomfort with using graphic sexual terms did not prevent him from forcing Joan to recount the assault in vulgar, explicit language.

GRIFFIN: He pulled you down and told you to do it; did you know what he meant?
LITTLE: No.
GRIFFIN: What term did he use?
LITTLE: He told me to suck him.

Griffin pressed on, but his attempt to trip her up backfired. "Why didn't you twist away from him? He only had one hand on you," Griffin insisted. "And the ice pick in the other," Joan replied.

GRIFFIN: Did you at any time bite him, strike him in the genitals, or in some other way disable him?
LITTLE: No.
GRIFFIN: Why didn't you do that?
LITTLE: My only reason was to get that ice pick away from him so that he wouldn't have it pointed it at me as he did before.
GRIFFIN: Well, he could have broken you in two without any weapon at all couldn't he?
LITTLE: A man his size . . . I would say yes.
GRIFFIN: And you had an opportunity during this period of time to disable him by hitting him in the genitals, biting him?
LITTLE: I didn't have that much power over him, Mr. Griffin.[6]

The jailer's sixty-two-year-old widow, Elsie Wollard Alligood, had her own spin on Little's physical ability. She just could not believe that a "little nigger girl" could have killed her husband alone. Perhaps hoping to restore some measure of masculine honor to her deceased husband, Alligood's wife, who claimed that "he didn't like coloreds that much," was convinced that Little had helped someone else kill her husband "because she'd do anything to get out."[7]

Little stammered and wept openly as she finished her grisly account. But she stuck to her story. "He loosened his grip on the ice pick. I grabbed for it and it fell to the floor." As Joan described the details of the terrifying struggle, she broke down, stuffing a handkerchief into her mouth to quell her sobs. After the judge called a fifteen-minute recess, Joan resumed her testimony. When Alligood loosened his grip on the ice pick, she explained, it fell between the bunk and the sink in the tiny cell. Forced to the floor during the assault, Joan described how she used her body to block the jailer, who was now behind her, still seated on the bunk. "I reached for the ice pick and he reached for the ice pick. I got to the ice pick first," she said. Joan swung the weapon frantically over her right shoulder, hoping to land a blow and fend off her assailant. At first, she wasn't sure if she had hit him, but as the two continued to struggle, she struck him again. Alligood grabbed her wrists and shouted, "What the hell are you doing?!" Joan recounted. She was never sure how many times she had actually hit him; but she was certain she had struck him at least once in the head. "It was not my intention for him to stay there and die," she insisted. Finally, Alligood released his hold on her wrists and fell to the floor on his knees, blood trickling down the right side of his face. Joan jumped to her feet and bolted from the cell. She hastily pulled on a pair of jeans and donned a blue blouse. Glancing quickly over her shoulder, she saw Alligood standing with the same "silly looking grin" he had when he had entered her cell earlier that evening. Terrified that he might come after her, Joan slammed the automatic door behind her, grabbed the jail keys and fled. Outside, headlights appeared in the parking lot. "I just threw the keys and kept running," she said.[8]

Little's excruciating testimony was convincing, especially to the women on the jury. She never wavered, despite the prosecution's attempts to reveal contradictions or inconsistencies in her version of events. Instead, her interrogators came across as crude and belligerent. In his summation to the jury, the lead prosecutor, William Griffin warned the jurors not to be swayed by sympathy for Little and asked them to consider, "Did she use excessive force?" One of the assistant prosecutors, Lester Chalmers, tried to diminish the sexual assault while simultaneously acknowledging Joan's version of events. Conjuring Inez García, who killed her rapist after the attack, Chalmers insisted that Joan killed Alligood not in self-defense but as vengeance. "This murder was not in defense of an assault. The assault had already been committed. This murder was committed in *retaliation*." For good measure, Chalmers quoted Proverbs, ignoring that the judge had overruled premeditation: "The wicked flee when no man pursues, while the righteous stand bold as a lion."[9] Meanwhile, another prosecutor, John Wilkerson, hoped to paint Joan as a ruthless killer. "Why was it necessary to stab him 11 times?" he demanded to know. "Red-faced" and roaring, he charged that Alligood had "bled like a pig." Like Chalmers, Wilkerson also tried to diminish Alligood's sexual assault and undermine Joan's claim of self-defense. "An unnatural sex act is not rape," he announced to the court. "It is a detestable, horrible thing, but it's not the statutory crime of rape, and it is not punishable by death."[10] Not for white men assaulting Black women, he might have added. But scores of African American men had been brutalized by lynch mobs or given a death sentence in kangaroo courts while white sympathizers conjured up the myth of the Black beast rapist threat to white womanhood as justification. In the end, the prosecution's behavior simply reinforced the defense strategy of painting the Beaufort County Jail as a backwater, poorly run outfit, managed by a bunch of incompetent, abusive white men, and the state of North Carolina as mired in centuries-old racist stereotypes.

Joan Little's defense team was not content to rely on the bumbling ineptitude of the prosecution, however. In his closing remarks to the jury, Jerry Paul returned to the themes of respectability and defiled Black womanhood. Quoting Martin Luther King Jr. and invoking the memory of Rosa Parks, he positioned Parks, Joan Little, and Karen Galloway under the rubric of honorable and upright Black womanhood and depicted all three women as heroic freedom fighters. Hoping the twelve men and women would see a version of the seasoned activist in Joan's act of self-defense and compelling testimony, he underlined Little's courage in turning herself in to authorities and testifying in detail about Alligood's sexual assault. "Joan Little is like Rosa Parks," Paul intoned. "If Rosa Parks had obeyed the law of the land. . . . you wouldn't be serving on this jury today," a direct appeal to the Black women on the jury. "If Rosa Parks had not have refused to sit in the back of the bus, you'd still be riding in the back of the bus . . . and you wouldn't have a job and it wouldn't be possible for Karen Galloway to stand up here and be a member of my law firm and go to Duke Law school and defend Joan Little. . . . So sometimes you have to stand up for morality and sometimes God chooses people . . . just like he chose Rosa Parks, just like he chose Joan Little." Paul skillfully tied Rosa Parks's decision to break a Jim Crow law to Little's act of lethal self-defense and cast both women's behavior as feats of moral bravery. He reminded the jury that the people in Nazi Germany had insisted that the "law is the law and must be enforced, while they sent six million Jewish people off to death, and nobody said a word." Most important, the attorney derided both Alligood—an officer of the law—and the state as criminals. "Where was the law to protect Joan Little that night in that cell? I'll tell you where the law was. The law was back there forcing her to do an unnatural sex act. That's where the law was that protects us."

Paul also underlined the larger significance of the trial for women: "This case compels . . . the world to see that women, black women, deserve justice; that women are victims of rape and that rape is not a sex crime. . . . It is a crime of violence, of hatred." Paul painted Little as an inspiration to the women's antirape movement: "She stood up, and that's why women all over this Nation are finding the courage to talk about rape and what happened to them. And organized rape crisis centers and organized women's groups where they meet and start to talk about some of these problems because of what people like Joan Little did." Little was not a criminal, Paul insisted. "She was a hero . . . because she stood up for what was right and had the courage to come back and tell you about it. And if you don't think that takes courage—in North Carolina . . ." Answering Chalmers's quote from Proverbs, he added, "She had a right to run. . . . She better run from eastern North Carolina or they'd have killed her."

At the end of his summation, Paul returned once again to Rosa Parks and Martin Luther King Jr., reminding that jury that both had broken laws. He also linked the state of North Carolina to the opponents of the civil rights movement: "These same people that said King was a criminal because he marched and spoke for freedom and was a freedom fighter are the same people that's trying to put Joan Little in jail." When the prosecution interrupted him, Paul apologized to the court: "I'm sorry if I'm emotional. It's been a hard battle." Finishing his summation, the lead defense attorney dropped his pointer to the floor and returned to his seat, his head bowed, totally spent.[11]

Perhaps the most effective and powerful defense summation, however, came from cocounsel Karen Galloway. She drew on the history of Black women's resistance against sexual violence and the lessons of NOW members Mary Ann Largen and Cathy Ellison, who had helped prepare her for this moment. Under North Carolina law, rape was narrowly defined and oral sexual assault was not included. Thus, the judge had refused to allow testimony from antirape experts, leaving that responsibility to the defense. Galloway had turned to the two NOW women for assistance. During her closing argument, the young attorney painted a vivid picture of Clarence Alligood overpowering a terrified Joan Little. To underline Joan's vulnerability, Galloway used tape to mark off a five-foot-by-seven foot "jail cell" on the court room floor. She asked the jury to imagine themselves "in Joan's shoes," trapped in her tiny cell, alone in the women's section of the Beaufort County Jail with Alligood the only guard on duty when he entered her cell. The young attorney dramatically reenacted Little's desperate self-defense on that terrible summer night. She wanted the jury to understand "what it was that a rape victim felt at the time." Several of the female jurors, especially the Black women, wept during Galloway's eloquent summation. She had touched a nerve. They knew all too well the sexual vulnerability and fear that Black women faced, whether through their own personal experiences or the warnings whispered by generations of elders to scores of young Black girls.

It was the same fear that had prompted Black mothers and fathers to keep their daughters out of white households and factories, hoping to protect them from white men's sexual advances. And it was the same defiance that had fueled the creation of the National Association of Colored Women in 1896 and Black women's determination to defend their reputations themselves. Much of this had been passed down through the decades, as African American women spoke out and organized against the sexual degradation and abuse of Black women. The group New York Radical Feminists might have sponsored the first public "speak-out" against rape in 1971, but as historian Danielle McGuire has noted, they were standing on the shoulders of the Black women antirape activists who preceded them, whether they knew it or not. And despite the whitewashing of that groundbreaking event, often heralded as the start of the feminist antirape movement, Black women were there too, speaking out against rape alongside their white counterparts.[12]

When Galloway finished her twenty-minute closing, silence filled the courtroom. Several Black women jurors wiped away tears. "I thought I had done something wrong," Galloway said. After the jury filed out of the courtroom, Galloway ran to the women's restroom and burst into tears. It was only the second time during the long ordeal that she had allowed herself that kind of emotional release. The first had been when State Bureau of Investigation officials brought the tiny Joan Little into court in shackles, her limbs in leg irons and handcuffs.[13]

But Galloway needn't have worried. After the five-week trial in the summer of 1975, the majority-female jury, evenly divided between Blacks and whites, deliberated seventy-eight minutes before acquitting the young woman. None of the jurors, who had been sequestered during the entire trial, thought the prosecution had presented convincing evidence of Little's guilt. "What bothered me was that all the evidence wasn't there," explained Annie Hunter, a sixty-six-year-old Black tobacco worker. For Donnell Livingstone, a twenty-two-year-old African American water bill collector, "the investigation was very sloppy.... We realize they don't have facilities like in New York City," he said, "but they could have done better." One of the white male jurors, a Raleigh attorney, claimed that "we didn't feel it was a racial case or particularly a sexual case." However, Pecola Jones, a forty-nine-year-old African American machinist, said she identified with Joan Little: "If her testimony was true it was a bad thing for a young woman to go through. I could only think about myself being in the same position." Jennie Lancaster, a white twenty-five-year-old youth counselor, acknowledged that in the end no one could be certain about what precisely had occurred in Little's cell that

Joan Little (left) and attorney Karen Galloway. This was Galloway's first trial after graduating from Duke University Law School in 1974. Courtesy of the North Carolina State Archives and the *Raleigh News and Observer*.

night; and some of the jurors did not believe all of Little's testimony. Yet all twelve jurors felt that Joan was vulnerable in that jail. In the end, they simply decided that the state had failed to prove its case.[14]

Most of the media sided with the not-guilty verdict. Editors at Little's hometown newspaper, perhaps still stinging from the change of venue, insisted, "Exactly the same result would have been achieved right here in Beaufort County." But not everyone thought she was innocent. Pulitzer Prize–winning Chicago columnist Mike Royko found Joan's version of the killing "almost laughable," and thought it "was just as easy to believe she had set up the old geezer for murder and escape as it was to believe he forced her to defend herself."[15]

Outside the courtroom, aides to the defense team rushed around the parking lot yelling, "Freedom! Freedom!" while other supporters, who presumably threatened violence if Joan was convicted, chanted, "We're so happy, we don't what to do." The *Afro-American* summed up the feelings of many when it announced, "Another Victory for Equal Justice Under the Law."[16] But none of this had come easily and victory seemed a remote possibility when attorneys Jerry Paul and Karen Galloway first agreed to take on Joan Little's defense.

Despite the courtroom victory in Joan Little's rape-murder trial, some of the details surrounding the sexual assault and Alligood's death remain murky to this day. The prosecution's incompetence, at least as much as the defense attorneys' skills, may have been a crucial factor in Joan's acquittal. Not only was the police investigation of the crime scene undermined. The prosecution also failed to pursue several inconsistencies in Little's testimony or other damaging details that could have suggested a motive for the killing and Joan's escape from the Beaufort County Jail. For example, the deadline for her appeal and release on bail for the original felony theft conviction that landed her in the Beaufort County Jail to begin with was due to expire the day of Alligood's death. According to the prosecution, the court session had ended the previous Friday, August 23, 1974, thus leaving her no opportunity for an appeal. During court testimony however, Joan insisted she had told several other prisoners and two of the guards on or about August 23 that she had spoken to a bondsman, Roger Bernholz, and to Julius Rogers; both informed her she would soon be bailed out. Her mother and Rogers similarly reassured her that they were working to raise bail and that she would be going to court the week of August 26. Joan testified that Alligood told her on the evening of August 26 that court was still in session. She added that one of the other guards repeatedly said that court had been extended for several weeks due to an overcrowded docket. Little explained that because she was the only one in the women's section of the jail at the time, she had no way of knowing that court was no longer in session. However, the courtroom was in the same building as the jail and the absence of sounds of people coming and going might have alerted her that the court was in recess.[17]

Other discrepancies also went unchallenged by the prosecution. Joan testified that Alligood said he "wanted to have sex with me again." Her use of the word "again" was ambiguous. Joan had testified that Alligood first approached her for sex two or three weeks after she was jailed in June 1974 and that she had rebuffed him. Jerry Paul maintained that Alligood had sexually assaulted her only once, though the jailer had repeatedly propositioned her. Marjorie Wright, who had helped Joan escape from Little Washington to Chapel Hill and Durham after fleeing the Beaufort County Jail following Alligood's sexual assault, reported in an interview shortly after the trial that Joan had told her that she was tired of "that man making her have oral sex" with him. However, years later, Joan negated many details of Wright's account, raising questions about whose recollections were more accurate. Beaufort County sheriff Davis also believed that Alligood "had been screwing" Little and in an interview with Morris Dees, he admitted that the jailer had been acting strangely on August 26 and 27, the night he died. To be sure, the number of sexual encounters that may have occurred or even Little's alleged and unproven consent did nothing to alter the coercive and unequal power relations between the prisoner and the jailer. However, it might have buttressed the prosecution's theory that Joan lured Alligood into her cell with promises of sex, all the while planning to attack him and escape. Did Little's use of the word "again" in her court testimony suggest that what happened that August night was not the first sexual contact between the two? Or was it an unartful sentence construction, a reference to the jailer's third return to her cell that night with cigarettes and sandwiches, before pressing her once more for sex and then finally assaulting her? The prosecution let the ambiguity slip.[18]

Presumed missing evidence also marred the case. For example, Joan had made notations in the margins of several books about daily events in the jail, and she testified that she had recorded Alligood's repeated sexual advances in one of her novels. When the book was finally produced, there were no notations, but pages 6–78 were inexplicably missing, suggesting evidence tampering by officials. Joan's testimony and an interview with her mother, however, made up for these lapses. Joan testified that she had told her mother, Jessie Williams, about Alligood's advances, shortly after she arrived at the jail. And while Joan was still on the lam, the local paper interviewed Williams, who reported that Joan had called her about a week before her escape and complained that male jail personnel "were bothering her."[19]

Most intriguing of all was another tantalizing tidbit that never found its way into the courtroom: a news clipping allegedly discovered in Joan's prison Bible. The clipping featured an Old Testament story in which Jael, an Israelite woman, lured the leader of an opposing army into her tent, fed him, and let him rest. Then as he slept, she drove a huge nail though his temples, killing him.[20] To some observers, Jerry Paul's waving the seemingly incriminating Bible clipping in front of the media after the trial cost Joan's appeal on her earlier felony theft conviction several months later. Others were incredulous that her lead defense attorney would taunt the courts by insinuating that his client may well have been guilty of premeditated murder. Yet Paul claimed that he mentioned the Bible clipping only to underline the incompetence of the prosecution and the injustice of the legal system. "They all want to hear that the Joan Little case proves that the system works, and they get uncomfortable when I say I tricked the system into working," he said.[21]

Yet even granting the prosecution's unproven contention that Joan had "lured" Alligood into her cell with promises of sex, sexual activity between a jailer and a prisoner could never be wholly consensual. Thus either way, Joan Little was a victim. Charlene Mitchell, the African American woman who headed the National Alliance Against Racist and Political Repression, which supported Little, pointed out that the prosecution's definition of consent was highly problematic: "No one can ever consent to have anything to do with their jailer. There was a weapon involved and this man was doing something that he had no business doing." Even a source in the sheriff's office conceded that Alligood had no right to enter Joan's cell that night.[22] In effect, the failure to protect Joan from sexual assault constituted state-sanctioned violence against the confined young woman. Moreover, the sworn testimony of several former Black women prisoners who stated that Alligood had repeatedly fondled them and tried to have sex with them lent credibility to Joan Little's version of events. Ida Mae Robinson, one of the three, responded to Alligood's advances with threats: "I said if he come in here I'd kill him," she testified. Alligood never bothered her after that, but she said she contemplated suicide because of his harassment. In court testimony and in a pretrial interview by Morris Dees, Phyllis Moore recalled that Alligood made frequent sexual remarks to Joan—such as "Do you need a man?"—and that Little always rebuffed him. Moore, who had been jailed briefly with Joan in July 1974, claimed that Alligood came into the women's cells to bring items when he easily could have passed them through the bars. Moore also recalled that Little was very modest, putting up blankets on cell bars for privacy. One of Alligood's former neighbors corroborated the women's testimony, noting that the jailer "had an eye for women." Little also had passed a polygraph test, though such evidence was inadmissible in court.[23] Finally, Joan Little's own gripping testimony was highly persuasive, especially to the women jurors.

Joan's acquittal in the murder case did not signal an end to rampant racism and discrimination in the criminal legal system. The verdict had been bought, not won, Paul insisted. Citing the $325,000 defense fund, he boasted, "I can win any case in this country given enough money."[24] Simply put, a top-notch fundraising effort and the ability to orchestrate sympathetic press coverage, rather than the search for truth or justice, was at the heart of America's criminal punishment enterprise and the reason for Joan's acquittal, the attorney maintained. Others would point to the nationwide Free Joan Little organizing campaign and international attention. Both the feminist and Black press echoed Paul's critique, underlining the challenges of seeking justice through the courts, especially for poor Black women who accused white men of sexual violence. "We celebrate her victory, but know that Joan is free, not because of the judicial system in this country, but in spite of it," opined the editors at *off our backs*. In New York City, the *Amsterdam News* similarly noted the limitations of Joan's courtroom victory. Comparing the Little trial to the Attica Prison rebellion several years before, the Black weekly charged that "brutality against women in the prison system [was] only casually investigated prior to the celebrated trial." Cautioning against the dangers of short memories, the editors warned that "what happened to Joan Little will happen a thousand times again—if the public turns its back and forgets."[25]

Following her acquittal, Little remained free while her attorneys appealed her original felony theft conviction. However, the North Carolina Court of Appeals struck down the appeal and in December 1975, the state Supreme Court, with no explanation, denied her motion for a new trial. Louis Randolph, a Black city councilman in Washington, North Carolina, who had helped raise money for Little's murder defense, had his own explanation. Randolph believed that Jerry Paul's mockery of the criminal justice system, both during and after Little's 1975 murder trial, had hurt her chances of an appeal and squelched any chance of a reduced sentence when she was returned to prison on the felony theft conviction.[26]

Joan Little's rape-murder case continued to resonate throughout the 1970s and beyond. In some respects, it mattered little whether she was "just like Rosa Parks"; for the unusual acquittal in a southern courtroom of a low-income Black woman accused of murdering her white male jailer inspired scores of activists. Attorneys then and now often remark that trials are seldom vehicles for social change. But mass-based defense campaigns rooted in care and longer-term struggles for social justice can, as activist Mariame Kaba notes, provide "popular education to strengthen our movements." They can "connect people in a heartfelt, direct way that teaches lessons about the brutality of prisons."[27] Both the prisoners' and the antirape movements of the 1970s and 1980s were stirred by the Joan Little case, joining their own demands with the plight of the young woman from eastern North Carolina who had garnered so much attention.

PART TWO

THIS ARMY OF THE WRONGED

FORGOTTEN WOMEN AND PRISON ORGANIZING IN THE CIVIL RIGHTS–BLACK POWER ERA

7

Child, Why Are They Bringing You to Trial?

The Prison Movement and the Joan Little Case

Joan Little might have beaten the murder charges and escaped North Carolina's gas chamber, no small feat for a young southern woman who was both poor and Black. As noted earlier, she did not fare so well with her felony-theft conviction, however. After losing her appeal in the North Carolina Court of Appeals in December 1975, Joan returned once again to the North Carolina Correction Center for Women (NCCCW, or "Women's Prison") in Raleigh to serve a seven-to-ten-year and possible fourteen-to-twenty-year sentence for the felony theft conviction. This was not Joan's first stint at Women's Prison; she had spent over five months there while her supporters raised bail and her attorneys crafted her legal defense for the rape-murder trial.[1]

At Women's Prison, Little encountered a prison movement that swept the country in the late 1960s and into the 1970s. As countless brown and Black bodies were subjected to ever-more-punitive penal polices, they did not remain quiescent. The protest movement they mounted, at times in concert with their white counterparts, was an unprecedented undertaking then and one that the country has not witnessed since. Prisoners at NCCCW, along with the men at Central Prison in Raleigh, were in the vanguard of these efforts in the South.

One of the key players in the North Carolina women's prison movement was Celine Chenier, a founder of the Free Joan Little campaign. Chenier had been a prisoner advocate long before she took up Joan Little's cause. Also known by the Nigerian name Tamu Amaka Emoli (meaning "beautiful one") or simply "Tamu," to the prisoners she worked with, Chenier was a thirty-seven-year-old African American woman from a middle-class Black-Creole family in New Orleans. She insisted that she was "no radical. . . . I'm not that kind of person—too sensitive to be good at it, probably." Raised as a devout Catholic, Chenier had once considered training to become a singer of liturgical music. Later she even flirted with the idea of becoming a nun. Instead, she found her way to New York City, working with heroin addicts for seven years before she was invited to Durham by the one Black psychiatrist in the city. Her interactions with women addicts, many of whom were on parole, inevitably had brought Chenier face-to-face with the brutality of prison life. "They didn't want to talk about drugs, but about conditions in the prisons, and that's how I got involved," she explained. "Conditions" included the sexual vulnerability of incarcerated women, and Chenier routinely received countless letters from prisoners who had been raped. She also had friends who had been raped in prison. But they never came forward. "Who would believe it?" she asked rhetorically. "They were black, they were inmates, and they were women." Thus, even if she had never met Joan Little, Chenier was sure she "would have been involved in the prison struggle." But "perhaps the issue would not have interested the public as much."[2]

After losing her job at Carolina Friends School, Chenier worked full-time on Joan Little's defense. She traveled around the country, speaking at various venues trying to elicit support for Little's upcoming murder trial. When Little finally made bail in February 1975 after nearly six months in prison, Chenier accompanied her to Beaufort County where they visited Joan's great-great grandmother, a woman then in her nineties whose father had been enslaved. Few words were exchanged, but the sordid history of Black women's sexual abuse at the hands of white men was written on the older woman's face. As she looked at Joan, Chenier thought her pained expression seemed to say, "'Child, why are they bringing you to trial?'" Celine Chenier may not have thought of herself as a "radical." Yet her efforts proved vital not only to Joan Little's fate but also to the prison movement and those incarcerated at the North Carolina Correctional Center for Women.[3]

While it has been given scant recognition in the scholarship on the Free Joan Little campaign, the prison movement was critical to Little's defense, especially in the early days. However, attention to prison organizing, especially among women, does more than flesh out

Little's rape-murder case: First, it challenges the declension narrative of the late 1960s which claimed that the Black freedom struggle was over by the end of the decade, and pushes the chronology of the "long civil rights movement" forward into the 1970s. Second, women's prison organizing moves beyond the hypermasculinity often associated with Black Power, which had a major impact on the prisoners' movement; and it broadens the male focus of much of the prison movement scholarship by illuminating the politicization and resistance of incarcerated women. Third, it highlights how distinctions between criminal prisoners and political prisoners were increasingly blurred during these years. Finally, centering the efforts of Black women, on both sides of the prison walls, reveals the continuities in African American women's activism, including the Black Left, and provides a more multifaceted picture of 1970s women's liberation, often called "second wave" feminism.[4]

Many of the local women who were among Little's earliest supporters were themselves part of the prison movement. Black women in North Carolina formed two organizations in direct response to Little's indictment for first-degree murder: Concerned Women for Fairness to Joan Little, which later changed its name to Concerned Women for Justice (CWJ), and Action for Forgotten Women. CWJ was a statewide group established by two veteran Black women organizers whose activism dated to the 1940s: Christine Strudwick, a Durham civil rights activist, and Velma Hopkins, a militant Congress of Industrial Organizations labor leader from Winston-Salem. CWJ raised money for Little's defense, sponsored a citywide prayer vigil for Little and the Wilmington Ten in Raleigh two days before Little's murder trial began, and submitted a resolution to the North Carolina governor protesting conditions at Women's Prison. Following Little's trial, CWJ chapters spread across the state and remained active in prisoner-support work, especially on behalf of the prisoners at NCCCW. Their prison visits and programs for incarcerated women, such as the CWJ Prison Christmas Project, were reminiscent of generations of both Black and white female reformers. However, CWJ also established prisoner-release programs, organized voter-registration drives, and supported African Americans who faced discrimination in the criminal legal system. And they condemned Governor Jim Hunt for simply reducing the sentences of the Wilmington Ten, accusing him of "officially legitimizing an error of political oppression."[5]

Chenier formed another local Black women's organization, Action for Forgotten Women, shortly after Little's indictment. Like Concerned Women for Justice, Action for Forgotten Women advocated for the prisoners at NCCCW. The group tended to attract younger women than CWJ but also drew seasoned activists such as Charsie Hedgepath, one of the leaders of Durham's Black boycott of white merchants and a founder of the Malcolm X Liberation University in the city in the late 1960s. Triangle Area Lesbian Feminists, a predominantly white, grassroots group in Durham organized prior to the Little case, also eagerly lent its support. All three groups—Concerned Women for Justice, Action for Forgotten Women, and Triangle Area Lesbian Feminists—were among the most important local participants in the Free Joan Little campaign; and they continued to advocate for incarcerated women and for racial justice in North Carolina long after the Joan Little case receded from public memory.

Many of these women also had links to national organizations and were part of a nationwide network of Black activists. For example, Celine Chenier was a member of the National Alliance Against Racist and Political Repression (National Alliance) and alerted two leading Black women prison activists, Angela Davis and Charlene Mitchell, to Joan Little's case. Both Mitchell and Davis were especially important in attracting radicals to the campaign. Davis, a member of the Communist Party, was the most-celebrated female political prisoner of the era; Mitchell was a veteran communist leader and head of the National Alliance, which organized numerous campaigns on behalf of political prisoners. Mitchell also was a role model for Davis and had been the executive director of the National Committee to Free Angela Davis.[6] But the two activists did more than organize national support for Joan Little, especially within the Left. Both women worked closely with attorney Jerry Paul to develop a defense of Little; and Davis attended the Raleigh trial and helped to prepare the young woman for her court testimony and grueling cross-examination by the prosecution.[7] In effect, the participation in Little's defense of seasoned Black women activists such as Velma Hopkins on the local level and Charlene Mitchell on the national level demonstrates the continuities in Black women's activism as well as the generational links between the Black Left of the 1940s and 1950s and the radical Black protest politics of the 1970s.

Prior to the Little case, the National Alliance had focused on North Carolina's use of the criminal legal system against Black activists, including the Wilmington Ten, and the state's racially discriminatory death penalty.[8] During a visit to North Carolina on behalf of the Wilmington Ten, Angela Davis learned about the Little case through Celine Chenier. The decision of Davis and the National Alliance, including its North Carolina chapter, to lend support to Joan Little underscored the degree to which prison activists increasingly challenged the rigid lines between "political" and "criminal" (also referred to as "common" or "social") prisoners. Other radical groups did likewise. The Black Panther Party linked the Little case to that of George Jackson, one of the most controversial political prisoners of the era. The experience of imprisonment frequently politicized "common" criminals, especially prisoners of color, similarly blurring such distinctions. Moreover, Alligood's assault on Little in the Beaufort County Jail underlined the state's failure to protect her and constituted state-sanctioned violence. Joan the "common criminal" thus morphed into a quasi-"political" prisoner and an icon of the prison movement.

Although Angela Davis had previously developed a radical intersectional analysis of sexual oppression and violence against Black women, including rape, historian Genna Rae McNeil notes that Davis did not immediately seize upon Little's ordeal as representative of these issues. "I can't say that was the reason why I was attracted to the case," Davis acknowledged. But she did feel a sense of solidarity with Little based on gender, race, and her own experience of confinement. "It was a sister who obviously was in need of assistance." At the same time, Davis did not initially view Little as a political prisoner.[9] However, Davis's support, particularly her exposé about the case in *Ms.* magazine, helped to galvanize broader feminist endorsement of the Free Joan Little campaign, especially among white women, and to shine a light on the sexual vulnerability of female prisoners.

By the 1970s, female activists on both sides of the prison walls drew on the women's liberation, civil rights, and Black Power movements to fashion a politics that included incarcerated women. Throughout the decade, prisoner advocates in North Carolina and across the country provided services to women inmates, brought public attention to prison conditions, and even fought for prison abolition. In Chicago, the National Alliance of Black Feminists (NABF) drafted a Black Woman's Bill of Rights in 1976 that included preventive measures against sexual abuse and called for justice in the courts, penal institutions, and work-release programs "free of discrimination based on race, sex, and socio-economic status." The following year the group resolved to create a resource bank for offenders and ex-offenders alike. The NABF's logo was a pair of clenched fists in handcuffs, evoking both enslavement and imprisonment; one cuff was marked "sexism," the other labeled "racism." In Michigan, Women Against Prison organized to halt the construction of a new women's prison. The Santa Cruz Women's Prison Project took direction from women inmates in devising their programs, while offering a radical critique of crime and imprisonment. Local activists, largely women of color, and feminists from a women's studies class at the State University of New York in Buffalo organized a women's prison abolition group. And the Puerto Rican Women's Prison Project provided daily programs for women at Rikers Island jail in New York City, where Joan Little was held during her extradition battle.[10]

Lesbian and feminist prison activists, as well as women inmates themselves, drew inspiration from the Joan Little case to highlight the pervasive sexual abuse of jailed women. In California, Indiana, New York, Ohio, and elsewhere, women prisoners protested state-sponsored sexual violence though writing, filing lawsuits, and organizing prisoner strikes. In Florida, over 100 women inmates "rioted" in 1975 to protest sexual abuse by male guards. In New York, the feminist collective Women Free Women in Prison strategically reversed the "deviancy" label that stigmatized suspected lesbians by calling out the "'many perversions in prisons' perpetuated against female inmates by 'degenerate' male guards" who sexually abused women prisoners.[11]

Even mainstream feminist groups like the National Organization for Women began to focus on the sexual vulnerability of jailed women. National NOW president Karen DeCrow not only proclaimed the group's support for Little but also urged local chapters to lobby legislators on the dangers of prisons for women and the mistreatment of poor women in the criminal punishment system. Members were encouraged to visit women prisoners, hold press conferences, and organize teach-ins on issues of concern to incarcerated women. DeCrow also called on the federal government to undertake a study of the sexual abuse of women in prison.[12]

Across the nation, both male and female prison activists rallied to Little's defense. In California, Sisters of Motivation, a prisoner aid group, sent a message of solidarity when Little appeared at a 1975 Panther rally in Oakland. Her case was publicized in prisoner newsletters including the *Midnight Special* and *Attica News*. It even attracted the backing of Prisoners Against Rape, a group of convicted rapists in Virginia who were dedicated to combatting sexual violence. While Joan awaited bail in Women's Prison before the murder-rape trial, a Muslim prisoner in Indiana, who claimed he was an attorney, offered legal support and suggested that he and Little write to one another. From Auburn Prison in New York, the White Panthers Criminal Justice Committee made the Little case a priority and helped to publicize it in nearby Buffalo.[13]

The Prisoners Solidarity Committee, a national group of ex-prisoners, their families, and other allies founded by Youth Against War and Fascism to support prison rebellions at the Attica and Auburn prisons in New York, sponsored rallies and defense funds for Joan Little in cities across the country, including New York, Cleveland, Philadelphia, Boston, Milwaukee, and Rochester, among others. The Prisoners Solidarity Committee held that prisons were "concentration camps for the poor" and that most prisoners were guilty of "crimes of survival." A large majority of the incarcerated were impoverished and/or people of color, the group observed. Therefore, all prisoners were political prisoners and "all jails should be torn down." In Richmond and Norfolk, the committee collected thousands of petition signatures demanding that the charges against Little be dropped; and it sent buses of observers from Richmond, Norfolk, and Baltimore to Little's murder trial in Raleigh.[14] The relationship between the Free Joan Little campaign and the prison movement thus was reciprocal, as each reinforced the other. An organized prisoners' movement helped to fuel the creation of the Free Joan Little campaign, which in turn brought greater scrutiny to North Carolina as well as to national penal policies, including the vulnerability of confined women to sexual abuse and a racist criminal punishment system.

These efforts were part of a vibrant prison movement that gained momentum in the 1960s and 1970s. By the mid-1970s, the movement was an eclectic group of reformers, prison abolitionists, gay and lesbian liberationists, feminists, radical academics, artists, leftists of various stripes, religious communities, and Black Power activists, among others. Even former U.S. attorney general Ramsey Clark joined their ranks. In a 1979 address to the annual conference of the Southern Coalition on Jails and Prisons, an alliance of prison reformers from nine southern states, Clark noted the class and racial disparities in imprisonment. "We are grinding up persons in a criminal justice system that never heard the word equality," he said.[15]

Black prison activists in particular built on a long tradition of African American protest against police brutality, a discriminatory legal system, and harsh prison conditions. As historian Dan Berger has observed, "Alongside their experiences of literal imprisonment, black activists and artists have used the prison as a metaphor for describing their confrontations with the American state."[16] African American singer-songwriters, from renowned blues singers Ma Rainey, Bessie Smith, and Leadbelly to B. B. King, James Brown, Gil Scott-Heron, and Public Enemy, among many more recent artists, have made police brutality, anti-Black vigilante violence, and incarceration a central motif in their accounts of Black life both inside and outside the prison walls. White supremacist violence, often carried out with official complicity if not outright participation, also drew the attention of Black cultural artists. Billie Holiday's 1938 "Strange Fruit," a searing indictment of lynching, became her signature song, while Nina Simone's 1964 "Mississippi Goddam!" excoriated white supremacist violence across the South. It became an anthem of the civil rights movement, and was even banned in several southern states. Bernice Johnson Reagon, former SNCC activist and Sweet Honey in the Rock founder, was one of the few cultural activists in the 1970s to center Black women's prison experience. Reagon's lyrics to "Joanne Little," originally recorded as a fundraiser for the Little defense, indicted the entire country: "Joanne is you, Joanne is me / Our prison is the whole society."[17]

In the 1950s and 1960s, the jailhouse was a central metaphor for racist brutality, in both the North and the South. Black leaders from Martin Luther King Jr. to Malcolm X alluded to confinement as both a place and symbol of anti-Black oppression. "America means prison," and the U.S. president was "just another [prison] warden," Malcolm declared. During the Montgomery Bus Boycott, King professed that Blacks "were tired of going through the long night of captivity" and exhorted his people to reach out "for the daybreak of freedom and justice and equality." SNCC leader Stokely Carmichael declared before a Swedish audience in 1967, "I was born in jail." Civil rights activists made the jailing of Black bodies a major tactic in the campaign to dismantle southern segregation. When a judge tried to release the pregnant SNCC activist Diane Nash from jail, she declared, "Since my child will be a black child born in Mississippi, whether I am in jail or not, he will be born in prison."[18] Turning imprisonment on its head, "showed that the prison could be made public and turned into a source of power where prisoners could trump their literal and figurative jailers," Berger claims. "If jail could not break the movement, nothing could." And yet, although African Americans had long been disproportionately arrested, convicted, incarcerated, and executed by the state, neither the transformation nor the abolition of the prison system was a primary goal of the civil rights movement.[19]

If prison reform was not a central demand of most civil rights organizations, the jailing of activists, especially women, brought renewed attention to prison conditions and the vulnerability of Black women prisoners. African American women from Rosa Parks to SNCC members Ruby Doris Smith Robinson, Fannie Lou Hamer, and scores of others, subverted gendered, class-inflected respectability politics by literally putting their bodies on the line and subjecting themselves to imprisonment. Women protesters faced not only similar brutality as their male comrades but the danger of sexual abuse as well. In fact, alarm over women's sexual vulnerability led the National Council of Negro Women to create the short-lived Youth Emergency Fund in the mid-1960s to protect jailed female activists. By reducing and even eliminating the stigma normally associated with arrest and imprisonment, Black women activists laid the groundwork for the Free Joan Little campaign and organized protests of other incarcerated women in the 1970s.[20]

Historically, campaigns involving African American boys and men, most notably the 1930s Scottsboro Boys case, drew the bulk of national attention. However, in the early twentieth century, Black women activists including Ida B. Wells, Mary Church Terrell, and Salena Sloan Butler pushed the National Association of Colored Women to protest the exploitation and sexual abuse of Black women prisoners, leading eventually to the abolition of the hated southern chain gang. African American reformers and clubwomen also initiated the "Black child-savers" movement to press for more humane treatment of confined Black youth. Individual Black women's cases attracted activist assistance and sometimes even national visibility years before the Joan Little case. For example, Rosa Parks, who founded a Joan Little Defense Committee in her adopted city of Detroit in the 1970s, had organized against racialized sexual violence in the 1940s and 1950s. One of Parks's early efforts in behalf of southern Black women rape survivors was the formation of the 1944 national campaign to defend Recy Taylor. Taylor had been abducted and gang-raped by a carload of white men in Alabama. Her campaign received an important boost from women in the left-leaning Southern Negro Youth Congress, where Angela Davis's mother, Sallye Belle Davis, was a national officer and leading organizer. While the men were never brought to justice, historian Danielle McGuire points out that African American women like Recy Taylor "used their voices as weapons against white supremacy . . . helped expose a ritual of rape in existence since slavery, inspired a nationwide campaign to defend black womanhood, and gave hope to thousands suffering through similar abuses."[21]

In 1948, Rosa Lee Ingram, a widowed Georgia sharecropper and mother of twelve, was sentenced to death along with two of her teenage sons after they defended her against an attack by a white man. The case highlighted the discriminatory use of capital punishment. But it also shone a spotlight on Black women's sexual vulnerability at the hands of white men. Ingram's supporters turned the trope of the endangered white woman on its head. It was not Black men who menaced white women, as lynching apologists had long maintained, but rather white men who had victimized African American women for centuries. Like the Little case, the Ingram trial also spurred the formation of two Black women's organizations: the Women's Committee for Equal Justice, and Sojourners for Truth and Justice. Both were offshoots of the leftist-oriented Civil Rights Congress. Although Sojourners for Truth and Justice was short-lived, a number of its former members were active in the Joan Little case, once again underscoring the connections between Black Left feminism of the 1940s and Black feminism in the 1970s. These linkages not only reveal the continuities between activist generations of African American women. Black women's early theorizing and organizing around sexual violence also challenge the foregrounding of white women's experiences as the basis for "second wave" feminism and antirape activism in the 1960s and 1970s.[22]

8

The Police Would Follow Our Van as We Picked Up Kids

Black Power, State Repression, and Carceral Politics

The Black Power movement was undoubtedly one of the most important factors spurring the expansion of the prison movement in the 1960s and 1970s. Prison activism was rooted in a long legacy of African American protest against racist police brutality and injustices throughout the criminal legal system. In the 1960s and 1970s it was also a response to the increased harassment and incarceration of Black activists, especially those denounced as "militants," "radicals," or "revolutionaries." As the decades-old "condemnation of blackness" was recast in the "law and order" rhetoric and "tough on crime" policies of the 1960s and 1970s, Black activists were criminalized and subjected to brutal policing and lengthy prison sentences. Thus prison issues were a key component of the Black Power agenda from the beginning.[1]

The Black Panther Party—a movement more than an organization, according to scholars Joshua Bloom and Waldo Martin—was the most influential Black Power group of the era. It was also a key player in the prison activism of the period. When the Party was formed in 1966 in California, its original name was the Black Panther Party for Self Defense. Members patrolled Black neighborhoods in Oakland with open weapons to thwart police brutality and the Panther's Ten Point program called for the release of "all Black people held in jails." Many of the Panthers' early recruits had been in juvenile detention centers, the euphemism for youth jails, and altercations with police helped fuel Panther membership. Some Black radicals and revolutionaries, such as George Jackson, who joined the Panthers from prison, were politicized as a direct result of their incarceration experience. But the Panthers were not the only organization targeting prisons. The Nation of Islam (NOI) had long made the jailhouse a focus of membership recruitment, and even the Panthers' demand to release all Black prisoners was derived from a similar NOI principle. Malcolm X was unquestionably the most celebrated NOI prison recruit. Eldridge Cleaver, a convicted rapist, also joined the NOI in prison. Upon release, Cleaver drifted toward the Panthers, becoming minister of information. Jackson, Malcolm, and Cleaver all were convicted of "criminal" rather than "political" offenses, a distinction that became increasingly blurred by the 1970s, and all three were radicalized in prison.[2]

Ironically, criminalizing and imprisoning Black freedom fighters also helped to radicalize "common criminals" in jails and prisons. When activists landed in jails and prisons, they often provided political education to fellow prisoners; others helped to initiate prison strikes, petition drives, rebellions, or other collective actions. In response, officials transferred activist "troublemakers" to other jails and prisons, often multiple times. Yet transferring activist prisoners also created new opportunities for politicizing and organizing more of those behind bars. Official reprisals thus inadvertently helped to spread the prison movement.

As activists personally experienced the injustices of the legal system and the harshness of prison life, they brought greater public scrutiny to incarceration. By the late 1960s and 1970s, a series of highly publicized prison uprisings, strikes, and escapes, alongside several high-profile trials of Black radicals such as Huey Newton, Angela Davis, and the Soledad Brothers, spurred a wide range of groups to push for reform and even abolition of the prison system. One of the first efforts to educate the broader public about prison abolition was a 1972 public forum, "Tear Down the Walls," at the University of California at Berkeley. That same year, the Black Panther Party joined the chorus to "tear down the walls" of the nation's prisons. However, according to historian Dan Berger, the abolitionist movement was marred by its failure to formulate clear policy alternatives and was no match for ever-increasing "tough on crime" policies and the conservative ascendency sweeping across the country, especially in the white suburbs.[3]

State-sanctioned violence and harassment of the Black freedom movement was not only a local police function. It was also promoted at the highest levels of government. Under the auspices of the FBI's Counterintelligence Program (COINTELPRO), the federal government launched a largely illegal assault on Black nationalist and civil rights organizations. Even Martin Luther King Jr.'s SCLC came under federal surveillance. FBI director J. Edgar Hoover's observation in 1969 that the Black Panther Party was the "most influential" revolutionary group in America was largely on the mark; but when he added that the Panthers were therefore the "greatest threat to internal security" of the United States, a new federal imprimatur was given to the policing and imprisonment of Black bodies. Panther chapters across the country were targeted by over 230 out of nearly 300 COINTELPRO initiatives against African American organizations. Alongside the FBI's focus on the Panthers, President Nixon's attorney general, John Mitchell, set up an independent task force to target the Panthers and considered using the Smith Act to arrest and convict members for subversion against the federal government.[4] The police murder of Illinois Black Panther Party leader Fred Hampton while he slept in his bed, and the shooting death of California inmate-turned-revolutionary George Jackson by prison guards fueled particular outrage across Black communities, even among those who opposed the Panthers and radical Black politics.[5] Although men received most of the public attention, African American women, especially activists, also felt the long arm of government retaliation. Angela Davis, Erika Huggins, Assata Shakur, Afeni Shakur, and Joan Bird were just some of the Black women radicals and revolutionaries who faced imprisonment on trumped-up charges during these years.[6]

The FBI often worked in tandem with local police. Police raids in cities such as Chicago, Baltimore, Cleveland, Boston, and Winston-Salem, North Carolina, frequently focused on Black Panther Party community programs. Known as "survival programs," they included free breakfast programs, free health clinics, and other services, often run by local Panther women. Historian Tracye Matthews has persuasively challenged activists and scholars who dismissed the survival programs as nonrevolutionary "support work" in contrast to "real" political activity. FBI director Hoover certainly understood the political implications of the Panther survival programs. Hoover singled out the Free Breakfast Program, calling it "the best and most influential activity going for the BPP [Black Panther Party] and as such is potentially the greatest threat to efforts by authorities . . . to neutralize the BPP and destroy what it stands for." Hoover's condemnation justified attacks on Panther Breakfast Programs across the country.⁷

In North Carolina, the FBI and local police targeted the Winston-Salem Black Panther Party, including its Free Breakfast Program. Like many Panther chapters, police killing of an unarmed Black man was the immediate catalyst for the formation of the Winston-Salem Black Panther Party. In 1967, a forty-two-year-old African American man was arrested on an intoxication charge and beaten in police custody. When he later died, infuriated Winston-Salem residents looted and burned local businesses, causing an estimated $750,000 in damages before the National Guard was called in to quell the disturbance. Soon after, Larry Little (no relation to Joan Little) and two other Black men formed the Organization of Black Liberation, which later became an official Black Panther chapter.⁸

Larry Little's experience of police surveillance, harassment, and arrest likely drew him to Joan Little's case. He became a leader in the Free Joan Little campaign and often accompanied Joan on her speaking tours. Larry had grown up in Winston-Salem's public housing projects and was politicized in the 1960s after witnessing police brutality against Black student protests at Dudley High School and North Carolina Agricultural and Technical College in nearby Greensboro. He was arrested numerous times, largely on trumped-up charges, and was targeted by a self-confessed FBI and police informant. Larry even claimed that the FBI had offered to pay one of his friends to shoot him. The harassment of Larry Little and the Winston-Salem Black Panther Party was so severe that it exhausted the financial and legal resources of the organization and thwarted almost all its community service programs. Although the Free Breakfast Program hung on, it too was harassed by law enforcement. "With the breakfast program, the police would follow our van as we picked up kids," Larry explained. When Panther drivers beeped their horns to call for the children, "the police would then arrest the party members for unnecessary use of the horn."⁹ In 1970, under Hoover's direction, the FBI launched a disinformation campaign against the Winston-Salem Panthers, suggesting that male members were sexually molesting young girls in the Breakfast Program. That same year, Larry Little was arrested on a felony theft charge that was likely initiated by the FBI. He secured legal representation from Joan Little's future attorney, Jerry Paul. "They set the whole thing up to destroy the breakfast program," Larry claimed.¹⁰

Evictions, refusals by local phone and insurance companies to provide services to the Winston-Salem Panthers, and a host of other retaliatory tactics backfired. Instead of ostracism, the Party enjoyed growing popularity, especially among the Black poor. Panther assistance to low-income Black women, which was widely reported in the local press, also helped to build community support for the Party. But perhaps no event cemented the Panthers' local reputation more than the events surrounding the death of Alan Denby, a local Black teenager. The fifteen-year-old died after ambulance workers first arrived late and then refused to treat his injuries. In response, the Winston-Salem Panthers bought a hearse and turned it into an ambulance. Tellingly, they named the ambulance after Joe Waddell, a twenty-one-year-old Panther who had died in a North Carolina prison under suspicious circumstances in 1972. Three years later and a month before her murder trial opened, Joan Little commemorated Waddell at a Winston-Salem Black Panther Party rally where she accepted a "Woman of the Year" award from the group and spoke out in "support for all political prisoners."[11]

These kinds of experiences helped draw the Panthers into the prison movement both in North Carolina and across the nation. Initial efforts often focused on prisoner-support programs, such as free prison commissaries. Local Party chapters, including Winston-Salem's, instituted free transportation to prisons for family members, enabling prisoners to maintain connections to relatives and communities. Despite state efforts to thwart the free busing program, it remained popular with local residents across the country, many of whom lived long distances from prisons. As with other survival programs, Panther women were frequently key to the success of the busing program. In Cleveland, JoAnn Bray's Panther prison busing program enjoyed such widespread local support that it continued even after the local Party chapter collapsed.[12]

In sum, stepped-up policing and imprisonment increasingly became weapons in the war against the Black freedom movement in North Carolina and throughout the country. From officially sanctioned disinformation campaigns and heightened surveillance to infiltration, disruption, and violence, federal and state officials along with local police greatly weakened much of the 1970s Black radical organizational base.

Individual activists and racial justice groups were not the only targets of heightened policing, however. As the postindustrial economic downturn of the late 1960s and 1970s took its toll on inner-city African American communities, low-income urban areas across the country exploded in rebellion against the horrid conditions, often in response to police violence. Officials used these racial disturbances, erroneously labeled "riots," to initiate violent crackdowns, such as the round-up and jailing of 7,000 mostly Black residents during the 1967 Detroit uprising. As Dan Berger argues, criminalizing

Black activists and the mass arrests of urban "rioters" thus became a dress rehearsal for the mass incarceration policies that swept the nation in subsequent decades.[13]

Such measures found greater federal support among both Democratic and Republican politicians. Conflating urban violence with Black protest, lawmakers used both as rationales for harsh anticrime legislation. As noted earlier, the 1965 Law Enforcement Assistance Act (LEAA), and the 1968 Omnibus Crime Control and Safe Streets Act, signed by President Lyndon Johnson and reauthorized under Richard Nixon, distributed billions in federal funds to local law enforcement, donated large amounts of military equipment to police departments across the country, and soon fueled a massive prison boom. Although the federal government had been inching toward national involvement in crime control since the 1920s, this level of federal anticrime support was unprecedented. Local police deployed military tactics and equipment not simply against criminal suspects but against a wide range of social justice groups and individuals, particularly African Americans. In California, Daryl Gates, a young police commander who later became a lightning rod for charges of widespread racism within the Los Angeles Police Department, initially created the special weapons and tactics (SWAT) teams in 1966 for use against Black activists. In Louisiana, authorities raided the Black Panthers' headquarters in New Orleans in 1970 with a tank purchased with LEAA funds. By the 1980s, SWAT teams proliferated in thousands of cities and small towns and were used in daily, routine policing, especially in the War on Drugs.[14]

Against such "tough on crime" policing and prison policies, reformers and activists scored a number of court victories. Prisoners used the 1871 Civil Rights Act, which allowed citizens to bring lawsuits in federal court against states for denial of their civil rights. After the Nation of Islam won a 1964 religious freedom appeal in the U.S. Supreme Court, a flood of prisoner lawsuits was unleashed, increasing from 218 in 1966 to over 18,470 by 1984. In at least nine southern states, federal courts declared prisons in violation of the constitution or placed them under federal court order. One of the most important prisoner rights legal victories was the *Ruiz v. Estelle* case, filed in 1972 by Texas inmate David Ruiz. Among the many issues at stake was the use of state-sanctioned prison rape as a means of control and suppression of the prisoner movement, making it one of the few legal attempts to reduce the sexual assault of male prisoners. Yet the impact of favorable court decisions was often short-lived. The most severe blow came in 1996 when Congress passed the Prison Litigation Reform Act, which severely curtailed prisoners' ability to file lawsuits. According to historian Robert Chase, "The thirty-year era of federal court intervention on behalf of the prisoners' rights movement came to an abrupt end."[15]

In fact, legal setbacks had begun two decades earlier, even as prison activists piled up court victories. In its 1972 *Furman v. Georgia* decision, the Supreme Court ruled that capital punishment as administered by the states was arbitrary and therefore constituted "cruel and unusual punishment." But the ruling was misleading for it did not outlaw the death penalty; it only objected to how the states administered it. North Carolina and other states quickly amended their statutes. In 1973, North Carolina adjusted its laws, making capital punishment mandatory for certain crimes. This was the revised statute that would have condemned Joan Little to death had she been convicted of first-degree murder in the Alligood rape-murder trial. By 1976, North Carolina had 120 prisoners on death row, more than any other state, and the majority were African American. The state was not unique as Black and brown men (and some women) were more likely to receive death sentences than white defendants, especially if their victims were white and often despite clear evidence of racial bias in jury selection and sentencing.[16]

The carceral state thus soon did the work of the lynch mob, and the South led the way. North Carolina's capital punishment ranking soon gave way to other contenders. By 1979, the Southern Coalition on Jails and Prisons, which opposed capital punishment, reported that Georgia led the nation in executions, while Florida had more people on death row, with Texas close behind. Of the 480 condemned prisoners in the country, 410 resided in southern prisons. As a prison-construction boom swept the nation, the prison population skyrocketed. The cost was astronomical, both in lives and resources. Incarceration spending rose from $6.9 billion in 1980 to $80 billion by 2010, but this included only the costs of running jails, prisons, probation, and parole.[17]

This was the wider context that attracted Black Power radicals, particularly the Black Panther Party, to Joan Little's case. Like Little, many of them also had felt the long arm of the carceral state. Although Joan Little's murder-rape trial attracted widespread attention and led to an unlikely acquittal, her broader experience in the criminal legal system, extending back to her teenage years, was far more typical of the Black and brown bodies deemed disposable by a society that was fast becoming a "prison nation."[18]

9

Slaves of the State

The Sisters Behind the Brothers and the North Carolina Prisoners' Labor Union

If many of the legal victories waged by prisoners and their advocates were short-lived, activists on the streets and in jails and prisons remained undeterred. With few exceptions, the public face of the prison movement in the 1970s tended to be male, in part because more men than women were imprisoned; and violent rebellions and escapes occurred more often in men's prisons. In just one year, between 1970–71, prisons in California, Minnesota, Kentucky, Nevada, Pennsylvania, Florida, Maryland, Indiana, Louisiana, and New York all witnessed prisoner strikes, takeovers, and escapes. Women rebelled too, and North Carolina witnessed its own prisoner revolts among both men and women. According to Dan Berger, "Across the country, prisons were experiencing low-intensity warfare."[1]

Although prison unrest had become a pressing issue by the early 1970s, the media tended to ignore or downplay conflict in women's prisons. Throughout the nation, however, confined women joined their male counterparts in staging a series of protests, some of which turned violent. Between 1969 and 1973, four "disturbances" erupted at a women's prison in Georgia. In 1971, women "rioted' at the Alderson Women's Penitentiary, the first federal women's prison, after which forty-five alleged leaders were transferred to a men's prison in Texas. That same year, over 300 mostly Black women staged a walkout and nightlong sit-in on the prison lawn to protest oppressive conditions at the Detroit House of Corrections. They demanded changes in low pay, dangerous working conditions, spoiled food, lack of medical care, and inadequate educational instruction. Prison officials responded by strip-searching the women and forcing them to undergo vaginal searches for presumed "concealed weapons."[2]

In Bedford Hills Prison in New York, a group of mostly African American and Latina women prisoners held seven of the prison staff hostage to protest the retaliation against Carol Crooks, an African American prison activist. Crooks had been brutally beaten and placed in solitary after she won a 1974 court injunction against Bedford Hills Prison. Male guards and state troopers were called in, ending the rebellion in less than three hours and injuring twenty-five women in the ensuing ruckus. Twenty-four women were transferred to Matteawan State Hospital for the Criminally Insane without the required commitment hearing. Such measures were part of a broader national trend. In what scholar Emma Thuma terms the "prison psychiatric state," discipline was medicalized by declaring protesters mentally ill and transferring them to prison psychiatric institutions, where they were often involuntarily drugged.[3]

The most spectacular and influential prison violence in the nation was the 1971 Attica prison uprising, which historian Heather Thompson has called "one of the most important rebellions in American history." Although Attica was a men's prison revolt, its effects rippled across the country for years, even touching Raleigh's Women's Prison, where Joan Little was confined. Nearly half of the 2,200 prisoners in the densely overcrowded Attica facility in upstate New York took forty-two hostages and held the prison for five days. The revolt started after officials repeatedly ignored written pleas for parole reforms, improved health care (they cited the case of a twenty-one-year-old prisoner with polio, which prison officials left untreated), and an end to racially discriminatory work assignments, among other demands. While many of the leaders of the revolt were members of the Black Panther Party and the Nation of Islam, the Attica rebels were a multiracial group, a pattern seen in other prison uprisings. New York governor Nelson Rockefeller refused to grant amnesty to the protesters. He did agree to send in outside observers, one of whom was Joan Little's future attorney, William Kunstler, to negotiate a settlement.[4] Before any agreement could be reached, however, the governor ordered state troopers to retake the prison. Stunned Americans were glued to their televisions as helicopters hurled tear gas and 500 troopers fired shotguns indiscriminately into prison catwalks and exercise yards. Within fifteen minutes, thirty-nine people lay dead, including ten guards and prison staff, who appeared to have been killed by state troopers. Two years later, the liberal Republican governor shored up his "tough on crime" bona fides by signing what became known as the Rockefeller drug laws. The legislation set mandatory sentences for low-level drug crimes and became a model for similar legislation in other states.[5]

Caught between the Scylla and Charybdis of overpolicing and underprotection, some African Americans welcomed the new legislation. It was the decades-old dilemma, especially for residents in crime-ridden urban areas. A number of mainstream Black leaders in Harlem, where drug-related street crime had worsened, supported the draconian measures and praised the New York governor. In Chicago, civil rights stalwart Jesse Jackson muted his critique of "law and order" Republicans: "We must be tough on crime. Handguns ought to leave. Dope pushers must be dealt with severely and the streets must be made safe for normal citizens." Even prior to the Rockefeller drug laws, many Black nationalists in majority-Black Washington, D.C., opposed methadone treatment for heroin addicts and the decriminalization of marijuana, and they frequently backed stiff penalties for drug crimes. Yet not all African Americans, including those hardest hit by "urban blight," supported harsh penal policies. Even hose who did want greater police protection also pressed for expanded drug treatment facilities and other antipoverty measures to reduce crime. Few of these demands were met, however. It soon became clear that Black support for tough-on-crime policies was little more than a deal with the devil. The Rockefeller drug laws not only served as a model for other states but also helped to fuel the mass incarceration of Black and brown bodies in subsequent years.[6]

To many observers, the Attica revolt, along with the Soledad Prison disturbance in California, marked the end of the prison movement. However, historians Heather Thompson and Robert Chase have shown that Attica actually inspired two decades of prison activism.[7] Prisoners at the North Carolina Correctional Center for Women would soon invoke the Attica uprising in their own protest and warned of similar carnage. New York City's Black weekly, the *Amsterdam News*, drew parallels between the Joan Little trial and the Attica rebellion, claiming they were of equal significance to African Americans. In the 1960s and in the years following Attica, increasing numbers of prisoners in North Carolina and across the country organized and revolted, sometimes with dire results. Indeed, the expansion of the prison movement in the 1970s and 1980s is but another neglected story that challenges the declension narrative of post-1960s activism.

Though not as dramatic or as well-publicized as Attica, North Carolina witnessed its own deadly prison violence several years before the New York uprising. On April 16 and 17, 1968, less than two weeks after Martin Luther King Jr. was assassinated and racial disturbances erupted in cities across the country, 500 prisoners in the men's Central Prison in Raleigh staged a peaceful sit-down strike to protest prison conditions. The 150-year-old facility, which had been segregated until 1965, was grossly overcrowded, a "crumbling edifice, infested with vermin." The men were particularly angry about the failure to implement the prison wage bill. While the Thirteenth Amendment, which abolished slavery, had stated that "those duly convicted" could be compelled to work without compensation, a 1967 state law mandated prisoner pay, not to exceed a dollar per day. Yet men received no wages at all.[8] Among their demands, the protesters wanted some of the men returned from solitary to the general population, more televisions, extended visiting hours, and three hot meals a day. They also wanted a grievance committee established that would meet with prison officials at least monthly and would include at least five prisoners. Finally, the prisoners demanded a meeting with state correction commissioner Lee Bounds. Bounds rejected all their demands: "The grievances of prisoners will not be complied with today or in the future, as long as they're couched in terms of demands." Instead, he called in 150 riot control police, claiming that prisoners threatened to burn buildings and harm guards, supposedly by making gestures at guards in the form of a gun. Prison officials positioned themselves with rifles on rooftops to thwart the alleged impending prisoner attack. The commissioner nonsensically insisted that the "crude weapons" the prisoners brandished (wooden clubs, makeshift knives) were "superior in lethal power to those in the hands of our officers." Bounds also called in the Raleigh Fire Department for added protection. He later reported that the prisoners started fires in trash bins, broke into a multipurpose room and used some of its contents to add to the trash bin fires, and threw flaming torches at guards. Although several fires were set, the protesters extinguished them, and no guards were harmed or injured by prisoners during the disturbance.[9]

Bounds acknowledged that many of the men had voluntarily returned to their cells. Nevertheless, prison officials fired several warning shots and then quickly opened fire on the prisoners. Ten minutes later, six prisoners had been killed and sixty-eight were wounded. Several state highway patrol officers and other prison officials were wounded by ricocheting bullets, but not seriously. Following the attack, Bounds boasted that he "could issue an order to shoot without wincing."[10] However, neither official brutality nor warnings deterred prison organizing and protest. And North Carolina would lead the way in the South.

Five years after the 1968 bloodbath at North Carolina Central Prison, 540 of the 700 prisoners at the men's prison launched the North Carolina Prisoners' Labor Union (NCPLU), the first in the South. Initial efforts to organize the union were thwarted when one of their outside supporters absconded with union funds and 5,000 membership cards. But the men persevered, attracting outside support from ministers and union officials; and in 1974 the state of North Carolina officially recognized the NCPLU. Memories of the deadly prison violence in 1968 were clearly on the minds of prison union organizers: "6 Dead, 77 Wounded, and 7 Years Later, No Pay for Convict Labor," announced a headline in the NCPLU newsletter.[11] Unlike some prison organizations, the men confined at Central Prison maintained control of the NCPLU, and the multiracial board included Black, Native American, and white representatives. While prison conditions fueled the creation of the NCPLU, the white union founder and president Wayne Brooks also understood that North Carolina had unjustly targeted and imprisoned Black political activists. Prisoners "should be sent to prison *as* punishment," Brooks asserted, "rather than *for* punishment."[12]

Although the NCPLU was established by the incarcerated men at Central Prison in Raleigh, they reached out to all those confined in the seventy-seven penal institutions throughout the state, for women as well as men. Moreover, the union's "goals and aims" specifically reflected the concerns of both "men and women incarcerated in the state prison of North Carolina"; and the *NCPLU Newsletter* included information by and about jailed women, including Joan Little's case. Initially, the women at the nearby North Carolina Correctional Center for Women (NCCCW, or "Women's Prison") were wary of working closely with the men. According to prison activist Robbie Purner, they "wanted nothing to do with the North Carolina Prisoners' Labor Union. So many of them were imprisoned due to domestic violence issues and rape issues. They were further traumatized by the guards. Why would they believe that men, even fellow prisoners, would care about their rights? Men had caused most of them to be where they were," she added. However, the men's success may well have influenced the women to organize their own protest. The following year, Women's Prison, where Little was also confined, witnessed a prisoner sit-down strike. Later the women joined with men at Central Prison in a lawsuit on behalf of imprisoned men and women throughout the state.[13]

The hypermasculinity of prison unrest tended to give prison organizing an almost exclusively male face. Ironically, women inadvertently reinforced this image. Female supporters working outside the prisons were largely responsible for keeping the concerns of male prisoners in the public eye. However, centering men obscured protest by female prisoners, giving the misleading impression that women were less resistant than men. Media attention to male prison protests also masked the critical efforts of women in the "free" world who were critical to prisoner organizing. As historian Rebecca Hill explains, a vast amount of prisoner-support work was gendered female. "Despite its importance in shaping revolutionary consciousness," prison organizing outside prison walls "was often defined as secondary to and diversionary from 'real' struggles over material issues."[14]

African American women, particularly mothers, had long organized public support for male prisoners and victims of state-sanctioned racist violence. During the Scottsboro trials in the 1930s and 1940s, several of the defendants' mothers joined nationwide defense tours. After fourteen-year-old Emmett Till was brutally lynched in Mississippi in 1955, his mother, Mamie Till Bradley, mobilized Chicago's Black activist network, secured widespread national and international press coverage, and even traveled from Chicago to Mississippi to appear at the trial of the two white men charged with his murder. Till's killers, who later admitted their guilt, were acquitted by an all-white, all-male jury. But Mamie Till Bradley insisted on an open casket, "so that all the world can see what they did to my son." *Jet* magazine's decision to publish the gruesome image of Till's disfigured body catapulted a generation of young Blacks into the civil rights movement. In another high-profile case nearly two decades later, Georgia Jackson, mother of Soledad Prison inmate George Jackson; attorney Faye Stender; and radical activist Angela Davis were instrumental in Jackson's defense campaign. Other female attorneys, including Elizabeth Fink and Frances Jalet, played key roles in the Attica Brothers Defense Fund and the Texas prisoners' litigation movement respectively.[15]

African American feminists also worked with male prisoners throughout the 1970s. One of the most striking centered on the Washington, D.C., Rape Crisis Center, where Black feminists agreed to partner with the men's prisoner-support group at Virginia's Lorton Prison, Prisoners Against Rape. In 1977, the National Alliance of Black Feminists in Chicago hoped to participate in a five-month Humanities Project at Sheridan Correctional Center for men. In a team-taught workshop with a philosophy instructor from Chicago City Colleges, NABF founder and director Brenda Eichelberger hoped to explore male-female power relations "regardless of race or color" to "reveal how the street-wise male uses his masculinity to manipulate both males and females." The workshop was also designed to explore a "similar phenomenon in a white, upper-middle-class environment."[16]

In North Carolina, women's outside support was crucial to the NCPLU's success. Had it not been for Robbie Purner, the second attempt to organize the men's prison union in 1974 may also have floundered. Purner, a Baltimore native, was a student at the Duke University Divinity School in Durham. After visiting her boyfriend in a Virginia prison, she became active in southern prison reform. By 1974, she was acting director of the North Carolina branch of Offender Aid, a national network of jail reform programs. A $14,000 grant she received enabled inmate Wayne Brooks to reorganize the NCPLU. Although prisoners initially were wary of another outsider swindle, they overcame their suspicions and Purner became state coordinator for the NCPLU. She operated the union's outside office and published the prison newsletter, which explicitly rejected any copy containing "racist or sexist prejudice." Purner also brought on legal aid attorney Deborah Mailman, who proved indispensable to the legal challenges brought by the prisoners. The attorney visited prisoners throughout the state, collecting evidence of violations that became the basis for the NCPLU lawsuit over prison censorship of mail and union literature. The women's advocacy led authorities to ban Purner and her assistant, Charles Eppinette, from jails and prisons throughout the state. Prison administrators relented, however, after Mailman threatened to sue the Department of Correction (DOC); but the state had other weapons of retaliation at its disposal. Eppinette was convicted for failure to carry his draft card; and Purner was harassed by both Durham police and the FBI, who urged her to relinquish her affiliation with the union. Meanwhile, DOC commissioner David Jones resorted to familiar red-baiting smears by accusing the union of communist influence. "It was a very, very unpopular thing to be doing," Purner recalled. "Back then, due to what had happened in Soledad and the other prisons in California, there was very negative press about the danger and violence posed by prisoners demanding any rights." Yet none of this compared to the reprisals the prisoners experienced. Throughout the state, NCPLU leaders were transferred to other prisons for union activity, and some of the men at Central Prison reported receiving death threats from guards.[17]

Despite the risks, the prisoners persevered. Labor issues and abolition rather than penal reform remained the NCPLU's focus. Prisoners also developed an expansive notion of freedom that reached beyond the prison walls to the wider society. The NCPLU maintained that "PRISONS CANNOT BE REFORMED. THEY MUST BE ABOLISHED." The union also called for the decriminalization of drug and alcohol offenses and for maximum sentences of twelve months. In addition to inmate wages, the union demanded worker

Demonstrators who supported Joan Little demanded an end to prisoner abuse and unpaid prisoner labor in both men's and women's prisons in North Carolina.
Courtesy of the North Carolina State Archives and the *Raleigh News and Observer*.

compensation for work-related injuries and unemployment insurance for ex-prisoners unable to land jobs. Members reasoned that the union would help maintain prison order and safety by creating a formalized mechanism for prisoner complaints. To secure these demands, the NCPLU believed that political education was "one of the most important tasks of any that we in the union must undertake." The group recommended establishing small study groups and reading lists that would include radical newspapers in particular; and they threatened legal action if authorities tried to censor reading materials. Prison official Fred Morrison dismissed their demands, arguing that prisoners "were not employees of the state, but just wards. . . . I don't think they have a right to a wage," he said. Purner pounced on Morrison's claims, pointing out that the term "ward" was a relic of slavery: "If a ward is not paid then he is a slave. . . . The state is raising a class of slaves," she charged. Purner's comment pointed to the disproportionate numbers of Black and brown bodies held at the men's Central Prison. It also echoed a prisoner discourse that increasingly equated imprisonment with slavery.[18]

The NCPLU's labor analysis condemned prison industries and the profit motive underlying incarceration. The union also linked collective bargaining to the inevitable dissolution of prisons and therefore the termination of prison industries. Noting the profits that the state accrued from unpaid convict labor in a variety of prison industries, the union reasoned that the state feared a minimum wage for prisoners achieved through collective bargaining would prove too competitive with "free" labor. The public would become so outraged by taxpayers undermining "free" labor that it would develop "real and meaningful community-based correctional programs" to replace prisons. However, unpaid and low-wage prison labor already posed competition with free labor, especially as restrictions against prison labor and prison products were increasingly weakened.[19] Nevertheless, the prisoners believed that their demands posed a real threat, which explained the state's determination to undermine the NCPLU.

Prisoners did not restrict their resistance tactics to union organizing or study groups. They also influenced organizing on the other side of prison walls and drew the support of radical organizations such as the National Alliance Against Racist and Political Repression (National Alliance). For example, the union was adamantly opposed to capital punishment and was instrumental in forming the North Carolina Coalition Against the Death Penalty. Several months before the NCPLU received official recognition from the state, the National Alliance, which became a key supporter of Joan Little the following year, organized a July 4, 1974, demonstration outside Central Prison. More than 6,000 demonstrators rallied against prison conditions, the death penalty, and an alleged medical "experimental" hospital at Butner. From the fifth-floor windows, Black prisoners shouted their encouragement to the protesters. The warden, perhaps recalling the 1968 uprising, hastily called in heavily armed police, who surrounded the prison. Officials cracked down by canceling all visitations and prisoner recreation, but the protesters remained defiant. "The over-reaction didn't stop us from doing what we could in support of the marchers," they explained. Inside, a group of Black prisoners organized a hunger strike to protest what they called "inhuman" prison conditions. Although the majority of those in Central Prison abstained from the hunger strike, undoubtedly due to fear of reprisals, the hunger strikers felt the demonstrations had a positive impact. "We think that some of the prisoners have seen the need to organize and come together to fight against the conditions that govern our lives," they said.[20]

With the lowest unionization rate in the country and its reputation as an antiunion "right to work" state, North Carolina was unlikely to countenance a prisoner's union. The Department of Correction refused to allow the union to meet or to recruit members and argued that the organization was redundant since the General Assembly had authorized the Inmate Grievance Commission in 1974. Prison official Fred Morrison, a former aide to Republican governor James Holshouser, headed the commission, which prisoners believed was formed deliberately to thwart their union. Denouncing the Inmate Grievance Commission as an administrative "puppet" of the DOC, the prisoners maintained that it effectively denied them their First Amendment right to freedom of expression. Their claims were strengthened when officials began to transfer prisoners in retaliation for union activity or for filing grievances with the commission—a tactic that was deployed against women prisoners as well. The strategy backfired. Moving prison organizers inadvertently enhanced their ability to spread information about the union throughout the state's prison system. For example, civil rights activist Jim Grant of the Charlotte Three was transferred several times, with each move offering a new opportunity to reach more prisoners. In less than a year, the NCPLU had grown to its previous size of 5,000 members and was publishing its own newsletter.[21]

The battle between the NCPLU and the state of North Carolina led all the way to the U.S. Supreme Court. The state hoped to squelch the union by relying on a 1959 state statute that prohibited collective bargaining between any trade union and state agencies. In effect, prisoner unions were permitted to exist—they simply were barred from engaging in negotiations with state officials. The NCPLU quickly regrouped and claimed it was a prison reform organization, not a labor union, although it kept the same name.[22] However, in a 1977 seven-to-two decision in *Jones v. North Carolina Prisoners' Labor Union*, the U.S. Supreme Court denied the NCPLU's First and Fourteenth Amendment claims. "A prison is most emphatically not a public forum," and imprisonment imposes "limitations on constitutional rights," Chief Justice William Rehnquist declared.[23] Perhaps equally devastating, the court upheld North Carolina's prohibition against prisoners recruiting other prisoners to the union. In their dissent, Justices Thurgood Marshall and William Brennan rebuked the court for taking a "giant step backward" toward a "discredited" 1871 Virginia case that determined prisoners were slaves of the state.[24] Despite the defeat, imprisoned activist Jim Grant signaled their determination to carry on the struggle: "It's not over," he said. "People inside will continue to organize. This doesn't mean we're going to stop. We'll go underground."[25]

The NCPLU struggled on for several more years, but with dwindling outside support, continued pressure from the DOC, and no legal standing, the union finally collapsed in 1981. Although it was short lived, the NCPLU was noteworthy for attracting broad support from groups like the North Carolina American Federation of Labor–Congress of Industrial Organizations, the state ACLU, and the Council of Southern Churchmen. In fact, the NCPLU was part of a nationwide prison-organizing effort spurred in part by California's United Prisoners Union and its underground prison newspaper, the *Outlaw*. By 1973, the paper reached 5,000 of those confined in jails and prisons across the country, and prisoner unions had formed in Massachusetts, Maine, Michigan, Minnesota, Wisconsin, Delaware, Pennsylvania, Ohio, and Washington, D.C. By the mid-1970s United Prisoners Union claimed 23,000 male and female members in state prisons across the country and its mailing list had expanded to 25,000. Most prisoner unions were created and run largely by African American prisoners who linked labor issues with civil rights demands.[26] Some unions focused more on prisoner rights and prison conditions than on labor rights or work rules. For example, women at Bedford Hills Prison in New York and at two other women's prisons sought certification as public employees. Others proposed alternatives to prisons.[27] In North Carolina, prison activists linked the Joan Little case to broader issues in the Raleigh Women's Prison. And like countless protests throughout the country, the women's demands were met first with silence and then with an eruption that observers on all sides could have predicted.

10

There Must Not Be Another Attica

Action for Forgotten Women and the Prisoner Strike at the North Carolina Correctional Center for Women

Like the men's Central Prison in Raleigh, the North Carolina Correctional Center for Women (NCCCW, or "Women's Prison"), where Joan Little was held during and after her rape-murder trial, witnessed peaceful protests and retaliatory violence by guards. Women's Prison opened in 1933 and reportedly was the "dullest and most brutal unit in the state's prison system." Like many women's prisons, the North Carolina women's unit was created to ease overcrowding in the men's Central Prison, where females—mostly women of color, immigrants, and those convicted of violent offenses—had been housed with male prisoners. Women accused of minor offenses such as prostitution, drunkenness, adultery, or theft generally had been sent to the North Carolina Industrial Farm Colony for Women in Kinston, which opened in 1929, and where many suffered involuntary sterilizations under the state's eugenics laws. When the state decided to separate the women from the men in Central Prison, the women were simply moved to barracks on the outskirts of the city that were previously used as a men's road camp for highway projects. The facilities were "primitive, consisting of two stories of open-dormitories with double-decker bunks." Initially, the women's camp was operated as a satellite of Central Prison, but in 1938 the North Carolina Correctional Institute for Women was established as an independent institution. Four years later, the DOC hired a woman superintendent, the first in the state, for the Raleigh facility. However, in 1956, dismal conditions and the death two years earlier of an eighteen-year-old Black woman who had died after guards bound and gagged her led twenty-six Black women to organize a protest in the prison that the press called a "riot." By the 1970s, Women's Prison was understaffed and operating in the "custodial mode," with few programs or work opportunities for the confined women.[1]

The NCCCW prisoners articulated their grievances in a discourse that was both racialized and gendered. "The Blacks and Whites are treated differently," one asserted. "Whites have the advantages, they are given the easy and safe jobs." Nine of the ten workers in the dangerous prison laundry were African American. Forced to work eight-hour shifts without pay and in temperatures that often reached 120 degrees, they endured conditions reminiscent of the abuse of enslaved women. "Yes, we are working just like slaves, and for what? Nothing! . . . We are women, not slaves," declared one woman. "We will not be slaves," insisted another. The rhetoric of enslavement was common across the nation among both prisoners and their supporters. "The prison system is a slave system," a San Quentin prisoner proclaimed. According to Angela Davis, African Americans had simply transitioned from "the prison of slavery to the slavery of prison."[2] The parallels between enslavement and imprisonment had a particular resonance in the South. Southern penal institutions could trace their roots directly to slave patrols, followed by convict leasing, the chain gang, and state-run prison farms. Across the region, prison activists framed "contemporary incarceration as the living legacy of slavery."[3]

Incarceration, like enslavement, masculinized and defeminized Black women's bodies through work assignments and even clothing. Female prisoners, historically and at NCCCW, protested the use of their bodies as state property and their labor as a resource for both prison profits and prison sustainability. Laundry workers at Women's Prison not only compared their treatment to slavery but also framed their grievances in gendered terms, accusing prison authorities of denying them protections as women. "This job is fit mainly for a man. We don't have the strength to be unloading trucks," one woman complained. Compelled to lift and push laundry carts weighing 200–360 pounds on dangerously wet floors, women suffered crushed fingers and toes when the heavy carts fell. Several women received burns from unsafe laundry conditions. Without any protective clothing, they were forced to handle diseased and germ-laden laundry from prisons and nearby hospitals. "We get other clothes from prison camps that carries [sic] maggots, crabs and other types of diseases and infections," one woman charged. "We are the first to come in contact with filthy clothes, bloody, shitty and diseased." After multiple complaints, they were finally issued rubber gloves; but when the gloves tore, staff refused to replace them.[4]

One particularly egregious case of abuse concerned Marie Hill, who lost several toes from untreated infections she picked up in the laundry. Hill was a twenty-five-year-old Black lesbian from Rocky Mount, North Carolina, with less than a sixth-grade education. Raised by foster parents, she may have been sexually abused and had several run-ins with the law as a teenager that sent her to the Kinston Training School, where Joan Little also had been confined. Like Little, Hill escaped from the juvenile jail, but, unlike Little, she was recaptured. In 1969, Hill was convicted by an all-white jury of murdering a white storeowner in Rocky Mount and was sentenced to death. She had been confined at Women's Prison since age seventeen, including two and a half years in isolation on death row. However, she insisted that she confessed under threats of death, and her case was cited for attention by the National Alliance Against Racist and Political Repression. Hill and the other laundry workers were vindicated when a federal investigation by the Occupational Safety and Health Administration cited the Department of Correction for hazardous conditions in the laundry and ordered that the violations be corrected by September 1975.[5]

The dangerous working conditions in the laundry were not the women's only concerns. Poor food, inadequate health care, racist medical personnel, and even sleeping arrangements all drew complaints. Medical treatment at Women's Prison, like in many correctional institutions, was especially gruesome. Edna Barnes received a hysterectomy after she was diagnosed with a minor vaginal infection. Another woman described an allergic reaction from medication for a kidney infection that made her face "so swollen it looked like I had been beaten." The nurse simply gave her more of the same medicine until a doctor intervened. Rosa Harrison complained of severe stomach pains but was repeatedly denied medical attention until her appendix burst, requiring her to wear an ostomy bag for the rest of her life. According to one of the prisoners, the prison nurse dismissed Harrison's complaints as an effort to avoid work detail. As one prisoner declared, "A change has got to come."[6]

Even Juanita Baker, the African American NCCCW superintendent, criticized the state's neglect. Since 1972, Baker had implored the state legislature to make improvements. "We're so small, they just forget we are here," she complained. "It's dull, psychologically," which "can be more brutal than the physical environment," Baker added. Prison official Fred Morrison, who headed the Inmates Grievance Commission, acknowledged Baker's criticism. Although the General Assembly granted millions of dollars for more prison construction to ease both overcrowding and the potential for prison unrest in men's facilities, the women's needs were ignored. Baker also publicly argued that the prison needed authentic inmate councils. She pointed out that the existing prisoners' council was discouraged by the authorities. Echoing the prisoners' demands, Baker's most scathing critique centered on the abysmal working conditions. The women were forced to work eight-hour shifts without pay. Instead of a wage, their "reward" was permission to attend night school for one hour, four nights per week. In contrast, male prisoners could receive vocational training, take educational courses, or attend off-campus classes at community colleges. "I'd probably be my own hardest case if I had to do this," Baker said. For her candor, Baker was fired shortly after her public remarks.[7]

Prison official Ralph Edwards acknowledged that "the work program at women's prison has hampered the rehabilitation program." He assured critics that changes were forthcoming and vowed to replace women workers with men in the prison laundry. "They would promise us they would check into it but nothing ever happened. . . . things got worse," one prisoner complained. Instead, officials blamed the women: "We need some way to determine what these women really want to do with their lives. . . . We simply don't know what they really want . . . or anything to offer them to prepare for that even if we did know."[8] Women prisoners would soon speak in a language that neither the authorities nor the public could misunderstand.

While prison officials dragged their feet, Celine Chenier organized a peaceful rally outside Women's Prison. The rally was planned for November 1974, two months after Joan Little arrived at the prison to await her trial in the Alligood murder case. Demonstrators strategically linked support for Little to demands for wider improvements inside the prison, including closure of the prison laundry.[9] About 100 demonstrators showed up at the rally, but Little had been moved to a different facility that day and was unable to hear or see her supporters' chants and signs beyond the prison walls. According to Chenier, the most important outcome of the rally was the formation of the new prisoner advocacy group, Action for Forgotten Women, based in Durham. "These women in prison had literally been forgotten, and this is true nationwide," Chenier noted. Protests continued both inside and outside the prison. One confined woman wrote a letter to the national prisoners' newsletter, *Midnight Special*, describing the dangerous laundry conditions,

Women protesters in November 1974 at a rally organized by Action for Forgotten Women, outside the North Carolina Correctional Center for Women in Raleigh (known as Women's Prison) where Joan Little was held, demand justice for Joan and the abolition of women's prisons. From *Break de Chains of Legalized U.$. Slavery*, courtesy of the Wisconsin Historical Society.

while Chenier appealed to the nationwide prisoners' movement. "There must not be another Attica," she warned, "and the inmates are ready to risk their lives."[10]

The women did risk their lives when their peaceful protest turned violent. At the time, Joan Little was out on bail, raising funds and awareness for her upcoming murder trial. However, she had her own grievances. Worse than the unsanitary conditions was the emotional torment. Initially placed in solitary confinement for several months while her supporters raised the $115,000 bail bond, Little reportedly was harassed by both hostile cellmates and prison staff. Yet during her public appearances to draw support for her upcoming murder trial, Joan linked her case to the plight of the NCCCW women. In one TV interview, Little noted that she was more concerned about her fellow prisoners at Women's Prison than about herself.[11]

The disturbance began on Sunday, June 15, 1975, more than a year and a half after prison officials had promised to address the women's concerns. At

8 p.m., the usual lock-up time, guards ordered the women to leave the yard and return to their dormitories or cell blocks. About one-third of the 450 prisoners refused to move and instead staged a peaceful sit-down strike. Like the men, they wanted wages for all prisoner jobs. Their demands included elimination of racist policies (especially the intake process and classification system), replacement of racist personnel, and permanent installation of the Black acting superintendent, Morris Kea, whom the women said "had their respect." Seemingly aware of the low pay for prison staff or perhaps hoping to attract more competent personnel, they also sought raises for prison guards and matrons. Their support for prison staff was not altogether atypical. Yolanda Ward, a Black activist who served on the board of the Washington, D.C., Rape Crisis Center, supported female guards who brought sexual harassment complaints at Virginia's Lorton Prison. These efforts suggest that women's prison activism and Black women's antirape organizing went beyond advocacy for prisoners or sexual assault survivors. Other grievances of the Women's Prison protesters centered on visitation, church services, food, and health care (specifically behavior-modification drugs in food), and the indiscriminate use of tranquilizers. And finally, they demanded the immediate closure of the prison laundry. As the sit-down strike began, the women also called for a meeting with prison officials and the governor.[12]

The multiracial group of sit-down participants had carefully prepared for their protest by asking Celine Chenier and Action for Forgotten Women to monitor the strike. Framing their call for help in the language of human rights discourse, the women demanded protection regardless of their status as unfree persons: "'Celine, we're human beings. Just because we committed a crime, that's no reason to be treated like a beast,'" declared one of the prisoners.[13] Action for Forgotten Women answered the call, together with members of Triangle Area Lesbian Feminists and other supporters. A group of about twenty women arrived. As they prepared to maintain an all-night vigil outside the prison, they shouted encouragement to their confined sisters. Soon women on both sides of the fence raised their voices in song, each group fortifying the other for whatever lay ahead. Meanwhile, the strikers wrapped themselves in blankets, placed the pregnant women in the middle of the group, and huddled behind makeshift barricades as the night closed in around them.[14]

While the women slept in the prison yard, officials planned their response. Guards were called in from surrounding prisons and equipped with riot gear, helmets, tear gas, mace, and billy clubs. At 5 a.m. on June 16, the guards ordered the sleeping women to move inside to the gymnasium. The

Women prisoners organized a sit-down strike at Women's Prison in Raleigh, where Joan Little had been held. The protest erupted in violence when the strikers refused to leave the yard and guards attacked them. From *Break de Chains of Legalized U.S. Slavery*, courtesy of the Wisconsin Historical Society.

women refused, fearing that they would be beaten. The presence of the tear gas had prompted some of the women to bring wet towels and sheets to shield themselves in the event of an attack. As guards began to remove the prisoners, some of the women decided to walk. From outside the prison, witnesses shouted legendary civil disobedience instructions urging the women to remain calm and to go limp: "Lie down. Don't resist," they coached.[15] Once inside and out of sight, the guards unleashed their fury. Screams and breaking glass were heard outside. Marie Hill broke out and ran to the fence crying, "'Celine, they're beating them down there.'" But these were not the nonviolent protesters of the early 1960s sit-in movement who allowed themselves to be burned with cigarettes and scalded with hot soup. More than 100 women fought back with whatever they could find. Baseball bats, hoes, rakes, chunks of concrete, and even shards of glass all became weapons of self-defense. Several women used a volleyball net with a concrete stand to kick in the gym door, enabling prisoners and guards to pour into the yard. As one woman explained, "Yes, we fought our way out, because the state had first used violence on us." Even Joan Little's hometown newspaper conceded that "conditions at Central Women's Prison have been ripe for an explosion for a long time."[16]

The fracas ended when the guards withdrew, but the confrontation was not over. Ten women were brought to the hospital after prison medical staff refused to treat them, but according to prison officials all were released. Guards escaped with minor cuts and scratches. Rumors circulated wildly and the media eagerly consumed the stories, erroneously reporting that one protester suffered a miscarriage after she was struck in the stomach; others reported that prisoners had sustained broken ribs and back, leg, and kidney injuries.[17]

Over the next few days, both sides held press conferences. Two African American members of Action for Forgotten Women, Celine Chenier and Brooke Whiting (who several years later at the University of North Carolina at Chapel Hill would write her master's thesis on the Little case), had been briefly allowed inside the prison early on when even the press and two federal investigators from the U.S. Department of Justice were denied entry. As a result of its privileged position, Action for Forgotten Women hoped to dispel some of the misinformation that had circulated in the media, including the rumor about the pregnant woman's alleged miscarriage. Chenier became the embodied intermediary between the press and the prisoners as she shouted questions and answers back and forth, with the women often answering in unison:

"Are you receiving medical care?"
"The usual. 2 Tylenols."
"How long are you going to stay out of work?"
"Until our demands are met."

Late that afternoon, the striking women gathered near the fence. Forming a circle, they danced and sang "We Shall Overcome," and "We Shall Not Be Moved." Despite their earlier decision to strike back against guard violence, these legendary songs of the 1960s civil rights movement linked the prisoners' protest to the legacy of nonviolent civil disobedience. That evening one inmate spoke to Chenier by phone. Just as civil rights activists had often embraced both nonviolent direct action and armed self-defense, the prisoner informed Chenier that the women would not allow the guards or police to beat them again. Some of them were prepared to die, she warned. Action for Forgotten Women feared another Attica.[18]

Prison authorities signaled that they would concede to some of the protesters' demands, including "possibly" closing the laundry within ninety days. They also agreed to investigate complaints about prison staff and the grievance system. An announcement would be forthcoming in a few days, no later than Thursday, June 19, they promised. Although the women continued their work stoppage, on Wednesday, June 18, they honored the 8 p.m. curfew and returned to the dorms. The next day, in anticipation of the settlement, 150–200 supporters, organized largely by Action for Forgotten Women, gathered outside Women's Prison. Eight to ten busloads of additional guards, numbering about 200, also arrived and remained stationed just beyond the prison fences throughout the day. Inside, five prisoner representatives negotiated with officials, joined later by three members of Action for Forgotten Women: Celine Chenier, Brooke Whiting, and Charsie Hedgepath, a seasoned activist from Durham's Black freedom struggle. At about 7:30 p.m. Action for Forgotten Women representatives were ejected and the negotiations broke down. Some of the women came out in tears. When the prisoners were ordered back to the dorms, many refused; others reportedly found themselves locked out. According to one of the witnesses, city police surrounded the prison, blocking the view of outsiders as another melee ensued. Again, the women fought back, even setting fire to a laundry basket. When it was over, nearly twenty women were taken to the hospital, one with serious injuries, and between seven and eleven guards had been injured.[19]

On Friday, after five days of what Action for Forgotten Women called a "small-sized Attica," the press was finally allowed inside the prison. Thirty to forty of the strike leaders, the alleged "extreme trouble-makers," were transferred to Western Correctional Institute, a men's prison nearly 200 miles away. Considering the complaints from women prisoners of sexual abuse and the Joan Little trial that was just a month away, the retaliatory transfer of the women protesters to a men's prison clearly threatened their safety. Triangle Area Lesbian Feminists made the link explicit and called for supporters to participate in demonstrations during Little's trial: "One of the main issues in her case is that of rape and the right of women to defend themselves.... Joanne's case is so closely tied to the recent violent repression of a peaceful demonstration at Women's Prison." Nearly forty years later, Karen Galloway, Little's cocounsel, recollected that sexual abuse of incarcerated women in North Carolina was widespread at the time. Rape was also a problem in men's prisons in North Carolina, especially when men were forced to sleep in overcrowded dormitories. According to one prison official, the dorms became "no man's lands" at night. "A guard would not dare go in there—except in force."[20]

Transferring the women to a men's prison not only endangered the women's bodily integrity, it defeminized them as well. Sixty additional women who remained at Women's Prison were placed in "segregation" (solitary confinement). Prisoners were forbidden visitations, others had their sentences extended, and some were denied parole on the grounds that they had incited to riot. Accused by prison official Edwards of being "outside agitators," Action for Forgotten Women was banned from the prison. Deborah Mailman, the attorney with the North Carolina Prisoners' Labor Union, was told by guards that "her credibility was questionable" and was also denied entrance. Meanwhile, protests continued at prisons throughout the state and the nation. Like the NCCCW women, male prisoners in Jackson, North Carolina, protested conditions in the Sampson County Prison laundry. After a year of filing grievances, seventeen of them, soon to be known as the Whiteville Seventeen, were sent to "administrative segregation" (solitary) and transferred to Odum Prison Farm.[21]

Despite the reprisals, many of the women remained defiant and undeterred. They sent letters to feminist newspapers and to prisoner newsletters. Marjorie Walsh, an African American woman, wrote from the Western Correctional Institute, where she remained for six weeks after her transfer from Women's Prison: "We have not changed our position or determination in our attempt to expose the department and its deceit to the people." Another wrote, "We haven't given up. We signed grievances to have a hearing on police brutality."[22] Some of the strikers harassed the guards as they passed by, chanting "pigs, oink, oink" and singing "We Shall Overcome." Their verbal protests combined both the Black Panther moniker for police, as well as the anthem of the nonviolent civil rights movement. But the guards used the women's protest to accuse them of using "obscene language" and making "threats," thus justifying their placement in solitary confinement. According to Anne Willett, one of the striking white prisoners, the women were denied hygiene items, sheets, and showers, and given cold food. According to the *Midnight Special*, Willett had been injured by one of the guards and then denied medical treatment. She described the despair that overcame her in solitary confinement: "The steel-barred door of my brick cell casts a shadow over my entire body; it follows me; there is no escape. . . . This is my 21st day in the hole. The food is still cold. I am away from everyone and powerless to get help. . . . The rats still squeak and the shadow continues to follow me." But the collective determination of the other women sustained her: "What gives me the courage to endure this? The beautiful love and unity of my sistahs."

She ended with an appeal for outside support: "Our love for each other is strong enough to crack this steel, but we need your help and support too!"[23]

Defiance was not their only response. In December 1975, Action for Forgotten Women filed a $25 million suit in U.S. District Court in Raleigh on behalf of the NCCCW prisoners, alleging unlawful, brutal, and excessive force by prison guards and violation of prisoners' constitutional rights in the aftermath of the sit-down strike. The National Conference of Black Lawyers and Prisoners' Rights Organized Defense agreed to represent the confined women.[24] The plaintiffs and Action for Forgotten Women sought public support as well. "The inmates' struggle is not just for incarcerated individuals but for oppressed society in general and women in particular," Action for Forgotten Women announced. "Unite and help the people stamp out sexism, racism, repression and our oppression." Several days after the Women's Prison lawsuit was filed, state correction commissioner David Jones took to the airwaves to announce that charges would be brought against the women protesters for "assault on guards." The women dismissed the move as designed to intimidate them into withdrawing their suit.[25]

Joan Little was not personally involved in the sit-down strike or the Women's Prison lawsuit. However, activists drew on Little's notoriety to bolster the women's legal action, noting that she was still imprisoned at NCCCW following her acquittal in the murder trial. Indeed, despite the seeming defeat of the sit-down strike, the protest had succeeded in drawing both local and national attention to the conditions at Women's Prison. A member of the local Women's International League for Peace and Freedom who had witnessed the strike, described the violence at the league's national conference, and sent letters to Congress, the press, the North Carolina governor, the U.S. Commission on Civil Rights, and activist groups. "I was shocked and appalled at the brutal force used against sleeping and peaceful women," she wrote. Assata Shakur, soon to become one of the most celebrated and most wanted political exiles in the country, penned a note of female solidarity from her own confinement at Rikers Island Prison in New York City: "The struggle that you have waged in North Carolina is an inspiration to other sisters who are imprisoned all over amerika." The embattled revolutionary evoked the allusions to enslavement that had become a trope of prison writing: "The pain that you have endured under the lash has been felt by many and has educated many people," Assata noted. Meanwhile *Attica News* urged supporters to write to Governor Holshouser to "protest the treatment of these sisters" in Women's Prison.[26]

Much as they might have wished to ignore the women's concerns, politicians and prison authorities were forced to respond to the violence that erupted at the North Carolina Correctional Center for Women. Legislators established a commission to investigate the causes of the rebellion while the Department of Correction turned to its so-called Inmate Grievance Commission, dismissed by prisoners as a mouthpiece of prison authorities. Neither group responded in any meaningful or substantive manner, and their recommendations were nonbinding, leading to little if any real change. However, the North Carolina General Assembly introduced a bill stipulating that male guards be replaced by female matrons in women's prisons, responding to a problem raised not only by the NCCCW protesters but by Joan Little's attorneys during her rape-murder trial.[27]

Both the General Assembly's Legislative Research Commission and the Inmates Grievance Commission convened a series of public, televised hearings, ostensibly to deal with the strikers' grievances. Brooke Whiting from Action for Forgotten Women, along with formerly incarcerated women from across the state and many of the "extreme troublemakers" who had been transferred to the men's Western Correctional Institution nearly 200 miles away, testified at nine separate hearings. At one of the public sessions, fourteen women prisoners appeared in ill-fitting, ankle-length brown prison dresses, surrounded by armed guards. The women testified that their complaints had been systematically ignored, leaving them no recourse but nonviolent protest. Their descriptions of horrendous and brutal medical treatment, including one woman's detailed account of being chained and shackled while she gave birth (a practice still used in many prisons), brought tears to several observers. Many of the women complained about the arbitrary use of "indefinite non-punitive segregation" (solitary confinement) by prison staff. According to prison activists, solitary confinement had become a favored retaliatory tactic against prison unrest across the country in the post-Attica era. The legislative commission began to worry that these policies violated the Fourteenth Amendment and warned that "such inhumane treatment ... has no place in the prison system of North Carolina." Commission members seemed equally worried about the impact of publicly airing abusive prison practices: "It is unnecessary to list here all the deprivations suffered by inmate isolation," they wrote.[28]

While the commission fretted about possible legal and political repercussions of the hearings, NCCCW administrators resorted to other measures. Prison officials Ralph Edwards and David Jones relied on the time-honored strategy of blaming "outside agitators" for the violence at Women's Prison.

Correction officials as well as some state legislators assured the public that an investigation was underway to uncover "subtle" communist influences inside the North Carolina prison system. Similar allegations were echoed by conservative politicians across the country, who insisted that radical influences, not prison conditions or the use of imprisonment as a political weapon against activists, were responsible for inmate discontent and prison rebellions. For example, in 1973, the House Committee on Internal Security blamed Marxist revolutionaries for the Attica uprising and for the violence at Folsom and San Quentin Prisons in California. Indeed, many conservatives were either convinced or found it politically expedient to insist that there was a deliberate communist plot to take over all the prisons. The confiscation at the San Quentin Prison mail room of a forty-six-page pamphlet describing how to make explosives from simple materials did little to quell such charges.[29]

Despite its efforts at obfuscation, the Inmates Grievance Commission administrators agreed to several prisoner demands, including returning all transferred women and those in solitary to the general prison population. But rather than recommending closure of the prison laundry, the commission merely recommended "incentive pay" for laundry workers. Most important, since the commission's role was merely advisory, none of its recommendations were binding. According to Action for Forgotten Women, the public hearings were simply a "pacification" tactic and "safety valve" designed to give the appearance of addressing prisoner grievances. However, the prison laundry eventually was closed, giving the protesters at least a partial victory and removing the Black women laundry workers from dangerous working conditions.[30]

Meanwhile, the legislative commission issued a report outlining its own recommendations to improve conditions at NCCCW. While failing to acknowledge racial discrimination explicitly, the report conceded that "inequality of treatment is probably the most certain way to foster resentment and bitterness among inmates." Commission members expressed support for rehabilitation, or as they stated it, creating "a stabilizing influence," through "work, schooling, [and] vocational" training. Foreshadowing a growing trend in privatization and for-profit prison labor, the report also suggested contracting with private industry. Much of the funding for the commission's proposed "reforms" was to be provided by federal grants, again underscoring the growing influence of federal dollars on local and state penal policies.[31]

Many of the commission's proposals were myopic at best and reified conventional gender roles for women. For example, commission members advocated converting the prison laundry building into a vocational training center. Seemingly oblivious to the growth of the women's movement(s) and the Equal Rights Amendment campaign that had recently focused national attention on North Carolina, the commission promoted vocational training in cosmetology, laundry work, and "secretarial science," in other words, traditional low-wage "women's" jobs. Endorsing training for jobs that increasingly were either outsourced to ever-cheaper labor overseas or were fast becoming outmoded by technology was even more short-sighted. For those ineligible for work-release, the commission suggested placing them in state institutions such as psychiatric hospitals. The experience presumably would prepare the women for nurse's aide positions upon their release from prison. Action for Forgotten Women dismissed the training programs, claiming they simply prepared "ex-convicts" to work as "scabs" under the state's antiunion "right-to-work" laws.[32]

The commission's gendered myopia was typical. A 1983 survey of women's prisons revealed that clerical skills, business education, food services, and cosmetology were the most common vocational training programs. In the 1980s, prisoners across the country, including women at NCCCW, brought sex discrimination suits charging unequal training opportunities for men and women prisoners. Spurred by the rebirth of feminism, the "parity" movement, as it was known, had only limited success despite numerous court victories. As state budgets were strained and harsh penal policies were enacted by politicians, programs were eliminated for both men and women. Feminists and other prisoner advocates soon realized that parity did nothing to stem prison population growth and even legitimized incarceration by making prisons seem more humane. Equal treatment reforms also worked against noncarceral efforts, including prison abolition and community-based alternatives to imprisonment. In the words of one woman, parity became simply "equality with a vengeance." Perhaps most ominous, gender "parity" led to more male prison officials in women's prisons. Thus, despite Joan Little's courtroom victory in her rape-murder trial, incarcerated women remained vulnerable and sexual abuse in prisons remained rampant well into the next century.[33]

In response to the legislative commission's recommendations, the state Division of Prisons agreed to implement vocational training at Women's Prison. However, prison officials claimed that many of the commission's proposals were already in place, that they had inadequate state funding to implement many of the suggestions, and that they were forced to rely on volunteers and erratic private donations for many programs. Their most vehement disagreement concerned the conversion of the building used for "disciplinary segregation" (punitive solitary confinement). Arguing that 42 percent of the prisoners were there for "assaultive crimes," prison authorities claimed that both the commission as well as the public were "unaware of the abuse to which certain inmates can subject not only staff but other inmates."[34]

An addendum in the Division of Prisons report was both peculiar and revealing. No doubt in light of the massive publicity surrounding the Joan Little case, officials acknowledged the problem of sexual and physical assault at NCCCW. Still, it was a curious disclosure, especially since sexual assault was never broached in the commission's report. Yet acknowledgment did not necessarily mean accountability. Instead, officials remained silent about male guards' abuse of women and implied that inmate-to-inmate physical and sexual assault was the main problem. Their solution: "hiring additional correctional officers."[35]

While prison administrators equivocated over most of the commission's recommendations, the prisoners lambasted the report, the governor, and prison officials. Marjorie Marsh, writing from solitary confinement, pointed to the power of collective protest: "Why hasn't their attention been focused here before? Because there has never been pressure from the people before; . . . because the interest of the establishment was not threatened before."[36] Even the reforms that were implemented were dismissed by the women as little more than window dressing designed to appease public criticism of the prison. Marsh excoriated Governor Holshouser for praising the modernization of the infirmary. Despite the improved facilities, only two nurses were responsible for 450 women, and a single psychiatrist was on duty for just five to ten hours per week. "A new dental chair with no dentist is useless; a newly installed examining table chair with no doctor is useless," she charged.[37]

Control, surveillance, and confinement rather than reform remained the priority of prison administrators; and politicians followed suit. The issue assumed ever-greater importance as federal and state "tough on crime" policies fueled a growing prison population. Although the expansion began slowly in the 1970s, increasing exponentially in the 1980s and 1990s across the nation, North Carolina was already feeling the strain. By 1977, the state's inmate population had reached the "breaking point." Its maximum operating capacity of just under 11,000 now held 14,200 prisoners. Two years earlier, the North Carolina Prisoners' Labor Union had charged that overcrowding was deliberately created through a "dramatic reduction in parole and guided releases" for both women and men, often in retaliation for an inmate's "history of protest/activism." Newly elected Democratic governor Jim Hunt acknowledged "the inhumane, overcrowded conditions in our prisons." At a September 1977 press conference, the governor assured residents that "today I want to report to you that North Carolina is on the road to reforming its prison system." But his solutions were contradictory at best. In addition to adding inmate beds by building more prisons, Hunt proposed a special rehabilitation school for young prisoners, more guards, and using local jails to ease prison overcrowding. He also noted legislative changes that promised to deter crime and ease prison population increases through restitution and speedy trials. Imprisoned activist Jim Grant derided the governor's "reforms," noting that whether a "'right wing fanatic' or a 'moderate'" was in charge, "the prison system operates for the same purpose." In 1980, five female prisoners brought a lawsuit demanding the same privileges and opportunities as male prisoners. Key among their complaints was inadequate medical care, which they claimed had resulted in one woman's death. And in 1997, Prisoners' Legal Services filed a class-action suit on behalf of nineteen prisoners at NCCCW charging "a lack of timely treatment, inadequate emergency services, poor care for inmates with chronic diseases, and a failure to follow the recommendations of outside specialists."[38] Meanwhile, the women at NCCCW had turned to another outlet to press their demands: the written word.

11

We Will Savor the Sweetness of Freedom

Prisoner Intellectuals and the Power of the Word

Few of the demands emerging from the sit-down strike at the North Carolina Correctional Center for Women (NCCCW, or Women's Prison) received any meaningful response. The nonbinding recommendations of the General Assembly's Legislative Research Commission were both shortsighted and reinforced conventional gender norms—such as training programs for disappearing or traditional low-wage "women's" jobs—or were ignored by corrections officials altogether. For the few prisoner concerns the commission did address, including medical care, its recommendations were inadequate at best. Although peer literacy programs do not appear to have been among the protesters' demands, prison authorities did permit writing groups, study groups, and, most remarkable of all, a radical publication by the prisoners themselves. This was surprising considering the power of the word to enhance prisoner communication, politicization, and protest. Joan Little and her fellow prisoners made ample use of the opportunity that prison writing presented.[1]

Support for prisoner reading and writing activities at Women's Prison may have been a holdover from the earlier bibliotherapy movement, which had gained national attention in 1930s and spread more broadly into penal circles in the 1950s. The idea that reading specially selected texts, particularly sacred readings, could foster rehabilitation, was initially adopted in early nineteenth-century reformatories. The therapeutic value of reading had been recognized since the ancient Greeks, but in the United States only white male prisoners were deemed worthy of redemption through education or literacy. Not until after the Civil War did reformers push for educational materials for women's reformatories. When the first National Prison Congress convened in 1870, it promoted the creation of libraries and prison libraries began to increase. However, Black women were largely excluded from women's reformatories, and authorities generally refused to make literacy programs or reading materials available to African American prisoners. Literacy thus was further racialized as a crucial aspect of white identity. In the late nineteenth century, African American clubwomen in New Orleans and Atlanta, whom literary scholar Megan Sweeney calls "literary activists," tried to fill the gap by distributing reading materials to Black prisoners in road camps, chain gangs, and prison farms. In the twentieth century, Sarah "Sadie" Delany, the African American chief librarian at Tuskegee Veterans Hospital from 1924 to 1958, was instrumental in shaping later penal bibliotherapy. Her work with Black veterans and with "delinquent" youth in New York City promoted literacy and reading as keys to Black empowerment and citizenship. From the 1950s to the 1970s, prison libraries enjoyed their greatest expansion after reformers and prison officials adopted bibliotherapy, including novels, as principal modes of rehabilitation. Even then, correction authorities strayed from Delaney's use of literacy to work through trauma and instead deployed it as "a normalization technique," treating prisoners as "passive recipients of literary medicine."[2]

Across the country, the conflict between officials and prisoners over reading materials ultimately led penal authorities to discard the idea that prisoner reading could be therapeutic. By the 1980s as the prison-building boom took off and jails and prisons became increasingly overcrowded, prison libraries became a low priority. Instead, televisions were deliberately installed as a pacification tool beginning in the 1960s and accelerating throughout the 1970s. Although the introduction of televisions (and telephones) led to the decline of reading and writing among prisoners, the measure backfired by enhancing prisoner knowledge and communication with the outside world. For example, California corrections staff deleted news of the 1964 Watts rebellion from prison newspapers until they realized that prisoners were watching coverage of the disturbance on the evening news. As the principle of rehabilitation was replaced by more draconian policies and mass incarceration came to dominate the American penal landscape, "bibliotherapy became a relic of the past," Sweeney observed. By 2007, when she interviewed staff and prisoners at the NCCCW and at women's prisons in Ohio and Pennsylvania, not one prison librarian had ever heard of bibliotherapy.[3]

Ironically, the 1970s were also known as the "golden years of prison library service," when prisons received block grants to expand or create libraries. Indeed, the promise of federal funds may explain NCCCW authorities' support for the women's literacy activities. At the same time, the prisoners' movement began to see reading as a vehicle for prisoner radicalization. A number of NCCCW prisoners, including those who had participated in the sit-in protest, formed their own study groups, reading radical texts, often about Third World liberation struggles.[4]

Print culture was one of the most important means of communication and radicalization among confined women and men and was the "backbone of prison organizing" in the mid- to late 1970s. Jailed protesters often targeted prison libraries, demanding freedom to choose their own reading materials, and censorship became a major battleground between the incarcerated and prison officials. Conflicts over prisoner access to legal materials also found their way into the courts, but legal victories did not always compel compliance. For example, North Carolina failed to observe a federal court order requiring law libraries for prisoners. Despite the deadly seriousness of the issue (disputes over prisoner reading and writing could and did erupt in violence), some of the disruptions seemed almost comical: in one instance prisoners destroyed obviously useless books, such as 500 copies of the *Coin Collectors Handbook* at the Manhattan House of Detention (known as the "Tombs") in New York City.[5]

Prisoner and social justice publications were particular points of contention. Several prisoner and activist newspapers, including the *Midnight Special*, the *Outlaw*, and the *Black Panther*, were frequently banned by officials. Yet they remained popular among prisoners and often were smuggled into jails and prisons across the country. Gay publications, including the *Gay Community News* and the lesbian feminist *off our backs*, were routinely prohibited and officially barred by the Federal Bureau of Prisons in 1977. It took court action to permit the *Outlaw* into California prisons in 1972 and more than a decade of litigation by the American Civil Liberties Union, the National Gay Task Force, and the Lambda Legal Defense Fund to allow prisoners the right to receive LGBTQ publications in 1980. However, as historian Regina Kunzel points out, despite the legal victories, officials continued to deny prisoners access to these materials.[6]

The feminist press, including publications by radical women of color, highlighted the abysmal conditions and protests in women's prisons. In North Carolina, *Feminary*, published by a Durham–Chapel Hill feminist collective from 1969 to 1982, provided extensive coverage of criminal justice issues, including the Joan Little trial and the protests at NCCCW. In one of its earliest issues, the publication drew attention to the campaign to free Marie Hill, the young Black woman imprisoned in Women's Prison who was sentenced to death for the alleged murder of a white storeowner in Rocky Mount. The feminist newspaper framed her case as an example of racist oppression and called on the women's movement to lend its support: "While the Marie Hill cause is primarily a battle against racism (rather than sexism), the FL (Female Liberation) movement should demonstrate its readiness to invoke moral (and, if at all possible, material) support to any woman in her fight against discrimination."[7] Many of the white women active in the lesbian feminist movement in the Triangle continued their literacy efforts with those confined at Women's Prison well into the 1980s and 1990s. For example, Alabama-born Mab Segrest, a prominent lesbian-feminist activist, scholar, and antiracist ally ran a literature and writing workshop at Women's Prison. Evelyn Machtinger joined Motheread, a project founded in 1987 to help incarcerated mothers at Women's Prison improve their literacy as a way of maintaining contact with their children.[8]

Women's activist newspapers such as *Triple Jeopardy*, which turned the woman's symbol into a Black fist brandishing a rifle as its logo, was published by the Third World Women's Alliance. *Triple Jeopardy* and the feminist *New Women's Times* helped to publicize the cases of individual women behind bars, including Joan Little. Similarly, *Aegis*, a publication of the women's antirape movement, covered the trials of Joan Little, Dessie X. Woods, Yvonne Wanrow, and Inez García, all women of color whose cases involved lethal self-defense against sexual violence. Many of these publications, including the *Lesbian Tide* and the Seattle-based *Through the Looking Glass: A Women and Children Prison Newsletter*, solicited writing from female prisoners who contributed creative pieces and exposés on incarceration.[9] Thus not only reading but writing too was a form of inmate empowerment and protest.

Prison writing has a long and celebrated literary history, and it gained heightened visibility in the 1960s and 1970s. Black prison writers joined a distinctive African American literary tradition rooted in slave narratives and the power of testimonial. Like the narratives of enslaved men and women, Black prison writing "preserves the natural speech patterns of the one who is telling the story" and frequently "rested on the importance of the story itself rather than the literary form in which the story is conveyed. It captures the irony, wit and wisdom frequently exhibited in African American storytelling."[10] From King's "Letter from Birmingham Jail" to George Jackson's *Soledad Brother*, most prisoner writing has been given a male face.[11] But incarcerated women also wrote from their perspective as "caged" subjects and frequently offered astute analyses of life behind bars, the criminal punishment system, and the wider society. Presaging what would soon be called the prison-industrial complex, NCCCW inmate Suzan Stuart condemned the "profit-making" motivations behind prison labor. The "forced labor" of North Carolina prisoners had earned the state's Division of Prisons $13 million in profits in 1974–75 alone, Stuart charged; and she pleaded with taxpayers to deny official requests for increased funding.[12] Imprisoned civil rights activist Jim Grant, writing for the *Southern Patriot*, echoed Stuart's accusations. Prisons were North Carolina's "biggest business," and jailed men and women were "a tremendous resource of slave labor," he wrote. North Carolina's prison farms produced millions of dollars of food, supplying most of the state's hospitals and schools. This clear financial incentive, Grant argued, was responsible for the horrendous conditions and the rise in the prison population: "The more prisoners inside, the more free labor available and the larger the profits."[13]

Some incarcerated women managed to create their own publications.[14] One of the most remarkable examples of female prison writing was the publication of a 1976 booklet, *Break de Chains of Legalized U.$. Slavery*. The sixty-eight-page collection of poems, exposés, photographs, and drawings showcased the uncensored, multiracial voices of women at the NCCCW. Proceeds from sales of the booklet were returned to the confined women to cover legal expenses and other personal needs. Initiated by the prisoners themselves, *Break de Chains* was published by the Triangle Area Lesbian Feminists in cooperation with the North Carolina Hard Times Prison Project. The editors made no changes whatsoever to the prisoners' submissions. *Break de Chains* thus reflected a more democratic publishing process, especially compared to the better-known prison writers who had ties to professional editors and publishers. Although Joan Little was not a contributor to *Break de Chains*, some of her prison writings appeared in various radical, feminist, and prisoner publications. In claiming a public voice through the written word, Joan Little and the NCCCW writers explicitly and often forcefully struck back at the forces both inside and outside the prison that sought to dehumanize and degrade them; and they did so on their own terms.[15]

With the decision to publish the unedited and sometimes profane expressions of the female prisoners, *Break de Chains* signaled a shift from the politics of respectability that had shaped decades of Black women's activism. These prison writers seemingly felt little compulsion to adhere to class-inflected modes of propriety as a precondition for demanding justice. Creating their own "epistemology of refusal," they defied North Carolina's culture of "civility," a mode of interracial relations that sought to blunt the harsher edges of white supremacy. Civility and respectability still mattered in some quarters, but, by the 1970s, the civil rights, Black Power, gay liberation, and women's movements had generated a new discursive space for formerly marginalized and stigmatized voices. Perhaps nowhere was this more evident than among the forgotten women in North Carolina's Women's Prison.[16]

The cover of the 1976 pamphlet depicted a seminude African American woman with the large Afro or natural hairstyle favored by Black Power activists. On her shoulders, she held a large globe featuring an oversized map of the United States that encompassed half the earth. Her cuffed wrists were attached to chains forming a prominent X superimposed over the U.S. map. The bare-breasted, shackled, and kneeling figure with head bowed and eyes downcast evoked slavery's auction block. But the figure was also a Black female Atlas shouldering the weight of the world, a visual representation of the heroic strength and resilience of the undefeated, strong Black woman. The sketch was an uncanny presaging of one of the most famous passages in Zora Neale Hurston's 1937 novel, *Their Eyes Were Watching God*. The novel would be reissued for the second time in 1978, two years after *Break de Chains* appeared, no doubt spurred by Alice Walker's 1975 *Ms.* magazine essay, "In Search of Zora Neale Hurston." In the novel, Nanny tells her granddaughter Janie, "De nigger woman is de mule uh de world as fur as Ah can see." However, the cover depicted more than modern-day slavery and the exploitation of African American women. Behind the kneeling woman, the red, green, and black Pan-African liberation colors invoked the legacy of Black resistance and African independence movements.[17]

In another parallel to Hurston, the title, *Break de Chains*, echoed and celebrated southern Black working-class dialect. It also underscored the writers' rejection of class-based and racially charged respectability politics. *Break de Chains* was likely borrowed from an appeal under the same title by defenders of Assata Shakur, a Black Liberation Army activist imprisoned on multiple trumped-up charges. From behind bars, Shakur had written an open letter in support of Joan Little that was published in the Durham-based *Action for Forgotten Women Newsletter*.[18] The use of the title, as well as the booklet's

Break de Chains of Legalized U.$. Slavery

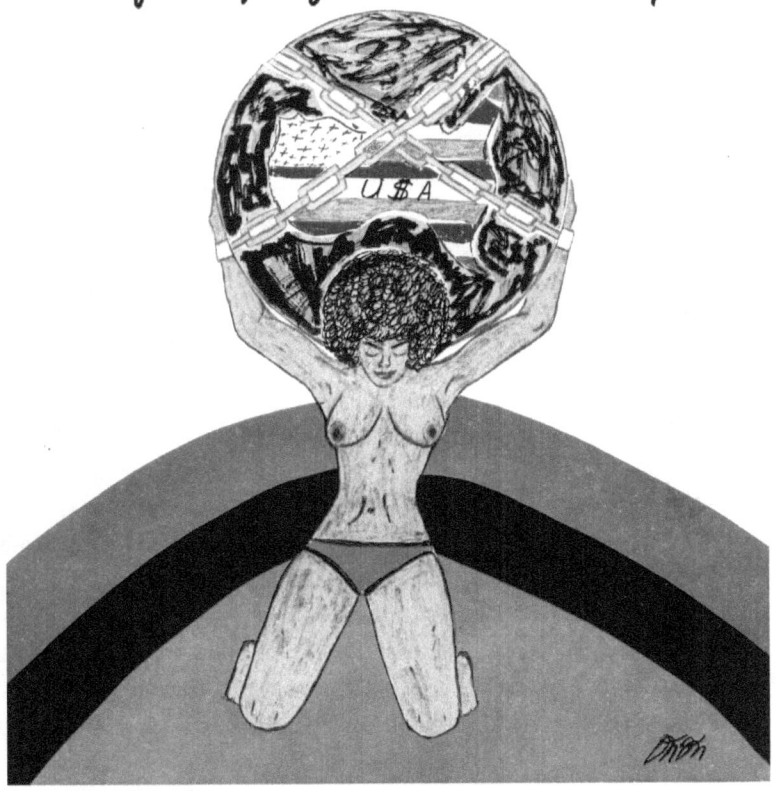

The cover of this booklet, produced by the prisoners at Raleigh's Women's Prison, equated Black women's unpaid prison labor with slavery and pointed to the financial incentives underlying incarceration.
Break de Chains of Legalized U.$. Slavery, courtesy of the Wisconsin Historical Society.

content, thus linked the prison writers to a broader, radical Black freedom movement beyond the prison walls. Most important, the imperative "Break de Chains" was a command, a call to action.

"Legalized U.$. Slavery" indicted the modern prison as a form of enslavement and gestured toward the Thirteenth Amendment's loophole, which had abolished slavery "except as punishment for crime" for persons "duly convicted." And the dollar sign replacing the "S" in "U.S." highlighted the profit motive embedded in the growing prison-industrial complex and rising incarceration rates. In short, the cover was a visual representation of the radical carceral politics of the mostly African American women authors featured in *Break de Chains*.

The contributors to *Break de Chains* frequently expressed their analyses in language that was popular in leftist polemics of the 1960s and 1970s. But this was more than just abstract revolutionary rhetoric. Their insights stemmed from their lived experience both inside and outside the prison walls, and showcased their intersectional understanding of patriarchy, white supremacy, and poverty as key components of their oppression.[19] The women forged an interracial sisterhood as unfree persons, and they linked their protests to liberation struggles against racism, class exploitation, misogyny, and imperialism. They also situated themselves within the larger prison movement. Most, if not all, of the contributors had participated in the Women's Prison sit-down strike; and they received communiqués of support from incarcerated men and women in California, Illinois, Maryland, Ohio, and throughout North Carolina. Even prisoners from Holland sent letters of encouragement. Perhaps motivated by fellow prisoner Joan Little's case, the authors drew attention to Dessie X. Woods and Cheryl Todd, two Black women who were arrested on charges of robbery and murder after they defended themselves against a sexual attack by a white man in Georgia.[20]

The women writers also drew parallels between their own confinement and incarcerated African American activists such as Assata Shakur and the San Quentin Six, collapsing the line between "social criminals" and "political prisoners." Self-naming similarly signaled their identification with Black radical and revolutionary struggles. Like Shakur, several women adopted African names, rejecting their given names as relics of enslavement. For example, one writer signed as "Comrade Aminah Aliyah s/n [slave name] Bessie Bouler."[21] The authors' deliberate misspelling of Amerikkka, Kapitalism, and NKKKW (for NCCCW) was a bold and provocative condemnation of anti-Black violence, especially in the South. The stylistic device mimicked other radical writings of the era and was adopted by Shakur in her 1987 memoir.[22]

Some of the visual images in *Break de Chains* both summoned and reappropriated iconic symbols of American freedom and liberty. A line from the Emma Lazarus poem inscribed on the Statue of Liberty, "Give me your tired, your poor, your huddled masses, yearning to breathe free," appeared alongside a sketch of a prison guard depicted as a KKK member armed with a three-foot baton. The baton was a direct reference to the weapons used by guards against the women during the sit-down strike.[23]

Illustrations like this one juxtaposed the racism and brutality of imprisonment with the promise of the Emma Lazarus poem inscribed on the Statue of Liberty: "Give me your tired, your poor, your huddled masses yearning to breathe free." From *Break de Chains of Legalized U.$. Slavery*, courtesy of the Wisconsin Historical Society.

Prison writers also appropriated orations from the civil rights and Black Power movements. Marjorie Marsh, one of the plaintiffs in the joint NCCCW–Central Prison lawsuit, invoked Martin Luther King Jr.'s "I Have a Dream" speech. But she rejected King's strict adherence to nonviolence, although even King was not opposed to armed defense of his home after it was firebombed during the Montgomery Bus Boycott. Instead, Marsh reiterated Malcolm X's provocative call for racial justice "by any means necessary" and threatened armed revolution if more peaceful methods failed: "Our dream is to expose [and] destroy the Oppressor scheme / And get justice by necessary means. / Be it negotiations or M-16!"[24]

Tarishi Maisha (aka Shirley Herlth) recast the 1960s civil rights anthem "We Shall Overcome" in her protest poem, "Till We Overcome!!!," published in the national prisoner newsletter *Midnight Special* prior to its appearance in *Break de Chains*. Maisha/Herlth had been singled out as a ringleader of the Women's Prison strike. Following the protest, she reportedly was dragged by guards, tearing the skin off her knees, placed in solitary for months, and transferred to Morganton men's prison. Written behind bars in the men's prison, the eighteen-year-old's poem was part lament and part profane condemnation of prison officials and the North Carolina governor, all of whom she accused by name. Calling them "filthy bastards" and "dirty bums" for the abuse they inflicted on the confined women—"you ruin lives / . . . you make it where / we barely live"—the young poet was not content merely to unleash her rage against the more powerful. Instead, Maisha/Herlth turned the tables. Threatening her abusers with the collective power of organized women, she reminded them that the prisoners outnumbered their keepers: "but this is a warning / . . . cause you got a whole lotta sistas / on your mutha-fucking ass." Most important, the young prison writer conveyed the newfound determination and perseverance of incarcerated women: "and we ain't giving up / and we ain't gonna run / we gonna keep on trucking / till we overcome."[25]

Several *Break de Chains* authors denounced poverty and other forms of injustice on both sides of the prison walls. In a stunning reversal, the "caged" women judged not only their keepers but society for its callous indifference to children. Maisha/Herlth's moving poem "What Do You Say to Hungry Children Amerikkka?" was a powerful indictment of Black childhood poverty in "Amerikkka." In her rhetorical refrain, "I ask you, what do you say to a hungry child?," the poet found "Amerikkka" guilty of denying food, shelter, education, employment, and equality to poor Black children. Although society blamed individual "criminals" for the choices they made, Maisha inverted the guilty charge by transposing guilt to the state: "Is this what you say, Amerikkka?" By failing to provide basic needs for impoverished African American children, "Amerikkka" was responsible for creating crime and criminals, she charged. Maisha/Herlth's rebuke was a reminder of the bitter legacy of enslavement and the generational impact on Black families of decades of thwarted opportunity: "You are to blame. / You put Those chains on him Before he was born. / His Daddy Wore them too."[26]

As unfree people, prison writers were uniquely positioned to expound upon the nature of freedom. For both Maisha/Herlth and Marjorie Marsh, incarceration was the measure of a nation's moral fabric. "I believe firmly in the saying 'you can determine the humanity of society by entering its prisons,'" Marsh wrote. Her essay on freedom was not simply a personal plea for release from confinement. Rather, Marsh blurred the lines between imprisonment and freedom, metaphorically erasing the prison walls that separated the free and the unfree. She insisted that those who believed they were "free" under "kapitalism" were deluded. "Can we have partial freedom? Can some of us consider ourselves 'free' (the petty bourgie capitalist) when others continue to starve/be brutalized/murdered?" Marsh asked. Such "freedom" was "imaginary," she concluded. According to Aminah Aliyah / Bessie Bouler, the jailed and the free were inextricably bound. "We are the captives of society's dungeons. Our problems are your problems. . . . Your problems will never be solved until and unless we are also recognized and treated as human beings."27

Tarishi Maisha / Shirley Herlth's "Open Letter to Amerikkka," written from "Morganton Slave Kamp" (Morganton Prison), denounced American wealth and economic inequality in a scathing critique of racial capitalism. Her "Letter" focused attention on the devastating consequences for poor Black women and children after Governor Rockefeller ordered the violent suppression of the 1971 Attica prisoner revolt: "Do you know, while rockefeller orders men to go kill men, that those men's wives scrub floors to feed their children and now those babies go fatherless?" Maisha similarly juxtaposed President Gerald Ford's lavish banquet for the Ghanaian president with her own mother's impoverishment, a woman forced to "sell little hand-made jewelries just for a can of split pea soup." Maisha thus set Black women's exploited labor against the murderous abundance of powerful white men. In so doing, she exposed the relational nature of dominance and subjugation, privilege and exploitation. She leveled her most biting critique at hypocrisy in America, the "land of the free." Although Maisha overlooked the fact that North Carolina's license plate motto, "First in Freedom," conveniently elides its history of slavery and Jim Crow, she condemned the state's penal policies, which incarcerated teens as young as fourteen and put more people on death row than any other state.28

White prison writers also excoriated the injustice of American society writ large. Anne Willett, a white plaintiff in the NCCCW prisoners' lawsuit, denounced social Darwinist capitalism and called for a global struggle to usher in a new socialist world: "We live in a capitalist system wherein only the strong survive," she wrote.[29] Linking poverty and crime, she noted that most incarcerated women (including those like Joan Little) were imprisoned for nonviolent property crimes. She too deployed creative misspellings to decry American racism and economic exploitation and called for reparations for the poor. "Most of us are here because our only means of survival was to take what is/was rightfully our share of Amerikkka's crop." This was not merely a justification for crime, however. It was a critique of a capitalist political economy that built its riches on the backs of exploited labor and put profits before people in a battle between the "haves" and the "have-nots." And it was a call for redistributive justice. Although Willett offered an essentialist notion of women's importance as mothers, hers was an assertive rather than a submissive or passive conception of motherhood. Most important, her vision of radical interracial sisterhood took its inspiration from a long legacy of Black women freedom fighters and incarcerated women. Willett urged her female readers to join the women's liberation movement and the "beautiful army of comrades/sistas such as Harriet Tubman, Sojourner Truth, and Assata Shakur, and the sistas of N.K. Women's Koncentration Kamp [NCCCW]."[30]

Only one of the prison writers featured in *Break de Chains* appears to have been a more conventional "political" prisoner. Ellen Amana Porter, a nineteen-year-old Black woman, was sentenced to thirty years for armed robbery, a crime she insisted she did not commit. Porter claimed that she never handled or fired the weapon and that the aggrieved party never showed up in court during her trial. Her codefendant apparently received a shorter sentence, while she was encouraged by her court-appointed attorney to take a plea bargain. With no prior offenses, her lawyer assured her that she would receive probation. She believed the harsh sentence was retaliation for her affiliation with Black on Vanguard, a Republic of New Afrika group that gained a footing among prisoners in North Carolina and elsewhere. Tellingly, Porter was the only writer to outline the specifics of her offense. And yet like the other writers, her lament was not primarily an appeal for individual sympathy or relief. Rather, she hoped to expose the injustice of a criminal punishment system that targeted Black activists, and the vulnerability of a young, impoverished Black woman.[31]

In a show of militant, interracial female solidarity, *Break de Chains* closed with a coauthored piece by two women, one Black, one white. The epistolary call to revolution by Marjorie Marsh and Anne Willett was based on one of the illustrations in the booklet. The simple, penciled sketch showed an interracial, armed sisterhood, comprised mostly of Black women, dressed similarly, perhaps in prison garb. The accompanying caption read, "Liberation" and underneath, "Revolution in Our Time." The "Emory" on the handle of one of the machine guns was likely an homage to Emory Douglas, the Black Panther minister of culture and a graphic artist, who had made a similar sketch, but with an armed Black man in front.[32] Marsh and Willett opened their appeal with a familiar Black Power salutation, "Greetings Our Bruthas/Sistahs." Black Power and revolutionary discourse permeated their missive: "The time is now at hand to *seize the time*," a reference to both the Elaine Brown song and Bobby Seale's book, Seize the Time, the latter appropriately dictated by Seale from a California jail in 1969 and 1970.[33] But in another piece, "Revolutionary Style," Marsh denounced inauthentic Blackness: "It's the style now to be black, to cry a fake love for the people . . . to rap revolutionary rhetoric, but still rip off the people . . . to feel sorry for the prisoners, yet feel us inferior . . . *Revolution has no style—color or sentiment!*" she asserted.[34] Marsh and Willett detailed the personal transformations they had undergone as prisoners and testified to the politicization of incarceration: "Our time here has been spent in growth . . . mentally, spiritually/comradely." Even their mistakes and disappointments, along with the other's betrayals, "contributed to our growth," they insisted. Marsh and Willett showcased an emancipatory pedagogy grounded in their lived experiences. Rejecting "alleged liberal sympathizers" who pacified them, they sought "hands that will teach us and learn from us." Out of "pain/suffering/sacrifice"—which paled before the "suffering of the oppressed people throughout the world"—Marsh and Willett vowed to keep alive their freedom dreams: "We will savor the sweetness of freedom," they declared. The imprisoned writers closed with a promise to remain vigilant: "Our assurance is to you, our people that we remain unyielding yours always, In Love, Devotion and Continuous Struggle," and it was signed Comrade Marsh and Comrade Willett.[35]

Print culture offered confined women a free space and a voice as prison intellectuals. But their emancipatory pedagogy was not without danger. All the writers featured in *Break de Chains* chose to sign their contributions. By identifying themselves in the public domain of print media, these prison writers not only demonstrated their collective rejection of state authority but also made themselves potential targets for official retaliation. Those who participated in the 1975 Women's Prison strike already had suffered reprisals from guards and prison officials; and they were still incarcerated. Their decision to raise their voices against all odds thus constituted both oppositional and courageous action. One woman wrote to Feminary, "I am afraid for the

Liberation

Many of the contributors to *Break de Chains* had participated in the Women's Prison strike. Sketches like this one conveyed their multiracial, woman-centered revolutionary politics. From *Break de Chains of Legalized U.$. Slavery*, courtesy of the Wisconsin Historical Society.

women who wrote Break de Chains. . . . I am also a little afraid for the women who printed and are distributing the book. I hope my fears are groundless."[36]

Such trepidations were not unfounded. One African American prisoner, Alice Wise, described a harrowing experience that may have been a deliberate effort to terrorize the women and send a warning to the "troublemakers." Wise, along with sixty other women, had been segregated from the other prisoners as punishment for participating in the sit-down strike. Although the women were physically confined, they weaponized their voices by invading the guards' aural spaces with verbal taunts. Three of the women were placed in solitary confinement as punishment. When Wise and several other women loudly complained after witnessing three male guards enter a woman's cell without the required female matron, the guards decided to teach Wise a lesson. She was stripped of everything, denied even a mattress, and she too was sent to solitary confinement. The next day, after a foam mattress had been delivered, prison guard Max Barbour and Superintendent Louis Powell came into her cell. A female guard, Sargent Satterwhite, reportedly stood by observing what happened next. "Words cannot possibly convey the feeling of terror which surrounded me," Wise wrote. "I was away from all prisoners and powerless." "With a wild look in his eye," Barbour cut out a piece of foam from her mattress. It was in the shape of a heart. The guard then "put his fingers across my lips and told me that I talked too much and I saw too much," Wise reported. The incident may have shaken her, but it did not silence her. Wise penned an urgent plea for assistance: "I am alive," she wrote, "but the next time Max Barbour pulls out his knife to passively assault me, I may not have the strength to overcome. Your help is needed now."[37] Despite or perhaps because of her fear, Wise chose to publicly recount her abuse and name her alleged abusers. Publicity and media attention had often protected Black freedom fighters throughout the South, especially when they were arrested for civil rights activity, and Wise may have felt this was her best chance for protection and survival.

Wise was not the only inmate to name alleged abusers and victims. Aminah Aliyah / Bessie Bouler described fellow Pauline Caldwell's "multiple bruises . . . wrists and face are swollen from the beatings she received Tuesday night—3/23/76—by six guards . . . while she was handcuffed." Brought to the "hole" (solitary confinement), Caldwell was sleeping naked with only a single blanket, Aliyah/Bouler asserted. "Have we been forgotten so easily and quickly?" she wondered. Feeling abandoned and near despair, she lamented, "Where are our supporters/our comrades/our people?"[38]

Whether knowingly or not, the creators of *Break de Chains* reflected the legendary African American "blues impulse," voicing their "isolation and despair," all the while refusing to succumb to those feelings and asserting Black humanity in a world based on what Martin Luther King Jr. called the "thingification" of human beings. A term coined by novelist Ralph Ellison, the "blues impulse" is not only a musical form but also keeps "the painful details and episodes of a brutal experience alive in one's aching consciousness, to finger its jagged edges, and to transcend it, . . . an autobiographical chronicle of personal catastrophe expressed lyrically."[39]

As cultural theorist Michael Hames-García has observed about prison writers during this period, "these prison intellectuals' analyses shift attention from individual actions to the role social structures play in limiting individual choice, but without excusing or justifying individual actions or underestimating the importance of subjective agency." Even more important, despite their lack of formal education, such obscure prison writers "are among the most insightful, nuanced, and visionary political philosophers of our time." Not only the more celebrated and erudite prison writers of the 1960s and 1970s, such as George Jackson and Angela Davis, but also the "unknown" contributors to publications like *Break de Chains* represented "a continuation of transformative social theory among activists involved in the most oppressed and exploited communities."[40]

Although Joan Little was not a contributor to *Break de Chains*, she too took pen to paper from a cell in Women's Prison. Like her fellow authors, Little used her prison writings to challenge those who would dismiss her as simply a common street criminal with little or no political awareness.

12

So Now I Take My Stand

The Prison Writings of Joan Little

Joan Little may not have been a "political" prisoner in the narrowest sense. Yet she entered Women's Prison in September 1974 with a political consciousness reflected in both her published pieces as well as her unpublished prison writings and sketches. Her contemporaneous interviews with various media outlets offer similar evidence and corroboration of her political views. Indeed, Little's prison writings belied those who claimed that if she could be considered "political" at all, it was imprisonment that politicized her. The Black Panther Party called her "a revolutionary born in jail," and Panther leader Huey Newton likened her incarceration experience to his own. While she may have entered prison as a convicted criminal jailed by a system that was itself criminal, she emerged a revolutionary, Newton claimed. Meanwhile the Nation of Islam insisted that although Little was "without political aspiration" and "had no politics," she was "no less a political prisoner" than Angela Davis had been. Even Celine Chenier claimed that "Joan didn't have political awareness." But, Chenier added, "she has it [now]," alluding to Little's ordeal in the rape-murder trial. "Joan speaks now as though she's been in it for years."[1]

Little spent nearly six months in Women's Prison in the fall of 1974 and early winter of 1975, while supporters raised her $115,000 bail bond. Within weeks of her arrival, she joined a prisoners' writing group and produced a slew of poems, other writings, and sketches that revealed her knowledge of current events and African American history while offering a critique of American racism and U.S. foreign policy. One of Little's earliest poems, "Murder," is dated September 25, 1974, just weeks after a grand jury indicted her for first-degree murder of her former jailer, sending her to the Raleigh prison to await trial. The date suggests that she was far from the naive, apolitical prisoner that even some of her supporters claimed she was. While Little was neither the most lyrical poet nor an activist, she did not need revolutionary theory or a literary degree to understand what her lived experience had taught her: that those who wielded political and economic power against the marginalized and oppressed were as guilty (and perhaps even more so) than those behind bars. Thus, Joan Little joined her "caged" sisters in claiming a public space and voice to craft an emancipatory pedagogy that exposed and condemned the injustices she both witnessed and lived.[2]

Several of Little's prison writings were published in activist outlets. Some conveyed gratitude to those who defended her, while others were political in nature. One piece, which she called "not a poem, just the facts," appeared in the national prisoner newsletter *Midnight Special*. It was also published in the lesbian feminist *off our backs* in January 1975, while she was awaiting release on bail from Women's Prison. The "non-poem" was printed alongside a letter of appreciation to her female supporters: "It is people like you at *oob* and around the country that have given me the strength to go on. . . . I want to thank each and every one of you. Peace and love be with you." She closed in her own handwriting, "In Sisterhood and the Struggle, JoAnne Little." In her "non-poem," Little denounced the deprivation suffered by the poor. "What's funny about no jobs and living / in roach filled two room shacks?" she asked. Perhaps seeing herself in her depiction of those victimized by an exploitative and unjust world, she lashed out at the debilitating conditions that thwarted so many lives. "The people who have the power to change things aren't doing a thing," she charged. In an autobiographical essay in *Southern Exposure*, a Durham-based journal published by a multiracial group of former southern civil rights activists, Little recounted her experiences growing up in the rural segregated South.[3]

Little's prison writings and drawings, however, remained largely unpublished and included poetry handwritten in beautiful cursive penmanship and sketches penciled on lined state Department of Correction paper. In several poems she challenged detractors who dismissed her as a conniving and lowly street criminal who had killed a defenseless man. "I Am Somebody," written from Women's Prison in Raleigh while awaiting her murder trial, painted an intriguing self-portrait.[4]

"I Am Somebody" opens with an unapologetic declaration, "I killed a white in self-defense / But the jury doesn't care," countering those who insisted that Little had lured Clarence Alligood into her jail cell with promises of sex, murderous intentions, and an escape plan. While also acknowledging the "bad company" in her past, she recast her choices, coupling her illegal "stealing" with the more acceptable and racially subordinate "begging": "I got in with 'bad company' begging / stealing for what I thought was / right." Still, the "bad company" was ambiguous. Little placed it in quotes, implicitly rejecting middle-class ideals of Black respectability. But her use of "right" was evocative. The language pointed to the historic denial of Black citizenship rights, but it also challenged the idea of "stealing" as criminal. In redefining "stealing" as right behavior, Little flipped the script on the legal protection of private property rights, suggesting that stolen property was ethically "right," a just recompense for poverty and racism. The image drew on a rich legacy of slave resistance and a moral economy in which "theft" became at least partial restitution for stolen Black bodies and exploited Black labor. Thus, her justification of "stealing" can be read as a demand for reparations in the "afterlife of slavery." (That Little was convicted of breaking into Black-owned trailers complicated the moral economy of her claims.) Most striking was Little's insistence that, despite her past behavior, she was entitled to all the protections and claims of citizenship. The last line of the poem, "That didn't make me less—I am still somebody," affirms her humanity and dignity. It was a defiant rejection of the historic African American uplift ideology and politics of respectability that too often required proper behavior—especially for women—as a necessary precondition for racial justice and Black freedom. Finally, Little's poem was a bold indictment of a criminal legal system—a jury that "doesn't care"—that was inclined to grant her neither protection nor justice.[5]

Little addressed similar themes in other writings. In an undated poem, "Joan—Walks with Dignity," handwritten on lined, state Department of Correction paper, she proclaimed her innocence and predicted that one day she would "be a part of the freedom ride." Unlike "I Am Somebody," "Joan—Walks with Dignity" declared "self-defense," rather than "stealing," as "right": "I am a woman who did what I thought was right." Little described herself as "caged," evoking the dehumanization of captivity and suggesting that she had been unfairly imprisoned simply for defending herself: "I struggled in self-defense / now—I'm caged behind a prison fence." Still, she remained unrepentant, defiant, and determined: "so now I take my stand." As in "I Am Somebody," Joan again asserted her humanity, insisting that she would

This sketch by Joan Little was dated just weeks after she was indicted for first-degree murder and sent to Women's Prison in Raleigh to await trial and the result of efforts by the Free Joan Little campaign to raise her substantial bail.
Courtesy of the Joan Little Papers, David M. Rubenstein
Rare Book and Manuscript Library, Duke University.

"continue to walk in dignity," regardless or in spite of those who would defame her. Although she remained indicted and detained on a first-degree murder charge, she positioned herself with the "law-abiding citizens," calling on them to "fight" against injustice, and by implication against the sexual abuse of women.

A chilling sketch titled "Joan Little, From Cell 9, N.C.C.C.W." was dated September 30, 1974, less than a month after Little entered Women's Prison to await her rape-murder trial. The sketch featured a sea of faceless people in a crowd standing below a gallows with an empty hangman's noose. On each of ten faceless heads, she printed one of the letters of her first and last name. In the right-hand corner, she paraphrased an excerpt from the Gospel of John: "He who is without sin, let him cast the first stone."[6] The sketch summoned the gruesome history of southern lynching, while the Gospel passage was an appeal to a southern populace steeped in Biblical scripture. But it also erased the line between Joan, the indicted murderess, and those who were not "without sin" but would condemn her to death.

Little's September 25, 1974, poem, "Murder," was composed less than a month after her fatal encounter with jailer Clarence Alligood. Addressed "To the people," it was uncannily similar to a missive by imprisoned Black revolutionary Assata Shakur. Shakur had released her taped message, "To My People," a year earlier, on July 4, 1973, American Independence Day. It was widely broadcast on many radio stations and later printed in total in her autobiography. Most remarkable was how closely Little's poem hewed to Shakur's letter, at times adopting the same language and themes. For example, both women critiqued the hypocrisy of American imperialist violence in Southeast Asia and Africa, indicting "Nixon and his crime partners [who] have murdered hundreds" of thousands of "third-world Brothers [and] Sisters in Vietnam-Cambodia, . . . Mozambique, Angola and South Africa" Both rebuked the "top law enforcement officials in this country"; Shakur called them a "lying bunch of criminals" who were "implicated in the Watergate crimes" while Little dismissed them as "nothing but a bunch of criminals, murderers and thieves." The two jailed women contrasted elected officials' criminal behavior with a penal system that indicted Shakur and Little as murderers. Little's "Yet they call me a murderer" paralleled Shakur's collectivist "They call us murderers." Little followed with lines taken nearly verbatim from Shakur, changing Shakur's "we" to Little's first-person "I": "but I didn't kill over 250 unarmed [Black] men, women and children in the riots they provoked during the 60s." Shakur wrote, "but we did not murder Martin Luther King, Jr., Emmett Till, Medgar Evers, Malcolm X, George Jackson . . ."

while Little penned "I didn't murder Martin Luther King, Emmit [sic] Till, Medger [sic] Evers, Malcolm X or Bro. George Jackson." Little's "we are the victims, not the criminals" echoed Shakur's "we are the victims . . . and not the criminals." Other lines were similarly lifted from Shakur. In the same language, both women excoriated those who murdered "millions of Indians by / Ripping off their homeland; / Then call[ed themselves] pioneers."

Little's decision to condemn the recent police shootings of three unarmed Black children in "Murder," as Shakur had done in "To My People," was revealing. In separate incidents in 1972 and 1973, New York City police, including a plainclothes officer, fatally shot sixteen-year-old Rita Lloyd, eleven-year-old Rickie Bodden, and ten-year-old Clifford Glover (whom Little calls Flower). Bodden and Glover were shot in the back. The killings provoked protests in Black communities and underlined northern anti-Black police violence, frequently downplayed by those who preferred to point a finger at the South. The targeting of three Black children might well have resonated with Little's own experience of police surveillance, harassment, false arrests, and the other injustices she had weathered in the criminal punishment system as a teenager.[7]

Joan Little's adoption of portions of Assata Shakur's "To My People" does not suggest simple plagiarism. "Murder" was never published or distributed publicly. Like many young poets, Little may have wanted to mimic the more experienced writer. But why did she choose Shakur, a seasoned activist and member of the Black Liberation Army, to imitate? Might she have shared an affinity with the older woman, who, like Little, was imprisoned and awaiting trial after being indicted for first-degree murder of a white male law enforcement official? Shakur's taped message was much longer than Little's poem, and Little borrowed only a small number of lines from it. The younger writer's selection of specific themes and her decision to replicate some of Shakur's language verbatim attests to Little's political consciousness. That she did so within weeks of arriving at Women's Prison indicates that Little did not arrive as a "tabula rasa" with no political awareness.

Joan Little did not need Assata Shakur to instruct her on what her own experiences in the Jim Crow South and in the criminal legal system had taught her about white supremacy and the abuse of power. By fusing the assassinations of well-known activists such as King and Evers with the prison murder of George Jackson and the recent fatal police shootings of three unarmed Black youth, as Shakur had done, Little similarly chose to link anti-Black vigilante violence, murderous prison guards, and police brutality.

It is not clear whether Little learned about Shakur's letter prior to her arrest on the felony theft charges or following her arrival at Women's Prison. But that Shakur's revolutionary message was in circulation at Women's Prison is in itself remarkable and may explain how the prisoner-authored booklet, *Break de Chains*, discussed in the previous chapter, was created in a tightly controlled space like Women's Prison. Perhaps Little had followed the spate of recent murders of Black activists on her own before entering Women's Prison or prior to her summer in Beaufort County Jail. She undoubtedly knew about Malcolm X, Martin Luther King Jr., and others whose murders had received wide media coverage.

Assata Shakur was not Little's only inspiration, however. She inscribed her handwritten poem "Murder" over a penciled clenched fist shackled with a heavy chain. Little's sketch depicted the militant Black Power fisted salute while the shackles summoned the history of slavery and the reality of imprisonment.

Other poems similarly showcased Little's racial consciousness and her affinity with oppressed people of color. In "The Mystery of Black," Little reversed the white-centered Tarzan epic. Rejecting a whitewashed story of heroic American settler colonialism, she reimagined the defeat of the iconic hero by Indigenous people: "Black is—when you root for the natives to beat the devil out of Tarzan." In "To the People, from Lincoln's Gettysburg Address," she juxtaposed the nation's broken promises to African Americans with two of the most cherished symbols of American democracy and freedom: excerpts from the former president's most celebrated speech and lyrics from "My Country 'Tis of Thee":

> "We here resolve that these dead shall not have died in vain"
> but my people little of this promise remains.
> "That this nation under God, shall have a new birth of freedom"
> My people where is all this sweet liberty . . .
> "My country tis of thee"
> What is left in this land for you and me?

Joan Little clearly did not enter prison as an uninformed young woman. Nor did imprisonment suddenly politicize her, as many of her defenders claimed. However, Little's experience of incarceration transcended her immediate, individual suffering and alerted her to the pressing concerns of confined women, including the dangers of sexual abuse. Although her political views vacillated—she even occasionally attacked some of her supporters—she used her notoriety and the Free Joan Little campaign to highlight the conditions at Raleigh's Women's Prison. "No matter how my trial comes out, I'm going to be behind those sisters," she promised. Speaking before large crowds in anticipation of her upcoming murder trial, Little framed her own case in the larger context of women's sexual vulnerability behind bars. She hinted that some prison deaths may have been cover-ups for sexual violence. Angela Davis made a similar observation. Few would have noticed or cared if the deadly ice pick struggle between jailer Clarence Alligood and prisoner Joan Little had ended differently. "Justifiable homicide" would have sealed the case, Davis asserted; just another dead Black woman, and an allegedly disreputable one at that.[8]

NCCCW prisoners reciprocated Joan's efforts to draw attention to Women's Prison abuses by publicly demonstrating their support for her. One sent an anonymous letter to *Feminary* threatening more disturbances if Little was convicted: "We are all with her even though we are locked up. I believe hell will break loose in the prison if any shit gets flaky at that trial." Another woman found hope and inspiration in Little's acquittal in the murder trial. "Sister Joan's victory has renewed old strength and given to the non-believer new strength." The writer hoped that the publicity surrounding Little's case and the attention it brought to prison conditions might help the women's class-action suit against North Carolina prison officials. "Give her the many thanks from her struggling comrades. As the power of the people has freed sister Joann, so shall it free the many brothers and sisters of the dehumanizing conditions and treatment we are currently forced to endure."[9]

The feminist newspaper *off our backs* also connected Little's case to the NCCCW prisoners by asking readers to write not only to the well-known Joan Little but to other imprisoned women as well. Correspondence was especially meaningful to the women who were denied visitations as punishment for their protest. "I just got your letter and was very glad to hear from you," one wrote. "I love my sisters and corresponding with them is one of my few pleasures. . . . . It's lonely here but every time they take something away from me, I get stronger." Families also felt the consequences of the Women's Prison strike. "I got a letter from my sister. She said the parole people had come to our house." Because the prisoner had been involved in the protest, the family was apparently informed that she would be denied parole. "I guess I must be one of the ones that's a risk to society."[10]

Following her acquittal on the murder charge and awaiting the outcome of her appeal on the felony theft conviction, Little kept her word and continued to speak out on behalf of the women at NCCCW and other victims of sexual violence. During a trip to California sponsored by the Black Panthers less than a week after her acquittal, she addressed a Panther Victory Rally in Oakland. "When I was in prison for six months, I saw the kinds of conditions human beings are living under," Joan told the crowd of 1,200 supporters. Drawing on her experience of sexual assault to expose the pervasive sexual abuse of Black women, especially prisoners, Little exhorted women to resist, even violently if necessary. "When the White man came to my cell and tried to take advantage of me, I stood up and said 'no.' Black women are not going to take this anymore. We're going to stop it now. . . . . If that means we have to stand up with guns in our hands and lose our lives—we've lost our lives for a good cause."[11]

Tellingly, Little also linked her case to some of the best-known political prisoners of the era, including George Jackson. During her California visit, she attended the trial of the San Quentin Six and visited one of them, Johnny Spain, in prison on August 21, 1975, the fourth anniversary of George Jackson's death. "The way I saw him [Spain] shackled and chained really got to me. . . . He was chained like a dog the entire time I sat there talking to him." Little observed the similarities between the treatment of prisoners in California and in North Carolina, erasing any apparent differences between regional penal policies. She even struck a militant tone, adopting Panther rhetoric by calling prison guards "pigs." "I'd take an atom bomb and drop it right in the middle of San Quentin Prison," she commented to a reporter, adding, "First I'd make sure that Johnny [Spain] and all the other prisoners were out of there, but I'd make sure that the warden and all the other pigs were in there so I'd get them."[12]

However, Little was more inclined to advocate for peaceful protest, even as she condemned state violence, the weaponization of the criminal punishment system against Black activists, and discriminatory policing practices that targeted African Americans in particular. "If we stand together, they won't railroad another JoAnne [sic] Little to the gas chamber. They won't kill another George Jackson." Little also collapsed the distinction between the "caged" and the "free," understanding that "freedom" for Black people was illusory. "I'm not free," she said. "None of us are free. As long as they shackle Johnny Spain, we will never be free. As long as they shoot down 14-year old kids, as long as they take half of our pay checks, as long as they kick 72-year-old women out of their houses, out of their shacks, we're not free. . . . I walked out into an invisible prison. I'm still in prison. You are still in prison." She urged everyone "to come together . . . because the time for us to seize our freedom is now," she said. "We're asking that Black people have a say so about what is going on in this country. Then, and only then will we be able to say that we are free." The overflowing crowd leapt to its feet in a standing ovation. The twenty-one-year-old newly minted celebrity spent the next forty-five minutes signing autographs and receiving congratulations from well-wishers, but her nearly eighteen-month legal ordeal had left its mark. Little might not have been a political prisoner in the conventional sense; nor had she been an activist prior to her murder trial. But neither was she simply an apolitical street criminal, as many of her supporters as well as her detractors maintained. However, she had sharpened her political acumen about freedom and incarceration, especially regarding the sexual abuse of imprisoned women. And the Free Joan Little campaign had honed her newfound embrace of collective struggle: "This just goes to show that if we stand together . . . we can do something because we have always done the impossible," Little announced. Joan Little had survived her near-fatal journey through the legal system, and the scores of activists who had stood by her could take some of the credit.[13]

Their bodies may have been "caged," but Joan Little and the "forgotten women" in North Carolina and in jails and prisons across the country were transformed by incarceration. Some entered prison with an analysis of anti-Black oppression and systemic injustice. Others were politicized by their carceral experiences. Nearly all had felt the long arm of the law and its many abuses. Scholar and activist Dylan Rodriguez asks, "What, then, is the significance of political praxis for people whose right to exist has been eliminated? What is an appropriate 'methodology' of engagement with this lineage of . . . political subjects who are, by force of condition, putative 'non-subjects'?"[14] For female prisoners, their engagement was to challenge their presumed civil death and the state of nonbeing that the U.S. Supreme Court reaffirmed in its 1977 curtailment of the North Carolina Prisoners' Labor Union. Their vantage point as carceral nonsubjects, they insisted, gave them special insights about power, freedom, and exploitation on both sides of the prison walls. Asserting a political consciousness no less authentic than the more recognizable political prisoners, these "social criminals" claimed a subjective agency in word and in deed that demanded liberation and justice for both the captives as well as the nominally free.

The women deployed nonviolent tactics of civil disobedience and sometimes resorted to violent protest, usually in self-defense. Others utilized the power of the pen to craft a liberatory pedagogy that recast their stigmatized and despised status as carceral nonsubjects. Some activists, both inside and outside prison, worked to ameliorate harsh and discriminatory prison conditions, often turning to the courts for relief. These female freedom fighters demanded their unalienable citizenship rights, regardless of their status as unfree persons. The more militant captives among them went beyond calls for mere citizenship rights, rejecting the legitimacy of a country that had exploited and then brutalized their communities. Instead, they demanded human rights as oppressed peoples of the world, framing their struggle within the context of Third World liberation movements. Others sought to "tear down the walls" of prisons entirely. Simultaneously proclaiming and rejecting their "slave status," these twentieth-century prison abolitionists clamored for public support much as their nineteenth-century abolitionist forbears had done. Modern abolitionists—on both sides of America's prison walls—pressed the nation to break the chains of legalized slavery and to resolve at long last the devastating flaws of the Thirteenth Amendment, reaffirmed by a nineteenth-century U.S. Supreme Court that had made prisoners "slaves of the state."

The larger society may have dismissed them as "forgotten women" and abandoned them in "forgotten places."[15] Yet the captive women in North Carolina articulated their grievances and formulated their political analyses on their own terms, joining a vibrant prison movement that drew inspiration from a broad range of liberation struggles. The relationship was reciprocal, as activists outside the prison walls increasingly linked their own demands to the concerns of their sisters and brothers languishing behind bars. One of the most important of these was the women's antirape movement. And Black women, walking in the footprints of their foremothers and inspired by the Joan Little case, fashioned their own distinctive response to the sexual abuse of African American women.

PART THREE

WHO WILL REVERE THE BLACK WOMAN? . . . TO WHOM WILL SHE CRY RAPE?

CARCERAL POLITICS AND ORGANIZING AGAINST SEXUAL VIOLENCE

13

Bringing This to the Attention of the Nation and the Movement

Third World Women, Sexual Assault, and Lethal Self-Defense

"Rape is rape," announced a *Ms.* magazine cover story, as if its meaning were self-evident. Yet rape has a long, sordid history, with shifting legal definitions as well as changing social and political meanings.[1] Joan Little's rape-murder trial highlighted this history, including the narrow, legal definition of rape that excluded most forms of sexual violence. Because oral sex was not legally defined as "rape" under North Carolina law, Judge Hamilton Hobgood refused to allow expert testimony on rape during her murder trial. Not until 2012 would the federal government adopt a more expansive definition of rape.[2]

American jurisprudence on rape was rooted in the seventeenth-century British jurist Matthew Hale's statement that rape was "an accusation easily to be made and hard to be proved and harder to be defended against by the party accused, tho never so innocent." Hale's prevarications, however, were rarely extended to Black men and women.[3] Intertwined with racialized conceptions of manhood and womanhood, rape has shaped the parameters of who was included and excluded from citizenship rights, who was afforded legal protections from violence, and who could expect justice in court proceedings.

Indeed, for African Americans this history has been particularly punishing. Bought and sold as breeders and laborers, enslaved women were painted as immoral, lascivious seductresses who were sexually available, a reprehensible ideology that marked both the Atlantic slave trade and centuries of racial slavery in the Americas.[4] While the lack of protection from sexual violence for enslaved women has been widely recognized, scholar and cultural worker Thulani Davis argues that the danger of sexual assault actually increased for Black women following Emancipation. Leaving plantations for public spaces and workplaces, freed women became even more vulnerable. No longer valued as human "property" and lacking assurances of legal recourse or full citizenship rights, Black women's bodies were now fair game. "The sexual dangers facing African American women and girls should be seen as a condition of their emergence into freedom in the South: more black females were exposed to sexual assault in more situations by an increased number of assailants." During this period, Black women occasionally turned to the courts for redress, though few found relief there. In North Carolina between 1865 and 1886 at least twelve Black women brought rape charges against men; however, almost all were for intraracial attacks and none of the men seem to have been convicted.[5]

If Black women were demonized as unrapable Jezebels, white women were generally dismissed as pathological liars; that is unless the white woman's alleged assailant was a Black man. Following the Civil War, Black men were criminalized as rapists, and false rumors of African American men assaulting white women fueled an epidemic of lynching and a white supremacist reign of terror across the South.[6] While Black men were the primary targets of lynch mobs, Black women did not escape this racialized brutality and other forms of anti-Black violence. Historian Crystal Feimster estimates that between 1880 and 1930 about 130 African American women were lynched, often for defending themselves against sexual assault by white men. "Many more were tortured, mutilated, tarred and feathered, shot, burned, stabbed, dragged, whipped, or raped by angry mobs all over the South," she adds.[7] As historian Chana Kai Lee reminds us, generations of Black women learned the cruel lesson that "their bodies were never theirs alone." Moreover, racialized rape ideologies legitimized the economic and political subjugation of Blacks in the Jim Crow South, while lynching and other forms of racialized terror often thwarted the possibility of Black protest. For all Black men and women, public space remained fraught with peril well into the twentieth and twenty-first centuries. Writing in the 1970s, James Baldwin cast blame on the entire nation: "There's a price this republic exacts from any Black man or woman walking, and that is a crime."[8]

Not all African Americans heeded the terrorist message, and some of the most courageous dared to speak-out and organize against anti-Black violence. Following the Civil War, Black men sometimes protested the sexual abuse of Black women by white men. Some threatened and even engaged in retaliatory violence against white Union soldiers and police; and in Alabama and Virginia Black men filed complaints against the sexual abuse of Black women by jailers and police.[9]

While the heightened abuse of African American women frequently was ignored by the larger society, the Black press widely reported these "outrages." Ida B. Wells—one of the very few Black female journalists and newspaper owners in the late nineteenth century—was among the first to publicly expose the racist lies about so-called Black male rapists that rationalized anti-Black violence. Although she has been widely celebrated for her anti-lynching investigations, the fearless "Princess of the Press" also pioneered post-Reconstruction investigative reporting on the rape of Black women. And yet, much like Rosa Parks's antirape organizing, Wells's efforts to protect Black women from sexual violence are scarcely recognized outside of scholarly circles.[10]

In the face of scurrilous stereotypes about Black male rapists and unrapable Black Jezebels, African American women often had only themselves for protection. In order to defend their reputations and shield their private lives, many adopted what historian Darlene Clark Hine has called a "culture of dissemblance," in which Black women frequently remained silent about sexual violence. Yet, from the enslaved Celia, sentenced to death by a Missouri court in the 1850s for killing her white owner after he repeatedly raped her, to the early twentieth-century efforts by the National Association of Colored Women to protect imprisoned Black women from sexual abuse, to Rosa Parks's organization of national campaigns on behalf of Black women rape victims in the 1940s, to Betty Jean Owens's testimony that helped to convict four white men of rape in a southern courtroom in the 1950s, African American women also fought back, organized, and testified when they could.[11]

It is unclear how much Joan Little knew of this history, though she may well have heard the stories about sexual abuse that southern Black families typically passed down to their daughters. Unwittingly or not, Little was part of the long arc of Black women's self-defense and testimony against sexual assault. Like untold numbers of her foremothers, she fought back to defend herself against sexual violence and then testified about it in court.

The African American women who initiated the Free Joan Little campaign built on this distinctive legacy of Black women's antirape organizing. They also influenced antirape activists across the country who linked the Little case to the self-defense murder trials of Yvonne Wanrow Swan, Inez García, and Dessie X. Woods. Wanrow was Native American, García was Latina, and Woods was African American. Each became embroiled in high-profile trials that sparked defense campaigns among broad swaths of supporters throughout the 1970s. Antirape activist Nkenge Touré, one of the first Black women at the Washington, D.C., Rape Crisis Center in this period, recalled how these efforts, spearheaded by African American, Indigenous, and other women of color, were instrumental in bringing the sexual abuse of their sisters "to the attention of the nation and the movement."[12]

Throughout the 1970s, the Wanrow, García, Woods, and Little cases fueled the debate over a woman's right to lethal self-defense against sexual violence. They also spurred the formation of diverse coalitions among feminists and other social justice activists. Unwilling to rely on inadequate or abusive police and criminal justice protections, African American and other women of color, sometimes in partnership with white feminist attorneys and other activists, pushed for pathbreaking legal precedents regarding violence against women. According to Loretta Ross, the Black feminist director of the Washington, D.C., Rape Crisis Center, court victories and antiviolence legislation of the 1970s rested "largely on the backs of black women."[13]

Yvonne Wanrow and the "Woman's Self-Defense Case"

Almost exactly two years before Joan Little fought off a sexual assault from jailer Clarence Alligood, Yvonne Wanrow used lethal force against an accused child molester in Spokane, Washington. Wanrow's trial would become known as one of the first "women's self-defense cases."[14] However, by the time her case made its way through the courts in the 1977 landmark *State v. Wanrow* decision, it had little impact on Inez García, Dessie X. Woods, or Joan Little, whose self-defense murder trials ended prior to the ruling. Moreover, the justices' failure to consider race or culture in *Wanrow* too often meant that courtroom justice remained a hollow promise for many women, especially those who, like García, Woods, and Little, were nonwhite and low-income.

In August 1972, Yvonne Wanrow, a Colville Indian, fatally shot Bill Wesler after he allegedly had tried to kidnap and molest her eight-year-old son and

Yvonne Wanrow (Swan). The Wanrow case was linked to the Joan Little, Inez García, and Dessie X. Woods trials, as well as other cases of women of color who had defended themselves against sexual violence in the 1970s. Courtesy of the Museum of History and Industry, Seattle, Seattle Post-Intelligencer Collection, 2000.107.222.03.02, photo by Tom Brownell.

made a lewd remark to her young nephew. Since 1969, at least three sets of parents had reported Wesler to the Spokane police, claiming that he lured their children with promises of candy and other treats and then sexually assaulted them. Although Wesler had been previously arrested on child molestation charges and confined to a psychiatric ward, police refused to make an arrest because the children were unable to recount the exact dates of the assaults. Wesler was also suspected of raping the seven-year-old daughter of Wanrow's friend, Shirley Hooper. The suspect lived next door to Hooper, whose daughter, Mildred, had contracted a sexually transmitted disease (STD). Hooper's landlord claimed that Wesler had tried to molest another young boy, which, along with Wesler's previous arrest, lent credence to the children's claims. However, Mildred declined to identify the rapist; and so once again, police refused to intervene.

One evening several months after the attack on her daughter, Hooper discovered a man crouching beneath her window. The previous night someone had slashed the screen in her bedroom window for the second night in a row and unscrewed her porch light. That Hooper's house was located in a dimly lit, fairly isolated section of town next door to a suspected child molester, only increased her anxiety.

On the night of the fatal shooting, Wanrow's young son Darren burst into Hooper's house, claiming that Wesler had tried to grab him. Wesler appeared on her porch insisting, "I didn't touch the boy!"[15] At that point, Hooper recognized Wesler as the prowler outside her window. Her daughter also recognized him and identified him as her rapist. Police arrived shortly and took Hooper's statement, but they again refused to arrest Wesler. Instead, they concurred with the landlord that Hooper could hit the intruder with a baseball bat if he tried to enter her home, but only after "he gets in the house."[16] Another officer suggested that she spread flour outside her bedroom window so that footprints would be visible in case Wesler returned.

Frightened and alone with the children, Hooper called Wanrow in a panic and asked her to bring her gun. Wanrow's sister and brother-in-law and their children also came along. When Wanrow arrived, her son showed her the bruise on his arm from where Wesler had grabbed him. Later that evening, Wanrow's brother-in-law confronted Wesler outside and accused him of being a pedophile. Wesler, who had been drinking, barged into Hooper's house. "I don't want that man in here!" Hooper screamed. But Wesler ignored the women's demands to leave. According to Hooper's testimony, he moved toward the couch where Wanrow's young nephew was sleeping. "My what a cute little boy," he reportedly leered. When Wanrow turned, the drunken six-foot-two Wesler was towering over her. Wanrow drew a pistol from her waistband and shot him. "I could have touched him," she later testified. To the five-foot-four, 120-pound Wanrow, whose leg was in a cast, "it seemed like he was coming right at me. He was just there, you know," she sobbed. When Wesler's friend, David Kelly, entered the room, Wanrow fired at him too, hitting him in the arm. The women dialed 911 and waited, still terrified that Kelly might return. When police arrived, they arrested Wanrow and charged her with second-degree murder in Wesler's death and first-degree assault for shooting Kelly. Urged by her public defender to plead guilty, Wanrow followed his advice. After securing another attorney, she withdrew her guilty plea, which was later amended to "not guilty by reason of insanity."[17]

The prosecutors in both the Little and Wanrow trials turned to well-worn racist stereotypes to disparage the women's character and undermine their credibility. Like Joan Little's detractors, the prosecution claimed that Wanrow had lured Wesler into her friend's home with plans to kill him. But rather than relying on the racist Jezebel trope, Wanrow's prosecutors drew on racially pejorative stereotypes of Native American savagery. Playing a recording of her call to the police, the prosecution claimed that the "deceptively calm, icy tone of her voice" was proof of intent: "No one could sound so cold unless she had planned it." The judge refused to allow evidence of Wesler's history of molestation or Hooper's daughter's STD. On Mother's Day in May 1973, Wanrow was convicted of first-degree assault and second-degree murder by an all-white jury of five women and seven men and sentenced to twenty-five years in prison.

Wanrow's trial attracted national support from the American Indian Movement (AIM), radical attorneys, and celebrities such as the well-known singer Buffy Saint-Marie, also of Native descent. William Kunstler, a member of Joan Little's defense team who would be ejected during her rape-murder trial, helped to convince two white feminist lawyers, Nancy Stearns and Elizabeth Schneider from the Center for Constitutional Rights, to take Wanrow's appeal. Both women had been active in the civil rights, antiwar, women's liberation, and radical student movements of the 1960s.[18]

In the 1977 landmark appeal, *State v. Wanrow*, the Washington State Supreme Court affirmed a woman's right to self-defense against a male attacker. In their five-to-three decision, the justices ruled that courts must consider gender when determining the "reasonable standard" of self-defense. "In our society, women suffer from a conspicuous lack of access to training in and the means of developing those skills necessary to effectively repel a male assailant without resorting to the use of deadly weapons," the majority wrote. To deny a woman the right to self-defense, including the use of weapons, "violates her right to equal protection under the law," the court ruled. The justices advised jurors to determine the "the degree of force which . . . a reasonable person in the same situation . . . seeing what (s)he sees and knowing what (s)he knows . . . would believe is necessary." Stearns and Schneider were stunned but also delighted that the court had adopted one of their arguments. However, their hope that the decision would have a broad impact on women in self-defense trials remained largely unrealized, especially for impoverished women of color.[19]

Still, the *Wanrow* decision opened up a new line of argument for self-defense cases by ruling that gender must be considered when assessing women's use of deadly force to protect themselves. While many courts across the country cited the *Wanrow* decision in subsequent women's self-defenses trials, others refused, even in Washington State in the immediate aftermath of the 1977 ruling. However, thirty years later, two justices who had dissented in the *Wanrow* decision changed course in another similar case. Explaining their about-face, they conceded that at the time of *Wanrow*, little was understood in legal circles about violence against women; perhaps especially among white male jurists, they might have added. Moreover, stereotypes regarding female self-defense cases, especially those involving battered women who killed their abusers, persisted. Too often courts viewed such women as "vigilantes."[20]

Despite Wanrow's legal victory, the state Supreme Court had ruled only on the gendered claims, refusing to consider the role of race and Indian culture. Wanrow's feminist attorneys had tried to enter these arguments. However, the judge barred expert testimony on Indigenous culture, including the presumed overprotectiveness of Indian mothers for children. Nor was testimony permitted concerning the history of tensions between local law enforcement and Native communities or the lack of police protection as factors shaping Wanrow's behavior and her decision to shoot Wesler. "Indian people were not popular [with the police in Spokane]. It seems like they were the ones that always got arrested and got put in jail," Wanrow recalled. "My brother was maced [and the police] would just beat them up whenever they could. I'm not saying all of the police, but [even] a little is too much racism." More than three decades later, Justice Robert Utter, who wrote the majority opinion in *Wanrow*, acknowledged widespread racial bias: "Those were the times of *strong* anti-American-Indian sentiment in Spokane County," he said.[21]

Wanrow's attorneys also noted the all-white jury and the hostile press coverage of her trial occasioned by the violent confrontation between the American Indian Movement and federal officials at Wounded Knee in 1973. Wounded Knee was the site of the 1890 massacre of 300 Lakota men, women, and children by U.S. troops on the Pine Ridge Reservation in nearby South Dakota. The site became a place of remembrance for Indigenous people, and the 1973 debacle there drew national attention. Thus, Wanrow's identity and experience as a *woman* was considered, but not her experience as a *Native American*. According to feminist legal scholars Donna Coker and Lindsay Harrison, "Wanrow's now-famous case enters law school textbooks on the issue of what constitutes a fair trial for *women*." Nearly four decades after the court's ruling, Coker and Harrison pointed to Kimberlé Crenshaw's conception of "intersectionality" to explain the limits of the *Wanrow* decision: "The courts who heard Wanrow's case failed to understand that gender and culture are not separate experiences, but rather 'intersecting experiences.'"[22]

Although Wanrow's court appeal had prevailed, her legal troubles were not over. The state filed new charges against her. Meanwhile, support for

Wanrow grew both nationally and even internationally, in South America, the Caribbean, Africa, and the Middle East. Once again, AIM and Native women, including the newly formed Women of All Red Nations, rallied behind her. So did singer and composer Bernice Johnson Reagon, who had written and performed "Joan Little." Marjorie Nelson, who had urged NOW members in North Carolina to support Joan Little, traveled to Spokane to secure backing from non-Native people. Schneider stayed on the case and was joined by Mary Alice Theiler, a criminal defense attorney from the left-leaning National Lawyers Guild, and Susan Jordan, who had recently defended Inez García in her self-defense murder trial.[23]

In 1979, just as her new trial was about to begin, Wanrow pleaded guilty to reduced charges and received a suspended sentence, five years' probation, and a year of community service. But her trial had transformed her. She dropped her married name, becoming Yvonne Swan, married AIM activist Floyd Red Crow Westerman, and had a daughter. She became an AIM activist herself, fighting to protect Colville land, traveling the globe, and presenting at the International Tribunal on Crimes Against Women in Brussels. "My case forced me to change," she noted. "When I was introduced to different people that were active in bringing about social justice in Indian country, I felt aligned with them, with their struggle.... I felt good and I felt optimistic. I felt strong. I didn't feel alone."[24]

"Inez Will Be Free Because Joan Is Free": The Inez García Trial

In March 1974, as the *Wanrow* case made its way through the courts, and just months before the Free Joan Little campaign would grab national headlines, Inez García was raped by Luis Castillo outside her home in Soledad, California. Miguel Jimenez, Castillo's 300-pound friend, blocked her escape and watched the assault. Following the rape, Castillo and Jimenez called García and threatened to harm her if she did not leave town. García grabbed a .22 caliber rifle and went looking for the men. In less than thirty minutes, she spotted her assailants, who were beating her friend, Fred Medrano. When Jimenez drew a knife and threw it at her, she shot and killed him. "I was just a little bit faster than him or else I would have been six feet under," she explained. García was indicted on first-degree (i.e., premeditated) murder. *Ms.* magazine's cover story called her "the rape victim who fought back."[25]

García was raised in Spanish Harlem in New York City in a devoutly Catholic Cuban and Puerto Rican family. At the time of the sexual assault,

García had recently moved to California to be near her husband, Juan, an anti-Castro Cuban who was serving time at Soledad Prison on a political bombing conviction in Los Angeles.[26]

Almost all accounts of the case claim that García did not immediately report the rape after her arrest on the murder charge, apparently due to cultural and religious feelings of shame and dishonor. However, this is only partially true, as would become apparent later. Because no medical evidence was available to substantiate her charge, the sixty-eight-year-old judge, Stanley Lawson, refused to allow the jury to consider García's rape allegations. "I don't see what rape has to do with the case," he said. Yet the judge did permit the prosecutor to question García about the sexual assault. In graphic detail, the prosecutor taunted and humiliated her, even asking, "Did you like it?" According to García, "It was like being raped all over again." Charles Garry, a well-known attorney who had defended Black Panthers, announced to the press that underpinning his defense strategy was the "unwritten law," or "the right of a woman who has been raped to take the law into her own hands to protect her integrity." However, in court, he presented García as a woman in "shock" and stressed her "illiteracy" and "emotional illnesses," rather than arguing for a woman's right to self-defense.[27]

Jane Odden, the female psychiatrist testifying for the defense, similarly explained that García had acted out of a "'diminished capacity' to cope," but she added that García's behavior was consistent with the aftermath of a sexual assault.[28] Odden pointed to García's incarceration at Hudson Prison and a short stint in the psychiatric wing of New York City's Bellevue Hospital when she was a young teen as evidence of the defendant's emotional deficiencies. The Free Inez García Committee objected to the defense strategy: "Any of us who acts [sic] as though we are free, as though we have self-determination, dignity, and the skills to defend ourselves, is labeled unhealthy, hysterical, and unlawful."[29]

As a teen, García was a chronic truant and, like Joan Little's, her youthful misdeeds were subjected to state control under the criminal punishment system. In 1957, at age thirteen, García was sentenced to a year at the New York Training School for Girls in Hudson (known as Hudson Prison). During her parole in 1958, she spent a short time at Bellevue. The use of psychiatry in García's case and her confinement was another way the state sought to control wayward youth, especially those who were nonwhite and/or low-income.[30]

During her 1974 trial, García grew increasingly frustrated as she listened. Finally, she'd had enough. Rising suddenly from her seat, she approached the bench and placed her fists firmly in front of the judge. "Why don't you just find me guilty and put me in jail," she exploded. "I killed the fucking guy because I was raped, and I'd kill him again today if I had to. [I'm only] sorry that I missed Luis," she added.[31] Although some jurors left the courtroom smiling at the outburst, others reportedly were "stunned" and shocked. Defiant, profane, and unrepentant—the mainstream press called her "tough" and "foulmouthed"—García's fate was sealed.[32] After deliberating for three days, the jury found her guilty of second-degree murder. Before sentencing her to the maximum five-years-to-life imprisonment, Judge Lawson again dismissed García's rape allegations and claimed she clearly showed an intent to kill, "going off on the prowl like a huntress."[33] After the trial, one juror commented, "You can't kill someone for trying to give you a good time."[34] Another boasted that he'd "have less fear of raping a woman now" and "that if I get shot she won't get away."[35]

Such attitudes were pervasive. A shopping center in Biloxi, Mississippi, advertised a similar insensitivity to rape, displaying T-shirts that read, "In case of rape . . . this side up." When the Biloxi NOW chapter demanded that the merchandise be removed, management simply placed the news clipping featuring NOW's protest alongside the T-shirt display. Meanwhile, town officials claimed they had no power to intervene. Farther north, a Milwaukee judge accused a sobbing rape victim of a "ploy" to curry favor with jurors and warned that if she didn't stop crying on the witness stand, he would dismiss the charges against her assailant.[36] This was the atmosphere, or what is now called "rape culture," that most women, especially women of color, faced in the 1970s and 1980s.

Like the Free Joan Little campaign and the Yvonne Wanrow case, the Inez García trial also drew a diverse array of supporters. The United Farm Workers, the Black Panther Party, the San Francisco Gay Latino Alliance, and the Third World Women's Alliance, among others, all lined up behind García. Other supporters included the Washington, D.C., Rape Crisis Center, the Feminist Alliance Against Rape, and the Washington, D.C., chapters of the National Organization for Women, the National Conference of Puerto Rican Women, and the League of United Latin-American Citizens. Her better-known feminist supporters included Gloria Steinem and Betty Freidan, National Black Feminist Organization (NBFO) cofounder Margaret Sloan, Angela Davis, and Simone de Beauvoir. The "Viva Inez" campaign specifically invoked the Joan Little trial: "Inez will be free because Joan is free" became its rallying cry.[37]

Women were especially infuriated by the verdict. Dorenda Moreno from the San Francisco Concilio Mujeres called the trial "the Inquisition. . . . We

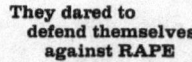

They dared to
defend themselves
against RAPE

NOW THEIR LIVES ARE AT STAKE!

Photo by Jill Krements
JOANNE LITTLE

AP Wirephoto
INEZ GARCIA

Joanne Little—facing a mandatory death sentence in North Carolina for killing the white jailer who raped her.

Inez Garcia—convicted and sentenced to five years to life on a second degree murder charge in California.

DEFENSE BENEFIT
WEDNESDAY-JUNE 25, 1975
CURTAIN TIME - 8:00 P.M.
FORD AUDITORIUM

*THE DEADLY NIGHTSHADE

*LINDA FURLOW
*MARGARET SLOAN   *GLORIA STEINEM

With a special performance by Detroit's own—

*LILY TOMLIN

Sponsored by . . .
Women's Defense and Education Committee
Marcia Elayne Davis, Chairwoman

Tickets Available at Grinnells   all Hudson Stores   Ford Auditorium Box Office

$12.50 — $7.50 — $5.50 — $3.50

Throughout the country supporters organized benefits like this one in Detroit to defend Inez García and Joan Little, both of whom were tried for murder after defending themselves against sexual violence.
Courtesy of University of Michigan Library, Joseph A. Labadie Collection, Special Collections Research Center.

are appalled; we are enraged at the outcome of the Inez García trial." At a teach-in sponsored by the Washington, D.C., Coalition to Support Inez García and Joan Little, Lourdes Miranda King from the National Council of Puerto Rican Women defended García's actions. "I would have done the same thing," she declared. Lila Gonzalez, coordinator of Chicano studies at the University of California, Berkeley, denounced the sexual stereotypes that afflicted Latinas: "Chicanas have for too long been considered sexual toys by the dominant society and have not been supported in the past when such cases are based on fundamental human rights." Her words surely rang true for Black women, for they had raised a similar lament in defense of themselves for decades. Infuriated protesters picketed Judge Lawson's house with provocative signs reading, "'Free Inez García! Rape the judge and see what he does!'" The Inez García Defense Committee in Oakland declared her a "political prisoner," insisted that "WOMEN HAVE THE RIGHT TO DEFEND THEMSELVES," and began a petition drive calling for García's immediate release. In February 1975, 250 protesters presented 2,000 signatures demanding that Governor Jerry Brown pardon García and create a multiracial women's commission to review the convictions of all women prisoners, especially those convicted of murder or manslaughter.[38] After serving fifteen months in prison, García's conviction was reversed on a technicality by the California Court of Appeals. But, like Wanrow, García was retried.

During her second trial in February 1977, Inez García was permitted to testify about the rape.[39] Other court testimony also refuted the earlier claim that she had never reported the rape. When García was arrested after shooting Jimenez, she did tell Soledad police that Castillo and Jimenez "got fresh with me." She explained, "[I] told them in my own way.... Any Latino person would understand." San Francisco clinical psychologist Dolores Jimenez (no relation to Miguel Jimenez), testified that in Latinx culture, sexual assault was seen as dishonoring the family, as well as the rape victim-survivor. But García had handed over her torn blouse and jeans to police. She also had called her extended family in Miami and told them about the attack before venturing out to find her assailants. Police never followed up on any of these details. A Salinas detective testified that law enforcement should have taken García's indirect statements more seriously.[40]

Medical authorities similarly failed to collect evidence of sexual assault. The first day after her arrest in 1974, as she awaited release on $100,000 bail in the Monterey Jail, García asked for a medical exam. The nurse said she could do nothing without a court order. When García finally saw a doctor, no exam was administered. The doctor simply dismissed her claims of rape, telling her, "It was all in [your] head and [will] go away."[41]

García's feminist legal team, led by Susan Jordan, emphasized that García had acted in "legitimate self-defense." Jordan also challenged popular myths about rape victims among the public and the jury pool who "had one standard for the bad girls who got raped, and another standard for their daughters."[42] In March 1977, García was acquitted; but Castillo was never arrested. Like Joan Little, García was also politicized about incarceration and the criminal legal system in new ways. "I never really knew before that I was a political person," García said after her second trial. "But I know that now. I met a lot of women in prison who I promised to help." She offered a view similar to the one that had gotten Little's defense attorney, Jerry Paul, in so much trouble. "In this country you have to buy justice," García said. "If you don't have the money you have to go to jail, that's the way they work it." But like Little, she was not the politically naive person that even some of her supporters saw in her. For example, in 1976, while out on bail and awaiting her second trial, García attended a gay pride march in San Francisco where she is pictured holding a Puerto Rican flag.[43]

It is not clear whether the publicity surrounding García's trial was the impetus, but in 1976, the East Los Angeles Rape Hotline was established, offering bilingual assistance to Latinas and Chicanas in the community. According to sociologist Nancy Matthews, it was one of the earliest and one of the few nonwhite antirape organizations. Because it was one of the only bilingual organizations in the area, the group was called upon to provide a multitude of services in addition to assisting rape victims. That same year in Boston, activists opened Casa Myrna Vasquez, named after a renowned Puerto Rican activist, to provide services for women who had been "battered, raped, evicted or burned out." A bilingual staff offered job training along with counseling, housing, and legal services. Forty percent of the women coming to Casa were "Hispanic," while the remaining 60 percent were split evenly between Black and white women.[44] Like their African American sisters, the women activists serving the various Latinx communities found that single-issue antirape advocacy was impossible. Instead, they adopted a more holistic approach to meeting the needs of rape victim-survivors.

Both García and Wanrow had shot their assailants *after* the alleged sexual attacks, rather than in the moment. Yet Wanrow certainly felt threatened by Wesler at the time; and García's attackers had threatened to kill her following the rape. And in both cases, police had failed to adequately investigate allegations of sexual violence. Most important, the two cases were hailed as establishing a woman's right to self-defense. The women's trials inaugurated the legal precedent that extended "imminent danger" beyond an immediate assault and laid the foundation for what would later become the "battered woman syndrome," allowing a woman to claim self-defense against her abuser even if she was not under attack at the time of the killing.[45] In subsequent cases, defense attorneys successfully utilized the battered woman syndrome to justify women's use of lethal force against their abusers. Still, the race and class of the assaulted woman too often determined the efficacy of the "imminent danger" and "battered woman's defense" in court proceedings, leaving far too many women convicted and imprisoned for fighting back against their assailants. Moreover, even if they eventually were acquitted, exorbitant bail kept too many women languishing in jails while awaiting trial.[46]

"Right Behind Joan Little": The Dessie X. Woods Case

Just months before the start of Little's rape-murder trial in the summer of 1975, two southern Black women, Dessie X. Woods and Cheryl Todd, were arrested and charged with the murder of Ronnie Horne, a white insurance salesman. The two women had traveled from Atlanta to Reidsville Prison in Georgia to check on Todd's brother. After arriving at the prison, Todd fainted from the intense heat and some blood pressure medication she had taken. Rather than offering help, police accused Todd of public intoxication and beat and arrested the two women. Three days later, they were released on bail.[47]

With no public transportation back to Atlanta, Todd and Woods decided to hitchhike. Horne offered them a ride. Initially the women refused. Horne drove past them again and told them he was a detective and that the police were following and would pick them up for hitchhiking. The two women got in the car. But after he drove in the wrong direction, Woods and Todd demanded that he stop the car. Instead, Horne continued on to a nearby restaurant and threatened them with arrest if they did not get back in the car. He then drove to a secluded area and attempted to rape them at gunpoint. Todd managed to run off and a struggle ensued between Woods and Horne; the gun went off, and Horne was killed. The women stole his wallet and fled, but police soon picked them up. Although their 1976 trial ended in a hung jury, the judge insisted that the jurors reach a verdict. Because she had taken Horne's gun, Dessie X. Woods was convicted of voluntary manslaughter and armed robbery. She was given two ten-year and twelve-year concurrent prison sentences. Todd was convicted as an accomplice, sentenced to six years' imprisonment, and released on bond pending appeal.[48]

As in the Joan Little case, Black female respectability was on trial. Although Horne apparently was known in the community for his attacks on Black women, the state painted Todd and Woods as disreputable. "Nice girls do not hitchhike, they do not have brothers in prison, they are not black, they do not defend themselves against attack," the feminist *New Women's Times* sneered.[49] Like the Little case, the Dessie X. Woods trial also garnered national attention. Defense committees sprang up from Atlanta to San Francisco, and Woods received letters of support from across the country, and from South America, Europe, and Canada.

According to scholar Emily Thuma, the National Committee to Defend Dessie X. Woods differed significantly from the Free Little Joan Campaign. Unlike the Little campaign, which encouraged a broad array of political supporters, the National Committee was headed by the African People's Socialist Party and deployed a Pan-African, anticolonial analysis of her case.[50] However, while the committee's revolutionary politics may have diminished media coverage, other factors were also at play. The judge, wishing to avoid the media frenzy of the Little trial, severely limited both the press and protest in the rural town where the trial was held. Despite these restrictions, prisoner publications, the Black Panther Party newspaper, and the feminist and antirape newspapers *off our backs* and *Aegis* covered the case. Local feminist groups, including the Atlanta Lesbian Feminist Alliance, Karate for Women, Dykes for the Second American Revolution (which compared Woods's case to Little's), and the Atlanta Socialist Feminist Women's Union, together with women from across the nation, rallied behind Woods.[51]

In another parallel to the Free Joan Little campaign, local groups drew links between the Woods case and broader concerns over women's incarceration. For example, the Women's Union, as the Atlanta socialist group was known, worked closely with the Georgia Alliance for Prison Alternatives and focused its efforts on women at Hardwick Prison in Georgia, where the majority were Black mothers. Even Laverne Ford, the first Black warden at Hardwick, conceded that three-quarters of the women there did not belong in prison. In another similarity to the Little case, Dessie X. Woods reported that sexual abuse of the women was rampant. "White women would come up to me in prison and say the warden raped me . . . [but] we can't do anything about it, because the women had sex with them (prison officials) for favors!

The guards raped these girls because they didn't want to be put isolation," Woods said.[52]

In a 1978 prison interview with antirape organizer Nkenge Touré, Woods revealed that a white man had attempted to rape her when she was twelve, but nothing was ever done about it. Later, after joining the Nation of Islam, she was sexually assaulted in her home at gunpoint. Afraid for her children, she did not struggle, but she vowed, "I was never going to let this happen again." Paradoxically, Woods also believed that her guilty verdict was directly related to Joan Little's acquittal. "Joann [sic] Little was the only black woman who was ever acquitted on self-defense," she said. "And my case came right behind Joann Little and they would not allow two women to be acquitted in a row. . . . I'm not guilty of anything except being a black woman defending herself."[53]

Dessie X. Woods's confinement, like that of so many jailed mothers, had a devastating impact on her two children. After her conviction, Woods's parents agreed to raise Calvin and Samantha, ages eleven and ten. But when Dessie's father died, her mother's meager Social Security check left the family in dire straits. When they were turned down for government assistance, Dessie's mother was urged to legally adopt the children so they could each receive financial assistance of $100/month, which was barely sufficient to meet the children's needs. To alleviate their plight, activists launched another campaign, Support for Dessie's Children's Trust Fund. Denied parole several times, beaten and threatened with a noose by prison officials, and transferred to Milledgeville mental hospital where she was heavily drugged, Woods was released in 1981 after serving six years. The warden, Mark Martin, was reportedly fired in 1981 for having sex with women prisoners.[54]

Although the Little, Wanrow, García, and Woods trials received the most publicity, other cases involving women of color, sexual assault, partner abuse, and self-defense also drew attention in the 1970s. In 1972, Linda Scott, a Black Texas woman, accused Peter Cole, a white man, of kidnapping, raping, and torturing her. Medical evidence, testimony from another young Black woman who claimed Cole had subjected her to similar abuse, and even Cole's admission of much of the torture all corroborated Scott's charges. However, Scott had a prior conviction for prostitution and in the minds of the all-white jury, including eight women, she may well have been viewed as disreputable, even "unrapable." Cole was acquitted in October 1974, the same week that Inez García was sentenced, and a month after Joan Little had been indicted on first-degree murder for defending herself against sexual violence. The feminist newspaper *off our backs* linked Cole's case with Joan Little's and Inez García's, noting how all three had been disparaged: "Like Inez García and JoAnne Little, Linda Scott is considered a 'criminal,' one of those 'bad women' by male society and by those women who have swallowed the line and struggle desperately to stay 'good.'"[55]

Following the verdict in the Cole trial, members of Dallas Women Against Rape immediately began arming themselves. The group, which had supported Linda Scott, soon formed Women Armed for Self-Protection (WASP), a multiracial, cross-class organization that held firearm instruction and safety classes. Black women constituted a critical mass and, at times, a majority of WASP members. One woman stressed the importance of weapons training, not just gun ownership, since attackers could easily disarm an untrained woman. "That old Southern belle mentality will get you every time," she said. Another member explained, "Personally I hate guns, . . . and as soon as the policemen and the truck drivers don't have guns, I will take the loaded .357 out from under my bed." But WASP advocated armed self-defense, not violent retaliation. Instead, many of the WASP members who had attended Cole's trial vowed not to shoot him but to leaflet his Dallas neighborhood and the railroad where he worked.[56]

Groups like WASP may not have been typical, but neither was it a total anomaly. Throughout the 1970s, antirape activists and feminists seriously debated and some even endorsed armed self-defense. In 1971, the Third World Women's Alliance declared that all "third world women have the right and responsibility to bear arms." That same year, a group of well-known feminists in New York City were invited to a secret meeting to discuss carrying weapons themselves in advance of the August Women's Equality Day March. Radical Black feminist lawyer Florence Kennedy, who would later fight Joan Little's extradition from New York to North Carolina, was one of those sounding the alarm. Kennedy warned the group that the FBI was training women to infiltrate women's liberation groups. Although the women decided to endorse nonviolence rather than armed self-defense, they left the meeting feeling shaken and afraid. Later revelations about the FBI's COINTELPRO targeting legal protest groups and individuals, including women's organizations, showed that such fears were not unfounded.[57]

In a special 1975 issue of *Ms.* magazine devoted to the Inez García case, Gloria Steinem worried about charges of "vigilantism" if feminists began carrying weapons. However, a few years later in 1979, the majority-white feminist antirape publication *Aegis* featured a cover with a large gun and the warning: "YOU CAN'T RAPE A .38; WE WILL DEFEND OURSELVES." In the late

1960s and throughout the 1970s, predominantly white feminist periodicals frequently deployed the imagery of Black women, sometimes armed, to project a revolutionary feminist politics. One drawing in particular, by Emory Douglas, minister of culture for the Black Panther Party, ran in numerous feminist periodicals. The drawing featured a Black woman in African garb, with an infant on her back and a rifle in her hand. Yet the use of Douglas's drawing by white women racialized women's self-defense in ways that also romanticized, exoticized, and even subtly criminalized African American women.[58]

Another 1970s case that spurred support among women across the racial divide was Cassandra Peten's 1979 trial. Peten was a young Black mother and Oakland shipyard worker who was charged with attempted murder in the killing of her abusive husband. The National Alliance of Black Feminists (NABF) in Chicago and other women's groups, including the multiracial Bay Area Defense Committee for Battered Women, rallied behind her, and she was finally cleared. According to Black feminist scholar Kimberly Springer, Peten's trial helped to establish the right of women to defend themselves prior to the legal recognition of the "battered woman syndrome."[59]

The self-defense trials of Wanrow, García, Woods, and Little prompted women attorneys at the Center for Constitutional Rights, some of whom had assisted in those cases, to establish the Women's Self-Defense Project in 1978. The project provided support in over 100 trials, mostly concerning women charged with killing an abusive partner, husband, or ex-boyfriend. In 1981, the project published *Women in Self-Defense Cases: Theory and Practice*, providing help for other women charged in violent self-defense cases. Amma Price of the Bay Area Defense Committee and a member of the Black American Law Students Association, described the influence of cases involving women of color, while also conceding that Wanrow, García, Woods, and Little represented the "mere tip of the iceberg."[60]

Black, Indigenous, and other women of color were not only key to some of the legal victories and organized protest concerning violence against women; they were also in the vanguard of resistance against sexual harassment. African American women have a long history of enduring sexual harassment, well before white feminists coined the term. Working as cooks, maids, and nannies in white households—the primary jobs available to Black women until the 1960s—they were especially vulnerable to sexual abuse. In fact, African American women laid the groundwork for legal protection against sexual harassment in employment. In 1977, Sandra Bundy, a Black single mother, won a federal lawsuit against the Washington, D.C., Department of

Corrections after claiming that she had been repeatedly sexually harassed by her superiors. According to court testimony, when Bundy complained to her superior he responded, "Any man in his right mind would want to rape you," and then propositioned her himself. Her victory on appeal recognized that sexual harassment comprised sexual discrimination. Another Black woman, Amma Price, was a plaintiff in a 1977 sexual harassment case at Yale University, charging professors with sexual intimidation of their students. Speaking at the first National Conference on Third World Women and Violence in 1980, Price claimed that over half the sexual harassment cases brought to court in 1977 were initiated by women of color.[61]

But bringing intraracial charges against Black men in particular often took a toll. Nkenge Touré recalled the scorn she received from Black men for her support of four Black women who accused a local African American minister of sexual harassment. Turning to time-honored denigrations of female sexuality, Touré's critics claimed she was antimale and a lesbian, and she was criticized for bringing down a "good man." Black feminist Barbara Smith brought the issue to a wider public in her 1979 open letter to white feminists asking for their support and condemning attacks on Black feminists from within African American communities. A similar dynamic would soon fuel an acrimonious national debate within Black communities when Anita Hill claimed in 1991 that she had been sexually harassed by the African American Supreme Court nominee, Clarence Thomas.[62]

As the nation took a sharper turn to the right in the 1970s and 1980s, accompanied by the emergence of a more robust neoliberal state and harsher penal policies, antirape activists faced even more hurdles. Yet Black women found innovative ways to continue their efforts to protect themselves and their sisters from sexual violence.

14

The Kind of History That Really Does Get Lost

Black Feminism, Multi-issue Organizing, and the Whitewashing of Women's Liberation

"The movement is broad, often unconnected and for the most part, undocumented," proclaimed Black feminist Loretta Ross. Ross was the director of the Washington, D.C., Rape Crisis Center in the 1970s. She and other Black feminists argued that scarce documentation has often obscured their antirape organizing and the feminist activism of African American and other women of color in the 1970s and 1980s.[1] Although frequently springing from different roots and the long arc of Black women's organizing history, Black feminists, including those who distanced themselves from the label "feminist," played key roles in what has erroneously been called the "second wave" feminism of the 1960s and 1970s. Though they sometimes joined with white women, they usually did so in *coalitions* rather than in the same *organizations*, often preferring to maintain their own groups, separate from both white women and African American men. "As opposed to outright rejection of feminist organizations most Black women believe in interracial coalitions, not interracial organizations," Ross explained, "so one would not necessarily expect the rising feminism of Black women to lead them into women's organizations in significant numbers."[2] Indeed, antirape activism among Black women in particular took place in a variety of organizations and among African American women who more often embraced a multi-issue approach to the prevention of sexual violence. Thus, searching for Black women's antirape activism in rape crisis centers, national feminist organizations, or women's antirape groups does not fully capture the full range of their efforts.

Other African American women have voiced similar sentiments about Black feminism. Linda Burnham, whose parents were part of the southern Black Left in the 1930s and 1940s, recalled her involvement in Black women's liberation after meeting another Black woman at an abortion rights rally in San Francisco in 1970. The woman led her to Black Sisters United, a consciousness-raising group with both heterosexual women and lesbians. Yet Burnham acknowledged that they failed to save or document much of their activity. "You know there were probably hundreds of groups like that across the country. That's the kind of history that really does get lost." Later, Burnham joined the West Coast branch of the Third World Women's Alliance, which originated from a Black women's caucus formed by Frances Beal in New York SNCC in 1968. The group changed its name to the Third World Women's Alliance in 1970 and expanded to include other women of color; and it was one of the many groups that generated support for Joan Little. In 1989, Burnham cofounded the Women of Color Resource Center in Oakland, California, where she served as director for nearly two decades.[3] Combahee River Collective cofounder and Black lesbian feminist Barbara Smith summed up the invisibility of Black feminist activism during this period: "Few know the details of what we accomplished. The story of our work remains untold."[4]

Centering Black feminism and Black women's antirape activism compels a reinterpretation of the women's liberation movement(s) or "second wave" feminism of the 1960s and 1970s. As numerous scholars have shown, the "wave" framework frequently obscures the activism of Black women by privileging white feminists. It also erases the long arc of Black women's separate and distinctive history of organizing against sexual violence. At the same time, African American women frequently played key roles in the various streams of the 1960s and 1970s women's movements, including mainstream organizations often dismissed as dominated by white, middle-class feminists who had little interest in or understanding of Black women's concerns. While the critique of white feminism is well-earned, the focus on white racial myopia too often eclipses key contributions of African American women, including accomplishments attributed primarily or exclusively to white women. In short, African American women's activism was both *a part of* and *apart from* the various streams of women's liberation from the 1960s to the 1980s.[5]

Black feminism, or feminisms, included radicals like Angela Davis as well as more mainstream leaders like Dorothy Height, who presided over the National Council of Negro Women for decades. A multitude of local groups like the one Burnham joined as well as national organizations including the Third World Women's Alliance, National Black Feminist Organization, Combahee River Collective, and Black Women's United Front were just some of the Black women's liberation groups of the 1970s. Though not all of these national groups adopted the explicit "feminist" label, all battled sexism and the multiple oppressions Black women faced; and nearly all lent their support to Joan Little during her rape-murder trial.

Black feminists also advocated for their sisters by working with more mainstream national women's organizations. Congresswoman Shirley Chisholm and attorney Pauli Murray were just two of the influential African American women who fought racial and gender discrimination, including sexual abuse. As noted earlier, Chisholm was an outspoken supporter of Joan Little during her trial, calling on the U.S. Department of Justice to investigate the sexual abuse of incarcerated women. Both Chisholm and Murray were founding members of one or more of several major national feminist groups in the 1960s and 1970s, including the 1961 President's Commission on the Status on Women, NOW, and the National Women's Political Caucus.[6]

Pauli Murray, an African American queer and transgender legal theorist, traced her activism to the 1930s and early 1940s. During this period, she defended Black men falsely convicted and condemned to death in the South, helped to organize an early sit-in in Washington, D.C., and was arrested for protesting Jim Crow seating on a Virginia bus. Murray coined the term "Jane Crow," to underline both the sexism and racism African American women endured, in work described by historians Daina Ramey Berry and Kali Gross as "an early version of intersectional Black feminism." Murray also was persecuted and denied employment due not only to race and sex discrimination but also to her radical politics dating to the 1930s, and rumors about her sexuality and gender identity. In the 1960s, she was instrumental in securing support for the addition of sex discrimination to Title VII of the groundbreaking 1964 Civil Rights Act, which enabled Black women like Sandra Bundy to win lawsuits against sexual harassment (as discussed in chapter 13). In 1965 Murray joined the staff of the American Civil Liberties Union, where she laid the foundation for the Women's Rights Project. There Murray mentored Ruth Bader Ginsberg, the late Supreme Court justice who is widely credited with pathbreaking legal theories opposing sex discrimination, often without noting Murray's key influence on Ginsburg.[7]

This 1970 pamphlet on Black women's liberation was coauthored by Maxine Williams, a member of the Third World Women's Alliance, and Pamela Newman, a Black student leader. Both were also members of the Young Socialist Alliance. Courtesy of the Atlanta Lesbian Feminist Alliance Papers, David M. Rubenstein Rare Book and Manuscript Library, Duke University.

The long arc of Black women's activism not only challenges the whitewashing of 1960s and 1970s feminism. It also disrupts the declension narrative of women's liberation which, until recently, historians dated from the mid- to late 1970s.[8] To be sure, feminism, including Black feminism, did suffer some significant setbacks in the 1970s and 1980s. The short life of the National Black Feminist Organization (NBFO), founded in 1973, and the demise of some of its most vibrant chapters, such as the National Alliance of Black Feminists in Chicago by 1981, seemingly fit the declension interpretation. And by 1981 the number of independent rape crisis centers had dwindled to 200–300, half the number from just five years earlier. But defeat does not tell the entire story. A 1972 national poll found that Black women supported feminist goals to a greater degree than any other group, including white women, and they maintained these attitudes into the 1980s, regardless of whether they embraced the term "feminist." (Some African American women adopted the term "womanism," coined by writer Alice Walker, to distance themselves from a feminist movement they saw as dominated by white women.) Moreover, despite the setbacks of the 1970s and 1980s and the dwindling number of rape crisis centers, Black antirape activists found numerous other outlets for their efforts.[9] Little of this history, however, has been well-documented, especially in the South, allowing some skeptics to dismiss Black feminism and antirape activism as irrelevant or ineffective. Consumed by movement demands and burdened by the vicissitudes of daily life, African American women often did not leave a paper trail of their accomplishments.

In fact, Black feminists scored some of their most impressive gains during the 1970s and 1980s, including the creation of rape crisis centers geared specifically to Black women and other women of color. As Kimberly Springer argues, African American women took the skills learned in the civil rights movement and applied them to Black feminist politics throughout the 1970s, 1980s, and 1990s.[10] One of the most important Black feminist organizations was the Combahee River Collective, founded in 1974. The group's widely circulated 1977 "Combahee River Collective Statement" articulated an early conceptualization of what legal scholar Kimberlé Crenshaw would later theorize as "intersectionality." In its outlining of the interlocking modes of oppression and systemic exploitation that Black women faced, the "Statement" became foundational for Black feminist politics throughout the 1980s and 1990s and for feminist theorizing more generally.[11]

The increasingly hostile political climate in the 1970s and 1980s, marked by a conservative backlash against social justice movements, often spurred innovative responses among Black feminists and antirape activists. Some African American women, even radicals, worked with white women, usually in coalitions, but occasionally in the same organizations. For example, the West Coast chapter of the radical Third World Women's Alliance, which joined the Free Joan Little campaign, abandoned its initial opposition to working with white women. Instead, the group incorporated the needs of low-income white women. However, the decision also created a rift, and several Black women left as the alliance evolved into a new multiracial group, the Alliance Against Women's Oppression (AAWO) in 1979. Linda Burnham was one of the Black women who decided to remain as the AAWO sought to influence the broader women's movement(s) on issues of race, class, and U.S. imperialism. The group also joined coalitions with feminist antirape organizations, such as New York Women Against Rape.[12]

Like Chisholm and Murray, other African American women participated in more mainstream efforts, sometimes taking leadership positions. In Philadelphia a Black woman coordinated a statewide education program of Women Organized Against Rape, ironically funded by the Law Enforcement Assistance Administration, the federal agency that helped to spur the disproportionate incarceration of Black and brown men and women. In 1976, the Detroit Rape Crisis Center had a Black administrator; and in New York City, a Black woman, Paulette Owens, headed the 1978 Mayor's Task Force on Rape.[13]

Many African Americans, especially in the South, chose existing institutions to combat sexual violence. From the late 1960s through the 1980s, Black women organized antirape campaigns and consciousness raising groups at campus Ys throughout the South and at historically Black colleges and universities (HBCUs), in what historian April Haynes has called "formative spaces in the construction of black feminism in the southern United States." In 1974, at Durham's North Carolina Central University, the first publicly funded liberal arts HBCU in the South, 500 students staged a sit-in to protest the lack of campus security following several campus rapes. The action may well have been inspired by the Free Joan Little campaign, which was organized just months earlier in Durham and had attracted several NCCU women students.[14]

For southern Black feminists, working within the conservative political milieu of the 1980s and in the heart of the Bible Belt brought its own challenges. For example, Dazon Dixon Diallo was the only Black woman at the Feminist Women's Health Network in Atlanta from 1984 to 1989, before starting Sister Love in 1989. Sister Love focused on Black women and

HIV-AIDS, linking the disease to reproductive justice and traumas Black women experienced, including sexual abuse and partner violence. Southern cultural and religious mores, however, frequently obscured sexual violence against Black women behind a wall of silence. "As southern women, and as southern black women we learned for generations that silence will save your life, because if you talk back, they might kill you," Diallo explained. "We have to get past that just to get to the table to be able to say our piece. We have to no longer be silent [because] silence kills." Southern-born Byllye Avery, who created the Black Women's Health Project (discussed below), voiced a similar sentiment: "We live in a conspiracy of silence."[15] This was a familiar refrain among Black women, North and South. Harlem-born Black lesbian feminist poet Audre Lorde issued a similar admonition to Black women at a 1977 panel at the Modern Language Association: "Your silence will not protect you." But African American women could never be sure their voices would be heard. Still, Lorde urged them to speak, for "we were never to survive," she reminded them.[16]

Speaking and visibility had its costs, not only for victim-survivors of sexual violence, but also for southern Black lesbians. According to Minnie Bruce Pratt, a southern white antiracist and lesbian activist, several Black lesbians were fired in the late 1970s from Fayetteville State University, a North Carolina HBCU, when their sexual identity was discovered. As president of the Fayetteville-Cumberland NOW chapter, Pratt helped generate support for Joan Little's rape-murder case; and in the 1970s, she and a Black woman, Izola Young, team-taught a Black women's studies class at Fayetteville State, "African American Feminism from the 1950s–1970s." Pratt was semicloseted at the time, and in a custody battle with her estranged husband. "Everybody was very afraid of losing their jobs," she recalled.[17]

Fear and vulnerability did not prevent African American women from finding creative ways to organize against sexual violence. Diallo's experience is emblematic of many Black feminists and underlines how searching for Black women's antiviolence activism solely within rape crisis centers may miss the mark. African American women challenged violence against women, as they had for generations, from within an array of organizations. Becky Thompson has shown that during the 1970s Black women worked to end violence against women in predominantly white feminist groups, in women's caucuses within mixed-gender groups, and in their own organizations. One report noted that between 1975 and 1985 the number of women of color organizations increased from 300 to over 1,000. While most began as sororities, mutual aid associations, and social clubs, during the U.N. Decade for Women, they shifted their focus from social service and educational work to issue- and policy-oriented efforts. Not all viewed themselves as "feminists," but Black women, whether feminist or not, frequently organized and spoke out about rape and battering.[18]

Recognizing the multiple burdens that African American women confronted, nearly all Black feminist groups, and Black women's organizations generally, promoted a multi-issue agenda. Many dealt specifically with sexual violence and the problems that Black women faced in the criminal justice system. The NBFO claimed that over 60 percent of rape victims were Black, mostly young women, and the organization adopted antirape education and reform of rape laws as key goals. Members also extended their recruitment and education efforts to incarcerated women. The Chicago branch of the NBFO, begun in 1974 and later changing its name to the National Alliance of Black Feminists, established a rape crisis committee that offered counseling to rape victims and escorts to hospitals and police departments. But the group also noted the importance of providing housing and self-defense groups for rape victims. In California, the Women of Color Resource Center under Linda Burnham's direction linked Black women's poverty and housing insecurity to the overlap between the welfare and criminal justice systems. The Combahee River Collective similarly promoted a broad-based agenda, including antirape measures, protests against police brutality, demands for lesbian rights, access to health care, and affordable housing.[19] By the 1980s Black feminists such as Diallo increasingly cast their work within an explicitly intersectional and human rights framework.[20]

To be fair, some of the white antirape activists in the 1960s and 1970s did understand that women's problems were interconnected, especially for those who were Black, poor, queer, or otherwise marginalized and vulnerable. And some white women, including those who backed the Free Joan Little campaign, intentionally adopted an explicitly antiracist political agenda. Yet signs were already apparent in the 1970s that the feminist antirape movement would be unable to overcome racial and class-inflected tensions, which were often exacerbated by ideological divisions. The assertion by many antirape activists that any woman could be raped and that all women were similarly at risk—a rallying cry of many in the Free Joan Little campaign—was a cornerstone of the feminist antirape movement. However, the feminist claim of universal danger also flattened the experiences of sexual assault, eliding differences among women. Moreover, African American women were increasingly unwilling to countenance white racial myopia.[21]

Black women's multi-issue analyses also sometimes influenced feminist organizing more broadly. For example, the reproductive rights movement frequently took its cues from Black women and other women of color in the 1970s and 1980s, transforming demands for a narrower understanding of reproductive rights that focused largely on abortion and birth control into a holistic vision of reproductive freedom and justice. Groups like the Committee for Abortion Rights and Against Sterilization Abuse adopted a multifaceted reproductive justice agenda and joined multiracial alliances such as the Reproductive Rights National Network (R2N2). Much like Black women's antirape organizing, reproductive justice activists connected the multiple needs of diverse women across lines of race, ethnicity, sexuality, gender identity, and class. Thus, reproductive freedom entailed not only access to legal abortion and birth control but also economic security, affordable health care, childcare, and housing, as well as protection for LGBTQ communities and an end to sterilization abuse, sexual violence, and intrusive welfare policies that criminalized poverty and fell most heavily on poor women of color. And yet Black women's participation in various streams of feminism and feminist coalitions, including antirape activism, has too often been obscured or unappreciated.[22]

In effect, the focus on rape crisis centers, rape hotlines, and the more visible and largely white feminist movements opposing violence against women, misses much of the antirape organizing of African American women in the 1970s and 1980s. Inspired by the Free Joan Little campaign and carrying forward their ancestors' legacy of protest against all forms of violence, Black women developed creative ways to address sexual assault. Although they frequently found work with white antirape activists untenable, opting instead for their own organizations, many were able to participate in short-term multiracial alliances, such as Take Back the Night marches. Thus, multiracial feminism and women's interracial antirape organizing were more likely to emerge from coalitions of diverse groups, rather than in single organizations.

In sum, African American women made major contributions to the myriad iterations of women's liberation in the 1960s and especially in the 1970s and 1980s. They were instrumental in achievements frequently attributed to white women; but more often they chose to work either with African American men or, when it came to sexual violence, in their own organizations and sometimes in multiracial coalitions. As we will see, throughout the 1970s and 1980s, Black women found various, often innovative ways to address the problem of sexual violence. That these developments occurred amid a rightward turn in American politics more broadly and the rise of a neoliberal carceral state makes Black women's perseverance and accomplishments all the more noteworthy. While confronting numerous barriers, from a decline in funding support and a conservative political milieu to the racial insensitivity of too many white feminists and the sexist blinders of too many Black men, African American women continued their antirape efforts, frequently on their own terms. Two of the most innovative organizations promoting these efforts were the Washington, D.C., Rape Crisis Center (RCC) and the National Black Women's Health Project (NBWHP).

15

That Space for Black Feminism to Grow and Flourish

The Washington, D.C., Rape Crisis Center

The Washington, D.C., Rape Crisis Center (RCC) was one of the most successful multiracial antirape organizations in which local activists transformed a predominantly white center into an interracial center with African American leadership. Started by white feminists in 1972 as one of the first RCCs, several of its features were replicated by other RCCs across the country. In 1975, it became the first center with a Black administrator, and by the following year it had three paid Black staff. As Anne Valk's masterful study has shown, the D.C. RCC was unique in many respects.[1]

Despite its exceptionalism, the D.C. RCC is a useful case study of how white women relinquished control of an institution they had created, enabling more than token Black and Latinx leadership and participation. The Black feminists who assumed leadership brought a radical inclusivity that went beyond identity politics and transformed how antirape service provision and advocacy were practiced. Most important, they promoted a more expansive understanding of violence against women that included not only sexual assault but also an analysis of state violence, policing, and the multiple needs of the women they served. As we have seen, these women, notably Loretta Ross and Nkenge Touré, were inspired by the Joan Little case; and both Ross and Touré led the effort to create a national and even international network of women of color antirape activists in the 1980s and beyond.[2]

When the D.C. RCC began it was essentially a hotline that volunteers operated out of their homes. Although Washington, D.C., was 70 percent Black in 1970, the RCC had difficulty attracting African American women. However, several years later, city and federal Comprehensive Employment and Training Act (CETA) and Volunteers in Service to America (VISTA) funds enabled the RCC to bring on paid staff, and the white women there decided that the first hire should be a Black woman. In 1974, two Black women joined as full-time, paid staff, and the following year saw an increase in African American volunteers. For Nkenge Touré, one of the Black volunteers and later a paid staff member, this move was crucial. "I think paying salaries is a priority," she said. Providing "salaries to Third World women is very important to assure that you have Third World women there." Several Latinx women and six African American women joined the staff. A Philadelphia rape crisis center saw a similar development.[3]

Three Black women in succession assumed key leadership positions at the D.C. Rape Crisis Center, beginning with Michelle Hudson, followed by Nkenge Touré and Loretta Ross. Hudson was the community education coordinator, which the RCC felt was appropriate since students of color were a majority in D.C. public schools. Hudson also created many of the materials used in rape prevention and education in the public schools. Both Touré and Ross later headed the D.C. RCC.[4]

In recent years, Touré and Ross have expressed their appreciation for white women's willingness to support Black leadership. "We wanted to keep that black thing going, but it was also part of the prophetic vision of white women to create that space for black feminism to grow and flourish," Ross said. Touré felt similarly: "Overall . . . I was very impressed with most of the people at the Center." They were "really trying to diversify and reach out to the community in a more concrete manner through having Black and Third World women playing a key role in this center." Ross insisted that the presence and influence of Black women in the first RCC in the nation was significant. "It not only birthed this black feminist thing, but we wrote a manual about how to start a rape crisis center." Thousands of copies were distributed around the world, "so a lot of groups used our model."[5]

Nkenge Touré was one of the first African American women to join the D.C. RCC as a volunteer in 1974, the same year as Joan Little's rape-murder case spurred the formation of the Free Joan Little campaign. Touré soon became the first Black woman to direct a rape crisis center in the country.

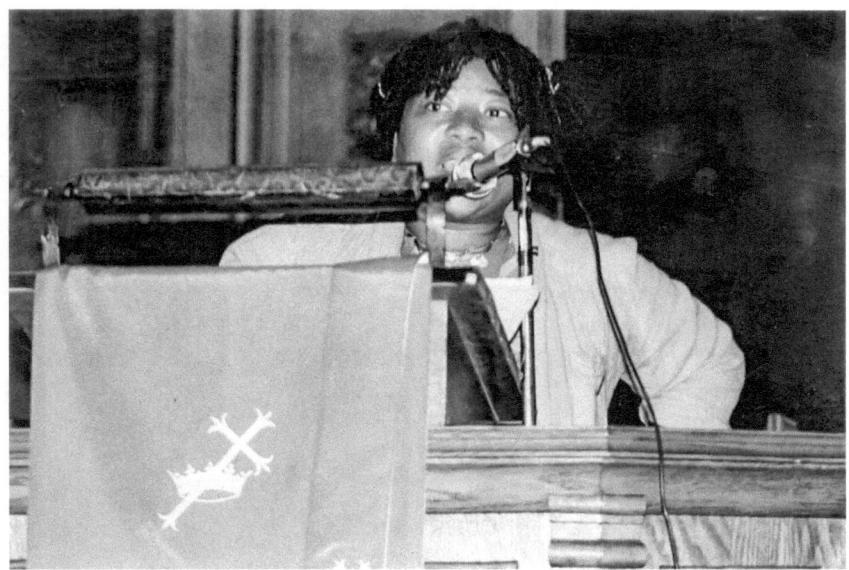

Nkenge Touré was one of the first Black women to join the Washington, D.C., Rape Crisis Center and soon took a top leadership position there. Courtesy of Nkenge Touré Papers, SSC-MS-00563, Sophia Smith Collection, Smith College Special Collections.

Born Anita Stroud in 1951, she grew up in Baltimore public housing. She later changed her name to Nkenge Touré and claimed to be a "Citizen of Record of the Republic of New Africa." After she was raped in high school, Touré turned to activism to channel her anger and depression. With a group of girls, she organized an underground organization, Black Voices, to protest institutional racism at Baltimore's majority-white Eastern High School for girls. During a student strike, Touré was maced in the face by police, arrested, and denied her diploma, unless she apologized for her participation. She refused and later earned her general education diploma.[6]

In high school, Touré had drifted toward the Black Panthers, joining the Party in 1970. Although she left the Black Panther Party several years later, Touré considered herself a Panther for life and embraced the Party's assertion that Blacks had a right to self-defense against racist violence. Touré worked in various Black Panther Party chapters, including the D.C. chapter, where she met her husband, Panther member John Wesley Stevens. Touré also worked in a Panther health clinic; after the clinic lost its funding, the couple started the Education for Liberation bookstore in D.C. The bookstore became a community meeting place and attracted several women who

Loretta Ross came to the Washington, D.C., Rape Crisis Center after meeting Nkenge Touré through tenant organizing, underlining how Black feminist antirape organizers advocated for the multiple needs of their communities. Photographer Charlene Eldridge Wheeler, c. 1987. Courtesy of Loretta Ross Papers, SSC-MS-00504, Sophia Smith Collection, Smith College Special Collections.

wanted to organize against a series of rapes that had occurred in the city. Touré's antirape organizing led her to the D.C. RCC, despite her wariness about working with white women. "I must admit I had reservations," she said. However, she was impressed by "the fact the women at the Center were trying to understand all kinds of women."[7]

Loretta Ross joined the D.C. RCC after meeting Touré at the City Wide Housing Coalition, which pushed for rent control and protested gentrification and the coercive relocation of poor Black and Latinx residents. By 1979, Ross was named executive director of the D.C. RCC. Before coming to the center, she had been active in tenants' rights organizing and Black nationalist politics; and she was a founder of the National Black United Front. Raised largely in Texas, Ross was raped at age eleven. After she was raped by a relative she became a single mother at age fourteen, and she was gang-raped in college. In 1970, at age sixteen, she again became pregnant. Although abortion was then legal in Washington, D.C., she needed parental permission. "By the time I got through fighting with my mom," she explained, she was forced to have a late-term abortion. At age twenty-three, Ross was involuntarily sterilized and subsequently became one of the first women to win a settlement against the Dalkon Shield manufacturers. These traumas attracted her to the reproductive rights movement, where she combined antirape and reproductive justice activism. After leaving the RCC, Ross organized a 1987 conference on Third World women and reproductive justice at Howard University (her alma mater); and she was one of the authors of the 1989 pamphlet *We Remember: African American Women for Reproductive Freedom*. From 1985 to 1989 Ross was director of Women of Color Programs for NOW, and in 1989 she became national director of programming for the National Black Women's Health Network.[8]

The activist histories and overlapping social justice networks of Ross and Touré were typical of many of the Black women who joined the women's antirape movement. As their foremothers had done for generations, they brought their skills, perspectives, and experiences as Black women to other organizations as well. Touré combined her antirape advocacy with her activism in the Women's Section of the National Black United Front, which she cofounded, pushing Black nationalist men to deal more directly with sexism. Similarly, both the Latinx D.C. RCC staff and Yolanda Ward, a Black woman who served on the center's board, worked on housing issues, linking rape prevention and safety measures for women to inadequate shelter.[9]

Ross had experienced housing insecurity and drug addiction, in addition to sexual violence, so she knew firsthand some of the day-to-day challenges

Black women navigated; and both she and Touré were instrumental in broadening the D.C. RCC's focus to make race and poverty central to the center's mission. Bringing a multifaceted analysis to antirape work thus enabled the center to address the various forms of violence that women of color faced. "An institution claiming to serve women had to connect those dots, or it was mostly serving a certain set of women who were mostly not subjected to these other forms of violence," Ross explained. She summed up the unique perspectives that a Black feminist standpoint brought to antirape organizing:

> Black feminism has always sought to connect the dots. We are much more able to articulate that with a more coherent analysis now, but the way we had to challenge the rape crisis center to not disconnect apartheid violence from state violence from personal violence. I mean, we were pushing that envelope in the 1970s. . . . That's what black women brought to the analysis of violence against women, that we had to talk about [all] the forms the violence takes.[10]

Government support together with a large African American and Latina clientele enabled rape crisis centers in Washington, D.C., and in California to diversity their paid staff and even their volunteers.[11] However, government funding, which was often crucial, came with strings attached or required alliances with mainstream health care institutions. Such arrangements too often sidelined grassroots organizations and women of color. The experiences of African American women at Atlanta's Grady Hospital Rape Crisis Center underlined the problem. All the center's volunteers were white, even though over 65 percent of its clients were African American in 1975. Black women reportedly had applied for the volunteer positions, but none were selected. The hospital also disregarded the perspectives of other Black antirape organizers. For example, in 1973 Portia La Sonde had organized the grassroots Metropolitan Rape Crisis Council, which was instrumental in starting the Grady Hospital RCC. But Grady officials increasingly limited the council's decision-making and input into staff and volunteer training at the hospital's RCC. That this dispute occurred at the same time and in the same city where activists organized a campaign in support of Dessie X. Woods—the young Black Georgia woman who, like Joan Little, killed her white male attacker after he allegedly attempted to rape her—was particularly troubling. The tension between La Sonde's organization and Grady Hospital was a prime example of the discord that frequently erupted between grassroots groups and more bureaucratic institutions, a trend that increasingly marked the women's antirape movement.[12]

In contrast to the Atlanta experience, establishing a critical mass of Black, Indigenous, and Latina women at the D.C. RCC had a ripple effect, most notably in the formation of a national and even international network of nonwhite antirape activists. Ross and Touré, working with other women of color, organized the first National Conference on Third World Women and Violence in Washington, D.C., in 1980. Organizers hoped to provide a national forum for Third World women activists to discuss how race and class shaped violence against women. Another goal of the conference was to create a space for women of color, who often felt isolated in majority-white RCCs, to share their experiences and strategies for meeting the needs of their communities. During the 1970s, small numbers of women of color worked in rape crisis centers in D.C., Chicago, Detroit, Philadelphia, and in California, mostly as volunteers. Several projects in North Carolina, Minnesota, and Boston attracted women of color who worked in community education and outreach.[13]

Prior to the D.C. conference, the Law Enforcement Assistance Administration (LEAA) and the National Center for the Prevention and Control of Rape provided one of the few national opportunities for women of color to gather in working conferences on "Issues Pertaining to Sexual Assault." Ironically, despite LEAA's role in policing and imprisoning increased numbers of Black and brown bodies, the federal agency funded several regional conferences in 1977 for "special populations" (the elderly and rural residents, African Americans, Spanish speakers, and the disabled). At the LEAA-sponsored gathering for African Americans, women discussed their isolation from other Third World women, and the seeds for the 1980 First National Conference on Third World Women and Violence were planted. Meanwhile, in Hartford, Connecticut, an African American and a Latina began an antirape project, and in Boston several Black women and Latinas developed a rape awareness program in a community mental health center.[14]

Seventy percent of attendees at the Third World Women and Violence conference were African American. The overwhelming presence of Black women led some Latinas, who made up about a fifth of participants, to complain that their concerns were not fully addressed, indicating that "Third World" women did not automatically find unity or consensus. Despite Black women's majority presence, Loretta Ross recalled that among the women present, only a handful were in leadership positions, and only she and one other Black woman were directors of RCCs. But nearly all participants expressed feelings of isolation working in a predominantly white, middle-class women's antiviolence movement, and they hoped to attract more women of color to the antirape movement. Although not all the attendees considered themselves feminists (believing the term carried an antimale, anti-middle-class stigma), they also acknowledged that the reemergence of the women's movement gave rise to a focus on the oppression of women of color "as women."[15]

Conference attendees pointed to Joan Little's trial and several other high-profile rape-murder cases involving women of color that inspired them to "organize around their particular victimization as women." The Little case in particular "aroused the anger of the Black community" and exposed the "injustices of the criminal justice system as it related to Third World Women," Touré recalled. The women believed that violence against women of color was poorly documented and vastly underreported, due largely to police racism and insensitivity to victims of sexual violence. Moreover, a collective history of police brutality and discrimination in communities of color made women reluctant to call the police; and one of the goals of the conference was to explore alternatives to the criminal legal system for rape survivors. This also marked a departure from earlier practices of the D.C. RCC in which staff and volunteers worked closely with city police, despite pushback from Black women. For example, in 1973, Mary Treadwell, cofounder of the Black nationalist Pride Inc. and wife of future Washington, D.C., mayor Marion Barry, critiqued the D.C. RCC's pursuit of legal reforms and its failure to consider racism, especially in the criminal justice system.[16]

Men's presence at the conference and in the antirape movement also sparked controversy. The ten males at the conference—all men of color—were working at RCCs or what were then called battered women's shelters. But some of the women present believed that men's participation reinforced male protection of women, rather than promoting female empowerment. Ross and conference organizers, however, stressed the importance of male allies in combatting sexual violence. At the time, Ross and other women in the D.C. RCC were allied with Black Men Against Rape, which patrolled several Black neighborhoods in the city. The D.C. women also worked closely with Prisoners Against Rape, a group formed in 1973 by Black convicted rapists at Lorton Prison in Virginia that supported Joan Little during her rape-murder trial. Several other prison and community programs in Washington State and Boston also worked with male perpetrators of sexual violence; and a small number of men of color had begun organizing vigilante groups in their communities to protect residents.[17]

Conference attendees examined many of the myths surrounding rape and race, including the notion that women of color were promiscuous, accustomed to violence, exceptionally resilient, and therefore largely unaffected by sexual assault. Unfortunately, these stereotypes were accepted not only by the larger society but by too many men of color as well. Participants challenged the widespread misperception that rape occurred largely in the ghetto, with its less-than-subtle racial implications.[18] The "ghetto" reference invoked the old "Black beast rapist" trope that had long plagued African American men and justified lynching in earlier decades. But it also masked another reality regarding incarceration. It was not that Black men were more likely to rape. Rather, even when innocent, African American men were more likely to be arrested, convicted, and given harsher prison sentences, including the death penalty, particularly if the alleged victim was a white woman. "The racist nature of the criminal justice system still has a drastic impact on Third World communities as non-white men are disproportionately jailed for sexual assault," Ross observed.[19]

An important outcome of the 1980 conference was the creation of a network of African American, Indigenous, and other women of color addressing violence against women. Ross explained how conference organizers reached out to activists like Beth Richie, who was combatting violence against Black women in New York City, and Cherrie Moraga, who was pressing Chicana issues in California. Both Moraga and Richie would become prominent lesbian scholars and activists advocating for the multiple needs of African American women and Latinas.[20] Other Black women started postconference projects in Philadelphia, Minnesota, and Florida. The publicity surrounding the conference also brought greater visibility to the D.C. RCC's local Anti-rape Week (later Anti-rape Month), which became a permanent fixture and a major annual fundraiser in the city. Several of the organizers and participants in the first conference, including Touré and Ross, joined with activists in New York and California to plan the Second National Conference on Violence Against Third World Women of Color for 1981 and then again in the later 1980s. Although another conference never materialized, other opportunities for cross-racial alliances and national gatherings among women of color did emerge.[21]

Despite Black women's influence and prominent leadership in the D.C. RCC, tensions surrounding race, class, and sexuality persisted. Black women were a majority of the staff, but the RCC volunteers and board of directors were mostly white. Because both Black and white lesbians had been part of the D.C. RCC since its inception, Ross found that sexual identity politics also had to be negotiated. But class and educational differences could be just as difficult to navigate. For example, a Black woman with a high school

Space for Black Feminism to Grow and Flourish

degree who hired and supervised a white woman with a master's degree in social work posed its own challenges. Other racial tensions came from white women outside the center. In one instance, a white police officer filed a reverse discrimination lawsuit against the center after she was excluded from the First National Conference on Third World Women and Violence. (White women provided support services such as childcare and transportation for the conference but did not attend as participants.) Another incident occurred when a group of white South African women visited the D.C. center. They had carefully read the D.C. RCC manual and wanted additional suggestions on starting their own rape crisis center. Upon arriving, the South Africans assumed the white receptionist was the director and were surprised when she pointed them to Ross. However, RCC staff turned the tables, underlining their focus on racial justice as well as sexual violence. For the next several hours, Ross and other RCC women grilled their white visitors, asking how their new rape crisis center would also fight the brutal South African apartheid system.[22]

While it was not without its own internal difficulties, the Washington, D.C., Rape Crisis Center became a space in which Black feminist leadership was created and nurtured. Although that model was not widely replicated in other RCCs, the organizing efforts of Black women like Loretta Ross and Nkenge Touré extended beyond the D.C. RCC. The 1980 conference on women of color and violence that they organized and the networks that emerged from that gathering were important examples of Black women's antirape activism in the 1970s and 1980s. As such, African American women not only carried on the legacy of foremothers Ida B. Wells and Rosa Parks but contributed to the long arc of Black women's activism and the women's liberation movements that continued throughout the 1970s and into the 1980s.

Reagan-era cuts to CETA and other social services, discussed in subsequent chapters, led to diminished financial support for local antirape services. By the late 1980s, the focus on women of color that activists had established at the D.C. RCC was also in decline, exacerbated by racial tensions and by political divisions among Black women. However, Black women antirape activists, including Ross and Touré, continued their efforts, finding new outlets to secure women's safety. One of the most successful Black women's antiviolence endeavors of the 1980s was the National Black Women's Health Project, the focus of the next chapter.

16

A Way to Free Themselves

Black Feminists and the National Black Women's Health Project

"The number one issue for most of our sisters is violence—battering, sexual abuse," asserted Byllye Avery, founder of the National Black Women's Health Project (NBWHP). "Same thing for their daughters, whether they are twelve or four." The NBWHP was a remarkable example of Black women's organizing against sexual violence and one of the most important Black feminist accomplishments of the 1980s. The organization emerged from a project that began in 1981 under the auspices of the National Women's Health Network, a largely white women's health alliance. Although the NBWHP did not focus exclusively on rape, its members viewed sexual violence as an integral part of African American women's health concerns. As such it underlines the necessity of looking beyond rape crisis centers for Black women's anti-violence organizing.[1]

Byllye Avery was a Black reproductive rights and women's health activist. Born Byllye Yvonne Reddick in Waynesville, Georgia, in 1937, she was the oldest of three children. The family moved to a farm in Florida near Daytona where Byllye grew up. Her mother, L. Alyce Ingram, was a graduate of Bethune-Cookman College, an HBCU started by the renowned Black clubwoman Mary McLeod Bethune. While her mother taught school, Byllye's father, Quitman Reddick, ran a neighborhood store. When Byllye was

Byllye Avery founded the National Black Women's Health Project, which adopted a holistic approach to Black women's health. In NBWHP workshops throughout the country, Avery found that violence, especially sexual violence, was frequently the number one issue that African American women wanted to address. Courtesy of Byllye Avery.

fourteen, her father was mysteriously killed, forcing her to assume much more responsibility for her younger siblings. In 1959, she graduated with a bachelor of arts in psychology from Talladega College, an Alabama HBCU, where she met her husband, Wesley Avery. They married the following year. After ten years of marriage, at age thirty-three, he died of a heart attack, leaving her a single mother of two young children and pregnant with a third. Her husband's unexpected early death as well as the trauma and stress Avery experienced prompted her interest in Black women's health and the holistic framework she developed to meet their needs.

In an interview, Avery explained that she became involved in the women's health movement through the issue of abortion. At the University of Florida, where she was working on a master's degree in special education in the late 1960s, campus women often turned to her and two other women for help in ending their pregnancies. Although there were then only a handful of Black students at the University of Florida, most Black women remained aloof from her. Their reticence stemmed from the stigma and silence in the African American community surrounding abortion, a key concern of feminist health activists during the years when abortion was illegal. "It's ok if you don't talk about it," Avery explained. So she began to meet with white women who were working on women's health and soon became a bridge between Black and white women's experiences. Avery discovered that the Black women on campus who shunned her had secretly admired her. "So I guess I sort of learned to move back and forth between the [two] worlds," she said. Avery began referring women to abortion facilities in New York City. New York legalized abortion in 1970, three years before the U.S. Supreme Court's *Roe v. Wade* decision, and the state had one of the most permissive abortion laws in the nation. But when a young Black woman approached the Florida group for help, she had no resources to make the trip to New York City. She later died from a self-induced abortion. "That really brought it home," Avery recalled, "and made us understand the importance of access." Avery credits her work with white feminist health activists in helping her to link abortion and rape, especially at the Gainesville Women's Health Center, which she cofounded in 1974, the same year as Joan Little's arrest for murder of her jailer. In 1978, through the Gainesville center, which also offered sickle-cell anemia testing for Black women, Avery helped to start Birthplace, an alternative birthing center featuring certified nurse midwives.[2]

Despite her accomplishments, Avery remained frustrated that these projects were not reaching enough African American women. At a community college CETA-funded job in 1980–81, she began working with young Black women, some of whom were teen mothers. "It was hearing these women's stories that led me to start conceptualizing the National Black Women's Health Project," she explained. Over a two-year period, and under the auspices of the National Women's Health Network, Avery and a planning committee of Black women organized the first national Black women's health conference in the country. The planning committee incorporated a collective form of leadership and decision-making adopted from feminist conscious-raising that both Black and white feminists had practiced during the 1960s and 1970s. They deliberately chose this model as an alternative to the charismatic male leadership that frequently had been the public face of the civil rights movement, most notably that of Martin Luther King Jr.[3]

The planning committee—which boasted women with PhDs as well as public housing tenants—initially intended to include white women allies from the National Women's Health Network. However, they also wanted to confront intraracial class differences among African American women and decided to include Black women only. The conference motto, "We're sick and tired of being sick and tired," echoed sharecropper and legendary civil rights activist Fannie Lou Hamer's well-known exhortation. It also signaled organizers' efforts to reach low-income rural as well as urban southern Black women who were provided funds to attend the 1983 gathering.[4]

The conference convened in Atlanta in 1983 at Spelman College, the distinguished Black women's HBCU. Ranging in age from young and middle-aged to elderly, conference participants included "women in uniform, Muslims, lesbians, political activists, women with straight hair, Afros and dread locks, women from all walks of life," according to one observer. "It brought poor black women and middle-class women, rural and urban women in dialogue that was enriching and exciting [to everyone]," Loretta Ross recalled. Workshops covered a wide range of topics from incest, rape, abortion, racism, and the blues, to lupus, teenage sexuality, and sickle-cell screening. The conference featured films, strategy sessions, and keynote addresses by Dr. June Jackson Christmas, the first Black woman to head the American Public Health Association in 1980, and Beverly Smith, cofounder with her twin sister, Barbara Smith of the Black feminist Combahee River Collective. Expecting several hundred participants, organizers were thrilled when 2,000 women showed up, including Dazon Dixon Diallo, Nkenge Touré, and Loretta Ross. Clearly, the conference had touched a nerve. Recalling the event more than twenty years later, Avery quoted Black feminist poet June Jordan: "We are the ones we've been waiting for."[5]

From the seeds of the 1983 conference, the NBWHP was born, later becoming the Black Women's Health Imperative, which is still in existence. While it was not specifically a rape crisis center, violence against women, including sexual assault, was a key concern. For Byllye Avery, violence against women, including battering and rape, were deeply personal issues. She grew up witnessing her father brutalizing her mother. The violence so traumatized the young Byllye that she wondered how she could ever leave her mother to attend college. In 1983, two weeks after Avery spoke at the Take Back the Night rally in Atlanta, her daughter was raped. Thus, Avery made sure to integrate an antiviolence perspective into the work of the NBWHP. "Let's deal with the number one issue. Violence," she insisted.[6] Black antirape activists such as Nkenge Touré and Loretta Ross joined the new organization and soon started a local NBWHP chapter in Washington, D.C. As these examples suggest, the NBWHP underlines the necessity of looking beyond RCCs for Black women's antirape organizing. Moreover, centering the activism of women like Avery, Touré, and Ross reveals the contributions of southern Black feminists, who are often invisible or marginalized in narratives of 1970s and 1980s feminism.

Both Black Power politics, including Black separatism, and feminism fueled the creation of the NBWHP. As Loretta Ross recalled, a meeting of 1,500 Black women "from the ground up" declared, "We don't want to be with these white women," and they pressured Avery to create a separate organization. "They were right," Avery laughed more than two decades later when recounting the skirmish. For Avery, "the race issue" prevented Black and white women from working together; and she advised white women to confront poverty in their own communities before "trying to articulate the concerns of the black community." However, after strenuous debate, white women were permitted to become members of the NBWHP if they provided financial support and attended an antiracism workshop series, "Sisters and Allies," developed by NBWHP organizer Lillie Allen.[7]

Black feminism also influenced the development of the NBWHP, even if Black women did not always recognize or embrace the term. "A lot of people don't want to believe it—that Black women are more feminist than white women," Avery noted. A national 1971 Harris poll had confirmed Avery's observation about Black women's support for feminist issues. The poll revealed that although many Black women eschewed the feminist label for themselves, both Black women and men backed the goals of women's liberation more than any other group, including white women.[8]

Avery herself viewed violence against women through a feminist lens. "Violence and sexism go hand in hand," she insisted. She called on men, especially African American men, to join the fight against rape, incest, and battering: "We need men to stop giving consent, by their silence, to rape, to sexual abuse, to stop violence. . . . For future generations, this has got to stop somewhere."[9]

Although Black feminism certainly shaped the work of the NBWHP, the group was less forthright about sexuality, especially same-sex desire. Lesbianism was not a major problem in the NBWHP, but neither was it openly discussed, something Avery regretted in retrospect. According to Loretta Ross, the most significant aspect of this silence was that it has obscured the role of Black lesbians in the creation of the Black women's health movement. Avery admitted that initially she was afraid of lesbians; but her involvement in the women's movement eventually enabled her to acknowledge her attraction to other women. However, her same-sex relationships created difficulties with some Black women, who presumably disapproved of gay relationships. In 2005 and after sixteen years together, Avery married Ngina Lythcott, whom she had met in Atlanta through the NBWHP.[10]

In contrast to its reticence about sexuality, the NBWHP made a more concerted effort to address poverty. To ensure that the voices of low-income women continued to be heard following the conference, Avery helped to create the Black Women's Wellness Center in the Mechanicsville section of Atlanta, which brought in women from low-income and public housing neighborhoods. "[If] you look at the positions of people who are having the hardest time in society and . . . when you change that, you change things for everyone," she said. Despite their efforts, Avery acknowledged that it was not always easy for low-income women to participate in NBWHP programs. But class location was a fluid and imprecise marker in Black women's lives. Some of the women involved in the NBWHP had college degrees but also struggled economically, Avery pointed out. At the same time, she also was careful not to perpetuate the stereotype that all Black women were impoverished. Nevertheless, "if we really want to make social change, if we really want to make economic change, . . . we have to first deal with the lives of the people who struggle at the bottom," Avery maintained.[11]

Avery's class-inflected belief that improving Black's women's circumstances would benefit the entire community had been echoed by African American women for decades. Educator Anna Julia Cooper, born into slavery in Raleigh in 1858, proclaimed in her 1892 *A Voice from the South*, "Only the Black woman can say, when and where I enter . . . then and there the whole Negro race enters with me." Cooper did not specifically mention poverty here; yet she understood that in the late nineteenth-century South and despite the growth of a tiny Black middle class, the majority of African American women remained poor. She also understood the pain of sexual violence. Cooper's white slave-owning father had raped her mother, but silence and shame had prevented her mother from speaking about the abuse. And yet for Cooper and other Black clubwomen of the era, it was precisely their collective history of sexual abuse and resilience that gave African American women the moral authority and strength to demand justice for themselves and the entire race. Black women's progress toward liberation would be the measure of race progress, they asserted.[12]

Much like their nineteenth-century foremothers, the women who organized the Black women's health conference understood the importance of addressing sexual violence. Sexual violence, including rape, incest, and intimate partner violence (usually referred to as "battering"), was a major issue for too many women. "When sisters take their shoes off and start talking about what's happening, the first thing we cry about is violence," Avery explained.[13]

The NBWHP responded to the realities of Black women's lives and adopted a holistic, multi-issue approach to improving Black women's health. Low-income Black women in particular found it impossible to separate sexual assault from the numerous difficulties in their lives. Avery and her coworker Ngina Lythcott worked for a while with a group of Black women in Chester, Pennsylvania, where the entire city and its public housing were in receivership. Poverty, violence, and incarceration scarred the lives of many of the residents. Lythcott, who was employed at nearby Swarthmore College at the time, was able to enlist the college's support to set up a women's wellness center in the community, which the local women had identified as a pressing need. For these young women, having a baby was viewed as a rite of passage and often was encouraged by their mothers, Avery recalled. But the young women also remained under the thumb of their male partners, many of whom were incarcerated. "We watched the lives of women whose men were in prison and how the men controlled the women's lives from prison," Avery remarked. Her observation underlined the ripple effects of imprisonment, particularly on impoverished Black women, their families, and communities in what later would be called "million-dollar blocks," a term that highlighted the geography and cost of mass incarceration.[14]

NBWHP organizers like Avery and Lillie Allen traversed the country, helping African American women form self-help groups. "People wanted to get together and talk to each other," Avery recollected. "White women had a sense of entitlement that we didn't have," she said, "and so we had to give ourselves permission to be entitled. . . . And give each other permission to be entitled."[15] Organizers stressed the value of Black women's self-empowerment, often achieved through storytelling. "It's in the process of telling our stories that can set us free and set us on the right path," Avery explained. Yet harrowing violence and trauma, including sexual assault, often lay at the core of the women's narratives. "So many women have been raped," Avery said. "So many women have been victims of sexual abuse and have had no way to talk about it, to heal." Breaking the silence of abuse broke the isolation that many Black rape victims experienced. Equally debilitating were the racist stereotypes about Black women's sexuality that too many had internalized. "We're the Jezebels," Loretta Ross explained. "So obviously we did something to deserve any sexual abuse that happens to us." According to Ross, the NBWHP gave Black women not just crucial information but also a sense of their own ability to use that knowledge for themselves, their families, and their communities. This renewed capacity was perhaps its most important legacy. "It wasn't enough to have the information," Ross insisted. "You have to feel empowered enough to use that information."[16]

Lillie Allen described how the NBWHP workshops liberated her from the need to maintain the culturally prescriptive "strong Black woman" identity:

> For a long time I had to hide out. I had to not show my feelings. I had to be "strong." When someone hurt me, I had to go somewhere and cry real hard and deal with that alone, then come back and always be consistently kind and stuff like that. . . . The "Black & Female" workshop is all of us, each and every one of us making that transition to move to the place where we've been struggling to get. It's all our stories, all our voices, all our cries, all our excitement, all our joys. What I've been able to do is provide the place for women to do that out loud. This is the commitment I've made to myself and to other Black women.[17]

Lillie Allen was the daughter of migrant farmworkers and had grown up in an all-Black community. Like Avery's mother, Allen also attended Bethune-Cookman College in Florida. Although it was an-all Black campus, Allen was subjected to colorism and felt especially hurt by feeling excluded in a place "that I thought was mine," she said. Later she earned her master's in public health at the University of North Carolina at Chapel Hill. Before joining the planning committee for the 1983 Black women's health conference, Allen had worked with teen pregnancy prevention programs in Atlanta's public housing projects. She developed a program based on art, dialogue, and dance that used self-expression for young women to envision how their lives could be different. From those efforts and reevaluation counseling, which incorporated dialogue and active listening to work through difficult issues, Allen created the "Black and Female" self-help workshops. In addition to offering support to Black women unable to afford more traditional counseling or therapy, the workshops politicized self-help.[18]

Thus, the NBWHP did more than promote healing and instill self-empowerment in African American women. Like participants in feminist consciousness-raising sessions, both Allen and Avery understood that Black women's storytelling about traumas, like sexual abuse, was part of a process of political consciousness regarding gender oppression: "What we learn in the presence of other Black women, [is] that . . . we have an institution of sexism that's going on in our lives that tends to oppress us, and that the only way we can get out from under it is to learn to how to unhook." Avery recalled the exhilaration of Black women who "totally change their lives." Sharing their stories, especially across generations and cultures, enabled women to place their experiences within a wider historical context that was culturally specific. For Avery, gathering cross-cultural experiences, especially the history of women's fertility control and antiviolence efforts, was crucial. "Sometimes that will be what will give us our courage and give us our strength, because . . . these women ran into difficulties," she said. The NBWHP newsletter, *Vital Signs*, not only provided health information but often carried political analyses, such as "The Roots of Black Women's Oppression," by Angela Davis, who was also a NBWHP board member. The NBWHP combined individual healing and empowerment with political education, thus bridging the separation between political action, educational projects, and service delivery.[19]

Many Black women activists were aware of their foremothers' struggles and achievements and drew on them for inspiration. For Loretta Ross, Black women's history could shine a light on controversial issues like rape, contraception, and abortion. "I felt one of the ways to break through the silence was [to] show that there were other times in our history when we weren't so silent, when we were more active, when we were not as cowed by the political situation."[20] Avery was similarly inspired and frequently invoked Black women's history in her work with other women. She understood that her efforts were part of a distinctive ethic of care that had enabled African American women to survive and persevere from generation to generation. Avery pointed to the legacy of Black granny midwives in the South and how they dealt with violence against women. She encouraged young women activists to learn this history, to see how those women "took care of women who had babies, how they helped women who had too many babies and didn't want to have [more children], how they handled women who had been victims of rape [and] victims of incest." Book knowledge was important, but younger activists must contextualize their work within women's everyday experiences, a hallmark of Black feminism: "Talk to other women," Avery urged young activists. "Have them talk to their relatives . . . so that we can stop . . . think[ing] that [our work] is something unique. . . . It's been going on throughout the ages, and it will continue." It has "no due date," she added. "Know that we're standing on the shoulders of many, and that we push this ball just a little further up the hill, and if we get it up there, there'll be some others who will come and push it further and further up the hill." Avery was articulating what historian Thulani Davis would later term the "emancipation circuit," a vision of freedom and a culture of resistance, forged in slavery, and honed in Emancipation and Reconstruction by Black southerners who passed it on to generations across time and space.[21]

The NBWHP did not limit its activism to African American women or even to the United States. For example, the organization helped Luz Martinez create the National Latina Health Project, while Mary Chung started the Asian Women's Health Organization. In 1985, a twenty-five-woman delegation represented the NBWHP at the Nairobi Third World Women's International Conference, where sexual violence was a key issue. African American women shared their stories of rape and incest with Kenyan women who had no word for "incest" in their language. By 1991, the NBWHP had chapters in twenty-five states, other chapters abroad, and was the fastest-growing Black women's organization in the United States. In 2002, the organization relocated its main office from Atlanta to Washington, D.C., and changed its name to the Black Women's Health Imperative to reflect its greater focus on policy. Avery felt it was time to move on. Influenced by a Puerto Rican woman, Avery began to reformulate Black women's health needs as a human rights issue and traveled globally, working with women in Belize and Brazil and in South Africa during the antiapartheid movement. She addressed the health priorities identified by local women, including sexual abuse and HIV-AIDS. "We gave them what they needed—a way to free themselves," she said. Avery looked back on the impact of the NBWHP: "We made a large enough ripple that it covered the pond . . . and the seeds are planted and things are happening. . . . We created not only a place for Black women to come and talk about their issues but we were able to pass along to women of color."[22]

"All the Women Are White, All the Men Are Black, but Some of Us Are Brave": Black Feminists Caught in the Middle (Again)

While many Black women activists chose to form all-female groups, others joined Black mixed-gender organizations. Yet working with men, especially around the volatile issue of intraracial sexual abuse, posed its own challenges. Pursuing antirape measures with white feminists frequently was no panacea for African American women either. The experience of scholar and activist Beth Richie is a case in point. Her decades-long activism in Black mixed-gender, majority-white women's, and Black women's groups illuminates how radical Black feminists formulated a transformative, multi-issue liberation politics that challenged both Black men's race-focused activism and white women's gender-centered advocacy, beyond the Joan Little case and into the 1980s.[23]

Richie's nuanced analysis of violence against women, including sexual assault and state violence, emerged from decades of antiviolence activism dating to the late 1970s. Like the NBWHP's, her efforts underline the links between political activism and service provision, too often viewed in opposition by those with more conventional notions of political activity. African American women such as Richie and longtime activists and supporters of Joan Little, like Angela Davis, would form new organizations based on an intersectional framework and an expansive understanding of violence against Black women, including those trapped behind bars.[24]

Richie was raised in a middle-class African American family where both parents were avid racial justice advocates. She recalled going to the 1963 March on Washington as a child, at that time the largest mass protest the nation had ever witnessed. After graduating with a social work degree from Cornell in 1979 and a master's in social work from Washington University in St. Louis the following year, she landed at a community health center in Harlem in the early 1980s. The health center ran a Head Start program and addressed a variety of difficulties confronting the local community including poor housing, education, employment and business opportunities, and the expansion of the prison-industrial complex. But the racial justice work she was engaged in failed to incorporate a gender analysis. Initially, Richie was silent, fearful of "being cast out by the [Black] community." Later she came to reject the "trap of silence" that equated "disclosure" with "treason." Even at the time, however, she noticed that Black women's input and experiences often were relegated to the margins.

Women "weren't articulating the vision. . . . their leadership, their voices weren't central to the analysis. . . . They didn't feel their power even though they were doing a lot of the work," Richie recalled. She observed something else about the women too: "They would come to meetings but then would be afraid to go home." She realized that many of the women had been victimized by partner violence or rape. "So I set up a support [group] to talk about why that was true."[25]

During the early 1980s, Richie sought out other women of color and the women's antiviolence movement, redirecting her activism toward rape, battering, sexual harassment, and economic exploitation. "The respite was brief," she said. She discovered a group called Battered Minority Women, which was associated with Third World organizations in Boston, Los Angeles, Detroit, and Atlanta. However, the group rejected feminism and the struggle against sexual oppression. Instead, members believed intraracial violence against Black women was the result of racism, that the men beat women because the men were oppressed. During this period, Richie cofounded the Leadership Institute for Women, which offered training for programs dealing with domestic violence and sexual assault. Richie also cochaired the Women of Color Task Force of the National Coalition Against Domestic Violence, hoping that it would form the basis for more diverse coalitions among antiviolence activists. For Richie, task forces were critical to building and supporting the leadership of women of color. But working with majority-white women's groups also brought disappointments. "We have learned that coalition work is complicated and time-consuming," Richie said. National women's antiviolence organizations too often focused narrowly on battering or rape and believed that gender oppression was the primary source of violence against women. "There was no analysis of racial injustice or poverty or of the need for meeting basic needs of food and shelter," she said. "The only discussion of shelter was shelter to get away from violence, not shelter because you're homeless, right?" Moreover, many of these groups failed to address state violence, the kind that poor women of color were often subjected to when social problems were criminalized. For example, during the 1980s in South Carolina, pregnant, mostly low-income Black women, were subjected to a "test and arrest" policy which allowed the arrest, often in shackles, of pregnant, drug-addicted women, even when no drug treatment programs were available.[26]

Richie tried to create a bridge between the Harlem men who ran the health center through a "racial only lens" and white antiviolence feminists who operated through a different "singular lens, a gender only lens." She found the challenge daunting, she admitted. The two groups "were so far apart. . . . People were just living in different worlds."[27]

After these kinds of frustrations, Richie decided to refocus her efforts. She and six other Harlem women secured grants to serve women of color who were victims of sexual harassment, rape, or intimate partner violence. But the grants were small and Richie and the other women were all volunteers. Like Dazon Diallo, Richie soon realized that addressing sexual violence in isolation was both impossible and ineffective. One day while she was delivering HIV-AIDS information to a group of women prisoners, she ran across a woman who had been in one of the counseling groups she had set up to deal with violence against women. Richie was surprised to find the woman in jail. But speaking with incarcerated women revealed that urging victims of violence to contact the police often made them even more vulnerable. As one prisoner explained, abused women didn't call the police because the police might arrest someone else in the house, "or the police won't come anyway, they don't respect us, they don't believe that we have really been hurt." A 1980 study confirmed this anecdotal evidence, finding that juries gave much lighter sentences to assailants of Black women compared to those convicted of raping or battering white women—especially if the white woman's attacker was African American.[29]

Richie summarized the lessons she learned from the jailed women: "'We are in jail because we were hurt by our boyfriend or partner or our landlord and we couldn't call the police and we couldn't go to shelter or services and those services weren't in our neighborhoods and we didn't even know that the movement was alive and beginning to provide some kind of remedies, [so] that we ended up being forced into illegal activities, sometimes including that we were criminalized for not reaching out for help.'" This was especially true in situations where children had witnessed violence or abuse. Richie realized that this was not a problem that could easily be solved "by raising a little bit of money and providing a little bit of service." Although some of the prisoners were discussing partner violence, a majority had experienced some form of abuse, including rape and physical violence.[29] Like Joan Little, many of the jailed women also had tried to defend themselves from sexual abuse and other forms of violence. But, unlike Little, they were more likely to find themselves facing long prison sentences for defending themselves against their assailants.

Other Black women made similar observations regarding the multiple needs of rape victims and poor women in their communities. The Rosa Parks Rape Crisis Center and the Compton YWCA Rape Crisis Hotline in California were established in the 1980s to provide services for African American women who experienced sexual assault. Both reported ongoing conflicts with funders over the ratio of dollars to number of clients served and financial allocations that were based largely on the experiences of white, middle-class women. The Southern California Rape Hotline Alliance similarly noted that serving a "predominantly ethnic minority population" entailed many more hours than the "average" time required "for a center that serves a predominantly white population."[30] Monica Williams, the African American director of the Compton Rape Crisis Center, described the multiple challenges faced by low-income women who were also rape victims:

> A woman may come in or call in for various reasons. She has no place to stay, she has no job, she has no support, she has no money, she has no food, she's been beaten, and after you finish meeting all those needs, or try to meet all those needs, then she may say, by the way, during all this, I was being raped. So that makes our community different than other communities. A person wants their basic needs first. It's a lot easier to discuss things when you are full.[31]

Like that of Williams and other Black women, Richie's analysis and activism bridged multiple issues. Working to stem violence against women seamlessly merged into prisoner support and HIV-AIDS work, especially for low-income women. Throughout the 1980s and 1990s, the United States was becoming what she called a "prison nation." In this political context, she saw that it was increasingly difficult to "find the political crossroads that link racial and economic justice with an analysis of gender."[32] By 2000 Richie joined longtime prison abolitionist Angela Davis and others to form INCITE! Women of Color Against Violence. The following year Critical Resistance, created in 1997 to combat policing and imprisonment as solutions to crime, poverty, and other social ills, issued a joint statement with INCITE! calling on the women's antiviolence movement to reject criminal justice solutions as remedies for personal and state violence against women.[33]

Despite the challenges, Black feminists and other Black women activists continued to struggle against sexual assault and other forms of violence against women and Black communities more generally, including the violence of poverty and the increasing criminalization of poor women. Walking in the footsteps of their foremothers, Black women did what they had always done: they simply "kept on keepin' on," trying to "make a way outta no way."

17

What Chou Mean We, White Girl?

White Women, Antiracism, and Sexual Violence

The national attention that the Free Joan Little campaign attracted with its diverse array of supporters seemed to promise a more multiracial, cross-class, feminist alliance, particularly among antirape activists. Antirape rhetoric was the thread with which Little's defenders, both activists and attorneys, stitched together the broad-based campaign. "Joanne is you, Joanne is me," sang the Black women's a cappella ensemble Sweet Honey in the Rock. The trials of Yvonne Wanrow, Inez García, and Dessie X. Woods had similarly drawn a wide range of defenders. Thus, at first glance, these high-profile cases would appear to be what sociologist Maria Bevacqua calls a "bridge issue," capable of uniting women and male allies across a broad spectrum of political differences, as well as racial, gender, and class divides. However, what made sense for a defense campaign and legal strategy posed challenges and frequently insurmountable obstacles to creating more diverse antirape organizations and an inclusive antirape movement going forward.[1]

As we have seen, African American antirape activists and other women of color often felt compelled to organize separately from both men of color and white feminists. For African American women, Black men's exclusive focus on racism and white women's emphasis on sexism were both limiting and often maddening. Black women's multi-issue organizing strategies and different priorities were also major impediments to interracial cooperation among female antirape activists. But other challenges of working with white women were just as daunting. In her now classic 1979 poem, "What Chou Mean We, White Girl? Or, the Culled Lesbian Feminist Declaration of Independence (Dedicated to the Proposition That All Women Are Not Equal, i.e. Identically Oppressed)," Black lesbian feminist poet Lorraine Bethel captured the anger and exasperation that many African American feminists experienced working with white women. Bethel lashed out at even the well-meaning white feminists who expected Black women, especially lesbians, to add some color and diversity to white feminist projects.[2]

Despite the admonitions of white antiracist allies such as Anne Braden, who had helped to organize support for Joan Little during the rape-murder trial, too many white women displayed an unconscious racial myopia and/or racist blind spots that thwarted possibilities for multiracial antirape efforts. Of course, there were always some white women who were steadfast antiracist allies. When women did manage to reach across these divides, however, they were more likely to join multiracial coalitions and one-time events such as Take Back the Night marches. For example, a 1981 Take Back the Night event Washington, D.C., organized by the D.C. RCC, D.C. Feminists Against Pornography, and Saphire Saphos [sic], among others, announced: "We are women of all races, all ages, all classes, all backgrounds united and marching to stop violence against women." In Ann Arbor Michigan the following year, a Take Back the Night event proclaimed, "Fight Back—stop sexist and racist violence against women."[3]

White feminist Susan Brownmiller's resurrection of the Black male rapist myth crystalized the kind of white women's racism that outraged Black women and made interracial organizing, especially against sexual violence, so difficult. Brownmiller's 1975 monumental study of rape, *Against Our Will* (published the same year as Joan Little's rape-murder trial), was both widely acclaimed and came under scathing criticism from African Americans, and some whites, for her racist assumption that Black males were more prone to rape than other men.[4] Especially infuriating was Brownmiller's discussion of the 1955 Emmett Till lynching in Mississippi. Till was a fourteen-year-old teenager who was tortured and murdered for an alleged remark he had made to a white woman. Like the Joan Little trial, the case drew international attention. But unlike the Little case, the Till trial was widely excoriated after the two white men, who later admitted they had killed the boy, were acquitted by an all-white, all-male jury. Brownmiller acknowledged the historic race-sex taboo that allowed white men nearly unfettered access to Black women's bodies while Black men were lynched, often over false accusations of raping white women, and even for supposedly "insulting" a white woman. Brownmiller also critiqued discriminatory capital punishment sentences for African American men who were falsely convicted of raping white women.[5] She might have added that Black men's alleged "leering" at a white woman, known as "eye rape," could just as easily trigger a lynching as well as a death penalty conviction in a kangaroo trial derided as a "legal lynching" by critics. A Black newspaper editor from North Carolina summed up the injustice when he quipped, "The death penalty for that crime [i.e., rape] . . . is 'for Negroes only.'"[6]

Although she condemned Till's killers, Brownmiller maintained that the teen's alleged comment "should not be misconstrued as an innocent flirtation." Rather, the case was a contest between men over access to women's bodies, she claimed. (Never mind that Till was only fourteen.) "Till's action was more than a kid's brash prank and his murder was more than a husband's revenge," she insisted. "In concrete terms, the accessibility of *all* white women was on review. . . . It was a deliberate insult just short of physical assault . . . a last reminder to Carolyn Bryant that this black boy, Till, had in mind to possess her." Brownmiller closed her discussion of the case by trumpeting her newfound liberation from men's verbal street harassment. Previously meeting unwanted sexual taunts from men with a steely smile, she had overcome her guilt feelings left over from the Till trial, she proudly confessed. Now, fifteen years later, Brownmiller could meet men's sexist street remarks with "a fleeting but murderous rage."[7]

Brownmiller's gross insensitivity and blatant racism enraged scores of young Black women who had been moved by Till's murder to join the Black freedom movement.[8] It was not that African American women were indifferent or unaffected by men's verbal abuse. However, they had far less disturbing and sometimes even creative responses. A woman writing for the National Black Women's Health Project newsletter described how she dealt with men's street harassment: "As I walked through a group of men, I declared out loud, 'This is a hassle-free zone and I will tolerate nothing more than a simple good morning or how are you.' Shocked that I would initiate these remarks, they quickly stepped aside, agreed to my request, honored my request, and I moved on feeling good because I was respected in the streets." Although she conceded that men did not always respond in this way, she insisted that "men can be different."[9]

Many, if not most, white feminists likely did not share Brownmiller's perspectives on the Emmett Till lynching. However, Anne Braden was one of the few white women to publicly decry the author's racist stereotypes of Black men; and she tried valiantly to educate white feminists about the history of white supremacy and rape. Braden covered Joan Little's trial for the *Southern Patriot* and the *Louisville Defender*. Working with the Kentucky Alliance Against Racist and Political Repression and a coalition of feminist, labor, and civil rights groups, Braden helped to deliver a petition with over 1,000 signatures to the North Carolina attorney general, Rufus Edmiston, demanding that he dismiss the charges against Little. The Southern Organizing Committee for Economic and Social Justice, a multiracial organization with Black leadership that Braden also helped found, urged members and friends to organize Joan Little Week across the region to coincide with the start of her murder trial in July 1975.[10]

Born in Kentucky in 1924 and raised in segregated Alabama, Braden was one of the South's most ardent white antiracist activists. Describing her own politicization around white supremacy beginning in the 1940s, Braden explained how abandoning "the Southern way of life" had freed her. Her moment of liberation came in 1951 at age twenty-six, when she joined the campaign to free Willie McGee, a Black man falsely accused of raping a white woman and subsequently executed in Mississippi before a crowd of 700 cheering whites. During the Willie McGee campaign, Braden explicitly rejected anti-Black violence as a defense of southern white womanhood. She was jailed for the first time, and when a police officer learned she was a southern woman, he said she "ought to be shot." It was the beginning of her deliverance from the stranglehold of patriarchal white supremacy. She had crossed over, relinquishing much of her class and race privileges to stand in solidarity with the "other America." Both Anne and her husband, Carl, endured intense government repression throughout the 1950s and 1960s, suffering arrests, trials, and prison time for their civil rights activity. Despite being maligned and marginalized, sometimes even by fellow activists, the Bradens remained staunch antiracist supporters of the southern Black freedom movement for decades, Anne until her death in 2005.[11]

Braden believed that Brownmiller's analysis of Black male rape had "become a weapon for racism," whether intentionally or not. Although she was critical of the feminist author's treatise on the history of rape, Braden acknowledged the book's contributions and noted that Brownmiller was no more "racist than the rest of us who grew up white in a racist society." Of particular concern was Brownmiller's heavy reliance on the criminal justice system. Increased convictions were not the answer, Braden insisted. "Such proposals ignore the nature of a court system which discriminates against the black and the poor and a prison system which does not control crime but increases it," she warned. "Such solutions put us objectively in alliance with the forces of repression."[12] The antiracist crusader's critique of activists who proposed "law and order solutions" to the problem of rape was both timely and prescient.

Braden's most urgent message, however, was addressed to white women in the South. Braden penned two "open letters" to southern white women, one in 1972 prior to Little's trial, and another in 1977, following Little's acquittal and the publication of Brownmiller's book. She believed that southern white women were uniquely positioned to confront white supremacy and "build a women's movement that is not at odds with the black liberation struggle." This was true "because historically we've had to deal with the issue of racism before we could understand anything else."[13]

Braden's first letter was an appeal to white women to support Thomas Wansley, a Black Virginia teen falsely accused of raping a white woman and sentenced to death in 1962. The alleged victim was unable to identify him, winning Wansley a new trial; but he was again convicted and given a life sentence.[14]

By the time she penned her "Second Open Letter" in 1977, Braden believed her worst fears had come true. Despite the gains of the civil rights movement, racism had intensified, she said. As field organizer and then co–executive director for the Southern Conference Education Fund and editor of its *Southern Patriot* for over fifteen years, Braden had seen firsthand the violent suppression of Black activists and their organizations by both officials and vigilante groups like the KKK. Yet even as she chastised white southern women, Braden refused to separate herself from them. Her "second open letter" was a call to action to her southern sisters, "because I believe we have a particular responsibility to help reverse this trend."[15]

While Anne Braden applauded the women's movement for exposing the problem of sexual assault, she also feared that many feminists had made it almost impossible to "struggle against the racist use of the rape charge." She outlined the "horrifying pattern that pervades Southern history": rape was considered a crime only if the victim was white and the alleged attacker was Black, but virtually ignored if the victim was Black, "no matter who the attacker." She described the historic conviction, imprisonment, and executions of Black men on false accusations of raping white women and noted similar contemporary cases, warning that "the list is growing." White women, in particular, must engage in a two-pronged struggle against both patriarchy and white supremacy, Braden insisted. Otherwise, they risked becoming pawns in a system of oppression that exploited not only African Americans but white women too.[16] Thus, while she did not downplay the racial privilege that white women enjoyed, Braden exhorted white women, "for their own liberation," to join the fight to free Black men who were sentenced to death for unsubstantiated charges of raping white women. She urged her southern sisters "to refuse any longer to be used, [but instead] to act in the tradition of Jessie Daniel Ames," the white southerner who founded the 1930 Association of Southern Women for the Prevention of Lynching. Ames was an odd choice for Braden to invoke, for while the Texas women's suffragist was hailed as a civil rights activist for her outspoken opposition to lynching, Ames did not oppose racial segregation, which Braden vehemently condemned. However, Braden may have referenced Ames and the ASWPL to remind white southern women that their forbears had stepped out on a volatile and controversial issue nearly a half century earlier. In any case, few seemed to heed Braden's call. Some "couldn't bear the thought of defending any man accused of rape," she acknowledged. Yet she warned that if white feminists failed to support Black freedom, they would find themselves at odds with the African American community and used once again by "the most reactionary social forces."[17]

Of course, false rape accusations against Black men were not a purely southern phenomenon. In 1978, in Dorchester, Massachusetts, a section of Boston with a large Black population, Willie Sanders was falsely accused and tried on charges of raping a white woman. Sanders was a thirty-nine-year-old African American, married father of four. In the late 1960s he had migrated from Alabama and worked as a painter for a local real estate company. After his arrest, Sanders was held as a serial rapist suspect, despite the fact that he did not fit the description of the rapist and the rapes continued while he was in custody. According to the *Baltimore Afro-American*, a number of prominent white feminists joined the Sanders defense campaign. Sanders fared better than scores of other Black men who had faced similarly unfounded charges. After a nearly two-year prosecution, he was finally acquitted in 1980. However, the ordeal left its scars, and Sanders remained embittered by the false accusation and the irreparable damage to his family. In a Boston TV interview following the trial, he compared his mistreatment to the notorious Scottsboro Boys case, in which nine Black teenagers were falsely accused of raping two white women in Alabama in 1931; Sanders even noted that he had met one of the Scottsboro defendants. But he also decried northern racism, claiming it was worse than in the South; whites in the North seemed to think all Black men were criminals, he told the reporter.[18]

Braden surely understood that the North was hardly free of racism, as the Sanders case clearly showed. But as a white southern woman, she believed her struggle against white supremacy had to be in her homeland. Braden also recognized the challenges that antirape activists faced; and as a radical, she knew that real security was not possible without a major transformation of American society. Still, women could not fight rape in ways "that feed the fires of racism," she insisted. Where were all the white women who had rallied behind Joan Little when Delbert Tibbs, wrongly convicted for murder and rape in 1974, sat on death row in Florida, despite evidence that he was 150 miles away when the crime was committed? she asked. Braden warned that society was moving toward "police state measures in the interest of 'order' and an elusive security. That's why it frightens me when I hear women calling for 'law and order' solutions to rape."[19]

Angela Davis couldn't have agreed more. Davis and Braden worked together in the left-leaning National Alliance Against Racist and Political Repression, founded in 1973, where Anne was vice chair. The National Alliance, including its North Carolina chapter, was instrumental in helping to launch the Free Joan Little campaign. In her 1975 *Ms.* magazine appeal for Little, Davis urged her largely white female readership to understand that a campaign in defense of Black women rape victims "must be explicitly anti-racist." Too many white feminists and antirape activists, while well-meaning, were guilty of gross racial insensitivity that alienated African American women, Davis charged. "If black women are conspicuously absent from the organized anti-rape movement today it is, in large part, their way of protesting the movement's posture of indifference toward the frame-up rape charge as an incitement to racist aggression," she asserted.[20]

Some white southern women did make antiracism central to their feminist politics in struggles against sexual violence and in prison activism. To cite just two examples, Minnie Bruce Pratt and Mab Segrest were born in the segregated South and became nationally prominent lesbian-feminist antiracist activists and writers. Both traced their activism to the 1960s, all were active in North Carolina's Black freedom struggles, and they remain staunch feminist, antiracist, and LGBTQ activists to this day. While their political stances were not identical, they adopted an intersectional analysis that linked gender, sexuality, race, and global, anticapitalist politics.[21]

Minnie Bruce Pratt was born and raised in segregated Alabama. In the 1970s, she became president of the Cumberland-Fayetteville, North Carolina, NOW chapter that backed Joan Little during her rape-murder case. The local chapter also helped bring attention to the conditions at Raleigh's

Women's Prison in the 1970s, including the prisoners' 1975 strike. Working with Black women in Fayetteville, often in coalitions, local NOW members cosponsored antirape events; and well into the 2000s, Pratt continued to organize and attend antirape Take Back the Night Marches. In 1978, as a graduate student at the University of North Carolina at Chapel Hill, she joined the *Feminary* magazine collective in Durham, founded by Triangle Area Lesbian Feminists.

Triangle Area Lesbian Feminists and *Feminary* were key supporters of both the Free Joan Little campaign and the Women's Prison strike in 1975. In the summer of 1978, *Feminary* announced its shift to a lesbian focus and an explicit commitment to antiracism: "We are committed to working on issues of race, because they are vital to an understanding of our lives as they have been, as they are and could be—and to an understanding and overcoming differences of class and age among lesbians as well." What was "so significant" about *Feminary* was that "we were all Southerners, and so dealing with racism was at the center of our agenda," Pratt recalled. "We were white Southerners, and it was at the center." In 1981, Pratt and Segrest coauthored a Womanwrites statement on racism and antisemitism; and in 1984, Pratt coauthored *Yours in Struggle: Three Feminist Perspectives on Anti-racism and Anti-Semitism* with Elly Bulkin and Black lesbian feminist Barbara Smith, a cofounder of the Black feminist Combahee River Collective.[22]

Like Pratt, Mab Segrest was born and raised in segregated Alabama. She attended Duke University as a graduate student in the 1970s and, like Pratt, soon found her way into the Durham-based feminist writing collective *Feminary*. In 1983, Segrest joined Black activist Christina Davis-McCoy to launch North Carolinians Against Racist and Religious Violence, where the two worked with a coalition of Black ministers and others to combat the resurgence of Ku Klux Klan and neo-Nazi violence in the state. As noted earlier, Segrest also taught a weekly writing class for prisoners at Women's Prison in the mid-1980s; a look at her curriculum indicates its less-than-subtle radical epistemology. In this period, Segrest worked with two other white southern LGBTQ activists, Carla Wallace and Pam McMichael, from the Kentucky branch of the National Alliance Against Racist and Political Repression, a multiracial alliance that boasted leadership by people of color. The Kentucky branch was a key supporter of Joan Little and, tellingly, both Wallace and McMichael were mentored by Anne Braden. In 1993, Segrest, Wallace, and McMichael joined Suzanne Pharr, another white southern lesbian feminist who had helped to organize a multiracial conference on domestic violence, and Mandy Carter, a Black Durham-based LGBTQ activist. Together they created Southerners Organized on New Ground (SONG), a multiracial, social justice organization that integrated LGBTQ liberation into various southern freedom struggles. The following year, in 1994, Segrest published *Memoir of a Race Traitor: Fighting Racism in the American South*.[23]

Unfortunately, little of the multiracial organizing history of these southern white antiracist feminists, especially lesbians, is well-known beyond activist circles. Like Black feminists, whose history has often been similarly obscured, white LGBTQ antiracists like Segrest and Pratt—among others—have worked in the trenches for over half a century, formulating a broad vision of social justice and struggling to create a more inclusive social order, particularly in the South. While sexual violence was not always their primary concern, their commitment to building intersectional movements linking the multiple ways that vulnerable communities are harmed, especially by white supremacy, violence, poverty, sexism, homophobia, and transphobia, have remained central concerns.[24]

Southern antiracist allies were not the only white women to address the links between sexism, racism, and rape. Santa Cruz Women Against Rape, a socialist feminist group, articulated an analysis quite similar to Braden's. In a published "Letter to the Anti-rape Movement," the group warned, "It is crucial that anti-rape groups fight the racist myths, stereotypes, and institutions that are associated with rape. And the first step . . . is to stop supporting the criminal justice system because, no matter what our intentions are, the system is racist through and through. We cannot turn our backs to the racism of the system when a Black man is being prosecuted, and expect that same racism not to be used against Joanne Little, Yvonne Wanrow, Inez García . . ." Deb Friedman, a member of the Washington, D.C., Rape Crisis Center and founder of the Feminist Alliance Against Rape (FAAR), penned a 1978 article in the *FAAR Newsletter* on the relationship between rape and racism: "The discriminatory prosecution of black men for the crime of rape and the gross lack of sanctions against the rape of black women (by white men particularly) constitutes the reality through which black men and women view rape," Friedman asserted. In Milwaukee, after authorities remained unresponsive to the demands of 3,000 participants in a 1979 Milwaukee Take Back the Night march, the protesters organized another march the following year that explicitly addressed the issue of race and rape. The antirape activists pointed out that Black women and other women of color, as well as poor women, were more likely to be raped and less likely to be believed than middle- and upper-class white women. Police often harassed Black and Latino men under the guise of searching for rapists, the organizers claimed; and African

American women were also racially profiled, leading to a high level of distrust between the police department and Milwaukee's Black community.[25]

Despite the challenges, some antirape activists throughout the country did manage to build fragile bridges across racial, ethnic, class, and political divides. As feminist scholars have argued recently, looking at single organizations, especially majority-white groups where African Americans and other women of color were few in number or absent altogether, misses the diverse alliances that antirape activists sometimes formed.[26] Antirape *coalitions* were more likely to be racially diverse than individual rape crisis centers (RCCs). For example, in New York City, the National Black Feminist Organization and 100 Black Women joined predominantly white feminist groups in the Women's Anti-rape Coalition, started in 1973. The alliance successfully lobbied state legislators to repeal the corroboration requirement for rape cases in 1974.[27] In Boston, Black Women for Wages for Housework and Wages Due Lesbians joined the Rape Action Project to stage a 1979 street trial of Massachusetts governor Edward King for his failure to respond to their antirape proposals. In Chicago, the National Alliance of Black Feminists worked closely with the city's Northside Rape Crisis Intervention. The Black feminist group also joined a citywide antirape coalition, the Chicago Council on Crimes Against Women, and a coalition of Chicago women's groups to endorse a 1980 Take Back the Night march.[28]

Antirape activist Nkenge Touré believed that coalitions were the most effective way for white women to engage with women of color. She urged white women to focus on their own communities, but also to share their more abundant resources. "White women cannot be responsive or sensitive by coming into an established Third World community and trying to organize to meet the needs of the women who live there," she said.[29] In 1971, Kathleen Cleaver, a leading figure in the Black Panther Party, had expressed a similar sentiment. Women must unite across racial lines, "on the basis of being women, not on the basis of being Black women or White women," she said. However, because Black women's relationship to Black men (who were "colonized") differed from white women's relationship to white men (who were the "colonizers"), and because their problems were "so completely diverse," Cleaver maintained that interracial unity among women "will have to be on a coalition basis and not on an integrated basis. [Their problems] cannot possibly be solved in the same type of organization nor met by the same type of activity." Black radical feminist attorney Florence (Flo) Kennedy, who often worked with white feminists and helped to forge alliances between Black Power and feminist struggles, echoed Cleaver's challenge. At a fall

1974 University of North Carolina lecture in Chapel Hill sponsored by Black students and the Association of Women students, Kennedy called on Black and white women to work together to support Joan Little in her upcoming rape-murder trial. However, she also encouraged Black and white women to work separately within the feminist movement.[30]

Like Cleaver and Touré, Anne Braden understood that African Americans and other people of color needed their own organizations if multiracial coalitions were to be effective. "Principled black-white coalitions don't work unless there is a strong group in the black community first," she said. But she also was wary of all-white groups since "white people are not oppressed as white people. That is the difference." Perhaps most important, Braden insisted that any interracial coalition must not be white-dominated or white-led. In a 2001 interview she asserted, "We need more whites who are willing to take action and to serve in organizations with people of color in the leadership. Those of us who are white have to be careful that we aren't trying to dominate. We are so used to running things." Despite the difficulties, the veteran organizer remained ever-optimistic. "To build multi-racial organizations in a racist society is virtually impossible. Impossible means it just takes a little longer," Braden said. "I tell people not to get discouraged if they try and fail, to try again."[31]

Establishing a multiracial rape crisis center, rather than a diverse coalition, may have been more difficult, not only for the reasons cited earlier. Peer counseling was a mainstay of early feminist RCCs; it was also one of the reasons their staff insisted on female counselors. Few if any dealt directly with the rape of men and boys. However, the Chapel Hill–Carrboro, North Carolina, Rape Crisis Center—which opened days after Joan Little turned herself in to authorities in September 1974—had male counselors for men who had close relationships with rape victim-survivors.[32] Peer counseling was appropriate in light of the extreme violation and trauma sexual assault victims experienced; and it gelled with the collectivist and nonhierarchical politics of feminist RCCs. Within this context, identity politics also made sense. Having a counselor of one's own race, culture, sexual orientation, gender identity, and/or class was potentially one less hurdle for rape survivors to navigate. Yet this cut both ways. For example, Black rape counselors in California feared that white women rape victim-survivors were reluctant to talk to them because they weren't white.[33]

Whether or not white feminists, including antirape activists, heeded Anne Braden's entreaties to make antiracism central to their efforts, Black feminists influenced various iterations of women's liberation more broadly.

The Combahee River Collective, whose members were not separatists and worked cooperatively with a wide range of women's groups and mixed-sex organizations, adopted a framework that addressed the overlapping and simultaneous oppressions in people's lives and the multiple concerns of African American women, their families and their communities. According to sociologist Benita Roth, the Combahee River Collective's "vision and activities—and those of other 'vanguard center' Black feminists—were never intended to stop at the borders of their groups, but were intended to be models for transforming the entire world."[34] In fact, the collective's 1977 "Statement" continued to shape Black feminist politics—and much feminist theorizing generally—well into the twenty-first century.[35]

18

The State Is in No Way Our Ally

Race, Sexual Violence, and the Dangers of Carceral Solutions

The Third World woman "is a nonentity with no rights in the American criminal justice system," announced Black feminist Loretta Ross in her keynote address at the 1980 First National Conference on Third World Women and Violence. Ross implicitly challenged the "every woman can be raped" mantra of much of the feminist antiviolence movement, which obscured racial differences. Women of color were "1.7 times more likely to be raped than white women," she claimed, and they made up 83 percent of the female prison population. Turning to law enforcement or the courts for protection or redress was not a viable option for most women of color, Ross added.[1]

Black women and other women of color figured in many of the pathbreaking legal victories against sexual abuse in the 1970s. Yet these achievements did not prevent more radical antirape activists from developing a broader critique of the criminal legal system or from questioning carceral solutions to violence against women. At the 1980 conference, participants pointed to the trials of Joan Little, Yvonne Wanrow, Dessie X. Woods, and Inez García, noting how each "exposed the injustices of the criminal justice system as it related to Third World women." They understood that even the limited victories in the four high-profile cases were anomalies and that most Black women and other vulnerable populations did not fare so well in the courts.

Nevertheless, these cases continued to spark dialogue among antirape activists about the relationship of the women's antiviolence movement to what would soon be called the prison-industrial complex and later the carceral state. Feminists across lines of race and politics also grappled with the dilemmas of redefining rape as violence rather than sex, and of accepting government funding for rape crisis services.[2]

Participants at the Conference on Third World Women and Violence questioned the supposed benefits of "more prisons, longer sentences, and increased convictions" for convicted rapists other than penalizing the "most disadvantaged of offenders."[3] Nkenge Touré, who worked with Ross at the Washington, D.C., Rape Crisis Center, acknowledged that "historically we (Black people) don't call the police." While urging attendees to find alternatives to penal remedies, she added, "If I'm not going to call the police, I want you all (the community) to get out there and kick his (the rapist's) ass." Yet this was not a rallying cry for vigilante violence. Instead, Touré, who was a rape survivor, challenged Black men, particularly Black activist men, to take seriously the sexual abuse of Black women. "It's a cop-out for our brothers to use racism to make us feel bad," she said.[4]

Recognizing the need for women's safety and security, however, some Black women, including feminists, reached out to Black police officers. In Chicago, the National Alliance of Black Feminists supported the Afro-American Patrolman's League discrimination lawsuit against the Chicago Police Department. The women hoped the League would work with their group "on criminal problems, especially in the area of rape." Similarly, in 1974, Ethel Payne, renowned African American columnist for the *Chicago Defender*, helped found the Coalition of Concerned Women in the War on Crime; the group called for the city to hire Black policewomen in order to assist African American rape victims. A three-month investigation by the *Chicago Sun-Times* in 1982 reported that rape in the Black community was a "plague." The investigation also found that in twenty-one of Chicago's suburbs, women faced a higher risk of being raped than in the city; and that aid for rape victims, especially Black women, was "sorely lacking." Noting that 75 percent of rape victims in Chicago were African American women, the National Alliance of Black Feminists (NABF) announced that it was "very dissatisfied with the way rape victims are treated by the hospitals, the power structure in the police department, and the courts." Police too often treated Black women in particular as if *they* were the criminals. Indeed, the racist stereotypes that had followed Joan Little were not simply a southern phenomenon. As the NABF explained, "When the victim happens to be Black, it is often assumed she is a prostitute." According to one African American female, "Young black girls are gang-raped every day, but no one gives a damn. It isn't sensational news when it happens to us."[5]

Securing protection against sexual violence and accountability for perpetrators without relying on the criminal punishment system was no easy task. There was a central contradiction as well as unintended consequences in the feminist redefinition of rape as violence. By recasting rape as male dominance and violence against women, rather than sex, antirape activists further criminalized rape and increased state involvement. After all, crime control and prevention were major government functions. But greater reliance on state power and resources was problematic for feminists who viewed cooperation with male-dominated institutions as a sellout and who feared that their feminist goals of female empowerment would be co-opted.

Black women had even greater reason to fear heightened state involvement. Historically, they had felt the long punitive arm of the state from involuntary medical experimentation to intrusive welfare and child protection policies. Policing in the South emerged from slave patrols and the confinement of both enslaved and free African Americans. Following Emancipation, new forms of control and imprisonment targeted formerly enslaved men, women, and children. In the North, policing historically had been deployed to protect private property, control immigrants and Black migrants, and to suppress labor protest. Thus, turning to police and the courts for protection or justice often offered little hope of either for disadvantaged communities.[6] Indeed, Black communities' extensive history of police brutality, combined with police underprotection and oversurveillance and a discriminatory legal system, left many African American women wary of cooperating with law enforcement. For Angela Davis, the growing reliance of the antirape movement on the criminal punishment system was especially problematic: "Too many innocents have been sacrificially offered to gas chambers and lifer's cells for black women to seek aid from police and judges. Moreover, as rape victims themselves they have found little if any sympathy from these men in uniforms and robes."[7]

As we have seen, not all antiviolence feminists in the 1970s and 1980s, including white women, demanded law-and-order solutions for rapists. The Feminist Alliance Against Rape (FAAR), a national clearinghouse on antirape activism that covered the cases of Little, Woods, Wanrow, and García in its newsletter, also questioned carceral solutions to rape. Jackie MacMillan, a white founder of the Washington, D.C., RCC, pushed activists to envision alternatives to incarceration, and many of the contributors to the *FAAR*

Newsletter believed that increased convictions did little to ensure women's safety or end sexual violence.⁸

In the 1970s, the Coalition to Stop Institutional Violence (CSIV), a broad-based, multiracial feminist coalition in Massachusetts, similarly rejected the "tough on crime" approach to male violence. As scholar Emily Thuma notes, the CSIV was inspired by high-profile cases like Joan Little's and offered alternatives to the criminal punishment system that racial justice activists would later reenvision as "community accountability," "restorative justice," or "transformative justice" programs. The Massachusetts women proposed community-based projects "without the intervention of the state" modeled on food coops, rape crisis centers, battered women's shelters, and other grassroots undertakings. Women were to remain in control of such programs and female victims of rape and battering would decide treatment for offenders, who would "learn to live as neighbors in caring communities." Though utopian and perhaps unrealistic, their remedies tried to deal with the fact that imprisoned rapists and batterers eventually returned to their communities. However, the CSIV conception of "community" remained abstract, and members failed to address the possibility that modes of domination and hierarchy also could be reproduced in community-based models. Despite these shortcomings, Thuma concludes that the "CSIV's anti-incarceration activism engendered a feminist politics of violence and safety that set it apart from, and against, current agendas for more aggressive policing and punishment of male intimate violence against women." As feminists in Brooklyn's Women Free Women in Prison noted, "The state is in no way our ally in the struggle against rape and battering."⁹

Just as Angela Davis and Anne Braden had feared, turning to the state for solutions to violence against women, including the reform of rape laws, frequently created divisions between racial justice advocates and antirape activists. And Black intraracial rape was especially contentious. Catherine Jacquet has persuasively argued that proponents of racial justice who had historically sought protection for Black men falsely accused or excessively punished for rape were frequently pitted against antirape activists seeking protection for women against sexual assault. As historian Estelle Freedman noted, "How to extend legal protections enjoyed by white male citizens to African American men without undermining women's rights to legal protections" remained a central dilemma for many seeking both racial and gender justice. Even landmark antirape legislation was double-edged, once again underlining the contradictions in turning to legal remedies. For example, rape shield laws, which protected a rape victim from cross-examination about her sexual history, were hailed as a victory by antirape activists. But these prohibitions could also impede a defendant's right to due process, particularly if the defendants were African American men and the victims were white women.[10]

Even feminist anticarceral measures could be problematic. For example, many feminist antirape activists shared the NAACP Legal Defense Fund's opposition to the death penalty for rape. However, some white women opposed capital punishment, not necessarily because it was reserved for Black men, but because it led to so few rape convictions, especially when juries were reluctant to render guilty verdicts that carried a mandatory death sentence. Still, not all white women opposed capital punishment or other harsh penalties for convicted rapists. In 1973, Miriam Slifkin, a Joan Little supporter, president of Chapel Hill NOW, and head of the Orange County Rape Crisis Center, publicly endorsed castration for rapists. Four years later, Myrtle "Lulu Belle" Cooper Wiseman, a retired country music singer and rape survivor then serving as a Democratic representative in the state General Assembly, called for "public hanging" for rapists. It was a not-so-subtle racist dog-whistle evoking the lynch-mob history of the South that had targeted Black men who frequently were falsely accused of raping white women. However, feminists in South Carolina were quick to denounce a judge's suggestion that three Black men convicted of raping a Black woman be castrated.[11]

No wonder conservative politicians often backed rape reform legislation, though they couched their support in law-and-order rhetoric. Having demanded legislative reforms for years, many feminists jumped on board.[12] Some politicians even used rape survivors in election campaign ads to underline their tough-on-crime bona fides. According to Bevacqua, "The politics of law and order and the politics of rape intersected at all levels of governments."[13] But crime control, always racialized in the United States, landed disproportionately on the poor and especially on Black and brown bodies; and antirape activists, however unwittingly, often were complicit.

For battered women, legal remedies could be even more problematic, especially for low-income women and women of color. For example, laws mandating that police arrest accused batterers or that prevented women from dropping charges against violent partners or spouses could make a difficult situation worse. A particularly pernicious policy fined landlords and/or required them to evict tenants who made too many 911 calls. The practice was widespread in Milwaukee, where domestic violence calls outnumbered all other assaults. The local ordinance posed special burdens for impoverished African American women, who made up the largest group of evicted residents and whose abusers often did not live on the premises.[14] Even gender-neutral statutory rape laws, long advocated by some feminists, had the effect of linking teen pregnancy, statutory rape, and welfare dependency, with devastating consequences for adolescent youth of color. In this political configuration, enforcement fell disproportionately on poor women of color, especially those who chose to give birth and were welfare recipients.[15]

In light of these ramifications, African American women found it difficult to address intraracial rape and other forms of Black male violence and abuse. But this does not mean that Black feminists did not try. Byllye Avery raised the particularly delicate issue of incest and teen pregnancy. "These girls did not get pregnant by teenage boys; most of them got pregnant by their mother's boyfriends or their brothers or their daddies," she charged. "We need to talk to our brothers. . . . They need to know that when they hurt us, they hurt themselves. 'Cause we are their mothers, their sisters, their wives; we are their allies on this planet."[16]

Loretta Ross and Yulanda Ward, an African American member of the Washington, D.C., Rape Crisis Center Board of Directors, also sought to break the silence surrounding Black men's sexual abuse of Black women. In 1979, they organized a program on women in the Black nationalist movement, sponsored by the D.C. Rape Crisis Center. The event aroused considerable controversy among those who thought it exceeded the RCC's mission.[17] However, to Ross and other African American women, intraracial rape as well as other issues of sexism within racial justice groups made it appropriate for the RCC to sponsor the program.[18] One out of every four Black women was raped by a Black man, Ross claimed; yet too many Black women, including activist women, were hesitant to raise the issue. It "was not being discussed . . . anywhere in the so-called political revolutionary work we were doing," she said. "I mean how can you mount a revolution when your army is at war with itself?" The failure to oppose violence against women "can't do anything but undermine your revolution," Ross concluded. In a 1984 letter to *UpFront*, a Black women's newspaper in Washington, D.C., another woman voiced similar concerns. Noting that most rapes were intraracial, she called on Black men to step up. "White men may ultimately determine our employment status, health care options and educational opportunities, but Black men can vastly reduce the likelihood of violence against women of which street harassment is a part," she said. "We cannot afford to have millions of Black women suffering the aftermath of rape and Black families torn apart by spouse battering and incest. Black men can and must rise above the self-hate that causes such behavior so that we as a people can be fit for the challenges ahead."[19]

In many respects, historical timing exacerbated such difficulties. The women's antiviolence movements of the 1970s and 1980s corresponded with the emergence of a conservative political climate and a backlash against social justice movements and ever-more-punitive anticrime measures that reached new heights in the 1980s and 1990s. While the policing and containment of Black bodies was decades old, unprecedented federal funding for local and state policing through the Law Enforcement Assistance Administration in the 1960s and 1970s provided new incentives for increasing arrest, conviction, and imprisonment rates. Low-income communities of color frequently became the targets, escalating the nation's move toward mass incarceration and a more punitive neoliberal state even after LEAA was discontinued in 1980.[20]

Ironically, by 1974, LEAA had also become a major source of funding for rape crisis centers as politicians focused greater attention on fighting crime, including rape. The creation of the National Center for the Prevention and Control of Rape under the National Institute of Mental Health in 1975 provided additional federal funding for antirape efforts. However, the institute's funds were designated largely for research and demonstration projects, not for ongoing services.[21] Mary Ann Largen, NOW's Rape Task Force coordinator who provided assistance to Joan Little's legal team, worried that there was no community accountability for government agencies like LEAA. Moreover, RCCs were required to team with hospitals or police departments in seeking LEAA grants, diminishing grassroots antirape efforts and feminist goals of empowerment.[22]

By the 1980s, cutbacks in social services and huge increases in crime control funding under President Ronald Reagan's administration had both positive and negative consequences for rape crisis centers. Most important, the federal funding available for rape crisis services was more likely to come from criminal justice sources. As many RCCs had discovered, self-help, volunteering, and peer counseling, while personally empowering for the women involved, went only so far. Moreover, these strategies frequently had racial and class-based implications, leaving many centers struggling for financial assistance and enabling only the more privileged women to participate. Again, contradictions abounded. On the one hand, as Nkenge Touré noted, government funding, whether local or federal, made it possible for RCCs to hire lower-income women and women of color. In California, the Office of Criminal Justice Planning, which stepped in after Congress phased out LEAA funding in 1980, provided support for two new RCCs in the 1980s, the Rosa Parks Rape Crisis Center and the Compton YWCA Rape Crisis Center. Both were in predominantly Black neighborhoods in Los Angeles.

On the other hand, while government support was welcome in some quarters, state involvement also carried strains of punitive social control. As rape crisis centers became more mainstream and received government funding, they often were compelled to adhere to narrower modes of operation and service delivery. Dependence on government funding also brought government oversight, and the neediest women, largely financially burdened women of color, were frequently medicalized, pathologized, or criminalized by a coercive and intrusive state. Some scholars have argued that rape crisis services became more hierarchical and bureaucratic, leaving little room for oppositional politics and instead reinforcing conservative policies that fueled the growing carceral state.[23] For example, when government funding provided victim services, such as counseling, the state also began to redefine rape as individual, psychological trauma.[24] This was partly an outgrowth of the victims' rights movement, which drew support from the Department of Justice and its LEAA-funded 1972 National Crime Victimization Survey.

Adopting a rights framework over a needs-based model placed victims' rights in opposition to prisoners' rights and reinforced more punitive, carceral measures. As political scientist Marie Gottschalk observed, LEAA funding created a "very particular kind of victims' movement, one that viewed the rights of victims as a zero-sum game predicated on tougher penalties for offenders." In contrast, some other countries adopted a "care ideology" or needs-based policies, bolstered by a strong welfare state that substituted civil law for criminal penalties. Alternatives to harsh penal practices were rooted in the idea that crime victims should be sheltered by a state safety net and offenders rehabilitated. Under this model, which had its roots in prison abolition and was advocated by Norwegian criminologists, the neighborhood and other local groups become the primary locus for dealing with crime. Mediation, reparations, social services, and crime prevention replaced more punitive measures. Yet few if any of these approaches were adopted in the United States.[25]

The focus on victimhood also undercut the feminist analysis of rape as a social consequence of patriarchy and reinforced notions of female powerlessness and subjugation. To counteract the disempowering victimhood model, feminists adopted the notion of "rape survivor."[26] The shift in nomenclature did not sit well with all women. For African American women, the "survivor" image reinforced the trope of the "strong Black woman," and discouraged them from seeking help. Black women faced pressures to "strain up" or tough it out, rather than seek help. "I think our image has always been of [being] strong and persevering and you can take it all," explained Monica Williams, director of the Compton YWCA. For Byllye Avery the "strong Black woman" imperative was exasperating. "If one more person says to me that black women are strong I'm going to scream in their face. I'm so tired of that stuff." The notion of Black women's inordinate strength placed a destructive burden on Black women: "We give a lot, but we don't get much back. . . . We have to do what's necessary to survive," Avery said. "But most of us are empty wells that never really get replenished." Like Avery, Williams also understood that violence was interwoven with other pressing needs for African American women. But for Black women who were assaulted, "usually their first concern was their children, or their home or their husband, or how'm I going to make ends meet. . . . they couldn't see that they were hurting too," said Williams. According to scholar Moya Bailey, the "strong Black woman" imperative has taken a toll on Black women's lives and bodies for generations.[27]

A long history of neglect and abuse of African Americans by medical authorities also created widespread cultural and class-based suspicions of mental health and other professional services. However, the erosion of historical, more informal sources of support in churches, families, and communities, along with the creation of RCCs in Black neighborhoods with Black staff, did prompt more women to seek help.

Unlike many of the predominantly white RCCs, those serving Black women often went beyond single-issue advocacy. The Rosa Parks Rape Crisis Center offered multiple services to meet the varied needs of their clients, such as support groups for victims of incest and drug addiction. In Los Angeles, locating the rape crisis program at the Compton Y also made sense. Like the Rosa Parks RCC, the Compton Y linked various kinds of assistance that Black women frequently needed, including a food program, drug counseling, a jobs program, and support group for families of incarcerated people. By addressing the harms that disproportionately affected Black women, the Compton Y, implicitly if not overtly, promoted the national YWCA's "One Imperative." Adopted in 1970 and echoing Malcolm X's call for Black liberation, the directive committed the Y's "collective power toward the elimination of racism, wherever it exists and by any means necessary."[28]

Despite the difficulties, RCC workers and even some politicians found ways to subvert state bureaucracies and mold guidelines to meet the needs of clientele. Some were pragmatic. Monica Williams explained her relationship with the Office of Criminal Justice Planning (OCJP), which distributed federal LEAA block grants. "They're our funding source. I need them," Williams said. "Without them I don't have a job and 6 or 7 people don't have a job, and my community goes unserved." Maxine Waters, now a long-serving member of Congress from California but at the time a state representative, ensured that the appointments to the OCJP committee responsible for distributing funds came from the Commission on Women. Thus, many of the rape crisis centers in California that received government support had more independence than others around the country. They also had greater access to funding when their services were consolidated under crime control and expanded in the 1980s.[29]

There were other differences among states. For example, Massachusetts, where rape crisis programs were funded under social services, saw deep cuts. Across the country, federal and state cutbacks to social services devastated grassroots antirape efforts. According to some scholars, the overall impact of these changes was a dramatic co-optation of RCCs' feminist goals. Sociologist Nancy Matthews claimed that "rape became depoliticized in the sense that the feminist analysis of gendered power relations was removed from the picture. In place of the goal of ending violence against women, rape crisis services now helped the state to manage it." For women of color the consequences were contradictory: government funding sometimes provided crucial resources, frequently for the first time, to underserved communities, but not always in ways that met the multiple needs of rape victim-survivors. Moreover, state intervention too often criminalized women's poverty and reinforced the expansion of the carceral state.[30]

While many feminists of all races and backgrounds resisted these changes, antirape activists of the 1970s and 1980s faced a dilemma that had parallels in some of the Black anticrime efforts of the 1960s: how to secure protection without causing harm, especially to the most vulnerable. Feminist antirape and Black anticrime groups often came to regret the growing reliance on government funding and especially on the criminal legal system, which had unintended consequences, including the growing mass incarceration of Black and brown bodies. Not surprisingly, Black feminists were among the first to protest and theorize the contradictions of antirape activists' harnessing their efforts to the carceral state and the dangers of ignoring the long history of racialized sexual violence.

In fact, the crime control component, not government funding for services per se, most undermined the antirape movement. In the past, federal funding could and did politicize local communities. In the 1960s, the federal War on Poverty's vague requirement that local antipoverty programs incorporate "maximum feasible participation of the poor" had the largely unintended consequence of organizing, radicalizing, and mobilizing large cohorts of low-income participants, often African American women. Black Panther Party "survival programs," frequently dismissed as "service work" rather than "real" political activity, had similar results. Illinois Panther Yvonne King explained,

> When we developed survival programs, service programs, programs to meet some of the basic needs of the black community, it was done not because we believed we could answer [or] we could meet all of the needs of black people. No. It was done more as an organizing vehicle. Our survival programs heightened the contradiction that existed between the black people and the government. When we were able to feed thousands of children every morning in various cities in the country, parents began to ask, why wasn't the government doing that? The government had all the resources.[31]

The lure of federal money was often irresistible. Even the Panthers accepted Department of Justice funds through LEAA to support their sickle-cell anemia campaign.[32] Thus, providing services to underserved communities was not necessarily apolitical or even counterproductive, as some scholars have claimed.[33] However, the War on Poverty and the Black Panthers' survival programs emerged amid vibrant protest movements that also helped politicize the programs' clientele, especially low-income Black women.[34] In contrast, the 1970s and, especially, the 1980s witnessed a conservative backlash against various liberation movements, often targeting those concerned with racial and gender justice. Within this political context, antirape activists across lines of race, culture, and class made hard choices, struggling to meet the needs of victim-survivors as best they could.

Frequently inspired by the Free Joan Little campaign, Black women pursued creative ways to address sexual assault. The focus on rape crisis centers, rape hotlines, and the more visible and largely white feminist movements opposing violence against women, therefore, misses much of the antirape work of African American women in the 1970s and 1980s. Black women more commonly organized separately and outside of majority-white rape crisis centers, and they did so in a wide variety of groups that recognized the multiple needs of Black women, their families, and communities. Although many found working with white antirape activists untenable, some African American women participated in short-term multiracial alliances or coalitions, such as Take Back the Night marches.

Like generations before them, most African American women refused to separate antirape activism from battles against racism. Their capacious vision of justice often linked protection from sexual violence to demands for affordable and safe housing, adequate income, quality education, health care access, reproductive freedom, decarceration, and other daily survival needs. They knew that a holistic approach was the only sensible and effective way to confront the pervasiveness of sexual abuse. And Black feminists typically connected all these issues directly to the struggle for Black women's liberation. Their intersectional perspective, which placed antirape activism within the context of Black women's lived experience and an understanding of the complex and varied needs of victim-survivors, demands a rethinking of "second wave" feminism, especially feminist antirape activism. Black women's organizing against sexual violence in the 1970s and 1980s was a continuation of the long arc of African American women's protest against rape and other forms of violence. Examining Black-female-centered and even multiracial activism, rather than the predominantly white-focused women's antirape efforts of these years, more fully captures the ways African American women carried on the work of their foremothers who sought to both protect and empower Black women.

EPILOGUE

The 1994 Crime Bill and the Violence Against Women Act

Searching for Safety in the Carceral State

Though two decades separated the momentous decisions made in a single day that brought them national and international attention, Joan Little and Rosa Parks shared more than one might first assume. Both were African American women from humble beginnings, born and raised in the Jim Crow South. Both may have been subjected to sexual abuse by white men. Both women have become iconic figures, mythologized, sanitized and revered for their willingness to fight back against more powerful white men. Whether on a de jure Jim Crow bus or in a de facto Jim Crow jail cell, the two decided the time had come to stand up to white supremacist patriarchy. In Parks's defiant act of refusal and Little's lone act of lethal self-defense, they spurred a groundswell of protest among veteran activists and those who would join struggles for Black freedom and women's liberation. Their lives were linked again, though hundreds of miles apart, when Parks headed the Joan Little Defense Committee in her adopted city of Detroit during Little's rape-murder trial. And in the decades since, new iterations of Black women's activism against sexual assault, the carceral state, and anti-Black violence have arisen with new urgency.

Twenty years after Joan Little was indicted on a first-degree murder charge for defending herself against sexual assault, Congress passed the Violence Against Women Act (VAWA). Tellingly, the pathbreaking legislation was included as Title IV under the $30 billion Violent Crime Control and Law Enforcement Act, signed by President Bill Clinton. The 1994 Crime Bill established sixty new death penalty offenses, limits on prisoner access to higher education, and mandatory "three strikes" penalties. Two years later, Clinton signed the Personal Responsibility and Work Opportunity Act, his signature "welfare reform" legislation, which imposed a five-year lifetime limit on benefits and other requirements, effectively severing the nation's social contract with some of the most vulnerable and destitute. Unlike Lyndon Johnson, who had linked his Wars on Poverty and Crime three decades earlier, Clinton's crime and welfare legislation had little impact on either crime or poverty—although the assault weapon ban did reduce firearm homicide rates and the VAWA helped stem domestic violence. However, the Personal Responsibility and Work Opportunity Act shredded America's already frayed safety net, making difficult lives even more desperate, especially for single mothers in extreme poverty. The 1994 Crime Bill—which Clinton later acknowledged "made the problem worse"—augmented the mass incarceration of Black and brown bodies already underway and, together with his "welfare reform" law, enhanced the buildup of the carceral state.[1]

Despite its inclusion in the crime bill, the VAWA offered some important benefits for women and drew broad support. The law recognized the prevalence of rape, battering, and other forms of gender violence as social problems rather than purely private, individual matters. Passage also signaled an effort to create a national policy on violence against women.[2] Cosponsored by Senators Joseph Biden (D-Del.) and Orrin Hatch (R-Utah), the VAWA received wide bipartisan endorsement and backing from organizations across the political and ideological spectrum. NOW's Legal Defense and Education Fund helped to organize over 1,000 groups to support the bill. Despite serious misgivings, twenty-six of the thirty-eight Congressional Black Caucus (CBC) members voted for the 1994 crime bill that included the VAWA. Fearing more draconian measures, civil rights legend John Lewis reluctantly agreed to bring the federal crime legislation to the floor, though he voted against it. Nearly twenty years later, Black women legislators supported the reauthorization of the VAWA. However, the CBC also introduced a substitute bill that included alternatives to prison, as well as demands for investments in jobs, quality education, and drug treatment. Moreover, African American officials never relinquished their long-standing protests against police brutality and other forms of anti-Black state violence.[3]

The legacy of the United States as a weak welfare state meant that the 1994 Crime Bill was generous on punitive measures and stingy on services. Only $1.6 billion was allocated for rape and battering prevention through education, and for shelters and hotlines for rape and domestic violence victims. By contrast, $10 billion was allocated to new prison construction. Thus, rape crisis and battered women's services were still forced to rely largely on volunteers and private or foundation funding. The bill also neglected to include resources for women to leave abusive situations, making less affluent women especially vulnerable. Other provisions required states to create registries for sexual predators and allowed prosecutors to bring a defendant's sexual crimes into court proceedings.[4]

The VAWA may have drawn wide and diverse support, but critics ranging from far-right white women like Phyllis Schlafly (famed opponent of the Equal Rights Amendment) and the National Rifle Association, to the American Civil Liberties Union and prison abolitionists, have raised objections to the act over the course of its legislative history. At the time of its passage, the National Black Women's Health Project noted the law's limitations, especially for poor women and women of color: "Without mechanisms to eliminate the serious gaps in access to health care and legal advocacy services that separate poor women, particularly women of color, from more affluent white women, the VAWA fails to address the full scope of the problem."[5]

Critiques have also come from Black feminists and academics and other women of color, including legal scholars Kimberlé Crenshaw and Mari Matsuda (who called it a "deal with the devil") and sociologist and antiviolence activist Beth Richie. For years, women of color had argued "against investing too heavily in arrest, detention and prosecution as responses to violence against women," Richie observed. "Our warnings have been ignored, and the consequences have been serious," both for the feminist antiviolence movement and especially for women "who fall outside of the mainstream," she charged.[6] Still, Richie was careful not to understate the serious danger that women faced from sexual assault or other forms of violence. "I do think that people need to be removed from a situation where they're about to harm someone," she said. "But I think long prison sentences don't make people safe and they don't prevent violence," she added. For Richie, political reeducation was critical, although she acknowledged that this made it harder for people trying to figure out "what to do right now." Despite her criticism of the VAWA, Richie worried that if it were defunded, shelters, crisis counseling, and other resources for victims of gender violence would disappear.[7]

Its benefits notwithstanding, the Violence Against Women Act was perhaps the most ominous collaboration between the women's antirape movement and anticrime politicians. Some feminists—more so within the battered women's than the antirape movements and more often among white middle-class women—viewed the state as a neutral arbiter of social problems. Even more worrisome, was their failure to understand crime control as social control, with embedded class and racial biases. For example, aligning themselves with tough-on-crime conservatives, many initial VAWA supporters turned a blind eye to racial injustice by failing to back inclusion of the Racial Justice Act (RJA) in the 1994 crime bill. The RJA would have allowed appeals based on racial discrimination for death row inmates. According to political theorist Kristin Bumiller, acknowledging the failure to support the RJA is not so much a criticism of feminists as it is a reminder of the constraints under which activists sought realistic solutions to the epidemic of violence against women. But it is also a cautionary tale about the perils of making alliances with government power, especially within a "highly regulated state and a dismantled social welfare system." Violence against women poses special problems when balancing criminalization against women's safety.[8] Still, some of the most adamant critics of the relationship between feminists and tough-on-crime proponents have adopted sociologist Elizabeth Bernstein's 2007 notion of "carceral feminism" to denounce "the commitment of . . . feminist activists to a law-and-order agenda and . . . a drift from the welfare state to the carceral state as the enforcement apparatus for feminist goals."[9]

For poor women of color, statutes meant to protect women often did the opposite. Mandatory arrests and policies prohibiting women from dropping charges against abusers could lead to dual arrests (especially if women were defending themselves against violent attacks), loss of children, or other involuntary intrusions by the state. On the local level, reform of state rape laws beginning in the 1970s brought only a slight increase in prosecution and conviction rates in subsequent decades. And most of these reforms emerged in the context of repressive law-and-order politics. When cases do proceed to trial, victims often receive little vindication. Not only have convictions been rare, but, as Bumiller notes, rape trials often "construct misogynist theories about women and pornographic stories about defendants' motivations." Nor is there solid evidence that more punitive legal measures make women any safer. A 2007 analysis of FBI statistics found that mandatory arrest laws actually increased intimate partner homicides, especially for unmarried women of color. Perhaps even more disappointing, research has been unable to measure the impact of antirape movements on actual violence rates.[10]

Of course, some feminists across lines of race, both then and now, have refused to endorse penal solutions for sexual violence. A number of prominent white feminist historians, including Linda Gordon, Elizabeth Pleck, and Judith Walkowitz, warned about the dangers historically posed to women from punitive legal solutions to rape.[11] As one feminist criminologist charged, the VAWA was "completely antithetical to anything that would be advocated by feminist criminology." Karen Tronsgard-Scott, executive director of the Vermont Network Against Domestic and Sexual Violence and a white lesbian from a working-class family, acknowledged the drawbacks of the VAWA: "The law was all about building our relationship to the criminal legal system so it could do a good job. That had really good and really terrible consequences." But too many survivors were excluded, and two-thirds of VAWA funds are allocated to the criminal legal system. "In order to access the services, you had to have the prosecution," she explained.[12]

In 2002, several years after Congress passed the VAWA, the Ms. Foundation convened a roundtable, "Safety and Justice for All: Examining the Relationship Between the Women's Anti-violence Movement and the Criminal Legal System." Academics and antiviolence activists, including Beth Richie, legal experts, and opponents of mass incarceration explored the impact on Black women and other vulnerable groups of overreliance on the criminal justice system for solutions to violence against women. In a subsequent report, the Ms. Foundation noted that no single policy works for all women. For example, increased legal advocacy reduced the likelihood of violence for married white and Black women but increased the potential for harming unmarried African American women. Thus, even well-intentioned state interventions posed myriad problems for women of color and other vulnerable groups. Alternatives to the criminal legal system, including community-based efforts, also were no panacea for ensuring women's safety from sexual abuse and other forms of violence. The two-day gathering ended with more questions than solutions, "perhaps even more frustration than inspiration." Yet participants urged the women's antiviolence movement to adopt a number of changes: First, the movement needed new leadership, particularly from Black, Indigenous, and other women of color. Second, single-issue advocacy would be ineffective. Finally, protection for women could be achieved only within a "broader context of safety and justice for all" and a comprehensive agenda that included investments in education, employment, housing, and other basic needs. This was the approach that scores of African American women had long advocated.[13]

Since passage of the VAWA, growing numbers of feminists have become more skeptical about carceral remedies to violence against women. Many have turned their attention to incarcerated women and the millions of other women—wives, sisters, girlfriends, mothers, or daughters of imprisoned men—"entombed in the carceral state." Others have turned toward nonpunitive solutions, such as restorative justice.[14] Yet according to most researchers, restorative justice and community-based alternatives to incarceration remain problematic. As Bumiller explains, these are suitable only "when tangible community support and resources back their processes." Antiviolence activists and prison abolitionists, like Mariame Kaba, have expanded this notion by calling for investments in communities rather than policing and prisons, and they often promote transformative rather than restorative justice, arguing that the latter fails to address the conditions that foster violence.[15]

Some proponents of the VAWA and the 1994 crime bill claimed that the harmful effects of the legislation were not deliberate. Disregarding the damage legislation or public policies wreak on African American communities, however, cannot merely be excused by labeling these "unintended consequences." Rather, such "blind spots" must be understood as furthering the institutionalization of racial bias and discrimination. According to a recent report from a roundtable sponsored by the Office of Violence Against Women, which included Beth Richie, "When decision makers in the criminal justice system are unaware of or allowed to include their biases in their decisions about the fate of Black women or girl survivors . . . violence against Black women and girls is perpetuated."[16]

Reauthorized four times since 1994, most recently in March 2022, the VAWA has been amended and expanded to include the federal government's more expansive definition of rape, as well as dating violence, stalking, and requirements for reporting when victims were targeted by gender identity, national origin, or other forms of bias. Despite the law's name, the text is gender-neutral, although there has been debate about how well it protects male, transgender, and gender-nonconforming victims of sexual violence. However, the 2022 reauthorization increased services and support for survivors from underserved and marginalized communities—including support for LGBTQ+ survivors of intimate-partner violence, dating violence, sexual assault and stalking; funding for survivor-centered, community-based restorative practice services; and increased support for culturally specific services and services in rural communities. Housing assistance and some protections for immigrant and Indigenous women have also been added. However, the VAWA remains within the Department of Justice, and the most recent reauthorization ramped up criminal justice responses. It is not the vision promoted by feminist antiviolence prison abolitionists. Instead of relying so heavily on "carceral strategies," Richie would prefer "abolitionist solutions" that address "the power imbalances that breed gendered violence through guaranteeing housing, employment training, childcare, food services, health care." Richie believes we need to think more creatively: "There are many well-meaning advocates who are deeply committed to the work of liberation and freedom," she said. "But we've been limited in our imagination, and we have to think and build beyond the current system that's more likely to criminalize than help survivors."[17]

The VAWA has not been the only legislative disappointment. For example, the 2003 Prison Rape Elimination Act (PREA) promised to protect all prisoners from sexual abuse, regardless of gender. However, Republican opposition weakened and delayed implementation until 2012, and even then compliance by corrections facilities was voluntary. Moreover, the law has been used mostly against consensual sex among prisoners, making LGBTQ prisoners especially susceptible to exploitation and danger under the PREA. According to a recent report on the PREA, "Rape continues unabated inside our nation's correctional facilities." Nearly a half century after Joan Little was sexually assaulted by her white male jailer, "there is no evidence that the new rules have reduced the gender-based and sexual violence against incarcerated people that is perpetuated most frequently by correctional staff. Yet it is clear that the regulations have increased punishment of incarcerated people."[18] Violence, including sexual assault, against impoverished African American women remains a pressing problem, both in prison and in the larger society.

North Carolina's prison system faces its own challenges. There are no law libraries in the state's prisons, jailhouse lawyers are a rarity, and legal services for the thousands of prisoners who seek assistance are understaffed and underfunded by the state. In 2009, North Carolina passed its own Racial Justice Act, permitting death row prisoners to reduce their sentences to life imprisonment without parole if the sentences were found to be racially biased or if African Americans had been excluded from juries. However, the following year, Republicans gained a supermajority in the legislature and immediately weakened the RJA, then repealed it entirely in 2013. The lawmakers made the repeal retroactive, sending prisoners who had gained a reprieve back to death row and prompting litigation against the retroactive repeal for over seven years. In June 2020, the North Carolina Supreme Court, largely due to Chief Justice Cheri Beasley, the first Black woman to hold the top position in the state, vacated the retroactive provision. Although the RJA was not restored, prisoners who filed an appeal in 2009 were able to proceed with their cases. Currently, 130 of the state's death row prisoners, or about 90 percent of the total number on death row, are legally permitted to file appeals based on race. If they succeed, they will be eligible only for life without parole (LWOP). As one observer lamented, "At best, LWOP is a muddled victory against racist prosecution. At worst, it's silent execution."[19]

Despite the obstacles and setbacks, calls for racial and gender justice from Black and Indigenous women and women of color have not abated. Many of the women featured in these pages have continued to bring their energy, creativity, and capacious understanding of women's needs to the struggle against sexual violence. In 1989, Dazon Dixon Diallo became founding president of SisterLove, the first women's HIV-AIDS and reproductive justice organization in the Southeast. In 2001, she opened a SisterLove program in South Africa. A board member of the National Women's Health Network, she also is a member of In Our Own Voice: National Black Women's Reproductive Justice Agenda Partnership; and for twenty years, Diallo hosted a local radio program, *Sistas' Time*, in Atlanta.

Byllye Avery has maintained her work on behalf of Black women's health and reproductive justice in the United States and globally. She has been an adviser at the National Institutes of Health and is a cofounder of Raising Women's Voices for the Health Care We Need. In 1989, Avery received a MacArthur Foundation "genius" grant for her pioneering work on behalf of Black women's health. In 2002 she established the Avery Center for Social Change in Harlem to promote health care for everyone.[20]

As if coming full circle, many of the women who had worked with the National Black Women's Health Project helped to start the SisterSong Women of Color Reproductive Justice Collective, a southern-based, national membership organization. Founded in 1997 in Atlanta, its African American, Latinx, Native American, and Asian American members have built a network of organizations promoting reproductive justice policies to improve the conditions of marginalized communities. SisterSong's intersectional framework brings together the myriad concerns that Black women have *always* connected, from abortion rights and contraception to prenatal care, a living wage, and women's right to physical safety. Byllye Avery's vision has lived on and the work continues.

Nkenge Touré also has been active with SisterSong and currently works with women substance abusers, women and babies living with HIV-AIDS, and women in transitional housing. After leaving the Washington, D.C., Rape Crisis Center in 1988, she hosted *In Our Voices* on a local Washington,

D.C., radio station, showcasing women's issues in the nation's capital. From 1987 to 1994, she served as president of the local chapter of the National Black Women's Health Project; and she has been a board member of both My Sister's Place, a shelter for battered women, and the National Center for Human Rights.

Like Touré, Loretta Ross also joined SisterSong, becoming national coordinator from 2005 to 2012. Earlier, she worked with the National Organization for Women, launching the group's the Women of Color Program in the late 1980s. In 1990 she became program research director for the Center for Democratic Renewal / National Anti-Klan Network, researching hate groups and working against all forms of bigotry. In 1996, she founded the National Center for Human Rights Education in Atlanta. A leader in the reproductive justice movement, she was national codirector of the 2004 March for Women's Lives in Washington, D.C., the largest women's protest march at that time, with over 1 million participants. Currently she runs her own consulting firm, Lorossta Consulting LLC, sharing what she has "learned as a professional feminist," especially with Black women and other women of color, in the hope that others will "join our human rights movement that has rocked the world."[21]

Other African American women have protested the expanding carceral state, frequently linking the struggle against sexual violence to other forms of state violence. In 1993, following famed boxer Mike Tyson's appeal of his conviction for the rape of Desiree Washington, Black feminists in St. Louis organized a mixed-gender coalition to protest intraracial sexual assault in the Black community. While calling for protection of African American women from sexual assault, the women also drew attention to the perils of incarceration for Black men.[22]

In 1995, African American scholar and activist Ruth Wilson Gilmore cofounded the California Prison Moratorium Project and No More Prisons to halt additional prison construction and press for alternatives to incarceration; in 1998, Gilmore joined with Angela Davis to form Critical Resistance, which seeks to build a mass movement for decarceration. Two years later, Critical Resistance helped to spur INCITE! Women of Color Against Violence (since shortened to INCITE!). The organization emerged from a 2000 conference, initially designed for a small group of activists "fed up" with the failure of "racial justice *and* anti-violence organizations" to incorporate an intersectional analysis that addressed the full range of the needs of women of color. The INCITE! conference drew 2,000 participants and turned away 2,000 more. Like Byllye Avery's 1983 conference on Black women's health, planners had clearly struck a nerve. Local chapters and affiliates have spread across the country, and INCITE! activists have continued to meet at national gatherings, sharing strategies for ending state, community, and interpersonal violence simultaneously. To date, their work has spurred several anthologies and a politics that Angela Davis has called "abolition feminism."[23]

Despite their perseverance, the challenges can often feel overwhelming. In a recent interview, prison activist Robbie Purner, one of the "outside" founders of the North Carolina Prisoners' Labor Union, noted the toll of decades of struggle and defeats. "If I sound discouraged, I am. I'm extremely discouraged." But she tempered her despair with the understanding "that organizing is not simple. A lot of people have died to preserve freedom and human rights," she said. "It's an ongoing battle. There will be advances and then retreats. Advances and then retreats."[24]

Organized protest, like the Moral Mondays Movement in North Carolina, which was created in 2013 under the leadership of state NAACP president Rev. Dr. William Barber II, has spread to a number of states. Moral Mondays and Repairers of the Breach, a nonprofit organization also begun by Barber, bring together multiracial coalitions of organizations and individuals that reflect the kind of capacious, progressive, multi-issue organizing that Black women have nearly always promoted. Even though Barber, a male minister, started both groups, NAACP branches in North Carolina and across the South have always been fueled by Black women, who frequently make up a majority of the membership; similarly, a majority of Repairers of the Breach members are Black women. In North Carolina, Moral Monday participants have engaged in civil disobedience and been arrested for their efforts to press criminal justice demands, such as the reinstatement of the state's Racial Justice Act, along with voting rights, antipoverty measures, environmental justice, and protections for LGBTQ communities, workers, and immigrants. In the summer of 2021, women from across the country, many of them poor and low income, organized a Moral Monday Women's March in cooperation with the Poor People's Campaign. The demonstrators converged on Washington, D.C., to protest the continued denial of basic freedoms, and at least seventy-five of them were arrested. "We aim to learn from history, not simply mimic it," organizers proclaimed.[25]

Despite the difficulties, activist voices and organizing campaigns have made a difference. "In a little over a decade, women of color involved in the anti-prison and antiviolence movements in the United States have radically transformed our understanding of violence against women and the most effective ways to combat it," scholar and activist Julia Chinyere Oparah noted in 2016.[26] Like Avery, Touré, and Ross, they have forged connections and analyses that link imprisonment, multiple forms of violence, including gender violence, to similar transnational struggles. In the United States veteran organizers and scholars like Angela Davis and Ruth Gilmore have underlined the links between global neoliberal economic forces and the rise of the carceral state. "In fleeing organized labor in the US to avoid paying higher wages and benefits, [corporations] leave entire communities in shambles, consigning huge numbers of people to joblessness, leaving them prey to the drug trade, destroying the economic base of these communities, thus affecting the education system, social welfare—and turning the people who live in these communities into perfect candidates for prison." Meanwhile the economic demand for prisons and carceral jobs increases. "It is a horrifying self-reproducing cycle," says Davis.[27]

But even in the face of trauma and criminal neglect by their government, survivors of violence and incarceration have offered new ways of going forward. Indeed, in the wake of police and vigilante shootings of unarmed African Americans and legal battles over armed self-defense, a new spirit of outrage, protest, and movement-building has spread across the country. Both local and national efforts abound as increasing numbers of young people, especially youth of color, have joined with veteran organizers in heightened demands for social justice. Black women have frequently been in the forefront of these movements. For example, Mariame Kaba, a prison abolitionist and sexual assault survivor, summons us to envision new forms of accountability for harm and violence. Collective struggle is her touchstone, as she cautions against the human impulse for punishment and revenge, which affords neither security nor justice. Some have questioned the proposition that sexual violence survivors should avoid turning to the criminal punishment system for protection or redress. However, Kaba reminds us that policing and imprisonment have never made women or Black people safer. A better question, she suggests, is why we have no other well-resourced options for safety and accountability. When challenged about restorative justice as a goal for sexual violence survivors, Kaba responds that such justice must be voluntary, not coercive. "If your goal is to end rape through a criminal legal process then I would say that based on the numbers, the strategy has already failed." Few women report rape and fewer than 3 percent of assailants will ever see a jail cell. "If you are working with survivors of rape and you are promising them 'safety' through a criminal legal process then you are actually doing more harm than any [restorative justice] process could ever do," she insists. "We can keep going in the direction that we have been or we can prioritize the desires and needs of many rape survivors and develop models for seeking accountability for the harm experienced and also focus on healing. This is what I choose to do."[28]

Kaba has helped to create numerous organizations to combat violence against girls and women and to abolish youth incarceration. Her organizing work provided the foundation for Assata's Daughters, established in 2015 by radical Black women and gender-nonconforming young people in Chicago. Formed in the wake of the police killing of Eric Garner and named after Assata Shakur, the group organizes against police brutality and fights for prison abolition and Black liberation "in the radical political tradition of Black feminism." More recently, the organization has expanded its efforts to educate Black boys and men about the dangers of toxic masculinity for men, women, and the larger African American community.[29]

Youth of color, including transgender youth, while standing on the shoulders of their activist forbears, have also challenged some of their elders' ways of thinking and organizing. Some have adopted new terminology. Discarding the term "women prisoners," they prefer "people incarcerated in women's prisons." Instead of working to abolish "violence against women," they prefer "harm against female-bodied and women-identified people." Similarly, prison abolitionists have replaced "criminal justice system" with "criminal punishment system." In response to Nehemiah, a group in Madison, Wisconsin, working locally with formerly incarcerated people, the new county sheriff agreed to substitute "residents" and "people in our care" for "inmates," since the latter term is seen by many as dehumanizing and demeaning. While these language shifts may seem awkward and cumbersome, they reflect an insistence on inclusivity, a challenge to binary systems that are oppressive to LBGTQ+ communities and incarcerated populations, and a more expansive vision of harm.[30]

Despite the odds, sometimes such efforts claim tangible victories. In Madison, Freedom Inc. promotes racial and gender justice among low-income and no-income communities of color, and it works with Black and Hmong teenaged girls, many of whom are sexual assault victim-survivors. After a four-year campaign and following local protests over the 2020 police killing of George Floyd in Minneapolis, Freedom Inc. persuaded the Madison School Board and City Council to remove cops from local schools. While losing the battle over a new county jail renovation, local activists did win a demand for a new mental health diversion program to substitute for incarceration; the county is also considering a community justice center to replace some court proceedings and provide educational, housing, peer mentoring, and restorative justice services. Another local effort is spawning a worker cooperative to support formerly incarcerated people, who have also been instrumental in creating the program.[31]

In Los Angeles, a multiracial coalition was successful in preventing the construction of a new prison. And the county has agreed to reduce its incarcerated population, diverting some to mental health and drug abuse treatment, and eventually to close the men's jail.[32] Scores of groups like these exist in communities throughout the country.

The emergence in recent years of the MeToo, Black Lives Matter, Say Her Name, and Black Voters Matter movements—all initiated by African American women, some of whom identify as members of LGBTQ communities—demonstrate the ongoing legacy of Black women's battles against pervasive sexual abuse, anti-Black violence, and an expanding carceral state.

Whatever promise these efforts may hold, violence against women, African Americans, and transgender youth of color continues; so does the disproportionate "caging" of Black and brown bodies and our tendency toward carceral solutions to social problems. Nearly a half century after the Joan Little trial focused attention on sexual violence, racialized incarceration, and the particular vulnerability of impoverished and imprisoned African American women, these problems have become ever more urgent. The United States is the world's leading jailer, imprisoning more people than any nation in the world, despite a falling crime rate. A disproportionate number of those in the criminal legal system—that is, in jails and prisons or under court-ordered parole or probation—are people of color. Black women are the fastest-growing prison population, the majority of them mothers incarcerated for nonviolent crimes; and the sexual abuse of women prisoners in the United States is rampant.[33]

After President Barack Obama signed the 2010 Fair Sentencing Act and the nation witnessed a slight decline in imprisonment between 2016 and 2018, the federal government under President Donald Trump embraced more punitive penal policies and a new enthusiasm for the death penalty. Although executions by states declined, the federal government carried out more executions in 2020 than it had in a century.[34] In January 2021, nearly a half century after Joan Little faced a possible death sentence in North Carolina's gas chamber, a fifty-two-year-old white woman with a long history of trauma, sexual abuse, and mental illness was executed at the men's prison in Terre Haute, Indiana. She was the first woman executed by the federal government in almost seventy years. While only 2 percent of those on death row and 1 percent of those actually put to death are female, according to the NAACP Legal Defense and Education Fund, close to fifty women await execution in state and federal prisons throughout the country. Like Little, most are portrayed as "deviant" by prosecutors and blamed for their past traumas or mental illness.[35]

The COVID-19 pandemic has exacerbated these dangers, wreaking havoc on communities of color and on those in jails and prisons. In October 2020, the ACLU filed a class-action lawsuit charging that the federal prison in Butner, North Carolina—fifteen miles north of Durham—with over 1,000 cases and seventeen deaths, is "the deadliest of all federal facilities."[36]

As of this writing, President Joseph Biden and Vice President Kamala Harris, the first Black woman vice president, have been in office less than a year and a half. Their victory was due, in large measure, to Black women's grassroots organizing, especially in "swing" states including Georgia, Michigan, Pennsylvania and Wisconsin. Promising to undo much of the damage wrought by its predecessor, the Biden administration faces enormous challenges. Authoritarian impulses and threats of violence from scores of elected and appointed officials at the federal, state, and local levels—as well as actual violence from some of their supporters—imperil our admittedly flawed and fragile democratic institutions, posing formidable obstacles to securing a more just and inclusive social order. Throughout the country, state legislatures have passed laws restricting voter access and bans against teaching about "divisive" issues. Scuffles have erupted at public meetings over the presumed teaching of critical race theory in K–12 grades; and school boards and local libraries censor books addressing slavery, white supremacy, the Holocaust, and LGBTQ themes. Perhaps the most dramatic and dangerous of these developments was the insurrectionist mob of thousands, including self-described white nationalists, that stormed the Capitol on January 6, 2021, hoping to halt the Electoral College vote tally for President-Elect Biden. The full extent of this unprecedented attack is still under investigation. But in its wake, retired generals warn of a military breakdown, analysts weigh the likelihood of armed civil conflict erupting, and pundits from across the political and religious spectrum preach the coming of Armageddon, given a new urgency in the wake of Russia's invasion of Ukraine and the potential for nuclear warfare. Hanging over these almost unimaginable forecasts, a global climate crisis and pandemic show few signs of receding.

The path forward is both perilous and uncertain. The politics of race, sexual violence, self-defense, and imprisonment remain as divisive and contentious as ever. And yet, a new generation, unrelenting and in partnership with seasoned activists, has embraced radical hope, beckoning us with ever-bolder dreams of freedom.

Postscript

In the summer of 2021, Joan Little and I chatted over sandwiches and iced tea at a well-known diner in a large urban area outside the South.[1] Nearly ten years had passed since our first meeting at the church of a distinguished Black activist minister. Understandably curious and somewhat wary about my request for an interview in 2012, Joan had brought her brother Malcolm "Mike" Williams and a friend along to the church. I offered some brief details about myself and my work; when I added that several of my family members had been sexually assaulted and imprisoned, Joan and her brother exchanged knowing glances. "I thought so," she remarked. I also shared that I had attended a Joan Little defense rally in New York City decades earlier. I was young and have only a dim memory of the event, but it was most likely during Little's extradition fight in 1977–78 following her escape from Women's Prison in Raleigh. In subsequent get-togethers over the years, I listened as Joan recounted the details of her life and her ordeal in the criminal legal system. In between, we have kept in touch through occasional short texts and emails.

Despite the toll of her rape-murder trial and the difficulties she encountered after leaving prison, Joan Little has built a rich and rewarding life for herself. Both intellectually sharp and politically astute, she is a warm, generous woman with an affable, easygoing manner, quick to find humor in situations others might shrink from.

But life has not been easy. Following her release from Woman's Prison in 1979 and her mother's death, Joan raised six of her younger siblings while still in her twenties. She worked for a short time as a clerical assistant for the National Conference of Black Lawyers in Harlem and then for at a

Brooklyn auto company. However, Little's prison record and the publicity from her rape-murder trial made it difficult to land steady employment, and she turned briefly to welfare to support her large family. At one point, she moved briefly to Arizona with a boyfriend. In 1981, Little was involved in a mysterious shooting in Brooklyn that landed her in the hospital but merited only a brief mention in the press. Years later, she explained that a spat with her boyfriend led to the accidental shooting. To protect him, she refrained from informing the police and pretended that she was the unwitting victim of an unknown assailant. Another arrest in 1989 for an alleged stolen license plate, gambling paraphernalia, and an illegal weapon (a box cutter or straight razor) seemingly resulted in no charges or jail time.[2]

When Joan was in her forties, she adopted the infant grandson of Jerome Little, the brother who had turned state's evidence against her during their 1974 felony theft trial. Ever-resilient and resourceful, Joan also secured medical training along the way. She has found personal happiness too and boasts a thirty-year marriage.

In the early 1990s, Little disappeared from a Black women's church luncheon just minutes before her scheduled talk and vanished from public view. In 2010, she resurfaced suddenly in a Detroit church at Danielle McGuire's public reading of her award-winning book *At the Dark End of the Street*, which includes a chapter on the Joan Little rape-murder case.

In a sense, Joan Little has come full circle. For the past twenty-five years, she has provided health care for incarcerated women. Bringing her keen intelligence, professional training, wit, and, perhaps most of all, her experience of imprisonment to bear, she finds the work worthwhile and rewarding, if also challenging.

Now in her late sixties, Joan Little certainly can claim a life well lived. But the trauma of her early years in the criminal legal system lingers just beneath the surface. For many years, she avoided returning to North Carolina. When Joan finally ventured South, she drove past the Wake County Courthouse where the threat of a death sentence had loomed over her. Seeing the imposing structure, gut-wrenching memories came flooding back and she burst into tears. The wounds of the past are not so easily put to rest.

Family harm lingers too. Some of Joan's siblings have only recently begun to share their own pain, and she is learning new details from them for the first time. On that summer afternoon in 2021, as we talked in the diner, Joan entered some numbers on her cell phone and put her brother Malcolm on speaker. He spoke freely about the impact of Joan's 1974–75 rape-murder case and the often-invisible scars left on family members of prisoners. Malcolm recalled the hostile whites who terrorized them during and after the trial. One evening, a frenetic scrum of reporters and local whites descended on the family house in Chocowinity, a tiny town just outside of Little Washington. Fearing for their safety, Joan's stepfather, Arthur Williams, grabbed a rifle and chased the intruders off the property. At school, Little's brothers and sisters faced resentment and harassment from family members of the slain jailer, Clarence Alligood. Many more painful stories likely remain, perhaps shrouded in silence forever. In spite of the family's ordeal, Malcolm was quick to add that Joan's high-profile case, ironically, had also saved them. "You got us out of Little Washington, sis," he said. "You gave us a chance for a different life."

Whether Joan Little was "just like Rosa Parks," as her defense counsel claimed nearly a half century ago, is beside the point. Who among us can measure up to the iconic heroine, sanitized, and frozen in time? Like the clarion calls of the Black Lives Matter, MeToo, and SayHerName movements, Joan Little's life mattered then and matters still. "I Am Somebody!" Joan insisted from behind bars. Her defiance prevailed against overwhelming odds and the state of North Carolina that sought her execution for defending herself against sexual violence. Without Little's own riveting courtroom testimony, and the courage to subject herself to what most sexual assault survivors cannot bear to endure, her trial might have ended quite differently. Much of the credit for her acquittal also belongs to a well-financed defense team and the mass-based Free Joan Little campaign that inspired antirape and prison activists then and continues to do so today.

There have always been, and still are, countless, unknown Joan Littles, many of whom have endured sexual violence on both sides of the prison walls, long sentences for self-defense, and worse. For prison abolitionist and rape survivor Mariame Kaba, "History is instructive, not because it offers us a blueprint for how to act in the present, but because it can help us ask better questions in the future." Over a century ago, W. E. B. Du Bois penned an exhortation reminding us of our collective responsibility to address injustice. His appeal is as urgent now as it was then: "The burden belongs to the nation, and the hands of none of us are clean if we bend not our energies to righting these great wrongs."[3]

ACKNOWLEDGMENTS

If it takes a village to raise a child, it can take multiple villages to write a book. I have spent over a decade researching and writing this book and I owe an enormous debt to scores of people who helped and inspired me along the way.

First, of course, this would have been a very different book without Joan Little. There are no words to adequately express my appreciation for the countless hours Joan spent sharing her experiences with me. Joan's generosity, courage, and good humor eased the challenges of delving into such fraught material. That I met Joan was serendipitous. I have the friendship and collegiality of Danielle McGuire, whose masterful *At the Dark End of the Street* informed my study, to thank. When Joan appeared unannounced at a reading of Danielle's book in a Detroit church, Danielle gave her my name and assured her she could meet with me. I am deeply grateful to them both.

The activists who relentlessly organized against racism, sexual violence, and the injustices of the criminal punishment system, both historically and today, and the scholars who have documented their efforts, form the bedrock for this book. Without their work, much of it cited in footnotes and the bibliography, this book would not have been possible.

Cherished friends and colleagues sustained me and gave me constructive criticism on multiple drafts, conference papers, book and fellowship proposals, and articles. They all made this a much better book, though any lapses or errors are mine alone. Bill Chafe, Mary Ellen Curtin, Suzanne Desan, Kirsten Fisher, Barbara Forrest, Estelle Freedman, Kali Gross, Nancy Hewitt, Annelise Orleck, Heather Thompson, Tim Tyson, Anne Valk, Rhonda Williams, and an anonymous reader for the University of North Carolina Press offered astute insights and suggestions. I have had the good fortune to have Thulani Davis as a friend and colleague, an accomplished writer and cultural worker who reinvented herself as a historian and decided to come to the University of Wisconsin. She soon started a writers' group, the Fundis (from the Swahili *funda*, meaning to teach or learn); our discussions and the written comments from Christy Clark-Pujara, Thulani Davis, April Haynes, Brenda Gayle Plummer, and Ethelene Whitmire were priceless. Thanks to Brenda, who provided the final tweak on the book title. Other colleagues in the University of Wisconsin–Madison Afro-American Studies, History, and Gender and Women's Studies Departments gave welcome advice along the way. Not least of those is Craig Werner, generous editor and scholar of African American culture and history par excellence, who read the manuscript twice. Steve Kantrowitz gave advice on lodging for an early research trip to Boston and language for the best sentence on Indigenous peoples in chapter 1. Drinks, walks, and conversations with Steve, Simon Balto, Tim Tyson, and Pernille Ipsen all kept me going.

A winter walk and pep talk with historians Kirsten Fisher and Jennifer Morgan gave me the final push and encouragement to complete a long-overdue draft; and Kirsten read the entire manuscript in just days, providing helpful feedback. At a Rutgers University conference, Jennifer Morgan and Herman Bennett offered valuable insights as well.

The UW-Madison Institute for Research in the Humanities (IRH), the Center for Research on Gender and Women (CRGW), a Vilas Research Associates Fellowship, a Dean's Chairs fellowship and a sabbatical from the Afro-American Studies Department provided much-needed time off from teaching obligations; colleagues at IRH and CRGW seminars offered beneficial comments and support, especially Leslie Bow, Susan Friedman, Judith Houck, Janet Hyde, and Lynn Nyhart. At the University of South Florida, Sarah Lawrence College, and numerous academic conferences, participants asked thoughtful questions, helping me to think carefully about the difficult subject matter I was exploring.

No historian can conduct research without the assistance and expertise of dedicated archivists and librarians. I have had the good fortune to meet some of the finest in the profession, especially at the Wisconsin Historical Society, the Sophia Smith Collection, the Southern Historical Collection, and Duke Special Collections. Librarians at the University of North Carolina–Charlotte, George Washington University, the University of Illinois–Chicago, the Chicago Public Library, the Tamiment Library at New York University, and the Schlesinger Library at Radcliffe/Harvard also were kind and helpful.

Cynthia Bachhuber and Lisa Marine at the Wisconsin Historical Society provided last-minute crucial help on artwork. I owe a huge thanks to Vann Evans at the North Carolina State Archives, who did the same. Lee Grady at the Wisconsin Historical Society was also helpful; and Tanya Andersen at the UW Cartography Lab produced the North Carolina map. Graduate students in the Afro-American Studies Department, Robin Brooks, Vanessa Brown, and Shannen Williams provided valuable research assistance.

Tim Tyson and Perri Morgan, and Bill and Lorna Chafe opened their hearts and homes in North Carolina for my numerous research trips. Good ole boys Tim and David Cecelski accompanied me on my trip to "Little Washington," not sure a Yankee could properly navigate the rural South—never mind that I lived in the South for seventeen years and, thanks to David, served on the board of the Institute for Southern Studies in Durham for nearly a decade. They also gave expert advice on North Carolina history and culture (including the proper spelling of "wasn't," i.e., "won't"); and the best places to pick up some North Carolina barbecue if Tim's chicken wasn't available and, of course, some spirits to wash it down. Mary Ellen Curtin and Perri Morgan offered hotel rooms, good food, and great company on research trips to Washington, D.C., and Chicago. Lisa Watson, my oldest, dearest friend and "sister," provided food, shelter, her car, and unending good times on research trips to New York and Massachusetts.

The Duke Mafia and Feminist Tribunal (neither of which really exist and whose names shall go unmentioned) provided love, comfort, and both hilarious and sublime conversation over many years. Barbara Forrest and Suzanne Desan saw me through every personal crisis, fed me, introduced me to beautiful places for walks throughout Wisconsin, and cheered me on through every single part of this long process.

The editors and staff at the University of North Carolina Press are the best. Retired editor in chief Chuck Grench never stopped believing in this project, even when I finally sent him chapters just as he was heading out the door. Mark Simpson-Vos generously stepped in and took over, shepherding the book through the arduous process of turning a manuscript into a book, along with Maria García, Erin Granville, Brandon Proia, Lindsay Starr, and Dylan White. Mark and Maria patiently answered my endless queries and tolerated my technological incompetence. Erin went above and beyond in getting this through production. Rhonda Williams and Heather Thompson welcomed the book in their Justice, Power, and Politics series and provided careful readings and crucial suggestions. Alex Martin was a terrific copy editor and saved me from some embarrassing errors. I am grateful to them all.

For over four decades, Bonnie Johnson and I have spent hours—often late-night phone chats in between my trips to New York—collaborating and talking about Black women's history, and the meaning of interracial friendships and alliances. We met as graduate students years ago, eager to learn about women's history. Subsequently, we team-taught a free women's history course for a multiracial group of women activists at a social justice "school" in New York City, no longer in existence. Bonnie's brilliant and undercompensated work has gone largely unrecognized, first as the participant-historian of the 1970s Black Women's Retreat (a group that included pathbreaking women such as Barbara Smith, Audre Lorde, and Cheryl Clark); later as a trainer-consultant for multiracial nonprofits; and as an adult education instructor at the District 65 Labor College, the Cornell School of Industrial Labor Relations, and the City University of New York. I had the pleasure of sitting in on Bonnie's classes numerous times at all these places and witnessed how she touched the lives of hundreds of students, the vast majority working-class, adult women of color. They have benefited enormously from her knowledge of African American women's history and culture, and especially from her unique and radical pedagogy that seeks to empower, not simply to teach. This book is dedicated to her.

My family, including my five siblings—Stephen, Cathy, Susan, Chloe, and my late brother Jimmy—liked having a sister who wrote and taught about this kind of history, even if they weren't certain I would ever finish the book. My late mother and youngest brother, Stephen, braved an early Sunday morning Organization of American Historians panel to listen to a paper that became one of the chapters in the book. And my mixed-race nieces, Allie, Victoria, Tara, and Jennifer, were pleased that I undertook such a project. Ashley, Brian, and Damien, while not quite sure what I was up to, certainly thought it was worthwhile. Rachel Fon and Lyle Anderson, honorary family members, graciously forgave me for canceling holiday dinners so I could finish the book. I am thankful to them all for their faith in me.

Not a word could have been written without the unending love and support of "my boys," Jim Conway and Dylan Conway-Greene, who were forced to live once again with a seemingly never-ending book. They are my forever loves, first, last, and always.

NOTES

ABBREVIATIONS

ALFA Archives Atlanta Lesbian Feminist Alliance Archives, David M. Rubenstein Rare Book and Manuscript Library, Duke University
BP *Black Panther* (newspaper)
BWHI Records Black Women's Health Imperative Records, Sophia Smith Collection, Smith College Special Collections
CAB Papers Carl and Anne Braden Papers, Wisconsin State Historical Society, Madison
HHH Papers Hamilton H. Hobgood Papers, Southern Historical Collection, Wilson Library, University of North Carolina at Chapel Hill
JLC Collection Joan Little Collection, David M. Rubenstein Rare Book and Manuscript Library, Duke University
JRJ Collection James Reston Jr. Collection of Joan Little Trial Materials, 1975–1976, Southern Historical Collection, Wilson Library, University of North Carolina at Chapel Hill, https://finding-aids.lib.unc.edu/04006/.
LEAA Law Enforcement Assistance Act
LR Papers Loretta Ross Papers, Sophia Smith Collection, Smith College Special Collections
MBP Papers Minnie Bruce Pratt Papers, David M. Rubenstein Rare Book and Manuscript Library, Duke University
MS Papers Miriam Slifkin Papers, David M. Rubenstein Rare Book and Manuscript Library, Duke University
NABF Papers National Alliance of Black Feminist Papers, Carter G. Woodson Regional Library, Chicago Public Library
N&O *Raleigh News & Observer*
NBFO/NABF Papers National Black Feminist Organization / National Alliance of Black Feminist Papers, Special Collections and University Archives, Richard J. Daley Library, University of Illinois at Chicago

NCCCW North Carolina Correctional Center for Women (Women's Prison)
NCPLU North Carolina Prisoners' Labor Union
NOW National Organization for Women
NOW Papers National Organization for Women (NOW) Papers, Arthur and Elizabeth Schlesinger Library, Radcliffe Institute for Advanced Study, Harvard University
NT Papers Nkenge Touré Papers, Sophia Smith Collection, Smith College Special Collections
NWT *New Women's Times*
NYT *New York Times*
TJR Papers T. J. Reddy Papers, Special Collections and University Archives, J. Murrey Atkins Library, University of North Carolina, Charlotte
VAWA Violence Against Women Act

INTRODUCTION

1. Joan (pronounced "Jo-Ann") was spelled various ways—JoAnne, Joan, Joann—including by Joan herself. Out of respect for formerly imprisoned persons, I have chosen to forgo the term "inmate"—seen as demeaning by many—and to substitute "prisoner," except in rare cases.

2. Alligood was a farmer and former truck driver who worked as a night jailer. Rick High, "Relatives Pleased by Jury," *Carolinian*, August 23, 1975; "Editorial Viewpoint: Was Black Womanhood Liberated?," *Carolinian*, August 23, 1975; Exhibit A, Medical Examiner's Report, box 4, folder 4, HHH Papers. The Hobgood Papers were unprocessed when I initially consulted them, hence the inconsistency in citations. Rick Nichols, "Little Trial Testimony Begins," *N&O*; Cathy Steele Roche, "Medical Examiner Testifies Today," *Washington (N.C.) Daily News*, July 29, 1975.

3. Wayne King, "Focus of Slaying Trial Had Humble Origins," *NYT*, July 29, 1975; Richard Kluger, "Crime and Punishment," review of *The Innocence of Joan Little*, by James Reston Jr., *NYT*, December 18, 1977. Reston was living and teaching in North Carolina and covered the murder trial for *Newsday*.

4. Reston, *Innocence of Joan Little*, 55; Harry Golden, "Joanne Little and the Gas Chamber," *Chicago Defender*, March 1, 1975. The Fugitive Law was declared unconstitutional the following year. Beaufort County sheriff Otis "Red" Davis and Fred Harwell, an attorney and journalist born in Little's hometown of Washington, North Carolina, who attended Little's murder trial, both claim she was never declared a fugitive. Regardless, she knew her life was in danger, especially after learning that Alligood was dead. In an interview, Joan Little claimed that accounts of her hiding under a mattress in a local man's cabin shortly after her escape were untrue; however, in her court testimony, Joan offered these details herself. Little also revealed that she had read recent histories of her case by Genna Rae McNeil and Danielle McGuire; it is unclear how much these accounts may have influenced Joan's recollections. Harwell, *True Deliverance*, 81; Rick Nichols, untitled, *N&O*, February 16, 1975, news clipping, box 1, JLC Collection; Joan Little, interview by author, May 1, 2012; *State of North Carolina vs. Joan Little*, Testimony, August 11–13, 1975, folders 1–2, JRJ Collection; McGuire, *At the Dark End of the Street*; McNeil, "Joanne Is You." The

Reston Papers have recently been divided to create a second collection, the James Reston Jr. Collection of Joan Little Trial Materials, 1975–76, and many of these items are currently digitized.

5. Paul, who was also Chenier's lawyer, said he assembled a group of men and women at his house in Chapel Hill, mostly from the university, who had money and influence. He also asked Chenier to gather people who might be interested in forming a Joan Little Defense Committee. Multiple groups were established to support Little and to raise money for her defense, including the Durham-based Joan Little Defense Fund. To avoid confusion, I use the all-encompassing Free Joan Little campaign to refer to this support. Little's testimony as well as interviews with both Paul and Frinks reported that an all-Black group of women assembled in Chenier's apartment; Chenier recalled that the group was a racially mixed group of men and women. It is unclear whether the meeting at Chenier's apartment or Paul's house came first; and given the crisis and chaos of the moment, the four may have confused the two meetings. Reston, *Innocence of Joan Little*, 60–63, 78–87; Golden Frinks, interview by James Reston Jr., n.d.; Celine Chenier, interview by James Reston Jr., n.d.; Jerry Paul, interview by James Reston Jr., n.d.; all in JRJ Collection; *State of North Carolina vs. Joan Little, Defendant*, Joan Little Testimony, August 11–13, 1975, folders 1–2, JRJ Collection.

6. Reston, *Innocence of Joan Little*, 63, 93–95.

7. Reston, 94–95; "Miss Little Defense Aid Set Up," *N&O*, September 8, 1974; "Joanne Little Indicted," *Washington (N.C.) Daily News*, September 10, 1974. Gregory Simms, "Joan Little Fights to Avoid Death Sentence," *Jet*, May 8, 1975. With a Black population of over 40 percent, Durham had a long history of African American activism. By the mid-1970s, much of the more overt protest of the 1960s had quelled, but the activists and the protest tradition remained. Some of those activists from earlier struggles would take up Joan Little's cause. State law in North Carolina called for the death penalty for all first-degree murder convictions. There was a certain irony in the mandatory death sentence; in the interests of fairness and justice, a recent court ruling had forbidden judges from imposing arbitrary sentences without a jury. Greene, *Our Separate Ways*; Greene, "She Ain't No Rosa Parks."

8. *State vs. Joan Little*, Motion for Change of Venue, March 14, 1975; *Joan Little v. State of North Carolina*, 1975, Brief in Support of Motion to Dismiss the First-Degree Murder Indictment, box 33, folder 348, HHH Papers; McGuire, "Joan Little and Triumph of Testimony," 207; Ginny Carroll, "Miss Little's Bond Is Set at $100,000," *N&O*, October 1, 1974; Ginny Carroll, "Joan Little Freed on $115,000 Bond," *N&O*, February 27, 1975; Rick Nichols, "Little Defense Criticizes Jury List," *N&O*, April 18, 1975; "Joan Little's Trial Will Be in Raleigh," *N&O*, May 2, 1975; David Zucchino, "Jurors Say Evidence Too Thin to Convict," *N&O*, August 16, 1975.

9. "Joan Little to Come Up for Parole," *Jet*, January 27, 1977; "Dentist Says Little Didn't Want to Leave Prison," *Jet*, November 3, 1977; "Joan up for Parole Again," *Carolina Times*, September 24, 1977; "Widespread N.C., VA. Search for Joan Little Continues," *Carolina Times*, October 22, 1977; "Search for Joan Little Continues in North Carolina Prison Escape," *NYT*, October 17, 1977; James Reston Jr., "Southern Justice and the Case of Joan Little," *NYT*, January 6, 1978; "Joan Little Placed Under Tight Security," *NYT*, June 18, 1978; "Kunstler Assails Carey for Joan's Extradition," *Daily Challenge* (New York), February 24, 1978. Joan Little, interview by author, October 27, 2013.

10. "Joan Little Captured in Brooklyn," *BP*, December 17, 1977; "Joanne Little: 'I Told Them I Was Going to Escape,'" *BP*, December 31, 1977; "Joan Little Granted Bail—$50,000," *BP*, January 28, 1978; "'I Fear for My Life': N.Y. Judge Halts JoAnne Little Extradition," *BP*, March 4, 1978; Max H. Seigel, "Joan Little Is Seized in Brooklyn Chase," *NYT*, December 8, 1977, 57; "Deal Made to Turn Joan Little over to N.Y. Police," *Carolina Times*, December 31, 1977; Lucius Walker (National Council of Churches) to Honorable Hugh Carey, January 4, 1978, William Kunstler Papers, Tamiment Library and Robert F. Wagner Archives, Bobst Library, New York University; George Todd, "Joan Little's Fate in Hands of Governor," *Amsterdam News* (New York), January 14, 1978; "Don't Send Joan Back," *Amsterdam News*, January 14, 1978; J. Zamgba Browne, "Extradition Nears for Joan Little," *Amsterdam News*, April 1, 1978; New York City Assemblyman Al Vann (chair, Black and Puerto Rican Legislative Caucus) to Governor Hugh Carey, March 2, 1978, William Kunstler Papers, Tamiment Library and Robert F. Wagner Archives, Bobst Library, New York University. My thanks to Sarah Kunstler and Joan Little for allowing me access to Kunstler's papers, which are currently unprocessed and closed. Although Little claimed she was imprisoned at Rikers Island Prison with Assata Shakur, the dates of their imprisonment at Rikers do not seem to have overlapped. Joan Little, conversation with author, April 8, 2013; Shakur, *Assata*, xix.

11. Little has given various explanations for her escape from Women's Prison, including fearing for her life and objecting to harsh prison treatment. More recently she explained that her mother's death, which occurred while Joan was incarcerated, and the need to look after her younger siblings motivated her to escape. At the time, a psychiatrist allegedly maintained that she was suffering a delayed reaction to her mother's passing and was unable to respond to counseling in North Carolina due to her feelings about the prison system. Joan Little; interview by author, May 1, 2012; Rev. Herbert Daughtry, conversation with author, May 1, 2012; Malcolm Williams, conversation with author, May 1, 2012; "Joan Little Granted Bail—$50,000," *BP*, January 28, 1978. Joan Little, interview by author, October 27, 2013; "Appellate Court Sets $50,000 for 'Fugitive' Joan Little," *Daily Challenge* (New York), January 26, 1978; "Cary Says He Will Return Joan to N.C.," *Daily Challenge*, February 23, 1978; "Kunstler Assails Carey for Joan's Extradition," *Daily Challenge*, February 24, 1978. "Delay Joan's Departure for North Carolina," *Daily Challenge*, March 26, 1978; Max H. Seigel, "Joan Little Loses Extradition Ruling," *NYT*, March 24, 1978; "Joan Little in North Carolina," *NWT*, July 1978.

12. Roger Wilkins, "Race, Joan Little, Justice," review of *The Innocence of Joan Little: A Southern Mystery*, by James Reston Jr., *NYT*, December 17, 1977.

13. Of the 362 inmates executed in North Carolina between 1910 and 1961, 75 percent were African American; only 2 women were put to death, both African American. At the time of Joan Little's arrest, 68 people were on death row in the state, the highest in the nation, and 50 of them were African Americans. Another source gave the figure at 82 people on death row. The 2009 Racial Justice Act allowed prisoners to use statistical evidence to prove racial bias in jury selection and death sentences, but North Carolina repealed the law in 2013. Chris Behre, Exhibit 2, "A Brief History of Capital Punishment in North Carolina," Office of Correction, September 1973; "Inmates Presently Under Death Penalty," August 20, 1974, HHH Papers; Janover Madeleine, "Rape Is a Political Crime," *off our backs*, November 30, 1974; Rick Nichols, "National Issues Engulf Unlikely N.C. Celebrity," *N&O*, July 13, 1975; Davis, "Joan Little."

CHAPTER 1

1. "North Carolina American Indian History Timeline," North Carolina Museum of History, accessed June 8, 2021, https://www.ncmuseumofhistory.org/american-indian/handouts/timeline; Clagget, "Native American Settlement of North Carolina"; "Native Americans of Beaufort Co., N.C.," Carolina Algonkian Project, 2006-2009, http://www.ncgenweb.us/beaufort/boindian.htm.

2. Van Camp, *Beaufort County*, 7, 99. Black soldiers' contributions were finally recognized with a historic marker in 2017. Coffey, "African Americans Defend Washington, N.C."

3. In 1970, Beaufort County's population of nearly 36,000 was 33 percent African American. By 2019, the county population of 47,200 was 25 percent African American, nearly 66 percent non-Hispanic white, and 7.8 percent Hispanic. Just under 19 percent of county residents lived at or below the poverty level, compared to 12 percent nationally. Van Camp, *Beaufort County*, 7–8; *Beaufort County Land Use Plan*; U.S. Census Bureau, *1970 Census of the Population*; Data USA: Beaufort County, N.C., accessed April 16, 2022, https://datausa.io/profile/geo/beaufort-county-nc; *Beaufort County Census of Population and Housing*; Cecelski, *Along Freedom Road*, 36, 182n21, 183n27, 185n70; Little, "I Am Joan," 46.

4. Harwell, *True Deliverance*, 22, 23, 26.

5. On the similarities between de jure and de facto racial discrimination, see Theoharis, "I'd Rather Go to School in the South" and "They Told Us Our Kids Were Stupid."

6. Harwell, *True Deliverance*, 98–100; Rick Nichols, "Trial Publicity Raises Hackles in Beaufort County," *N&O*, April 27, 1975; Earls, Wynes, and Quatrucci, *Voting Rights in North Carolina*, 8, appendix section 7, 18.

7. Jerry Paul quoted in Reston, *Innocence of Joan Little*, 112–13, 13, 16, 18–19, 68, 77. Mark Pinsky, a graduate of Duke University, covered Little's murder trial for Reuters. Pinsky, "The Innocence of James Reston, Jr.," 40.

8. Joan Little, interviews by author, May 1, 2012, October 27, 2013; Little, "I Am Joan," 45.

9. Joan Little, interviews by author, May 1, 2012, October 27, 2013; Little, "I Am Joan," 45; *State of North Carolina vs. Joan Little, Defendant*, Testimony of Joan Little, August 11–13, 1975, folders 1–2, JRJ Collection.

10. Little, "I Am Joan," 45.

11. Joan Little, interviews by author, May 1, 2012, October 27, 2013; Joan Little, testimony; Little, "I Am Joan," 43; Joan Little, conversation with author, July 23, 2021.

12. Joan Little, conversation with author, April 8, 2013; Joan Little, interviews by author, May 1, 2012, October 27, 2013; McNeil, "Joanne Is You," 263.

13. Joan Little, conversation with author, April 2013; Milton Jordan, "Trial for Joanne Starts on Monday," *Afro-American*, July 12, 1975; Joan Little, interview by author, October 27, 2013. Cheryl Hicks has shown how Black parents who had migrated north often turned to the courts to control and protect their "wayward" daughters. Hicks, *Talk with You Like a Woman*, 182–203. Black southerners, well into the 1950s, also sought to control and protect their presumably unmanageable youth but often turned to Black-run "boot camps" rather than white law enforcement for assistance. Thulani Davis, conversation with author, January 15, 2016.

14. Purcell, "North Carolina," 198, 202–3.

15. A 1974 report from the University of Michigan found that North Carolina was one of six states without any state-funded community programs for juvenile offenders. "North

Carolina Among Six States Without Funded Programs for Juvenile Offenders," *Carolina Times*, January 10, 1976.

16. *State of North Carolina vs. Joan Little, Defendant*, Joan Little Testimony, August 12, 1975, folders 1–2, JRJ Collection; Little, "I Am Joan"; Harwell, *True Deliverance*, 26–28; Reston, *Innocence of Joan Little*, 154–55; Milton Jordan, "Making of a National Symbol—Joan Little," *Afro-American*, August 23, 1975.

17. Summary of Indictment and Appeals, folder 13, JRJ Collection; Harwell, *True Deliverance*, 29; Joan Little, telephone conversation with author, August 15, 2015.

18. "List," William Kunstler Papers, unprocessed, Tamiment Library and Robert F. Wagner Archives, Bobst Library, New York University; *State of North Carolina v. Joan Little*, Superior Court File no. 74-Cr-4176, Answer to Amendment to Defendant's Petition for a Writ of Prohibition, box 32, folder 343, HHH Papers; Harwell, *True Deliverance*, 29, 31–35, 49; North Carolina Court of Appeals, Second District, *State of North Carolina vs. Joan Little*, Brief for the State, July 14, 1975, folder 11, JRJ Collection.

19. Summary of Indictment and Appeals, folder 13, JRJ Collection.

20. In open court, the jury returned a verdict of guilty against Joan Little for three felonies of breaking, entry, and larceny; but both the bills of indictment as well as the clerk's certificate of court also showed that the jury had found her guilty of felonious possession. It is also unclear why she received two consecutive sentences when there were at least three felony convictions. This may have been just one of many problems with the trial. Joan still insists that Julius had nothing to do with the theft. Summary of Indictment and Appeals, folder 13, JRJ Collection; Joan Little, interview by author, May 1, 2012; Joan Little, conversation with author, April 8, 2013; Reston, *Innocence of Joan Little*, 157–58; Harwell, *True Deliverance*, 29, 31–35, 49.

21. Joan Little, interview by author, October 27, 2013. Discrepancies exist between Joan Little's court testimony and her recent recollections. In her 1974 confession, she testified that she and Jerome, together with Melinda and Wilbur Moore, broke into the trailers and transferred the loot—all except the food, the TV, and the rifle (which she later said was a BB gun, not a rifle)—to Jerome's nearby trailer. In a 2013 interview, Joan said she broke into only one trailer and speculated that perhaps Jerome and Melinda burglarized the other two trailers on their own. She confessed, she explained, because the theft was her idea and, as the older sister, she felt she should take responsibility. Summary of Indictment and Appeals, folder 13, JRJ Collection; Joan Little, conversation with author, April 8, 2013; Joan Little, text message to author, April 8, 2013.

22. Summary of Indictment and Appeals, folder 13, JRJ Collection; Karen Bethea-Shields, interview by author, November 11, 2013. At the time of the trial, she was Karen Galloway, which I have retained here for consistency with the documentary evidence.

23. Karen Bethea-Shields, interview by author, November 11, 2013; Brief for the State, July 14, 1975, folder 11, JRJ Collection; Joan Little, interview by author, May 1, 2012; Malcolm Williams, conversation with author, May 1, 2012; Joan Little, conversation with author, April 8, 2013; "Joanne Little: No Escape Yet," *off our backs*, January 1975. Using defendants against one another was a common prosecutorial tactic; but turning family members against each other was especially harmful and created strains within the Little family for decades. Joan's younger brother, Malcolm Williams, recalled repeated harassment in school, where family members of the slain jailer worked. For more recent examples of these prosecutorial practices, see Goffman, *On the Run*, 55–90.

24. *State of North Carolina v. Joan Little*, Superior Court File no. 74-Cr-4176, Answer to Amendment to Defendant's Petition for a Writ of Prohibition, box 32, folder 343, HHH Papers; *State of North Carolina v. Joan Little*, Summary of Indictment and Appeals, North Carolina Court of Appeals, May 19, 1975, folder 13, JRJ Collection; *State of North Carolina v. Joan Little*, Defendant's Appellant Brief, North Carolina Court of Appeals, June 25, 1975, folder 12, JRJ Collection; *State of North Carolina v. Joan Little*, Brief for the State, June 25, 1975, folder 11, JRJ Collection; Joan Little, conversation with author, April 8, 2013; Reston, *Innocence of Joan Little*, 157.

25. Reston, *Innocence of Joan Little*, 159. *Joan Little v. State of North Carolina*, Summary of Indictment and Appeals, North Carolina Court of Appeals, May 19, 1975, folder 13, JRJ Collection; *State of North Carolina v. Joan Little*, Wake County Superior Court file no. 74-Cr-4176, Answer to Amendment to Defendant's Petition for a Writ of Prohibition, box 32, folder 343, HHH Papers.

26. Summary of Indictment and Appeals, North Carolina Court of Appeals, May 19, 1975, folder 13, JRJ Collection. In 1979, before the state's Fair Sentencing Act was implemented, 49 percent of felons under the age of twenty-one were sentenced under CYO status. Nichols, "Criminal Procedure," 652n148, Table 1, 634–35; Reston, *Innocence of Joan Little*, 112.

27. Joan Little, conversation with author, April 8, 2013; Summary of Indictment and Appeals, North Carolina Court of Appeals, May 19, 1975, folder 13, JRJ Collection. Purcell, "North Carolina," 198, 202–3.

28. Reston, *Innocence of Joan Little*, 162, 105; Harwell, *True Deliverance*, 28; Little interviews with author, May 1, 2012, October 27, 2013; *State of North Carolina vs. Joan Little, Defendant*, Joan Little Testimony, August 11–13, 1975, folders 1-2, JRJ Collection. Little appears to have been aware of these rumors at the time for she jokingly made a remark about kissing a woman named Alexis. Jo Anne [sic] to Dear Toothless, n.d., box 1, JLC Collection.

29. Otis E. Davis, Complaint for Arrest, Joan Little, August 27, 1974, box 33, folder 345, HHH Papers. Pater Galuszka, "Jailer Found Slain," *Washington (N.C.) Daily News*, August 27, 1975.

30. Elaine Abelson, *When Ladies Go A-Thieving: Middle-Class Shoplifters in the Victorian Department Store* (New York 1989), quoted in Hicks, *Talk with You Like a Woman*, 154; Gross, *Colored Amazons*, 155. For changing conceptions of the "fallen woman," see Freedman, *Their Sisters' Keepers*. On the differential treatment of white immigrants and African Americans in the criminal justice system historically, see Gross, *Colored Amazons*, 121–25; and Muhammad, *Condemnation of Blackness*, 271, 273–75. On Black women's vulnerability to theft charges, see Gross, *Colored Amazons*, 34–35, 41–43, 54–55; on similar vulnerabilities of African American women in the South and elsewhere, see Hunter, *To 'Joy My Freedom*; and Blair, *I've Got to Make My Livin'*.

31. Quoted in Reston, *Innocence of Joan Little*, 6, 73; Archie Allen, conversation with author, August 14, 2006.

32. Harwell, *True Deliverance*, 28; Reston, *Innocence of Joan Little*, 112–14.

33. Karen (Galloway) Bethea-Shields, interview by author, November 11, 2013; Galloway (Bethea-Shields), quoted in NOW Rape Task Force, "The Case of Joan Little," n.d., box 210, folder 51, NOW Papers; Karen Bethea-Shields, interview by David Cecelski, n.d. I will discuss Joan Little's prison writings in part 2.

34. Rick Nichols, "Costs Soar for Little Defense," N&O, July, 3, 1975; Golden Frinks, interview by Melynn Glusman, January 1994; McNeil, "Body, Sexuality and Self-Defense," 241; Harwell, *True Deliverance*, 143–46; Reston, *Innocence of Joan Little*, 53–55.

35. Little, "I Am Joan," 42; Greene, "I'm Gonna Get You."

36. McNeil, "Body, Sexuality and Self-Defense," 242; Fergus, *Liberalism*, 184; Paul Jervay Jr., "Raleigh Native Worked Hard in Defense of Miss Little," *Carolinian*, August, 23, 1975.

CHAPTER 2

1. Chafe, *Civilities and Civil Rights*, 51, 58. Martin, quoted in Tyson, *Blood Done Sign My Name*, 229, 231, 268–70.

2. On the Oxford murder and trial, see Tyson, *Blood Done Sign My Name*. Anne Blythe, "Perdue Pardons Wilmington Ten," N&O, January 1, 2013. When the Wilmington Ten finally were pardoned in 2012, four of the defendants had died and Chavis had spent almost four years in prison. In another 1970s miscarriage of justice, three African American civil rights activists, who became known as the Charlotte Three, were falsely convicted of arson. The case was similarly denounced for corrupt police and criminal justice practices, and its most prominent activist, Jim Grant, was sentenced to twenty-five years for burning a horse stable. Both the Wilmington and Charlotte cases also helped to fuel the creation of the North Carolina Prisoners' Labor Union (NCPLU), discussed in more detail in part 2. For a firsthand account of the Oxford murder and the Wilmington Ten, see Chavis, "Wilmington Ten." "Pardon the Wilmington Ten," www.naacp.org. Schutz, "Burning of America"; Tibbs, *From Black Power to Prison Power*, 126–30. See also Berger, *Captive Nation*.

3. Bond, "Plea Bargaining in North Carolina," 830, 835. Nichols, "Criminal Procedure," 634, 649. The American Bar Association adopted similar determinant sentencing guidelines in 1993, arguing that parole boards were often discriminatory and that prison failed to rehabilitate prisoners. Marvel and Moody, *Impact of Determinant Sentencing Laws*.

4. Alexander, *New Jim Crow*, 89–93, 104–12.

5. I discuss the Central Prison disturbance and the NCCCW strike in greater detail in part 2. Legislative Research Commission, Nichols, "Criminal Procedure," 631, 650, 655. For a discussion that interrogates the rigid distinction between southern de jure discrimination and northern de facto discrimination, see Theoharis, "I'd Rather Go to School in the South."

6. Nichols, "Criminal Procedure," 631n4; French, "Incarcerated Black Female," 323, 326. By 2000, budgetary considerations had lowered the state's inmate population to thirty-first in the nation and second among southern states. Political scientist Marie Gottschalk notes that most prison costs are fixed and budget cuts frequently eliminate treatment programs, thus increasing recidivism rates and prison costs over the long-term. Gottschalk, *Prison and the Gallows*, 243.

7. Reston, *Innocence of Joan Little*, 112; French, "Incarcerated Black Female," 331, 333. The prison population was increasing during this period at about 100 inmates per month across the state. Nichols, "Criminal Procedure," 651n146. U.S. Census Bureau, "Table 48, North Carolina."

8. By 2010, the state's prison population of 40,379 was 7 percent female and 57 percent African American; an additional 112,000 offenders were under criminal justice

supervision, of which 24 percent were female and 45 percent were African American, although North Carolina's Black population is just under 23 percent. DOC figures are not broken down by both race and gender, making it difficult to determine the exact number of incarcerated Black women. "The Black Population: 2010," U.S. Census Bureau, "Table 5."

9. Some have argued that the baby boom was partially responsible for increased crime rates, while others pointed to the rise in Black unemployment. Although the crime wave, including the homicide rate, spiked in the mid-1960s, these statistics have been widely debated by scholars; and FBI changes in tracking crime make comparisons difficult. As Heather Thompson points out, crime was counted quite differently after 1965 in cities across the country, due largely to financial incentives that gave federal funds to local law enforcement, particularly if police departments could demonstrate rising crime rates. In fact, crime had been at higher levels in U.S. history prior to the 1960s. Nichols, "Criminal Procedure," 651n146. Thompson, "Why Mass Incarceration Matters," 727; Alexander, *New Jim Crow*, 41; Flamm, *Law and Order*, 125–29; Fergus, *Liberalism*, 140. For a discussion of how crime rates were racialized from 1890 to 1949, see Muhammad, *Condemnation of Blackness*.

10. For example, both Marie Gottschalk and Naomi Murakawa contend that the role of liberals and a weak welfare state (among other trends) are important factors in the emergence of the U.S. carceral state. Gottschalk, *Prison and the Gallows*; Murakawa, *First Civil Right*. Thompson, "Why Mass Incarceration Matters," 730. For a comprehensive examination of the links between the War on Poverty and the War on Crime, see Hinton, *From the War on Poverty to the War on Crime*.

11. Quoted in Murakawa, *First Civil Right*, 71.

12. Johnson, quoted in Law, *Resistance Behind Bars*, 159; Johnson, quoted in Flamm, *Law and Order*, 47, 52–54, 132–44. Jonathan Simon implicates Attorney General Robert Kennedy for increasing federal involvement in crime. Simon, *Governing Through Crime*, 49. Murakawa argues that "postwar racial liberalism"—that is, the liberal push to modernize policing and create supposedly race-neutral penal policies beginning in the post–World War II period—inadvertently enhanced the notion of Black criminality and both strengthened and legitimized the modern U.S. carceral state. Murakawa, *First Civil Right*, 11–13.

13. Murakawa, *First Civil Right*, 70, 71, 77. For differing scholarly views on African American responses to anticrime legislation and the War on Drugs, see Fortner, *Black Silent Majority*; Murch, "Crack in Los Angeles"; Forman, "Racial Critiques of Mass Incarceration"; and Forman, *Locking Up Our Own*.

14. Hinton, *From the War on Poverty to the War on Crime*, 9; Nixon, quoted in Beckett and Sasson, *Politics of Injustice*, 52. Both the Senate and the House of Representatives, with Democratic majorities, wanted to increase LEAA funding to $750 million or even $1 billion, over Nixon's $480 million request but settled on $650 million for the 1970–71 fiscal year. Peskoe, "1968 Safe Streets Act." Micol Seigel argues that LEAA enhanced the militarization of local police, private policing, and private-public ventures including think tanks, research and development tech firms, and private universities. Seigel, "Objects of Police History." See also Kohler-Hausmann, "Guns and Butter"; and Hinton, "'War Within Our Own Boundaries.'" For a scathing, scholarly indictment of how the War on Crime fueled urban "riots," more accurately described as "rebellions," in low-income Black communities, see Hinton, *America on Fire*.

15. Nebraska Republican senator Roman Hruska, quoted in Feeley and Sarat, *Policy Dilemma*, 47–48, 63, 111.

16. Flamm, *Law and Order*, 115–20, 133. When the bill was reauthorized in 1970, rural and suburban areas without racial disturbances—and with Republican majorities—also received funds; however, disproportionate funding still went to "riot" control and organized crime under LEAA allocations. Peskoe, "1968 Safe Streets Act," 98–99; Purcell, "North Carolina," 191–93; North Carolina Bar Association, "DOC Gets Largest LEAA Appropriation in Its History," January 1975, box 74, folder 146, HHH Papers. U.S. Congressional Budget Office, *Law Enforcement Assistance Administration*, xiii. In 1974, Congress amended the Safe Streets Act and mandated that some LEAA funds be used for juvenile justice and delinquency programs. Feeley and Sarat, *Policy Dilemma*, 60. Another report noted that North Carolina Republican governor James Holshouser Jr. had influence over issues that were of concern to him. The same report also noted that crime actually increased in the state; others countered that LEAA funds likely slowed the increase. U.S. Advisory Commission on Intergovernmental Relations, *Safe Streets Reconsidered*, table 7, 443, 429–49.

17. This is not to discount the impact of President Reagan's 1984 Sentencing Reform Law and 1986 Anti–Drug Abuse Act. Hoping to rectify the historic dilemma of overpolicing and underprotection that had plagued Black communities for decades, thirteen of the twenty Congressional Black Caucus members supported the 1986 law. However, only eight of twenty-four CBC members supported a similar law in 1988. Likewise, President Clinton's 1994 Violent Crime Control and Law Enforcement Act (which Clinton recently called a mistake before an NAACP audience) had an even bigger impact on the policing and imprisonment of disproportionate numbers of African Americans in the 1990s. Ironically, the 1994 bill also included the Violence Against Women Act (VAWA). See epilogue for more on the VAWA. Alexander, *New Jim Crow*, 48–58; Murakwa, *First Civil Right*, 124; Elizabeth Hinton, Julilly Kohler-Hausmann, and Vesla M. Weaver, "Did Blacks Really Endorse the 1994 Crime Bill?," op-ed, *NYT*, April 13, 2016. Historian Simon Balto persuasively argues that all the tactics associated with punitive policing practices in the decades after the civil rights movement were in place decades earlier, although these practices and policies were expanded in the Wars on Crime and Drugs. Balto, *Occupied Territory*.

18. Perkinson, *Texas Tough*, 302, 303. Some scholars argue that other regions and states led the way, with larger absolute numbers of prisoners. See, for example, Gilmore, *Golden Gulag*; and Lichtenstein, "Flocatex and the Fiscal Limits of Mass Incarceration."

19. Hinton, *From the War on Poverty to the War on Crime*, 2; Murakawa, *First Civil Right*, 71–72, 230n6.

20. Fergus, *Liberalism*, 140. In 2012, North Carolina spent $1.2 billion, or $30,000 per inmate. Vera Institute of Justice, "Price of Prisons."

21. The federal government provided no more than 50 percent of the cost for prison construction. It is uncertain, though likely, that LEAA funds were used to renovate the Beaufort County Jail. According to Governor Holshouser, there was little public appetite for funding correctional programs, even though the state's facilities and programs were "badly in need of updating," according to one federal report. However, in 1970 Congress amended the Safe Streets Act mandating that LEAA money also be spent on correctional programs. U.S. Advisory Commission on Intergovernmental Relations, *Safe Streets Reconsidered*, 437; Feeley and Sarat, *Policy Dilemma*, 144.

22. Harwell, *True Deliverance*, 39–40, 42; "Joanne Little: No Escape Yet," *off our backs*, January 31, 1975. Ironically, the arrest of civil rights activists in the South and the widespread

perception of southern barbarism as a holdover from slavery led to reforms in southern more often than northern prisons during the 1960s and 1970s, despite similarly horrific prison conditions in both regions. Improvements often meant modernizing but not necessarily humanizing incarceration. Thompson, "Blinded by a 'Barbaric' South." On racialized penal practices in the South in an earlier period, see, for example, Lichtenstein, *Twice the Work of Free Labor*; Oshinsky, *Worse Than Slavery*; and Curtin, *Black Prisoners and Their World*. On the incarceration of southern Black women in the nineteenth and early twentieth centuries, see Curtin, "'Human World' of Black Women in Alabama Prisons"; Haley, *No Mercy Here*; and LeFlouria, *Chained in Silence*. See also the special issue of the *Journal of African American History*, edited by Gross and Hicks, on Black women and the carceral state; and Gross, "African American Women, Mass Incarceration, and the Politics of Protection."

23. Reston, *Innocence of Joan Little*, 289–94; Harwell, *True Deliverance*, 42–54.

24. *Joan Little v. State of North Carolina*, Summary of Indictment and Appeals, North Carolina Court of Appeals, May 19, 1975, folder 13, JRJ Collection.

25. See, for example, McGuire, *At the Dark End of the Street*; McGuire, "Joan Little and the Triumph of Testimony"; McNeil, "'Joanne Is You'"; and McNeil, "Body, Sexuality and Self-Defense." More recent accounts of the Little case, such as Emily Thuma's *All Our Trials* and Catherine Jacquet's *Injustices of Rape*, cite my article on Little's felony theft conviction: Greene, "She Ain't No Rosa Parks."

26. Thompson, "Why Mass Incarceration Matters," 703–34. Robert Perkinson contends that scholarly focus on the North's penal history has obscured the southern roots of mass incarceration. Perkinson, *Texas Tough*, 4, 7–8. For the liberal roots of mass incarceration dating to the post–World War II era, see Murakawa, *First Civil Right*; Muhammad, *Condemnation of Blackness*; and Gross, *Colored Amazons*. For a recent work that traces the roots of racialized policing and the carceral state even earlier, to the Great Migration, see Balto, *Occupied Territory*. See LeFlouria, *Chained in Silence*, and Haley, *No Mercy Here*, on Black women and carceral practices in the late nineteenth and early twentieth-century South.

27. Thompson, "Special Report II." On female imprisonment and women's prison activism in the 1960s and 1970s, see also Thuma, *All Our Trials*.

28. Lee, *For Freedom's Sake*, 180; Harris-Perry, *Sister Citizen*, 189. See also Wallace, *Black Macho and the Myth of the Superwoman*, for a 1970s critique of how Black women's supposedly innate strength has been used to castigate them as domineering, emasculating matriarchs.

29. Davis, "Joan Little," 38; "Joann Little Rally, July 2," *Feminary*, July 20, 1975.

CHAPTER 3

1. Reston, *Innocence of Joan Little*, 77.

2. Peter Galuszka, "Change of Venue Sought," *Washington (N.C.) Daily News*, September 7, 1974; Rick Nichols, "Joan Little Challenged on Phone Calls," *N&O*, August 14, 1975; "Little Witness Labels Alligood Probe 'Inferior,'" *Afro-American*, August 16, 1975; Karen Bethea-Shields, interview by David Cecelski, n.d.; an excerpted version of Cecelski's interview appears in the *N&O*, January 12, 2003. My thanks to David for sharing his full interview with me.

3. "Brutal Murder," *Washington (N.C.) Daily News*, August, 28, 1975. *Daily News* editor Ashley Futrell claimed he knew nothing of this evidence when he wrote the editorial praising

Alligood and felt hoodwinked by local authorities. Later editions of the local paper included more complete coverage. Louis Randolph, interview by James Reston Jr., n.d., JRJ Collection; Rick Nichols, "National Issues Engulf Unlikely N.C. Celebrity," N&O, July 13, 1975.

4. Judge Henry McKinnon claimed he granted the change of venue because heightened publicity, not racism, made a fair trial nearly impossible. McConahay, Mullin, and Fredrick, "Uses of Social Science in Trials." *State of North Carolina vs. Joann Little*, Motion for Change of Venue, Superior Court Division, Beaufort County, March 14, 1975, box 4, folder 4, HHH Papers; McGuire, *At the Dark End of the Street*, 217.

5. McGuire, *At the Dark End of the Street*, 210; McGuire, "The Maid and Mr. Charlie"; Theoharis, *Rebellious Life of Mrs. Rosa Parks*.

6. These cases are covered more extensively in part 3. Free Joan Little Flyer, n.d.; "The Story of Dessie Woods," n.d, National Committee to Defend Dessie Woods to Dear Friend, June 25, 1979, box 10, ALFA Archives. On "Latinx," see chapter 9, note 3.

7. In response to Chisholm's appeal, observers from the Community Relations Service of the U.S. Department of Justice also attended the trial. The *Economist* editors recast the quip by former SNCC leader H. Rap Brown / Jamil Abdullah Al-Amin that violence was "as American as apple pie." Bevacqua, *Rape on the Public Agenda*, 128. "Radio Station Gives Little Defense $22,000," N&O, June 5, 1975; Rick Nichols, "National Issues Engulf Unlikely N.C. Celebrity," N&O, July 13, 1975; "Joan Little Supporters Stage Demonstration," N&O, August 2, 1975; Davis, "Joan Little," 49; "Huge Nationwide Rallies Mark Start of JoAnn Little Trial," *Muhammad Speaks*, August 8, 1975.

8. Bond, "Self-Defense Against Rape"; "B.P.P. Name JoAnn Little 'Woman of the Year,'" *BP*, June 30, 1975; September 1, 1975; "Newsmakers of the Year," *Chicago Defender*, December 27, 1975; Thuma. *All Our Trials*, 105; Lyle Denniston, "Joan Little Case: Biggest Civil Rights Trial of the '70s," *Washington Star*, July 13, 1975; Lyle Denniston, "An Easy Air Prevails at Little Trial," *Washington Star*, August 10, 1975, news clippings, box 3, HHH Papers.

9. McNeil, "Joanne Is You"; "People's Artists Perform at JoAnne Little Victory Rally," *BP*, September 1, 1975; Mel Gussow, "The Nightmare of 'Jo Anne' Is Staged," *NYT*, October 19, 1976, news clipping, box 3, HHH Papers.

10. Christine Strudwick, interview by Melynn Glusman, January 18, 1994; Karen Bethea-Shields, interview by David Cecelski, n.d.; Bevacqua, *Rape on the Public Agenda*, 128; Springer, *Living for the Revolution*, 91–92, 152, 205n49, 213n31; "Woman Inmate Kills Would-Be Rapist," *Triple Jeopardy*, January–February 1975; "Oakland Welcomes JoAnne Little," *BP*, September 1, 1975; "Political Activism" n.d. [ca. 1980], box 1, NABF Papers; Minutes of First Meeting of National Black Feminist Organization—Chicago Chapter, June 17, 1974; Statement of Purpose, NBFO, n.d., box 1, NBFO/NABF Papers; Dannia Sutherland, email to author, July 1, 2004; Karen Lindsey, "Joan Little's Trial: A Jail Killing Becomes a Cause Celebre," *Boston Phoenix*, July 15, 1975, news clipping, box 169, series 3, NOW Papers. The various references to Black feminists in Raleigh may be referring to the same organization.

11. Bevacqua, *Rape on the Public Agenda*, 12; Afi Phoebe to My Feminist Sisters, March 31, 1975; *NOW Minority Women and Women's Rights Task Force Newsletter* 1, no. 1 (June 975); Karen DeCrow, Speech on Joan Little [1975]; NOW Rape Task Force, "The Case of Joan Little," box 210, series 42, NOW Papers.

12. The Joan Little case also performed a valuable function for national NOW president Karen DeCrow, who was fighting her own internal battle over the organization's future and

the direction of the women's movement, which she hoped might become more sensitive to issues of concern to women of color, lesbians, and working-class women. However, NOW soon devoted most of its energies to passage of the ERA. On the divisions in NOW, see Wandersee, *On the Move*, 49–54; and Evans, *Tidal Wave*, 109–10.

13. Dree Lovell, "Joint Action, for Immediate Release," n.d. [ca. April 1975]; Shirley Chisholm to Attorney General Edward Levi, April 15, 1975; "A Call for Action," n.d. [ca. April 14, 1975], NOW Rape Task Force Memo, September 1976, box 49, NOW Papers; Mary Ann Largen and Del Dobbins, "Joann [sic] Little Actions," August 19, 1975, box 31, series 8, NOW Papers.

14. Bevacqua, *Rape on the Public Agenda*, 35–36; *NOW Minority Women and Women's Rights Task Force Newsletter* 1, no. 1 (June 1975); Marjorie Nelson, interview by Katie Weigand, 2005; NOW-NC State Convention Resolutions, n.d. [ca. July 1975]; "Women's Group Pledges Support to Joan Little," news clipping, n.d., box 169, NOW Papers.

15. Greensboro YWCA, "The Joan Little Case," April 1, [1975], box 31, series 8, NOW Papers; *Fayetteville-Cumberland NOW Newsletter*, September 1, 1975, February 25 [1976], box 94, MBP Papers.

16. Charlotte NOW Executive Board Minutes, March 6, April 11, 1976, *ACT NOW Charlotte NOW Newsletter*, August 1975, May 10, 1976, 2, "Highlights of Charlotte NOW Actions," handwritten resolution, July 18, 1972, Charlotte NOW Minutes, July 18, 1972, n.d., box 1, Charlotte NOW Papers, Special Collections, J. Murrey Atkins Library, University of North Carolina at Charlotte.

17. Dr. Cathy Ellison from New Jersey, an expert on sexual assault, also gave the defense team advice. Karen Bethea-Shields interview. At the time of the trial, Galloway (now Bethea-Shields) was one of the first Black women to graduate from Duke University Law School. The day she passed the North Carolina Bar Exam, Jerry Paul assigned her to be his cocounsel in the Little trial. In 1976, a year after the Little trial, the National Conference of Black Lawyers named her Lawyer of the Year, and in 1980 she became one of the first elected Black judges in North Carolina. "Karen Bethea-Shields, First Female Judge in Durham County, 1980–1986," Galleries, And Justice for All: Durham County Courthouse Wall Art, Durham County Library, accessed April 26, 2021, http://andjusticeforall.dconc .gov/gallery_images/karen-bethea-shields-first-female-judge-in-durham-county-1980 -1986.

18. Bevacqua, *Rape on the Public Agenda*, 128; Levine and Thom, *Bella Abzug*.

19. On letters sent to Hobgood, see "Hobgood Cited N.C. Court Flaws," *N&O*, September 21, 1975; and "Hobgood Reports on Sensational Trial," *Franklin (N.C.) Times*, November 13, 1975, clippings file, folder 380; see also folders 367–71, HHH Papers; McNeil, "Joanne Is You," 271.

20. "Frinks Erects Tents at Site of Little Trial," *N&O*, March 28, 1975.

21. Frinks claimed he needed funds in order to organize rallies and demonstrations in support of Little, which he believed was the only way to ensure that she got a fair trial. When Frinks initiated the lawsuit, Joan disassociated herself from him, calling him Golden "Freaks." He later dropped the suit but continued to support Joan "morally." Joan Little, conversation with author; Golden Frinks, interview; Louis Randolph, interview by James Reston Jr., n.d., JRJ Collection; Diane Sechrest and Jerry Allegood, "Dispute Erupts Among Little Supporters," *N&O*, March 14, 1975; Allegood, "Frinks, Attorney Split over Joan Little Case," *N&O*, March 17, 1975; Allegood, "Suit Filed to Block Joan Little Fund Use," *N&O*,

March 21, 1975; Kerry Sipe, "Little Denies Faking Illness," N&O, March 23, 1975. See photo of Little with bodyguard Russell McDonald, N&O, April 27, 1975.

22. Ginny Carroll, "Peaceful Courthouse Rally Marks Eve of Little," N&O, July 14, 1975.

23. Wake County Superior Court judge James Pou Bailey forbade all demonstrations on courthouse property. James H. Pou Bailey, Superior Court Division Order, July 18, 1975, HHH Papers (these papers were unprocessed when I first consulted them; this order can likely be found in folders 342–49); Ginny Carroll, "500 Stage Courthouse Rally," N&O, July 15, 1975.

24. Paul quoted in Reston, *Innocence of Joan Little*, 238; "Joan Little Trial Begins with Motions and a March," *Jet*, July 31, 1975.

25. Wilkerson claimed he did not represent Little, although he had represented her on several misdemeanor charges. During the trial for the three felonies, Wilkerson defended Little's brother, Jerome, who turned state's evidence against her. B. E. James [North Carolina State Bar] to Judge Hobgood, July 18, 1975; Beaufort County, *State of North Carolina vs. Joan Little*, Answer to Amendment to Defendant's Petition for a Writ of Prohibition, April 14, 1975, box 4, HHH Papers; Rick Nichols, "Jury Selection Begins in Joan Little Trial," N&O, July 15, 1975.

26. "Court Refuses to Hear Paul's Contempt Appeal," N&O, October 18, 1977; Little, "An Urgent Letter from Joan Little," NYT, August 24, 1975; "Jerry Paul Sentenced to Suspended Term"; Ginny Carroll, "Court Releases Jerry Paul Pending Appeals Ruling," N&O, news clippings, box 3, HHH Papers. Dees made his fortune selling cookbooks and participated in the appeal of three Black men in Tarboro, North Carolina, convicted and sentenced to death for the alleged rape of a white woman in 1973. Dees also made a name for himself in Alabama, where he challenged the state legislature's apportionment and won a victory that increased the number of Black legislators from three to fifteen. Dees, *A Lawyer's Journey*. Rick Nichols, "Judge Bans Lawyer in Joan Little Case"; Ginny Carroll, "Attorney Replies to Felony Charge," N&O, July 30, 1975; Carroll, "Dees Seeks Lawyers' Aid in Fighting Dismissal," N&O, July 31, 1975; news clippings, box 3, HHH Papers; Kunstler, quoted in Harwell, *True Deliverance*, 233.

27. Universal Studios was reported to have movie plans underway in the mid-1970s, and Jerry Paul even suggested that Cicely Tyson play Joan Little, while he cast Robert Redford as himself and Rod Steiger as Clarence Alligood. Wayne King, "Little's Lawyer: Justice Was 'Bought,'" *Washington Star*, October 20, 1975, news clipping, box 3, HHH Papers; Braden, "An Open Letter."

28. "Little Murder Charge Reduced," *Montreal Star*, August 7, 1975; Jane Gaskell, "Judge Saves Girl in Jail Rape Case from the Death Penalty," *Daily Mail* (London), August 7, 1975, box 3, HHH Papers; Jerry Paul, Closing Argument, August 14, 1975, folder 9, JRJ Collection.

CHAPTER 4

1. For the impact on public policy of representations of Black women historically, see, for example, Morton, *Disfigured Images*; Jewell, *From Mammy to Miss America*; James, *Shadowboxing*; and Roberts, *Killing the Black Body*. Portions of this chapter were presented previously in Greene, "Representations of Black Womanhood."

2. Historian Elsa Barkley Brown has observed that the failure to recognize racial and class differences can also impede female solidarity, a difficulty that emerged during the 1991 Anita Hill / Clarence Thomas debacle. By making Hill a "generic woman" and a "universal symbol" of the "common bonds of womanhood," white feminists perpetuated a "deracialized notion of women's experiences" and ignored "class-specific histories of women's sexuality and stereotypes and [women's] different histories of sexual harassment and sexual violence." Brown, "Imaging Lynching," 104, 105.

3. Paul claimed that a judge voiced this view in his chambers before he dismissed rape charges brought by a Black woman. Jerry Paul, interview by James Reston Jr., n.d., JRJ Collection; Paul quote in Karen Bethea-Shields, interview by David Cecelski, n.d.; Judge Walter Pickett, quoted in "Patriarchal Sex," *NWT*, July 1978; car dealer, quoted in Reston, *Innocence of Joan Little*, 6; sheriff, quoted in Roger Wilkins, "Race, Joan Little Justice," *NYT*, December 17, 1977.

4. Reston, *Innocence of Joan Little*, 53, 105; "Doctor Supports Defense Charge of JoAnne Little Rape," *BP*, August 11, 1975.

5. NOW Criminal Justice Task Force, Update—Joanne Little, August 10, 1975, box 209, folder 78, NOW Papers.

6. Tilda Hunting, "Joanne Little, When the Law Means Nothing Women Must Defend," *NWT*, February 1975; Karen Lindsey, "Little Goes on Trial," *off our backs*, August 31, 1975. See also Jacquet, *Injustices of Rape*. These issues are explored more fully in part 3.

7. Quoted in McNeil, "Joanne Is You," 259, 266.

8. Even though she was nowhere near the courthouse when the shoot-out occurred, the guns used by eighteen-year-old Jonathan Jackson in his attempt to free his brother George Jackson and fellow defendant-prisoners were traced to Angela Davis. Bond, quoted in Rick Nichols, "Officer Tells of Finding Body," *N&O*, July 29, 1975; Galloway quoted in Jackie McMillan, "Joanne Little: No Escape Yet," *off our backs*, January 31, 1975.

9. Harold 4x, "Joann Little Case Puts Plight of Women Prisoners in Focus," *Muhammad Speaks*, April 25, 1975.

10. Gregory Simms, "Joan Little Fights to Avoid Death Sentence," *Jet*, May 8, 1975; Ethel Payne, "Joan Little's Plight," *Chicago Defender*, December 6, 1975. Later Little complained that radicals like Angela Davis were using her to advance their own politics.

11. "Radio Station Gives Little Defense $22,000," *N&O*, June 5, 1975.

12. Wayne King, "Focus of Slaying Trial Had Humble Origins," *NYT*, July 29, 1975.

13. Testimony of Joan Little, August 1–13, 1975, folders 1–2, JRJ Collection; Harwell, *True Deliverance*, 257–58.

14. "Joan Becomes Nationwide Speaker," *Afro-American*, August 19–23, 1975. Joan's straightened hair may have been a wig. She had a wig in the Beaufort County Jail, which she often combed.

15. Karen often played older sister to Joan, and, like that of most siblings, their relationship was fraught with occasional tension as well as affection. Despite their class differences, Karen recognized a part of herself in Joan. Had it not been for her parents and her upbringing, she could easily have been in Joan's place. Years later, Galloway understood her presence as a role model, not necessarily as a substitute, for Joan Little, and she confessed to being slightly uncomfortable with this status. Joan recollected that there was also some tension in the relationship, in part fueled by class-inflected notions of respectability.

Reston, "Innocence of Joan Little"; McNeil, "Joanne Is You," 268; Joan Little, testimony, August 11–13, 1975, folders 1–2, JRJ Collection; Joan Little, conversation with author, April 8, 2013; Karen (Galloway) Bethea-Shields, interview by author, November 11, 2013.

16. Anonymous, "A Colored Woman, However Respectable, Is Lower than the White Prostitute," in Lerner, *Black Women in White America*, 166–69; Rick Nichols, "Lawyers End Arguments," N&O, August 15, 1975.

17. McGuire, *At the Dark End of the Street*, 212, 226.

CHAPTER 5

1. Black Power in the 1960s and 1970s was broad, diffuse, and multifaceted. While groups and individuals from cultural nationalists to Black capitalists to Pan-Africanists and armed revolutionaries embraced the label, Black Power adherents fundamentally promoted Black autonomy and control, self-determination, economic independence, racial pride, and often Black separatism and armed self-defense. For several syntheses of the Black Power movement(s), see Williams, *Concrete Demands*, which also pays special attention to women's contributions, and Joseph, *Waiting 'til the Midnight Hour*.

2. Black activists interpreted Little's trial in various ways. For many Black nationalist men and women, the Little case highlighted the racism in the criminal legal system. Rashhaad Ali, representing the North California Student Coalition Against Racism, told an Oakland rally that North Carolina was on trial, adding that "the crackers . . . must be taught to clean up their prison system." "'Free JoAnne Little' Rally Draws 500 to Learning Center," *BP*, 21 July, 1975. The prison movement is explored more fully in part 2.

3. Griffin, "Ironies of the Saint"; Taylor, "Elijah Muhammad's Nation of Islam"; Taylor, *Promise of Patriarchy*.

4. Karenga, "In Defense of Sis. Joanne," 37.

5. Brown, *Fighting for US*, 120–21, 128.

6. Karenga also refuted the myth of the Black matriarchy, which had received an official imprimatur in the 1965 Moynihan Report. Karenga, "In Defense of Sis. Joanne"; see also Karenga, "In Love and Struggle."

7. Eldridge Cleaver, minister of information for the BPP, was the most notable proponent of this stereotype in the 1960s and 1970s. On Black feminist critiques of Black nationalism, see, for example, Taylor, "Elijah Muhammad's Nation of Islam"; Taylor, *Promise of Patriarchy*; Ransby and Matthews, "Black Popular Culture and the Transcendence of Patriarchal Illusions"; Griffin, "Ironies of the Saint"; and White, "Africa on My Mind."

8. Karenga, "In Defense of Sis. Joanne," 39, my emphasis; Karenga, "In Love and Struggle"; Ogbar, *Black Power*, 29–30.

9. My emphasis. Abernathy reportedly responded to Little's attorneys with a callous boast: "We don't need the rape case because we have the best program for blacks and poor people in the country." Jerry Allegood, "Abernathy Leads Rally in Beaufort," N&O, April 5, 1975.

10. During Emancipation, Black women guarded weapons while Black men gathered in political meetings; but Black women also wielded knives and hatchets when traveling en masse to the polls in order to protect Black men's ability to cast ballots. Brown, "Negotiating and Transforming the Public Sphere." Similarly, antilynching crusader Ida B. Wells armed herself and averred that "a Winchester rifle should have a place of honor in

every [African American] home" as a defense against white racial violence. Wells, quoted in Giddings, *When and Where I Enter*, 20.

11. Karenga, "In Defense of Sis. Joanne," 42.

12. Karenga, "In Love and Struggle," 23. Scot Brown contends that the inclusion of women in Us paramilitary security operations led to greater gender equality in the organization by the 1970s. Brown, *Fighting for US*, 123.

13. "Abernathy Leads 2,000 in Support of Joanne Little," *Jet*, April 24, 1975; Tyson, *Radio Free Dixie*; Cobb, *This Non-violent Stuff Will Get You Killed*.

14. Bond, quoted in "Little Grasping 'Reality' of Staving Off Conviction," *N&O*, July 29, 1975. Karenga, "In Defense of Sis. Joanne," 39.

15. According to historian Estelle Freedman, "The most important target of the feminist antirape movement has been the legal system. The treatment of rape by police and the courts long resembled a second form of violence against women." Freedman, *No Turning Back*, 287; see also Jacquet, *Injustices of Rape*.

16. Karenga defined this as not only a "right" but a "responsibility." Karenga, "In Defense of Sis Joanne," 41.

17. David Du Bois, son of W. E. B. Du Bois, was hired in 1973 to edit the BPP newspaper and read the message from Newton. "Huey P. Newton: 'JoAnne Is the Living Spirit of George Jackson," *BP*, September 1, 1975. Julian Bond, "Dear Friend" letter from Southern Poverty Law Center, n.d., box 4, HHH Papers.

18. In 1996–97, the National Black United Front submitted a similar petition to the United Nations under the same name, "We Charge Genocide." Tilda Hunting, "Joanne Little, When the Law Means Nothing Women Must Defend," *NWT*, February, 1975; Joseph, *Waiting 'til The Midnight Hour*, 3, 5, 85, 98, 102, 112, 113. See also Anderson, *Eyes off the Prize*; and Plummer, *In Search of Power*.

19. "Elaine Brown: 'JoAnne Little Acted for Us All," *BP*, July 21, 1975.

20. My emphasis. Brown's references to rape in "our" (the Black) community also recalls the controversy surrounding Cleaver's admission that he had raped Black women as practice for raping white women. "Elaine Brown: 'We Must Keep on Thanking JoAnne Little,'" *BP*, September 1, 1975.

21. Brown, *Taste of Power*.

22. Giddings, "Last Taboo."

23. Tracye Matthews was one of the first historians to bring a gender analysis to the examination of Black Power. Historian Rhonda Williams has persuasively argued that Black women also deployed Black Power rhetoric and tactics outside of self-described Black Power groups, an argument I have also made elsewhere. Matthews, "No One Ever Asks What a Man's Role in the Revolution Is." Williams, "Black Women, Urban Politics and Engendering Black Power"; Greene, *Our Separate Ways*. See also Spencer, *Revolution Has Come*; Farmer, *Remaking Black Power*; and Taylor, *Promise of Patriarchy*.

24. Woodard, *Nation within a Nation*, 183; Baraka, quoted in Farmer, *Remaking Black Power*, 123; 115–25. Black women's antirape activism is explored in part 3.

25. "Editorial—JoAnne Little Case," *BP*, August 18, 1975.

26. Cleaver, *Soul on Ice*. Cleaver joined the Panthers in 1966 and became minister of information soon after. He fled the country to Cuba and then Algeria after a 1968 shoot-out with police. Following a dispute with Huey Newton in 1971, he broke with the Party.

27. James, *Shadowboxing*, 102; Spencer, "Engendering the Black Freedom Struggle," 100, 108.

28. Started in 1973 shortly after Angela Davis was acquitted, the National Alliance Against Racist and Political Repression focused on North Carolina's repression of political activists, especially African Americans and Indigenous peoples. Hannigan, Platt, and Davis, "Interview with Angela Davis."

29. Davis, "Joan Little," 37–40; Lyle Denniston, "An Easy Air Prevails at Little Trial," *Washington Star*, August 10, 1975, news clipping, box 3, HHH Papers; see photo of Davis and Little in Lonnie Kashif, "Common Suffering Links Activist, Rape Victim," *Muhammad Speaks*, June 20, 1975.

30. Davis quoted feminist Susan Griffin, who had theorized rape as a form of terror against women. Davis, "Joan Little," 39, 40.

31. Karenga, "In Defense of Sis. Joanne," 40.

32. Elaine Brown, "JoAnne Little Acted for Us All," *BP*, July 21, 1975. Davis, "Joan Little," 39.

33. Black women's antirape activism is explored more fully in part 3.

CHAPTER 6

1. *State of North Carolina vs. Joan Little, Defendant*, Joan Little Testimony, August 11–13, 1975, folders 1–2, JRJ Collection. Little testified over several days, and I have included only a small part of her testimony and cross-examination here. Scholarly debate continues concerning detailed descriptions of violence perpetrated on Black bodies in what sometimes has been denounced as "trauma porn." I have thought long and hard about whether to include this deeply disturbing and graphic material. In making my decision, I shared this chapter with numerous scholars, the majority of them African American women, some of whom have experienced sexual assault. Everyone thought that the material should be included, although I take full responsibility for including it. Several other considerations guided my decision-making. First, as a historian I worried that omitting this evidence risked sanitizing and erasing anti-Black violence and sexual abuse. Second, the testimony, while admittedly distressing and even triggering for some readers, is essentially a reflection of the prosecution's brutality, not a debasement of the defendant. Third, Little's experiences within the criminal punishment system were not atypical, especially for low-income Black women. And finally, Joan's testimony reveals her refusal to be reduced to the caricature of the wanton, seductress killer the prosecution hoped to create. It also shows her triumph over the stereotype of the helpless victim as she defiantly proclaimed her right to defend her womanhood. Despite the trauma of her ordeal both in a jail cell and later in court, Joan Little was always more than simply a victorious sexual assault victim-survivor, as subsequent chapters will demonstrate. For an opposing view from literary scholar and cultural critic Saidiya Hartman, see *Scenes of Subjection* and especially *Lose Your Mother*, in which she develops the paradigm of "the afterlife of slavery," which is especially applicable to Joan Little's predicament. See also Sharpe, *In the Wake*. My thanks to Ayanna Drakos for reminding me of this literature. For an insightful discussion of this issue from an African American sexual assault survivor and prison abolitionist, see Mariame Kaba, "Itemizing Atrocity," in Kaba, *We Do This 'Til We Free Us*, 82–87.

2. Reston, *Innocence of Joan Little*, 302, 306–7; *State of North Carolina vs. Joan Little, Defendant*, Joan Little Testimony, August 11–13, 1975, folders 1–2, JRJ Collection. After the trial, Paul told a reporter that he had instructed Joan to recount the sexual assault repeatedly to ensure that she would grow "bored" with it and so that the prosecution would be unable to anger her and cause her to contradict herself. Paul also claimed that at times he brought her to tears during these sessions. Wayne King, "Joan Little's Lawyer Scorns Legal System and Says He 'Bought' Her Acquittal," *NYT*, October 20, 1975.

3. *State of North Carolina vs. Joan Little, Defendant*, Joan Little Testimony, August 11–13, 1975, folders 1–2, JRJ Collection.

4. Little testimony, August 11–13, 1975.

5. "Karen Bethea-Shields: In Joan Little's Cell," interview by David Cecelski, *N&O*, January 12, 2003.

6. *State of North Carolina vs. Joan Little, Defendant*, Joan Little Testimony, August 11–13, 1975, folders 1–2, JRJ Collection; Reston, *Innocence of Joan Little*, 308–16.

7. Alligood, quoted in "Widow of Jailer Believes Joan Had Help in Slaying," *Afro-American*, August 9, 1975.

8. Cathy Steele Roche, "Joan Little Testifies Today," *Washington (N.C.) Daily News*, August 11, 1975; *State of North Carolina vs. Joan Little, Defendant*, Joan Little Testimony, August 11–13, 1975, folders 1–2, JRJ Collection.

9. William Griffin, Argument to the Jury, August 14, 1975, folder 8, JRJ Collection; Chalmers quoted in Reston, *Innocence of Joan Little*, 321; Rick Nichols, "Lawyers End Arguments: Case Goes to Jury Today," *N&O*, August 15, 1975. I discuss the Inez García case in part 3.

10. Cathy Steele Roche, "Little Defense Opens Today," *Washington (N.C.) Daily News*, August 7, 1975; Jury Argument of John Wilkerson, *State of North Carolina vs. Joan Little*, folder 10, JRJ Collection. Part 3 includes a fuller discussion of the changing definitions of rape.

11. Jerry Paul, Argument to the Jury, August 14, 1975, folder 9, JRJ Collection; Rick Nichols, "Lawyers End Arguments: Case Goes to Jury Today," *N&O*, August 15, 1975. Paul had been suffering from various health ailments throughout the trial and his ten-year-old son was a fighting a return of leukemia that would soon take his life.

12. The only trial testimony currently available has been placed in the JRJ Collection. Unfortunately, Galloway's summation was not included. After several inquiries, I was informed by court officials that the full trial transcript is no longer available and was likely destroyed. Karen (Galloway) Bethea-Shields, interview by author, November 11, 2013; McGuire, *At the Dark End of the Street*. Black women, as well as white women, testified at that New York City speak-out, frequently seen as the start of the "second wave" feminist antirape movement. Jacquet, *Injustices of Rape*, 10.

13. Karen (Galloway) Bethea-Shields, interview by author, November 11, 2013.

14. The jury initially comprised five white women, three Black women, two white men, and two Black men; later a Black male alternate juror replaced one of the white women. Rick Nichols, "Verdict Comes Quickly," *N&O*, August 16, 1975; David Zucchino, "Jurors Say Evidence Too Thin to Convict," *N&O*, August 16, 1975; "Joan Little to Speak from Coast to Coast," *Afro-American*, August 23, 1975.

15. "Long Night's Drama Closes Ugly Chapter," *Washington (N.C.) Daily News*, August 19, 1975. Royko quoted in Wayne King, "Joan Little's Lawyer Scorns Legal System and Says

He 'Bought' Her Acquittal," *NYT*, October 20, 1975. For editorials in a variety of North Carolina newspapers, see clippings file, box 36, HHH Papers.

16. Rick Nichols, "Verdict Comes Quickly," *N&O*, August 16, 1975; "Another Victory for Equal Justice Under the Law" (cartoon), *Afro-American*, August 19–23, 1975.

17. There was some confusion regarding exactly when the court session had ended and whether it had been extended. Harwell, *True Deliverance*, 270–73; Testimony of Joan Little, August 11, 1975. For other discrepancies and even the possibility that a third party, a sixteen-year-old trustee, was involved in Alligood's murder, see Reston, *Innocence of Joan Little*, 205–25, 330.

18. Reston, *Innocence of Joan Little*, 294; *State of North Carolina vs. Joan Little, Defendant*, Joan Little Testimony, August 11–13, 1975, folders 1–2, JRJ Collection; Wright, quoted in Reston, *Innocence of Joan Little*, 44. The tape of the Wright interview uses different language. Marjorie Wright, interview by James Reston Jr., n.d., JRJ Collection. Morris Dees, "Sheriff Davis" interview notes, n.d., box 1, JLC Collection. When I asked Joan about her testimony and use of the word "again," she said her lawyer had instructed her not to talk about it. Joan Little, interview, October 27, 2013.

19. *State of North Carolina vs. Joan Little, Defendant*, Joan Little Testimony, August 11–13, 1975, folders 1–2, JRJ Collection; Peter Galuszka, "Mother, Frinks Charge Jail Harassment," *Washington (N.C.) Daily News*, September 2, 1974.

20. Later Paul claimed he had misplaced the clipping and then thrown it away, and Joan said both then and more recently that she couldn't remember it. In a recent interview, Bethea-Shields (Galloway) also claimed to have no knowledge or memory of the clipping. Nor did Morris Dees or any of the three prosecutors. However, the local *Washington Daily News* did run the Jael story on June 15, 1974, according to Ashley Futrell, the paper's editor. "Defense Attorney Says Joan Little Acquittal 'Bought,'" *N&O*, October 21, 1975; Harwell, *True Deliverance*, 278–79. Joan Little, interview by author, May 1, 2012. Karen (Galloway) Bethea-Shields, interview by author, November 11, 2013. Reston quoted from the Old Testament verse, Judges 4:18–21, and said it appeared August 6 but didn't provide a year. Reston, *Innocence of Joan Little*, 281. Rick Nichols, "Miss Little Can't Recall Clipping in Her Bible"; Nichols, "Prosecutor Didn't See Clipping"; Wayne King, "Little's Lawyer: Justice Was 'Bought,'" clippings file, box 36, HHH Papers.

21. Paul, quoted in Reston, *Innocence of Joan Little*, 110.

22. Mitchell, quoted in McNeil, "Joanne Is You," 273; Rick Nichols, "Little Case Questions Unanswered," *N&O*, February 16, 1975, news clipping, box 1, JLC Collection.

23. Rick Nichols, "Ex-Inmates Testify in Little Case," *Raleigh N&O*, August 8, 1975; Benjamin E. Mays, "Joanne Little's Case," *Chicago Defender*, August 30, 1975; Reston, *Innocence of Joan Little*, 213–15. Morris Dees, "Phyllis Ann Moore" interview notes, n.d.; Nichols, "Little Case Questions Unanswered," *N&O*, February 16, 1975, news clipping, box 1, JLC Collection; *State of North Carolina vs. Joan Little, Defendant*, Joan Little Testimony, August 11–13, 1975, folders 1–2, JRJ Collection.

24. Paul, quoted in "Defense Attorney Says Joan Little Acquittal 'Bought,'" *N&O*, October 21, 1975.

25. "We Won Because I Could Buy the Things to Win," *National Observer*, n.d., box 36, clippings file, HHH Papers; *off our backs*, quoted in Reston, *Innocence of Joan Little*, 326; "A Big Little Victory" (editorial), *Amsterdam News* (New York), August 27, 1975.

26. Louis Randolph, interview by James Reston Jr., n.d., JRJ Collection; Reston, *Innocence of Joan Little*, 339; Harwell, *True Deliverance*, 277.

27. Mariame Kaba, "Free Us All: Participatory Defense Campaigns as Abolitionist Organizing," in Kaba, *We Do This 'Til We Free Us*, 116, 111.

CHAPTER 7

1. The title for part 2 is drawn from the following passage in *The Autobiography of W. E. B. Du Bois*, quoted in Davis, *If They Come in the Morning*, 1: "And of this army of the wronged, the proportion of Negroes is frightful. We protect and defend sensational cases where Negroes are involved. But the great mass of arrested or accused black folk have no defense."

2. Quoted in Reston, *Innocence of Joan Little*, 92, 90–92. Chenier reportedly lost her job at Carolina Friends School, a Quaker school located between Durham and Chapel Hill, because of her involvement in the Free Joan Little campaign. Her employer denied that Chenier's activism was the reason for her termination. Considering the Carolina Friends School's history of involvement in the civil rights movement, it seems unlikely Chenier was fired for this reason.

3. After she surrendered to authorities, Little remained in Woman's Prison from September 1974 until the end of February 1975, when she was released on $115,000 bail. Ginny Carroll, "Joan Little Freed on $115,000 Bond," *N&O*, February 27, 1975; Celine Chenier, interview by James Reston Jr., n.d., JRJ Collection; Little's great-great grandmother, quoted in Reston, *Innocence of Joan Little*, 93.

4. The "wave" metaphor itself has come under criticism for its centering of white women's experiences at the expense of Black women and other women of color. See part 3 for a fuller discussion of Black feminism. On the women's prison movement in the 1970s, see Thuma, *All Our Trials*.

5. Korstad, *Civil Rights Unionism*; Greene, *Our Separate Ways*; "History of the Concerned Women for Justice," typescript in author's possession; "Woman's Concern Eased on 'Chain Gang Rights,'" *Greensboro Daily News*, March 1, 1975; Marsha Lamm, "They're Prisoners' Link with Society," *N&O*, December 21, 1980; Flyer: Concerned Women for Justice Hazardous Waste Conference in Warren County, April 23, 1983, in author's possession. "Under the Dome," *N&O*, March 30, 1978. In the 1980s, CWJ worked with local Black women in majority-Black Warren County to protest a toxic waste dump, a campaign that birthed the term "environmental racism." Glusman, "Moment of Possibility," 59–67; Kaplan, *Crazy for Democracy*, 47–71. My thanks to Melynn Glusman for sharing these documents on CWJ.

6. McDuffie, *Sojourning for Freedom*, 140–41, 198, 215–16; Davis, *Autobiography*.

7. Jerry Paul to Charlene Mitchell, open letter, *Chicago Alliance Against Racist and Political Repression Newsletter* 11, no. 8 (November 1975): 7. Following her acquittal, Joan Little criticized both Charlene Michell and Angela Davis, claiming that they were late to support her and accusing the Communist Party of undermining her defense. Instead, she credited Celine Chenier, who had alerted Mitchell and Davis to Little's case, and then Larry Little with launching the Free Joan Little campaign. Although Joan believed that Davis was unduly influenced by whites, she felt that white feminists, especially poor white

women, were more supportive of her case. "JoAnne Little Talks with the Black Press," *BP*, September 8, 1975, 14–15, 25.

8. For an overview of how the courts and criminal justice system were used to suppress political dissent in North Carolina, especially among Blacks, see National Alliance Against Racist and Political Repression, *North Carolina*.

9. Following her acquittal in 1972, Angela Davis became one of the nation's most outspoken prison activists and abolitionists. McNeil, "Joanne Is You," 262, 268–69; *North Carolina Alliance Newsletter* 1, no. 1 (1974).

10. "Black Woman's Bill of Rights," NABF 1976, box 1, NBFO/NABF Papers; NABF Conference, October 21–27, 1977, Resolutions, box 1, NABF Papers; Lawston, *Sisters Outside*, 52–55.

11. Thuma, *All Our Trials*, 110; Kunzel, *Criminal Intimacy*, 202–5.

12. Karen DeCrow speech, n.d. [ca. 1975], box 201, NOW Papers. Despite this show of support for incarcerated women, NOW was preoccupied with its struggle to pass the Equal Rights Amendment (ERA), especially in North Carolina. The Tarheel State was viewed as a swing state in the final, ultimately unsuccessful, push to secure the landmark amendment and most North Carolina NOW chapters made the ERA campaign a priority in the 1970s. On the ERA struggle in North Carolina, see Matthews and De Hart, *Sex, Gender, and the Politics of ERA*.

13. "1,000 Rally for JoAnne Little at Trial Opening," *BP*, July 28, 1975; "We Have Long Way to Go Before We're Free: JoAnne Little's Address to Oakland Victory Rally," *BP*, September 1, 1975. "Trial Notes: Joan Little," *Midnight Special*, January 1975, 22; "Prisoners Against Rape Support Joanne Little," *Midnight Special*, March 1975, 8; "Trial Briefs; Jo Anne Little, December 9, 1975," *Midnight Special*, December 1975–January 1976, 29; "Joann's Trial Begins," *Attica News*, June 26, 1975, 5; Adrian D. X. to Dear Sister JoAnne, December 22, 1974; Alfred Juhl to Jerry Paul, June 1, 1975, box 1, JLC Collection.

14. Flyer, Prisoners Solidarity Committee Supports Joanne Little, August 7, 1975, box 36, HHH Papers.

15. Berger, *Captive Nation*; Berger and Losier, *Rethinking the American Prison Movement*; Johnson, *Inner Lives*. Clark, quoted in Paul Pierce, "Southern Coalition Probes Prisoners Rights," box 142, CAB Papers. In the early 1970s in California and elsewhere, activist-artists also performed in prisons. Personal correspondence with scholar and artist Thulani Davis, June 2016.

16. Berger, *Captive Nation*, 6.

17. "Joan Little" lyrics quoted in McNeil, "Joanne Is You," 259. Reagon also was inspired by women's prison music recorded in the 1930s at Parchman Penitentiary. She wrote the liner notes for a 1987 rerelease of the songs on the album *Jailhouse Blues: Women's a Capella Songs from Parchman Penitentiary*, calling the songs "the best singing lesson I have ever had in Black American vocal song style." Reagon, quoted in Haley, *No Mercy Here*, 216. "Joanne Little" was later recorded by Sweet Honey in the Rock. On the original forty-five recording, the flip side featured another song about Little, "On the Line." It was composed by John Loudermilk and sung by white southern folk singer and activist Anne Romaine as part of the Southern Folk Cultural Folk Revival Project. The project was a biracial group of activist performers who toured the South, including southern prisons. The first Southern Folk Festival was established in the 1960s and performed at civil rights rallies and colleges throughout the South. "Record Now Available," advertisement, *Southern Patriot*, June–July 1975, 4. Following the 2020 police murders of George Floyd and Breonna Taylor,

an outpouring of songs, performances, various visual culture creations, and fundraisers have emerged from Black hip-hop and other cultural artists.

18. Malcolm X, quoted in Marable, *Malcolm X*, 241; King, quoted in Berger, *Captive Nation*, 24; Carmichael, quoted in Olsson, *Black Power Mixtape*; Nash, quoted in Olson, *Freedom's Daughters*, 212.

19. Berger, *Captive Nation*, 28, 30, 25. However, the NAACP-LDEF did pursue legal challenges, mostly via the courts, concerning due process violations and other forms of discrimination in the criminal justice system. See Gottschalk, *Prison and the Gallows*.

20. White, *Too Heavy a Load*, 194; see also Colley, *Ain't Scared of Your Jail*. Rape in men's prisons began to receive increased attention in the late 1960s and 1970s, following the highly publicized wave of prisoner protest and violence that emerged in this period. The heightened focus was also highly racialized. Victims were overwhelmingly portrayed as white, including white activists, and the perpetrators as African American, a new twist on the Black beast rapist myth. Some writers and investigators, informed by feminist analyses of rape, asserted that interracial prison rape was politically motivated by racial politics: Black prisoners seeking racial retribution and asserting hypermasculinity through control, domination, and sexual abuse of white prisoners. Kunzel, *Criminal Intimacy*, 149–89.

21. This theme will be explored more fully in part 3. LeFlouria, *Chained in Silence*, 104–5, 143–44, 165. Haley, *No Mercy Here*, 120–41; McGuire, *At the Dark End of the Street*, 3–39. In 2011, when Taylor was in her nineties, the Alabama legislature officially apologized for the state's failure to prosecute Taylor's attackers. Sewell Chan, "Recy Taylor, Who Fought for Justice After a 1944 Rape, Dies at 97," *NYT*, December 29, 2017.

22. The SFTJ was an all-Black women's organization; but unlike the WCEJ, the SFTJ did not define itself as solely concerned with women's issues. Ironically, the debate over the participation of white women was partly responsible for the SFTJ's demise. McDuffie, *Sojourning for Freedom*, 171–82, 199–201. The WCEJ was technically a multiracial women's organization, although Black women, such as clubwoman Mary Church Terrell, held top leadership positions. Like their antilynching forbears, Black WCEJ women insisted that white women take a stand against white supremacy and understand that they "can truly protect their rights only when they join with their Negro sisters to protect the rights of all women." Quoted in Gore, *Radicalism at the Crossroads*, 92, 74–99.

CHAPTER 8

1. Muhammad, *Condemnation of Blackness*; Berger, *Captive Nation*; Chase, *We Are Not Slaves*; Felber, *Those Who Know Don't Say*.

2. Bloom and Martin, *Black Against Empire*; Marable, *Malcolm X*, 90, 123, 240–41; Berger, *Captive Nation*, 66–67; Joseph, *Waiting 'Til the Midnight Hour*, 212–13.

3. Berger, *Captive Nation*, 95, 66, 170–71, 189–91. Marie Gottschalk argues that the decline of the prison movement was rooted in a weak U.S. welfare state and the tendency to seek penal and legal solutions to social problems via the courts rather than securing remedies through an expanded welfare state. Ironically, prison reformers enhanced the creation of a carceral state by calling for better prisons rather than reducing or eliminating incarceration. Gottschalk, *Prison and the Gallows*.

4. Hoover, quoted in Williams, *From the Bullet to the Ballot*, 173. The Smith Act had been used to imprison communists in the 1950s. Joseph, *Waiting 'Til the Midnight Hour*,

241–42; Bloom and Martin, *Black Against Empire*, 186, 188–89, 210. This is not to suggest that the Panthers were always innocent, as Huey Newton's descent into drug addiction and thuggish authoritarianism reveals. However, Panther antipolice rhetoric was frequently more bravado than actual.

5. In 1969, Fred Hampton, the charismatic leader of the Illinois Black Panther Party, was asleep in his bed when Chicago police with the help of the FBI shot and killed him. In 1960 at age eighteen, George Jackson was convicted of a seventy-dollar armed robbery at a gas station. He received an "indeterminate" sentence in a California prison where he was radicalized, joined the Black Panthers, and became an acclaimed prison writer. In 1971 he was killed by prison officials in an alleged prison break under circumstances that remain controversial. Hill, *Men, Mobs, and Law*, 265–314; Williams, *From the Bullet to the Ballot*.

6. See, for example, Shakur, "Women in Prison."

7. Hoover, quoted in Matthews, "'No One Ever Asks What a Man's Role in the Revolution Is,'" 246. Other Panther survival programs included liberation schools, free clothing, health clinics, housing cooperatives, pest control, sickle cell anemia testing, renter's assistance, ambulances, and legal aid. Bloom and Martin, *Black Against Empire*, 179–98.

8. The Organization of Black Liberation received a charter from the National Committee to Combat Fascism and was harassed for several years by the FBI and local police before gaining official recognition as a BPP chapter in 1970. Freidman, "Picking Up Where Robert F. Williams Left Off."

9. Larry Little, quoted in Freidman, 61.

10. Larry Little, quoted in Freidman, 69. On Larry Little's legal troubles, see Fergus, epilogue to Williams and Lazerow, *Liberated Territory*, 283–86.

11. "B.P.P. Names Joann Little 'Woman of the Year,'" "JoAnn Little Talks with *The Black Panther*," *BP*, June 30, 1975, 1, 14. Larry Little quit the BPP in 1976 and the Party soon declined. He ran for Winston-Salem alderman in 1974 but was narrowly defeated, possibly due to election fraud, but later won election. His North Ward became known as the "permanent Panther seat" when another former Panther was elected after Little. Freidman, "Picking Up Where Robert F. Williams Left Off," 60–81; Fergus, *Liberalism*, 186.

12. Free busing for families to visit prisoners still exists in many places, a legacy of the Panther program. Nelson, *Body and Soul*; Bloom and Martin, *Black Against Empire*, 190–91.

13. Berger, *Captive Nation*, 44–46, 62; Gilmore, *Golden Gulag*, 274n7; Parenti, *Lockdown America*, 112–13; Hinton, *America on Fire*.

14. Thompson, "Why Mass Incarceration Matters." On LEAA funds in New Orleans, see Murakawa, *First Civil Right*, 73. Gottschalk and Murakawa trace the origins of the modern U.S. carceral state to earlier periods, pointing to a weak welfare state as key. Both also indict, although they do not blame, liberals for inadvertently exacerbating and failing to protest the rise of the carceral state. Gottschalk, *Prison and the Gallows*. Scholars debate which regions took the lead. Robert Perkinson and Alex Lichtenstein point to the South as a leader in the development of the carceral state; Lichtenstein joins Ruth Gilmore by adding California. Perkinson, *Texas Tough*; Lichtenstein, "Flocatex and the Fiscal Limits of Mass Incarceration"; Gilmore, *Golden Gulag*. For a recent example of the damage created by SWAT teams, see Kevin Sack, "Door-Busting Drug Raids Leave Trail of Blood," *NYT*, March 18, 2017.

15. In *Cooper v. Pate*, a suit brought by a Black Muslim inmate in Illinois, the Supreme Court ruled in 1964 that prisoners could not be denied religious materials; more important, it affirmed the right of prisoners to sue prison officials in federal court. Chase, "We

Are Not Slaves," 77–79, 84–85; Felber, "Shades of Mississippi." See also Felber, *Those Who Know Don't Say*.

16. Joseph Ingle to Alex Hurder, March 23, 1979, box 142, CAB Papers. North Carolina's death penalty was affirmed in *Waddell v. North Carolina* (1973) but was again challenged and struck down in *Woodson v. North Carolina* (1976). Guided by the Supreme Court's 1976 *Gregg v. Georgia* decision, which upheld Georgia's death penalty, North Carolina enacted a new capital punishment statute the following year. With some minor changes, it remains in effect to this day.

17. A 2017 report from the Prison Policy Initiative, *Following the Money of Mass Incarceration*, revealed that the true cost of incarceration, including what families and governments pay, is closer to $181 billion a year. According to the Sentencing Project, the trend toward mass incarceration showed no signs of receding until the second decade of the twenty-first century, and then only slightly. From 1976 to 2016, there were 1,427 executions in the United States. Of these, 1,161 were in the South, with the vast majority in Texas. As of December 2014, fifty-six women were on death row, and from 1976 to 2005 sixteen women were executed. Just as Donald Trump was leaving office in 2021, the first woman in nearly seventy years was executed by the federal government. Welty, "Death Penalty in North Carolina." In 2015, thirty-two states along with the federal government and U.S. military retained capital punishment statutes; nearly 60 percent of the 2,905 people on death row were nonwhite (e.g., Black, Latino, Native American, Asian) and less than 2 percent were female. In North Carolina, the numbers were similar; of the 156 persons on death row, nearly 60 percent were nonwhite. California had the most people on death row, followed by Florida and Texas. NAACP-LDEF, *Death Row U.S.A.*, 2015, https://www.naacpldf.org/our-thinking/death-row-usa/; Sentencing Project, https://www.sentencingproject.org/; Stevenson, *Just Mercy*, 16.

18. For a description of the "prison nation," including its impact on low-income Black women, see Richie, *Arrested Justice*.

CHAPTER 9

1. Berger, *Captive Nation*, 129. Victoria Law argues that scholars and activists alike have generally ignored prison protest by women, which was widespread. Law, *Resistance Behind Bars*, 13. The North Carolina Women's Prison strike is covered in the next chapter.

2. Law, *Resistance Behind Bars*, 13; "Women Prisoners Unite," *Triple Jeopardy*, September–October 1971, 10; Freedman, *Sisters' Keepers*, 157, 225.

3. "Nonnormative" gender presentation and sexual expression could also subject women prisoners to various forms of involuntary behavior-modification techniques. Law, *Resistance Behind Bars*, 11; Thuma, *All Our Trials*, 55–87, 95–96. On conditions and protests at women's prisons, including Bedford Hills, Rikers Island, and Alderson, see "A Difficult Prey," *Midnight Special*, May–June 1974, 1; "Women's Freedom Committee," *Midnight Special*, January 1974, 14; "Rikers Island Women's House of Detention Suit," *Midnight Special*, January 1974, 23; "Resistance: Women Prisoners Receive Same Treatment as Men Prisoners," *Midnight Special*, February 1974, 9; "Sisters Speak Out," *Midnight Special*, September–October 1974, 13; "Sisterhood Is Powerful," *Midnight Special*, October–November 1974, 1; "Sisters Fight On," *Midnight Special*, January 1975, 1. Controversy and debate among people of Hispanic descent regarding nomenclature continues;

some prefer "Latina/Latino" or "Latin@" over "Hispanic." More recently, some academics and activists have adopted "Latinx" for a more gender-inclusive, nonbinary term. Since "Latinx" was not in usage in the 1960s–1980s, the years this book focuses on, I have used both "Latina" and "Latinx."

4. Although Kunstler was ousted rather quickly from Joan Little's murder-rape trial after the judge charged him with contempt, he defended her during her extradition case and in later legal entanglements. He also was an attorney for the Attica Brothers Defense League.

5. Other Attica prisoner leaders included a white radical from the Weather Underground and Puerto Rican prisoners from the Young Lords. In 1997, Attica prisoners won a judgment against New York State for violation of their civil rights, although the state did not allocate the $8 million in damages until 2000. In 2005, guards and other prison workers won a judgment of $12 million. However, the state has yet to acknowledge its use of excessive force, the torture of prisoners who surrendered, or responsibility for any of the thirty-nine deaths by troopers. Heather Thompson, "The Lingering Injustice of Attica," *NYT*, September 8, 2011; Thompson, *Blood in the Water*, 45, 65–70.

6. Jesse Jackson, quoted in Fortner, *Black Silent Majority*, 11; Forman, *Locking Up Our Own*, 17–46. For a critique of Fortner and his response, see the Donna Murch and Michael Fortner exchange in the *Boston Globe*, October 6 and 23, 2015. For different responses to "tough on crime" policies," especially among working-class and poor Blacks (including Black mothers), see, for example, Murch, "Crack in Los Angeles." For a discussion of Mothers Reclaiming Our Children, see Gilmore, *Golden Gulag*, 181–240. Black elected officials, including members of the Congressional Black Caucus, were also divided on anticrime legislation, especially the new drug laws passed in the 1980s. Alexander, *New Jim Crow*, 53–54.

7. Thompson, *Blood in the Water*, 559–60; Chase, "We Are Not Slaves," 74–75; Chase, *We Are Not Slaves*.

8. Historian Adam Malka has shown how the forced labor loophole in the Thirteenth Amendment and some white abolitionists inadvertently planted the seeds for mass incarceration by heightening the criminalization of Blacks and exploding the arrest and imprisonment rates of Black residents after the Civil War. Malka, *Men of Mobtown*. Jim Grant, "In North Carolina Prisoners Organize Union," *Southern Patriot*, February 1975, 3. On prison conditions at Central Prison, see North Carolina Advisory Committee to the U.S. Commission on Civil Rights, *Prisons in North Carolina*; Taylor, *Central Prison*. According to state correction commissioner Bounds, prisoner wages were to be paid at the "discretion" of the Department of Correction. Bounds, *Riot at Central Prison*.

9. Bounds, quoted in Tibbs, *From Black Power to Prison Power*, 143; Bounds, *Riot at Central Prison*.

10. Bounds, quoted in Tibbs, *From Black Power to Prison Power*, 144. Several years later, the NCPLU claimed that seventy-seven had been wounded. Bounds's report noted seventy-eight casualties, with six listed as lethal. Bounds, *Riot at Central Prison*.

11. Thompson, "Rethinking Working-Class Struggles," 24. The NCPLU drafted bylaws, articles of incorporation, and a purpose and goals statement and applied for nonprofit corporate status in North Carolina. Tibbs, *From Black Power to Prison Power*, 137; *Raleigh Times*, March 6, 1973, news clipping, series 1, box 1, TJR Papers; "6 Dead, 77 Wounded,

and 7 Years Later, No Pay for Convict Labor," *NCPLU Newsletter* 1, no. 5 (August–September 1975): 11.

12. Brooks quoted in Tibbs, *From Black Power to Prison Power*, 140; J. L. Hill, "Manipulation Through Racism," *NCPLU Newsletter* 1, no. 3 (February–March 1975): 18. *NCPLU Newsletter* issues 2 and 3 are both dated February–March.

13. Michaels, "'If Free People Are Not Allowed to Have Unions"; Anne C. Willett, "In Our Peaceful Struggle," *NCPLU Newsletter* 1, no. 5 (August–September 1975): 1.

14. Hill, quoted in Berger, *Captive Nation*, 20, 7.

15. In the Scottsboro trials, nine African American teenage boys were falsely convicted and given death sentences for allegedly raping two white women on an Alabama train; their trials lasted for decades before the last defendant was finally released. Emmett Till was accused of making a lewd remark to a white woman and was lynched in retaliation. Goodman, *Stories of Scottsboro*; Tyson, *Blood of Emmett Till*; Hill, *Men, Mobs, and Law*, 293–99; Thompson, *Blood in the Water*, 232, 457–58; Chase, *We Are Not Slaves*, chap. 4.

16. Although Lorton Prison was in Virginia, in 1946 it came under the jurisdiction of Washington, D.C., and was ordered closed in the 1990s. Illinois Humanities Council Project Support Application, April 14, 1977, box 2, NABF Papers.

17. Tibbs, *From Black Power to Prison Power*, 137–38, 141–42, 151–53; *Durham (N.C.) Morning Herald*, December 1, 1974, news clipping, series 1, box 1, TJR Papers; Jim Grant, "N.C. Prisoners Union Harassed," *Southern Patriot*, December 1975, 8; Paul M. Baugh, "Overcrowded Prisons Created," *NCPLU Newsletter* 1, no. 2 (February–March 1975): 13. Eppinette's conviction was later overturned on appeal. Jim Grant, "In North Carolina Prisoners Organize Union," *Southern Patriot*, February 1975; Michaels, "If Free People." In some documents Robbie "Purner" appears as Robbie "Pruner."

18. "Goals of the NCPLU," n.d.; "NCPLU Political Education," n.d.; Robbie Purner memo to All Unit Reps., March 3, 1975, series 1, box 1, TJR Papers; Morrison and Purner, quoted in Jim Grant, "In North Carolina Prisoners Organize Union," *Southern Patriot*, February 1975.

19. "Incentive Wage Program Will Provide Prison Compensation"; *NCPLU Newsletter* 1, no. 2 (February–March 1975): 12; "6 Dead, 77 Wounded, and 7 Years Later, No Pay for Convict Labor," *NCPLU Newsletter* 1, no. 5 (August–September 1975): 11; "Union Condemns Prison Industries" *NCPLU Newsletter* 1, no. 3 (February–March 1975): 16,; Ernest McIntyre, "The Myth of Vocational Training," *NCPLU Newsletter* 1, no. 3 (February–March 1975): 13; Thompson, "Why Mass Incarceration Matters," 719–25.

20. Black Inmates of Central Prison, "Raleigh Demonstration," *Midnight Special*, September–October 1975, 12. On a prisoner boycott of Christmas dinner at Central Prison, see Pajoma Tutashinda, "Holiday Special," *Midnight Special*, March 1974, 24.

21. The DOC order was undermined when the union charged discriminatory treatment by pointing out that other prisoner groups, such as the JAYCEES and Alcoholics Anonymous, were permitted to function. Tibbs, *From Black Power to Prison Power*, 144–51, 158. In retaliation for his civil rights activism, Jim Grant was given a twenty-five-year sentence for burning a horse stable. After his conviction, he was hired by the Southern Conference Education Fund and wrote for the *Southern Patriot*.

22. Tibbs, *From Black Power to Prison Power*, 161.

23. Quoted in Tibbs, 178–79.

24. Lesley Oelsner, "Justices Back Curbs on Prisoner Unions," *NYT*, June 24, 1977, quoted in Tibbs, 179. In the 1871 *Ruffin v. Commonwealth* decision, the Virginia court ruled that the prisoner had "not only forfeited his right to his liberty, but all his personal rights except those which the law in its humanity accords to him. . . . He is for the time being a slave of the state." This translated into a "hands off" policy, signaling court reluctance to interfere with prison operations. The ruling left all prisoners, especially African Americans, vulnerable. The court began to reverse itself in the 1940s, slowly recognizing prisoners' rights. Even then, enforcement remained a problem, and Black prisoners often had little protection. *Ruffin v. Commonwealth*, quoted in Tibbs, 184, 185–95, 198.

25. Tibbs, *From Black Power to Prison Power*, 179.

26. The United Prisoners Union (UPU) formed in the aftermath of strikes at San Quentin and Folsom Prisons in 1970. In 1973, the Prisoners' Union (PU) split from the more radical UPU, which was headed by Popeye Jackson, reputed by one sociologist to be a "convict opportunist." Cummins, *Rise and Fall of California's Radical Prison Movement*, 219, 191, 199–204, 214–17. According to legal scholar Donald Tibbs, in nearly every prison where a union was organized, more than 90 percent of the prisoners joined, a figure that seems high. Tibbs also noted that from 1971 to 1975 over 11,000 prisoners in thirteen states claimed union membership. Tibbs, *From Black Power to Prison Power*, 155–56; Thompson, "Rethinking Working-Class Struggles," 23–25.

27. "Announcements," *Midnight Special*, May–June 1974, 23. Historian Robert Chase argues that the prison movement had three distinct branches: a prison abolitionist movement; a prison union movement; and a legal, civil rights, and social movement that focused on prison conditions and prisoners' rights. However, his focus is on male prisoners. Chase, "We Are Not Slaves," 75–76.

CHAPTER 10

1. In 1929, the Industrial Farm Colony for Women opened in Kinston, North Carolina, for nonfelons after a report noted the sexual abuse of women in local jails. It was closed in 1947. Rafter, *Partial Justice*, 56–57, 92, 62–63, 234n29; Harris, "Shadows Behind Bars," 14–27.

2. "Southern Blues," *Midnight Special*, May 1975, 16; "Trial Briefs: Joanne Little," *Midnight Special*, May 1975, 21; Anne Willett, "Our Peaceful Protest," in North Carolina Women's Prison Project, *Break de Chains*, 5. San Quentin inmate quoted in Cummins, *Rise and Fall of California's Radical Prison Movement*, 194; Davis, "From the Prison of Slavery to the Slavery of Prison," 75.

3. One of the key goals of southern prison activists was to overturn "the legal tradition of prisoners as slaves of the state." Chase, "We Are Not Slaves," 81, 75.

4. "Open Letter to the People," in North Carolina Women's Prison Project, *Break de Chains*, 28; Ann Finch, "Women Prisoners Protest Living and Working Conditions," *Southern Patriot*, April [June] 1975, 8; Jim Grant, "Resistance Sweeps N.C. Prisons," *Southern Patriot*, October 1975, 4. According to the North Carolina Advisory Committee to the U.S. Commission on Civil Rights, *Prisons in North Carolina*, 23, the laundry bins at Women's Prison weighed 360 pounds. On racialized and gendered prison labor policies that excluded Black women from the category "female" in an earlier period in the South, see Haley, "Like I Was a Man." On the use of men's prison garb to defeminize Black women

prisoners in southern convict leasing camps and on chain gangs in what Talitha LeFlouria has called "social rape," see LeFlouria, *Chained in Silence*, 88–92.

5. "She Came of Age on Death Row," *Charlotte Observer*, December 18, 1982, news clipping, series 1, box 2, TJR Papers; "News," *Feminary*, September 14, 1975, 7; Milton Jordan, "Marie Hill Knows of Life from Wrong Side of Tracks," *Afro-American*, May 6–10, 1975.

6. "Southern Blues," *Midnight Special*, May 1975, 16; "Letter from Prison," *Feminary*, September 14, 1975, 6; Marjorie Marsh, "Contradiction," in North Carolina Women's Prison Project, *Break de Chains*, 18; Hames-García, *Fugitive Thought*, 239.

7. Bill Noblitt, "Women's Prison Was Ripe for Explosion," *Washington (N.C.) Daily News*, July 1975, 15; "News," *Feminary*, December, 22, 1974, 3; Reston, *Innocence of Joan Little*, 106. In May 1974, of 435 women imprisoned at NCCCW, about 40 percent were white; the remainder were African American or Native American. Of 95 prison staff, 89 were white, and 17 were men, including the deputy superintendent. Only 24 prisoners were on work release. Prison recreation was "all but non-existent." U.S. Commission on Civil Rights, *Prisons in North Carolina*, 54, 11, 21–23.

8. Bill Noblitt, "Women's Prison Was Ripe for Explosion," *Washington (N.C.) Daily News*, July 1975; "Letter from Prison," *Feminary*, September 14, 1975, 6; "Southern Blues," *Midnight Special*, May 1975, 16.

9. Reston, *Innocence of Joan Little*, 89–94; "Fact Sheet on the Women's Correctional Institute [NCCCW], Raleigh, N.C.," box 93, MBP Papers. Little remained in Women's Prison from September 7, 1974, to February 26, 1975, when she was released on $115,000 bail. Other reports indicate the bail was $125,000. It is possible her bail was raised. Little, "I Am Joan," 47.

10. Reston, *Innocence of Joan Little*, 105, 106; "Southern Blues," *Midnight Special*, May 1975.

11. Karen Lindsay, "Little Goes on Trial," *off our backs*, August 31, 1975. Bob McMahon and Jim Grant, "The Case of Joanne Little," *Southern Patriot*, October 1974, 1, 7.

12. Loretta Ross, interview by Joyce Follet, 2004–5; Jini M. Stroman, "Morning When We Rise," *Midnight Special*, August–September 1975, 5; Ann Finch, "Women Prisoners Protest Living & Working Conditions," *Southern Patriot*, April [June] 1975, 8; Kathy Hyatt, "News from Women's Prison in Raleigh," *Feminary*, June 22, 1975, 5. Hyatt was one of the women who came as a witness after the prisoners called for help from Action for Forgotten Women. There is a long history of medical experimentation on prisoners. From the 1940s to the 1970s, prisoners were exposed to radiation, malaria, chemical warfare agents, and experimental cosmetics. Kunzel, *Criminal Intimacy*, 242n27. A number of studies published in the 1980s found that women and girls were more likely than male prisoners to be given psychotropic medication by prison doctors. Belknap, *Invisible Woman*, 174. See also Thuma, *All Our Trials*.

13. Quoted in Reston, *Innocence of Joan Little*, 106.

14. Jini M. Stroman, "Morning When We Rise," *Midnight Special*, August–September 1975; Reston, *Innocence of Joan Little*, 107; "Events at Women's Prison," June 15–20, 1975, box 142, folder 27, CAB Papers. A handwritten notation at the end of this document lists two women authors as observers and supporters, members of a "feminist/lesbian group" in Durham, most likely Triangle Area Lesbian Feminists. On the protest at Women's Prison, see also Shirley and Stafford, *Dixie Be Damned*, 219–47.

15. Mecca Reliance et al., "Raleigh Women Lose," *off our backs*, July 31, 1975, 26; "Events at Women's Prison," June 15–20, 1975, box 142, folder 27, CAB Papers.

16. Anne Willett, "Our Peaceful Protest," in North Carolina Women's Prison Project, *Break de Chains*, 4; "Events at Women's Prison," June 15–20, 1975, box 142, folder 27, CAB Papers; Bill Noblitt, "Women's Prison Was Ripe for Explosion," *Washington (N.C.) Daily News*, July 1975.

17. Jini M. Stroman, "Morning When We Rise," *Midnight Special*, August–September 1975; Reston, *Innocence of Joan Little*, 97, 98, 106–7; "Women Inmates Battle Guards in North Carolina," *NYT*, June 17, 1975, 18.

18. "Events at Women's Prison," June 15–20, 1975, box 142, folder 27, CAB Papers. It is unclear why Action for Forgotten Women was permitted inside the prison. Officials may have felt that the trust the group enjoyed among the prisoners could quell the protest.

19. Anne Willett, "Our Peaceful Protest," in North Carolina Women's Prison Project, *Break de Chains*; "Letter from Prison" and "News," *Feminary*, September 14, 1975, 6–7; "Events at Women's Prison," June 15–20, 1975, box 142, folder 27, CAB Papers. News reports gave various figures on the number of prisoners and guards injured. The *New York Times* initially gave lower figures and then reported that seventeen inmates and eleven guards were injured. "Officers Charge Women Inmates Staging North Carolina Protest," *NYT*, June 20, 1975, 32; Jini M. Stroman, "Morning When We Rise," *Midnight Special*, August–September 1975; Anne Finch, "Women Prisoners Protest Living & Working Conditions," *Southern Patriot*, April [June] 1975; "Events at Women's Prison," June 15–20, 1975, box 142, folder 27, CAB Papers.

20. "Sisters," *Feminary*, July 6, 1975; Karen (Galloway) Bethea-Shields, interview by author, November 11, 2013; U.S. Commission on Civil Rights, *Prisons in North Carolina*.

21. "Events at Women's Prison," June 15–20, 1975, box 142, folder 27, CAB Papers; Jim Grant, "Protests at Women's Prison," *Southern Patriot*, May, 1975, 7; Jim Grant, "Resistance Sweeps N.C. Prisons," *Southern Patriot*, October 1975, 4; "Sexism Racism, Repression and Oppression: Four Ways to Better Understanding," *Action for Forgotten Women Newsletter*, November 1975, 1.

22. Marjorie Marsh, "To the People," *Midnight Special*, October–November 1975, 1; "Letter from Prison"; Marjorie Marsh, "N.C.C.C.W. Update," *off our backs*, November 30, 1975, 7.

23. A guard had reportedly seriously injured Willett's arm, and she was being held in isolation without medical care. Anne Willett, "Sisters of Strength," *Midnight Special*, December 1975–January 1976, 6. Anne Willett, "NCCCW—1865" and "Life's Shadow," in North Carolina Women's Prison Project, *Break de Chains*, 22, 24. See note by Jini Stroman, who interviewed some of incarcerated women after the Women's Prison strike, in *Midnight Special*, October–November 1975, 2.

24. "N.C. Women Prisoners File Lawsuit," *Southern Patriot*, January 1976, 7; "Women's Prison Suit," *North Carolina Political Prisoners Committee Newsletter*, March 1, 1976, box 1, TJR Papers; "Local News" and "Women's Prison News," *Feminary*, November, 9 1975, 1; January 18, 1976, 2; "Actions Now," *Action for Forgotten Women Newsletter*, n.d., 2.

25. Marjorie Marsh, "The Enemy Speaks," in North Carolina Women's Prison Project, *Break de Chains*, 30; Brooke Whiting to Dear Friends and Supporters, December 30, 1975,

Prisoners Solidarity Committee to Dear Friend, January 5, 1975 [1976], box 142, folder 27, folder 26, CAB Papers.

26. Ann Shepherd to the Editor, June 21, 1975, box 142, folder 27, CAB Papers; Assata Shakur, "To My Sisters," *Action for Forgotten Women Newsletter*, November 1975, 7; "Inside the Walls—We Just Got Mad," *Attica News*, June 26, 1975, 5.

27. "News," *Feminary*, March 2, 1975, 6.

28. Legislative Research Commission, *Females in the Department of Correction*.

29. Mecca Reliance et al., "Raleigh Women Lose," *off our backs*, July 31, 1975, 26; Jim Grant, "Hearings Held on Conditions in N.C. Women's Prison," *Southern Patriot*, September 1975, 7; Cummins, *Rise and Fall of California's Radical Prison Movement*, 230, 195.

30. Jim Grant, "Resistance Sweeps N.C. Prisons," *Southern Patriot*, October 1975, 4; "The Grievance Commission," *Action for Forgotten Women Newsletter*, n.d. [ca. 1975].

31. Commission members were also troubled about the increase in youth incarceration and the fact that too many were housed with adult prisoners. Legislative Research Commission, *Females in the Department of Correction*.

32. Legislative Research Commission, *Females in the Department of Correction*; "Pacification-Repression on a Different Level," *Action for Forgotten Women Newsletter*, November 1975, 4. Both supporters and opponents of the ERA targeted Senator Sam Ervin (D-N.C.), who chaired the Senate Judiciary Committee and was one of the most powerful and influential ERA opponents. On the ERA battle in North Carolina, see Matthews and De Hart, *Sex, Gender, and the Politics of ERA*. In the eighteenth and early nineteenth centuries, native-born white women prisoners engaged in typical "female" tasks to support both themselves and male prisoners. Imprisoned African American and immigrant women faced greater restrictions and were relegated to laundresses, seamstresses, and servants. Manion, *Liberty's Prisons*, 32–41. My thanks to April Haynes for this reference. Talitha LeFlouria notes that, ironically, Black imprisoned women in the South following the Civil War were assigned a much wider range of tasks, including traditional "men's jobs." This contrasted with the occupational restrictions they faced in the free world marketplace, especially after Emancipation and the rise of convict labor in the South. LeFlouria, *Chained in Silence*.

33. Rafter, *Partial Justice*, 256n37, 185–90, 203, 206; Legislative Research Commission, *Females in the Department of Correction*; Bader, "Women Prisoners Endure Rampant Sexual Violence."

34. Prison officials agreed to train women in nontraditional jobs, including auto body repair and welding in off-site job sites, "when it is available." It is unclear if these concessions were implemented or, if so, how extensively. Legislative Research Commission, *Females in the Department of Correction*; North Carolina Division of Prisons, "Response to *Females in the Department of Correction*."

35. North Carolina Division of Prisons, "Response to *Females in the Department of Correction*."

36. Marjorie Marsh, "The Enemy Speaks," in North Carolina Women's Prison Project, *Break de Chains*, 30.

37. Marjorie Marsh, "Contradiction," in North Carolina Women's Prison Project, *Break de Chains*, 17.

38. Jim Grant, "Resistance Sweeps N.C. Prisons," *Southern Patriot*, October 1975; Paul M. Baugh, "Overcrowded Prisons Created," *NCPLU Newsletter*, February–March 1975, 13;

Governor James B. Hunt Jr. "Statement on Prison System"; Stella Dawson, "Medical Brutality: 'The Norm in Women's Prisons,'" *off our backs*, December 1980. The 1997 lawsuit ended in a settlement that resulted in some improvements but took more than five years to implement. Taylor, *Central Prison*, 180–81.

CHAPTER 11

1. The prisoner writing group appears to have been in place prior to the Women's Prison sit-down strike. North Carolina Division of Prisons, "Response to *Females in the Department of Correction*."

2. Sweeney, *Reading Is My Window*, 21–41; Cummins, *Rise and Fall of California's Radical Prison Movement*, 4–6.

3. Sweeney, *Reading Is My Window*, 1–2, 33–46; Cummins, *Rise and Fall of California's Radical Prison Movement*, 84.

4. Sweeney, *Reading Is My Window*, 37; North Carolina Women's Prison Project, *Break de Chains*, 2. Triangle Area Lesbian Feminists and the North Carolina Hard Times Prison Project also reportedly had been sending radical reading materials to prisoners at NCCCW.

5. Lura Tally and Lamar Gudger (chairs, North Carolina Legislative Research Commission) to Edward Knox, n.d. [ca. 1976], James B. Hunt Addresses and Public Papers, North Carolina Collection, Wilson Library, University of North Carolina at Chapel Hill; Berger, *Captive Nation*, 226; Sweeney, *Reading Is My Window*, 37. See also Rodrigues, *Forced Passages*.

6. One of the first gay male prisoner organizations, Men Against Sexism, was formed in Washington State in 1977 at the Walla Walla Penitentiary. A multiracial group started by Ed Mead and members of the George Jackson Brigade, it focused on protecting prisoners from violence and sexual assaults, which they believed were outgrowths of the hypermasculine prison ethos. Berger, *Captive Nation*, 226, 264; Cummins, *Rise and Fall of California's Radical Prison Movement*, 214; Kunzel, *Criminal Intimacy*, 206–7, 211–12.

7. Quoted in Gilbert, "*Feminary* of Durham–Chapel Hill," 16. *Feminary* had its origins in 1969 as the *Research Triangle Women's Liberation Newsletter* and underwent several name changes before adopting the name *Feminary* in 1974. Several prison activists from Triangle Area Lesbian Feminists had direct ties to *Feminary*, which likely influenced the newsletter's coverage of incarcerated women.

8. Finding Guide, Mab Segrest Papers, David M. Rubenstein Rare Book and Manuscript Library, Duke University, Durham, N.C. Motheread began as a one-year pilot project in the late 1980s. Still in existence (now as Motheread/Fatheread), it has spread to over twenty states and expanded beyond prisons. Machtinger worked with a mother's prison group in Massachusetts before her stint with Motheread at Women's Prison, where she has been almost since its inception, promoting the power of oral storytelling, parents' own stories, and print culture. Evelyn Machtinger, Northern Marianas Humanities Council, "Your Humanities Half-Hour," September 15, 2019, https://www.youtube.com/watch?v=jvPTSx_Ln8U; Motheread, accessed December 2021, http://www.motheread.org. The Motheread website expired in April 2022 and is awaiting renewal or removal.

9. See, for example, "Letter from Angela Davis," *Triple Jeopardy*, January 1972, 3; Tina Williams, "The Woman Offender," *Triple Jeopardy*, January–February 1974, 3; "Woman Inmate Kills Would-Be Rapist," *Triple Jeopardy*, January–February 1975, 7. "Another Case

of Rape and Racism," *NWT*, February 1976, 9; "Native American's Conviction Reversed," *NWT*, January 15–February 15, 1977, 6; "Garcia Acquitted," *NWT*, February 15–March 15, 1977, 1; "Shakur Gets 33 Years Added to Life Sentence," *NWT*, April–May 1977, 6. *Aegis* was originally published by a group of Wisconsin women in the battered women's movement; in 1978 it merged with the *Feminist Alliance Against Rape (FAAR) News*. FAAR was a predominantly white antirape group established in 1974 to provide information about the antirape movement. Valk, *Radical Sisters*, 167–68, 221; Kunzel, *Criminal Intimacy*, 206–7. For an outstanding examination of women's prison print media, see Thuma, *All Our Trials*, 88–122.

10. Although Jewelle Gomez here is comparing slave narratives to the Black "coming out" story, her insights are equally applicable to the writings of incarcerated women, particularly poor Black women, who made up the majority of NCCCW prisoners. As Gomez writes, "To speak of who we are as African Americans has traditionally been a sign of triumph over adverse conditions." Gomez, "Because Silence Is Costly," 169–70, 167.

11. For struggles over inmate writings in California, which often led to violence and to a series of court cases, see Cummins, *Rise and Fall of California's Radical Prison Movement*.

12. Susan Stuart, "An Open Letter to the Taxpayers of N.C.," in North Carolina Women's Prison Project, *Break de Chains*, 49–50. Stuart's first name is sometimes spelled "Suzan." While some formerly incarcerated people object to the term "caged," others use it deliberately to underline the dehumanizing intent of incarceration. See, for example, prison abolitionist Mariame Kaba, *We Do This 'Til We Free Us*. Little herself used the term in one of her prison writings, discussed below.

13. Jim Grant, "Resistance Sweeps N.C. Prisons," *Southern Patriot*, October 1975, 4. Although North Carolina statutes prohibited prison industries from competing with free labor, Heather Thompson has shown how federal and state laws enacted during the New Deal by pressure from the labor movement were successfully weakened across the country starting in the 1970s. By the 1990s, thirty-six states gave private companies total access to prison labor; and government services—including incarceration—were increasingly privatized. Thompson, "Why Mass Incarceration Matters," 717–24. There is disagreement regarding the profit-making potential of state prisons. However, the prison boom and mass incarceration spurred a huge increase in scores of subsidiary industries, from prison phone cards to food and laundry services. Private, for-profit penal institutions run by corporations emerged in the 1990s and expanded with the advent of mass incarceration, especially on the federal level. North Carolina is currently one of the few states to have ended its contracts with private prisons; in January 2021, President Biden issued an executive order directing the Department of Justice not to renew contracts with private prisons. Eisen, "Breaking Down Biden's Order"; Gotsch and Basti, "Capitalizing on Mass Incarceration." On prisons and economic and labor issues inside and outside the prison walls, see, for example, Lichtenstein, "'Labor History' of Mass Incarceration"; Gilmore, *Golden Gulag*; Herivel and Wright, *Prison Profiteers*; Chase, "'Slaves of the State' Revolt"; Chase, *We Are Not Slaves*; and Wacquant, "Place of the Prison."

14. For example, *New Dawn* was published by women at the Hudson Valley Women's Prison in Ypsilanti, Michigan. On Ypsilanti women prisoners, see *off our backs*, January 1981, news clipping, box 100, MBP Papers. On women's prison newsletters, see Thuma, *All Our Trials*, 88–122.

15. North Carolina Women's Prison Project, *Break de Chains*; "Local Women Make Books!," *Feminary*, November 21, 1976; "Two Perspectives on the North Carolina Women's Prison Book, 'Break de Chains of Legalized U.$. Slavery,'" *Feminary*, Winter Solstice (December) 1976. Although both Black and white prisoners contributed to the booklet, most contributors were African American. Little's prison writings are examined in the next chapter.

16. I have borrowed "epistemology of refusal" from Haley, *No Mercy Here*, 254. According to historian William Chafe, civility was the cornerstone of North Carolina's "progressive mystique." Civility valued good manners over conflict and justice, but it was reinforced by the threat and often the practice of white racial violence. The "progressive mystique" was characterized by white paternalism, a patron-client relationship between Black and white North Carolinians, and white attitudes of noblesse oblige toward African Americans. Civility marked the racialized attitudes of much of the nation, not only the South. Chafe, *Civilities and Civil Rights*.

17. The novel was "rediscovered" in the 1960s and then again through Alice Walker's 1975 *Ms.* magazine essay, "In Search of Zora Neale Hurston." Daley, "A Rocky Road to Posterity."

18. National Committee for the Defense of Jo Anne Chesimard [Assata Shakur] and David Squires, "Break de Chains," September 1973, Freedom Archives, Berkeley, California. Assata Shakur, "To My Sisters," *Action for Forgotten Women Newsletter*, November 1975, 7.

19. The Black feminist Combahee River Collective described the "interlocking" oppressions that Black women experienced in their everyday lives. The group's 1977 "Statement" was an early articulation of what Black feminist legal scholar Kimberlé Crenshaw would later call "intersectionality," and it had an enormous impact on women's liberation politics, especially among women of color. "The Combahee River Collective Statement," in Smith, *Home Girls*, 272–82; Crenshaw, "Mapping the Margins." Feminist historian Joan Scott has observed the power (as well as the limitations for historians) of writing and experience, especially by and of marginalized groups: "Writing is reproduction, transmission—the communication of knowledge through (visual, visceral) experience." Scott, "Evidence of Experience," 776. I discuss Black feminism and antirape organizing in part 3.

20. North Carolina Women's Prison Project, *Break de Chains*, 2.

21. Aminah Aliyah / Bessie Bouler, "Dungeons of Despair," in North Carolina Women's Prison Project, *Break de Chains*, 46.

22. North Carolina Women's Prison Project, *Break de Chains*; Shakur, *Assata*.

23. North Carolina Women's Prison Project, *Break de Chains*, 4.

24. Marjorie Marsh, untitled, North Carolina Women's Prison Project, *Break de Chains*, 12.

25. Tarishi Maisha / Shirley Herlth, "Till We Overcome"; note from Jini Stroman, *Midnight Special*, October–November 1975, 2. According to Stroman, who interviewed Maishe/Herlth in prison, Herlth had been placed in solitary for "obscene language" and threatening a guard after chanting "oink oink" and singing "We Shall Overcome." Alice Wise and Tarishi Maisha, "What Next?," in North Carolina Women's Prison Project, *Break de Chains*, 31.

26. Tarishi Maisha / Shirley Herlth, "What Do You Say to a Hungry Child, Amerikkka?," in North Carolina Women's Prison Project, *Break de Chains*, 41–43.

27. Marjorie Marsh, untitled, and Aminah Aliyah, "Dungeons of Despair," in North Carolina Women's Prison Project, *Break de Chains*, 60, 46.

28. North Carolina license plates were later changed to "First in Flight." Tarishi Maisha / Shirley Herlth, "Open Letter to Amerikkka," in North Carolina Women's Prison Project, *Break de Chains*, 8–9.

29. Anne Willett, "Our Peaceful Protest," in North Carolina Women's Prison Project, *Break de Chains*, 4.

30. Anne Willett, untitled, in North Carolina Women's Prison Project, *Break de Chains*, 26, 43–44.

31. Ellen Amana Porter, "The Court System, Fair or Unfair? An Inmate's View," in North Carolina Women's Prison Project, *Break de Chains*, 33–34; Berger, *Captive Nation*, 233–34.

32. Marjorie Marsh and Anne Willett, "Conclusions" and "Liberation, Revolution in Our Time," in North Carolina Women's Prison Project, *Break de Chains*, 64, 43; Douglas, *Black Panther*.

33. "Seize the Time" was a song written and performed by Panther leader Elaine Brown on an album released in 1969. Brown, *Seize the Time*. It was also the title of a book by Bobby Seale, recorded from a county jail by a San Francisco reporter in 1969–70.

34. Marjorie Marsh, "Revolutionary Style," in North Carolina Women's Prison Project, *Break de Chains*, 50; emphasis in the original.

35. Marjorie Marsh and Anne Willett, "Conclusions," in North Carolina Women's Prison Project, *Break de Chains*, 64.

36. "Two Perspectives on the North Carolina Women's Prison Book, 'Break de Chains of Legalized U.$. Slavery,'" *Feminary*, Winter Solstice (December) 1976.

37. North Carolina Women's Prison Project, *Break de Chains*, 19.

38. Aminah Aliyah / Bessie Bouler, "A Luta Continua," in North Carolina Women's Prison Project, *Break de Chains*, 48–49.

39. My thanks to Craig Werner for the blues insight. Ellison, quoted in Werner, *Higher Ground*, 7.

40. Hames-Garcia, *Fugitive Thought*, 227, 252.

CHAPTER 12

1. "Huey P. Newton: 'JoAnne Is the Living Spirt of George Jackson,'" *BP*, September 1, 1975; Lonnie Kashif, "Common Suffering Links Activist, Rape Victim," *Muhammad Speaks*, June 20, 1975. Celine Chenier, interview by James Reston Jr., n.d. Newton also linked Little's case to Inez García's rape-murder trial. I discuss Garcia's case in part 3.

2. Joan Little, "Murder," September 25, 1974, unpublished poem, box 1, JLC Collection.

3. Little, "I Am Joan," 42; Jo Anne Little, "Not a Poem . . . Just Facts," *Midnight Special*, March 1975, 8; Joan Little, "Dear Miss Janover" and "Not a Poem," *off our backs*, January 1975, 5. Little was part of a writing and acting program, Souls from Within, that Rebecca Ranson led at Women's Prison. But Little had joined another prisoner writing group prior to Ranson's arrival. Ranson was a southern lesbian playwright and prison, LGBTQ, and AIDS activist. She had taught at Attica, where the Joan Little case was often discussed and Joan was considered a heroine, especially among the prisoners from North Carolina.

Ranson seems to have arrived at Women's Prison after Little's murder trial and following Little's return to prison to serve her sentence on the felony theft conviction. For Little's unpublished prison writings, see box 1, JLC Collection.

4. Joan Little, "I Am Somebody," box 1, JLC Collection. An excerpt of the poem was quoted in Wayne King, "Focus of Slaying Trial Had Humble Origins, Joan Little," *NYT*, July 29, 1975, 12.

5. On the conservative implications of Black uplift ideology, see Gaines, *Uplifting the Race*. The "afterlife of slavery," a term coined by literary scholar Saidiya Hartman, is characterized by the ways "black lives are still imperiled and devalued by a racial calculus and a political arithmetic that were entrenched centuries ago." It includes "skewed life chances, limited access to health and education, premature death, incarceration, and impoverishment." Hartman, *Lose Your Mother*, 6.

6. Joan Little's unpublished poems, including "Murder," "Joan—Walks with Dignity," "The Mystery of Black," and "To the People, From Lincoln's Gettysburg Address," are in box 1, JLC Collection. Another epic poem, "Dropping a Dime," depicted a drug dealer, pimp, and police informer, Poor Pete, who was betrayed by the "man" and landed in the "joint." Several poems were written to her sister and to her mother, while others expressed the loneliness and desolation of prison life.

7. Joan Little, "Murder"; Assata Shakur, *Assata*, 49–53. Clifford "Flower" is likely Clifford Glover, sometimes erroneously listed as "Clover," which Joan may have confused with "Flower." Glover was a ten-year-old boy, only five feet tall and weighing less than 100 pounds, who was shot in the back by a plainclothes police officer in Queens, New York, in 1973. Bodden was also shot in the back by police; both murders spurred protests and, following the Bodden murder, led to two days of "minor riots," according to a local newspaper. The officer in the Glover shooting was charged with murder, acquitted, and later fired. Lloyd was standing on a Brooklyn corner with a girlfriend when police opened fire, wounding the friend and killing Lloyd. Police claimed the girlfriend had pointed a gun at them. No one was arrested or charged. Jim Dwyer, "A Police Shot to a Boy's Back in Queens, Echoing since 1973," *NYT*, April 16, 2015; David J. Krajicek, "Deaths of Two 10-Year Old Boys Shot While Running from Cops Were Wake-Up Call for NYPD Flaws," *New York Daily News*, March 11, 2017; Robert D. McFadden, "'Defensive' Police Shots Kill a Girl, 16," *NYT*, January 28, 1973.

8. "Joann Little Rally," *Feminary*, July 20, 1975; Davis, "Joan Little." Joan appeared to adopt more conservative politics when she affiliated briefly with the Nation of Islam. During a trip to California following her acquittal, she also criticized Angela Davis, Charlene Mitchell, and the Communist Party USA, claiming they hadn't done enough to support her. In addition to publishing her *Ms.* article, Davis attended Little's rape-murder trial, and Mitchell and Davis reportedly offered advice to Little's defense team. "JoAnne Little: 'The Time for Us to Seize Freedom Is Now,'" *BP*, September 1, 1975.

9. "Letter from Prison," *Feminary*, September 14, 1975; "Letters from the Inside," *Feminary*, August 31, 1975.

10. Jackie Macmillan, "Joanne Little: No Escape Yet," *off our backs*, January 1975; "Letters from the Inside," *Feminary*, August 31, 1975.

11. "'We Have a Long Way to Go Before We're Free': JoAnne Little's Address to Oakland Victory Rally," *BP*, September 1, 1975.

12. "JoAnne Little Visits Johnny Spain," *BP*, September 1, 1975. Johnny Spain was a BPP member and one of the San Quentin Six.

13. "'We Have a Long Way to Go Before We're Free': JoAnne Little's Address to Oakland Victory Rally," *BP*, September 1, 1975.

14. Rodriguez, *Forced Passages*, 37.

15. "Forgotten places" is from Ruth Wilson Gilmore: "The places where prisons are built share many similarities with the places prisoners come from. . . . These forgotten places . . . can be understood to form one political world, abandoned but hardly defeated." Gilmore, *Golden Gulag*, 247.

CHAPTER 13

1. Historian Estelle Freedman has explored the historical construction of rape and its shifting meanings throughout history. In patriarchal societies, rape has been a crime against family property, not women, while liberal societies often defined it as an individual crime of lust. Feminists, in contrast, have defined rape as a crime of power exercised by men over women. Today, Freedman notes, these three meanings coexist throughout the world. Freedman, *No Turning Back*, 279–80. The quote in the part 3 title is from Lincoln, "Who Will Revere the Black Woman?"

2. Since 1929, the FBI had defined "real" rape as "forcible rape," and its definition was widely adopted by police departments across the country. The legal definition excluded all other forms of sexual assault, including oral and anal rape, male rape, rape with objects, and rape of unconscious or inebriated victims, among other forms of sexual violence. Numerous groups, such as the Women's Law Project, had lobbied for changes in the legal definition of rape for decades. After a national campaign, No More Excuses, #RapeIsRape, was launched in 2011 by *Ms.* magazine and the Feminist Majority Foundation in collaboration with Change.org., FBI director Robert Mueller approved a new, broader definition of rape in 2012. Hallett, "Rape Is Rape." See also *Ms.*, cover October 19, 2011; and Mary Ann Largen, "The Case of Joan Little," NOW Rape Task Force, [1975], box 210, NOW Papers.

3. According to Freedman, race has been central to the "political history of rape" in the United States. Freedman, *Redefining Rape*, 2. Hale, quoted in Flood, *Rape in Chicago*, l. Hale's notion lingers on both inside and outside of courtrooms.

4. Historian Jennifer Morgan has shown that early sixteenth- and seventeenth-century European male travelers in Africa vilified African women as shameless and sexually promiscuous. While Europeans infrequently focused on African male genitalia as evidence of Black savagery, descriptions of female bodies were far more common. "Women's sexual availability [became] the defining metaphor of colonial accessibility and black African savagery. . . . Confronted with an Africa they needed to exploit, European writers turned to black women as evidence of cultural inferiority that ultimately became encoded as racial difference." Morgan, *Laboring Women*, 29, 49. Morgan has also shown that the rape of African women on slave ships was ubiquitous and that "the exposure of female captives to sexual predation and violation [was] foundational to the production of race and racial hierarchy." Morgan, *Reckoning with Slavery*, 162.

5. Davis, "'White Gentleman Commits Rape.'" My thanks to Thulani Davis for sharing this unpublished work with me.

6. Jacquet, *Injustices of Rape*. For a discussion of debates among historians about the emergence of the myth of the Black male rapist and the American South, see Sommerville, *Rape and Race in the Nineteenth South*, 219–59.

7. African American women were usually lynched for alleged violent offenses, often murder, which was frequently self-defense. However, they could also be lynched for resisting sexual assault by white men. Feimster, *Southern Horrors*, 159, 160, 162, 172.

8. Lee, *For Freedom's Sake*, 9–12; Freedman, *Redefining Rape*, 124; Baldwin's 1979 remark quoted in Geneva Abdul, "Lost Time," *New York Times Magazine*, July 4, 2021, 8.

9. Freedman, *Redefining Rape*, 76; see also Davis, *Emancipation Circuit*.

10. Feimster, *Southern Horrors*; McGuire, *At the Dark End of the Street*; Davis, "'White Gentleman Commits Rape.'" Wells was also one of the first to promote the notion of the "lying white women," which later was embedded in American jurisprudence and gained widespread popularity. Jacquet, *Injustices of Rape*, 17–18, 55–57.

11. Although Celia's attorney claimed his client used lethal self-defense against repeated rapes, the Missouri judge failed to instruct the jury that homicide could be legally justifiable. The National Association of Colored Women is widely known for its efforts to protect Black women's reputations, especially those of the middle class, but LeFlouria and Haley note Black clubwomen's campaign against convict leasing and the sexual abuse of imprisoned Black women. Hine, "Rape and the Inner Lives of Black Women"; Freedman, *Redefining Rape*, 28; McLaurin, *Celia, a Slave*; Haley, *No Mercy Here*, 119–41; LeFlouria, *Chained in Silence*, 103–5, 142–44; Theoharis, *Rebellious Life of Mrs. Rosa Parks*; McGuire, "It Was Like All of Us Had Been Raped."

12. Touré and Loretta Ross worked directly with Dessie X. Woods. After she was released from an Atlanta jail, Woods came to Washington, D.C., where the RCC provided immediate support, including clothing and housing. Loretta Ross, interview by Joyce Follett, November and December 2004, February 2005; Nkenge Touré, interview by Loretta Ross, December and March 2005.

13. Loretta Ross, interview by Joyce Follett, 2004, 2005. These roots were deeper than activists like Ross understood. The first court case prohibiting a husband from beating his wife was brought by a Black woman in Alabama in 1871, showing the southern origins of the domestic violence movement, usually attributed to northern white women. Davis, *Emancipation Circuit*, 331.

14. My discussion of the *Wanrow* case relies heavily on Coker and Harrison, "Story of *Wanrow*." Coker and Harrison interviewed Wanrow, currently known as Yvonne Swan, and other key players in the case.

15. Quoted in Coker and Harrison, "Story of *Wanrow*," 227.

16. Quoted in Law, "Sick of the Abuse," 39–40; "Rape: The Right to Self Defense, Native Woman Appeals Murder Charge," *NWT*, September 15–October 15, 1975, 9. Coker and Harrison, "Story of *Wanrow*." Coker, Harrison, and the *New Women's Times* give Wanrow's son's age as eight; Law says he was eleven.

17. "Rape: The Right to Self Defense, Native Woman Appeals Murder Charge," *NWT*, September 15–October 15, 1975, 1, 9. Trial testimony quoted in Coker and Harrison, "Story of *Wanrow*." 229. Because there was no legal precedent for a woman's lethal self-defense, this was often the only viable argument defense attorneys could make.

18. "Rape: The Right to Self Defense, Native Woman Appeals Murder Charge," *NWT*, September 15–October 15, 1975, 9. The Center for Constitutional Rights was formed in

1966 by a team of lawyers including Kunstler. In the late 1960s and early 1970s, the center pioneered the hiring of feminist lawyers to argue race and sex discrimination cases. One of these lawyers was Rhonda Copelon, who assisted in Little's trial. Coker and Harrison, "Story of *Wanrow*," 221–26.

19. Opinion quoted in Coker and Harrison, "Story of *Wanrow*," 240, and in "Native American's Conviction Reversed," *NWT*, January 18–February 15, 1977, 6.

20. Coker and Harrison, "Story of *Wanrow*," 247–55; Wanrow quoted on 218; Utter quoted on 252. For Black women defendants, see Richie, *Compelled to Crime*.

21. Quoted in Coker and Harrison, "Story of *Wanrow*," 252. Initially, all the other justices, except Utter, had wanted to uphold Wanrow's conviction.

22. A 1991 study revealed that 40 percent of domestic violence murder convictions of abused women who claimed self-defense were reversed on appeal largely because courts had been either unable or unwilling to properly apply the standard of reasonableness. Coker and Harrison, "Story of *Wanrow*," 214, 250–51, 255. See also Richie, *Compelled to Crime*, on African American women and intimate partner abuse.

23. Coker and Harrison, "Story of *Wanrow*"; Sherrie Cohen, "Native Women's Benefit to Free Yvonne Wanrow," *off our backs*, April 30, 1979; Thuma, *All Our Trials*, 43.

24. Thuma, *All Our Trials*, 41–43. Wanrow, quoted in Coker and Harrison, "Story of *Wanrow*," 257; 250.

25. García, quoted in "Garcia Acquitted," *NWT*, February 15–March 15, 1977, 13. Baxandall and Gordon, *Dear Sisters*, 201. According to Jacquet, Jimenez held García down while Castillo raped her; Jacquet, *Injustices of Rape*, 126.

26. Feulner, "'Women Have the Right to Fight!'" Ann Senechal, "Justice: A Political Case of Rape," *San Francisco Bay Guardian*, August 15, 1974, news clipping, box 10, ALFA Archives.

27. Baxandall and Gordon, *Dear Sisters*, 202; Law, "Sick of the Abuse," 42; Garry, quoted in Feulner, "'Women Have the Right to Fight!,'" 17.

28. Susan Rothaizer, "The Trial: Inez Garcia," *Plexus*, October 1974, news clipping, box 10, ALFA Archives; Feulner, "'Women Have the Right to Fight!,'" 15, 20.

29. Velasco, "Incorrigible Girl," 82.

30. On García's imprisonment at the Hudson Prison, see Velasco, 13. On the use of psychiatry and institutionalization of women as a form of social control, see Thuma, "Against the 'Prison/Psychiatric' State."

31. García, quoted in Susan Rothaizer, "The Trial: Inez Garcia," *Plexus*, October 1974, news clipping, box 10, ALFA Archives; and in Jim Wood, "Angry Inez Stalks Off Stand," *San Francisco Examiner*, September 27, [1974], news clipping, box 10, ALFA Archives.

32. Susan Rothaizer, "The Trial: Inez Garcia," *Plexus*, October 1974, news clipping, box 10, ALFA Archives; Jim Wood, "The Story Inez Didn't Tell Court," *San Francisco Examiner*, October 6, [1974], news clipping, box 10, ALFA Archives.

33. Lawson quoted in Feulner, "'Women Have the Right to Fight!,'" 21.

34. Inez Garcia Defense Committee excerpted the transcript of Radio KPFA's interview with the juror, Samuel Rhone, who made this comment. "Transcript," n.d., box 10, ALFA Archives; "For Crying Out Loud," *Big Mama Rag*, April 1984, 7.

35. Quoted in Bay Area Women Against Rape, n.d., box 10, ALFA Archives.

36. "Rape Is a Joke to Merchant," *NWT*, September–October 1977, 10. On rape culture defined, see Bevacqua, *Rape on the Public Agenda*. In a more recent incident showcasing

the persistence of "rape culture," a nationwide petition campaign was launched to recall a California judge in June 2016 for sentencing a white Stanford athlete to six months in jail after he was found guilty of raping an unconscious young white woman. The defendant was required to serve only half the sentence. The woman penned an anonymous but gruesomely detailed account of the impact of the rape that was so powerful it spurred a letter from then–vice president Joe Biden, author of the 1994 Violence Against Women Act. Jonah Engel Bromwich, "Biden Calls Victim in Stanford Rape Case a 'Warrior,'" *NYT*, June 9, 2016. White women are far more likely to elicit this kind of sympathy than Black, Indigenous, or other women of color.

37. Thuma, "Lessons in Self-Defense," 57; Thuma, *All Our Trials*, 34–37; Feulner, "'Women Have the Right to Fight!,'" 22. Jacquet claims that racial justice groups offered little support because Garcia's attackers were also men of color. Jacquet, *Injustices of Rape*, 214n71.

38. News clipping, n.d.; Inez Garcia Defense Committee Fact Sheet; Inez Garcia Defense Committee, Petition, box 10, ALFA Archives; Feulner, "'Women Have the Right to Fight!,'" 2; Thuma, *All Our Trials*, 37; Marlene Schmitz, untitled, *off our backs*, February 25, 1975; "Inez Garcia Acquitted of 'Rape-Related' Killing, *Washington Post*, online, March 5, 1977.

39. Susan Rothaizer, "Inez Garcia Acquitted," *off our backs*, April 30, 1977.

40. Rothaizer; Velasco, "Incorrigible Girl," 33.

41. Velasco, "Incorrigible Girl," 31.

42. Feulner, "'Women Have the Right to Fight!,'" 23; Baxandall and Gordon, *Dear Sisters*, 203.

43. Quoted in "Garcia Acquitted," *NWT*, February 15–March 15, 1977, 13. For the photo of García, see Velasco, "Incorrigible Girl," 50.

44. Matthews, *Confronting Rape*, 131; "Projects, Programs and Shelters," *Aegis*, September–October 1978, 9–10.

45. Law, "Sick of the Abuse," 43; Baxandall and Gordon, *Dear Sisters*, 202; Browne, *When Battered Women Kill*, 172; Richie, *Compelled to Crime*.

46. Kupenda, "Law, Life, and Literature." For a recent example of a Black woman imprisoned on Rikers Island for eighteen months before taking a guilty plea of second-degree manslaughter after killing her abusive partner, see Arlene Adams, "I Killed My Partner: It Saved My Life," *NYT*, September 8, 2019. Adams was released with five years of probation and later moved to North Carolina. In Wisconsin, a nineteen-year-old Black woman, Chrystul Kizer, was indicted for killing a white man, Randall Volar III, and setting his house on fire in 2018. At the time of his death, Volar was under investigation for child trafficking underage Black girls; and authorities had learned he had trafficked Kizer as a teen. Change.org has gathered 1.5 million signatures demanding that all charges against her be dropped. Supporters hope she will be acquitted under Wisconsin's "affirmative defense" law and that her case can set a precedent for trafficking victims accused of crimes. The prosecutor, Michael Gravely, who failed to arrest Volar but charged Kizer, recently refused to bring charges against the white Kenosha police officer who shot a Black man, Jacob Blake, seven times in the back. The shooting, which left Blake paralyzed, occurred less than three months after the 2020 police killing of George Floyd fueled protests and attracted national attention. At a demonstration in support of Blake, a seventeen-year-old

white male killed two and wounded a third with an AR-15 rifle he had carried across state lines. In November 2021 he was found not guilty. Jessica Contrera, "Chrystul Kizer, Sex Trafficking Victim, Accused of Killing Abuser Wins Appeal in Wisconsin Court," *Washington Post*, June 3, 2021; Julie Bosman, "What to Know about the Trial of Kyle Rittenhouse," *NYT*, November 19, 2021.

47. Todd's imprisoned brother claimed he had been injured and was not receiving medical attention. The women had previously approached the governor's office, the DOC, the Atlanta mayor's office, the district attorney, and the SCLC for help, to no avail. Up-date Fact Sheet on Dessie Woods, December 6, 1976, box 10, ALFA Archives.

48. Nancy Fithian, "Dessie Woods Speaks Out," *off our backs*, November 30, 1981.

49. Jane Dodds, "Supporting a Rape Victim," *NWT*, February 1976, 9.

50. In the early 1980s, several Black women members of the African People's Socialist Party accused its leadership and especially its founder, Omali Yeshitela (Joseph Waller), of physically brutalizing and exploiting several Black women members; and they demanded that "the criminal beating and rape of women in our movement . . . be stopped immediately." African Women's Committee for Community Education, "Women Fight Sexism in Black Liberation Movement," *Big Mama Rag*, November 1983, 5. A controversy erupted after *Big Mama Rag*, which ran a regular feature on incarcerated women, "Women in Cages," published the Black women's assertions against Yeshetela/Waller. Yeshetela claimed that one of the women who exposed his behavior undermined the Dessie X. Woods case.

51. Thuma, "Lessons in Self-Defense," 57–58; Thuma, *All Our Trials*, 39–40; Janis Kelly, "Cheryl Todd & Dessie Woods: A Staged Crime," *off our backs*, April 30, 1976; "Women's Union Works on Two Projects," n.d., box 100, MBP Papers; Dear Friend from Karate for Women, n.d. [ca. 1981], box 100, MBP Papers; Dear Sisters, from Dykes for the Second American Revolution, n.d., box 194, MBP Papers; "Stop Drugging Dessie," *Aegis*, May–June 1979; see also "Violence Against Women and Race," special issue of *Aegis*, March–April 1979, which also includes coverage of the Wanrow and Woods cases; "Victimized," *Midnight Special*, December 1975–January 1976, 5; "Dessie Woods Demonstration Held," *BP*, May 20, 1978.

52. "Women's Union"; Nancy Fithian, "Dessie Woods Speaks Out," *off our backs*, November 30, 1981. On prison rape reported in the radical prisoner press, see also "Sex + Violence = Rape," *Midnight Special*, May–June 1974, 18.

53. Law, "Sick of the Abuse," 43–45; "Dialogue with Dessie," *Aegis*, July–August 1978, 10, 12; Nancy Fithian, "Dessie Woods Speaks Out," *off our backs*, November 30, 1981. On the history of racism and abuse at Milledgeville, see Segrest, *Administrations of Lunacy*.

54. National Committee for the Defense of Dessie Woods (NCDDW) Bulletin, March 19, 1979, box 10, ALFA Archives; "Dessie Woods Beaten, Denied Parole," *off our backs*, January 1981, news clipping, box 100, MBP Papers.

55. "Coming to Terms," *off our backs*, January 1975, 2.

56. "News," *Feminary*, March 2, 1975, 6; Tracie Dejanikus and Janis Kelly, "WASP: On Target," *off our backs*, January 1975, 3.

57. *TWWA: Our History, Our Ideology, Our Goals*, 1971, box 3, Third World Women's Alliance Papers, Sophia Smith Collection, Smith College Special Collections; FBI, "Confidential" Report, October 6, 1971; and FBI Report, April 3, 1973, both in box 4, Third World

Women's Alliance Papers, Sophia Smith Collection, Smith College Special Collections; Showalter, "Rethinking the Seventies." On women's antirape squads, see Jacquet, *Injustices of Rape*, 90–92.

58. *Aegis*, cited in Gottschalk, *Prison and the Gallows*, 132. Some feminist periodicals also included Asian women, often in articles opposing U.S. imperialism and the Vietnam War. Beins, "Radical Others."

59. Handwritten note, n.d., box 1, NABF Papers; Thuma, *All Our Trials*, 52–53; Springer, *Living for the Revolution*, 89.

60. Coker and Harrison, "Story of *Wanrow*," 244; "Fighting Back: Winning Self-Defense Cases in Court," *Aegis*, September–October 1978, 52–54; Price, quoted in Thuma, *All Our Trials*, 53.

61. Brown, "Imaging Lynching"; Tracie Dejanikus, "First National Conference on Third World Women and Violence," *off our backs*, December 1980; Berry and Gross, *Black Women's History*, 202; Lynora Williams, "Third World Women Decry Violence," *National Guardian*, September 10, 1980, news clipping, box 100, MBP Papers. It is possible that Amma Price has been confused with Pamela Price, also a Black Yale Law School student who joined the sexual harassment suit against Yale professors in 1977. Price, Statement, *Alexander v. Yale*.

62. Loretta Ross, interview by Joyce Follett, 2004, 2005; Nkenge Touré, interview by Loretta Ross, December and March 2005; Barbara Smith, "Dear Sisters," news clipping, September 1979, box 100, MBP Papers. Smith's letter was printed in many feminist newspapers; see, for example, *Big Mama Rag*, September 1979. On the Hill-Thomas debacle, see Smitherman, *African American Women Speak Out*; and Chrisman and Allen, *Court of Appeal*.

CHAPTER 14

1. Loretta Ross, interview by Joyce Follett, 2004, 2005.
2. Ross, "Notes, 1982–1992," box 5, LR Papers.
3. The term "third world people" generally referred to nonwhite, oppressed people of color in the United States and throughout the world. Burnham's parents, Louis and Dorothy Burnham, were well-known activists in the Black Left in the 1930s and 1940s and had worked with Angela Davis's family and the Southern Negro Youth Congress in Birmingham. Linda joined CORE as a teenager in Brooklyn and then the Angela Davis Defense Committee in 1970. In the early 1970s, she made two trips to Cuba under the auspices of the Venceremos Brigade, underlining the multiple concerns of Black feminists. Although Burnham has never used the term "feminist" for herself, largely due to her critique of white, middle-class feminism, she does not object to others using the term to describe her. Moreover, she believes that in the 1980s and 1990s women of color transformed feminism. Linda Burnham, interview by Loretta J. Ross, 2005. Frances Beal, interview by Loretta J. Ross, 2005.
4. Smith, "Some Home Truths," 259. See also White, "Mining the Forgotten."
5. Black women were among the first to critique the "wave" paradigm for privileging nineteenth- and twentieth-century white feminists. Springer, *Living for the Revolution*, 7–10. For other critiques of the "second wave" framework by white women's historians, see, for example, Evans, "Women's Liberation"; see also Hewitt, *No Permanent Waves*,

especially the essays by Becky Thompson, Ula Taylor, and Premilla Nadasen on Black feminism. There has been an outpouring of scholarship on Black feminism in recent years. Cade, *Black Woman* (1970), is one of the earliest publications in this era and now a Black feminist classic. Other classic works by Black feminists published in the 1980s include Davis, *Women, Race and Class*; Smith, *Home Girls*; Lorde, *Sister Outsider*; and Hull, Bell Scott, and Smith, *Some of Us Are Brave*. In addition to Springer, some of the early Black feminist scholarly works include hooks, *Ain't I a Woman*; hooks, *Feminist Theory*; Collins, *Black Feminist Thought*; Guy-Sheftall, *Words of Fire*, and Roth, *Separate Roads to Feminism*.

6. Chisholm also gave one of the keynote addresses, along with Florynce Kennedy and Margaret Sloan, at the 1973 NBFO Eastern Regional Conference. Aileen Hernandez, an African American labor leader, was elected NOW president in 1970. Neither Murray nor Hernandez remained with NOW very long because of the group's failure to adequately address Black women's issues. Giddings, *When and Where I Enter*, 337–40; Springer, *Living for the Revolution*, 33, 93–96; Strum, "Pauli Murray's Indelible Mark."

7. Berry and Gross, *Black Women's History*, 169; Strum, "Pauli Murray's Indelible Mark"; Bell-Scott, *Firebrand and the First Lady*, 215, 325–27, 329–34. Murray also formulated the theory that became the basis for the 1954 *Brown v. Board of Education* decision. Some writers insist that Murray should more accurately be identified as transgender and referred to in nonbinary terms, "they" and "their" instead of "she" or "her." This is a persistent dilemma facing historians: imposing presentist categories of identity and analysis on historical subjects who did not have this framework available at the time. Because Murray did not reject gender-binary language, I have chosen to adhere to the limits of the historical period in which she lived and worked. For an opposing perspective that argues how this erases trans history and is transphobic, see Jude Ellison S. Doyle, "We're Still Not Seeing Pauli Murray," September 28, 2021, https://judedoyle.medium.com/were-still-not-seeing-pauli-murray-b6b73dca8869.

8. Recent scholarship has demonstrated the ongoing impact of the women's movement(s) and the subsequent gains made in the 1980s and beyond, despite the rise of a conservative backlash to feminism. "Many early leaders believed by the mid-1970s that their movement was in decline, but they were wrong. It was changing so much that the transformations made it hard for some to recognize," writes historian Sara Evans. During the 1980s "feminism not only persisted but flowed into new channels." Evans, *Tidal Wave*, 127, 176.

9. Gottschalk, *Prison and the Gallows*, 124; Roth, *Separate Roads*, 78. More recently, Black feminists have embraced the term "misogynoir," coined by Moya Bailey, to specify misogyny directed at African American women, especially on digital media. Bailey, *Misogynoir Transformed*.

10. Springer, *Living for the Revolution*, 4, 154–55. Linda Burnham believes that the more conservative 1980s and 1990s did thwart youthful activism and that a generation of more dedicated activists may have been lost. Most of the activists she worked with were either women of her generation who came of age in the 1960s and 1970s or women who are now in their twenties and early thirties. Linda Burnham, interview by Loretta J. Ross, 2005.

11. Harris, "From the Kennedy Commission to the Combahee River Collective," 290–91, 293; Crenshaw, "Mapping the Margins."

12. See Roth, *Separate Roads to Feminism*, regarding the better environment for multiracial feminist coalitions in 1980s; and Orleck, *Storming Caesars Palace*, for a

1970s–1980s multiracial coalition of Black welfare rights mothers, white feminists, and labor. Reagon, "Coalition Politics"; Frances Beal, interview by Loretta J. Ross, 2005; "Summation of Local AAWO R2 [Reproductive Rights] Work," January 1986, box 7, Alliance Against Women's Oppression Papers, Sophia Smith Collection, Smith College Special Collections.

13. Nkenge Touré, "Report from the First National Conference on Third World Women: An Overview of Third World Women and Violence," August 1980, box 34, LR Papers; Sam Walton, "Black Woman Heads City Anti-rape Unit," *Amsterdam News* (New York), April 29, 1978.

14. *Durham (N.C.) Morning Herald*, November 7, 1974, news clipping, box 9, MS Papers; Haynes, "'Sex-Ins College Style,'" 38.

15. Diallo continued this work into the 1990s and to the present. Dazon Dixon Diallo, interview by Loretta J. Ross, 2009. Baxandall and Gordon, *Dear Sisters*, 132.

16. Lorde, "Transformation of Silence"; Lorde, "Litany for Survival."

17. The firing does not appear to have elicited a public outcry. Southern Black lesbians felt particularly vulnerable, and the women may have wished to avoid further victimization. Pratt came out as a lesbian in the late 1970s, which led to the dissolution of her marriage and loss of her children in a custody battle. Minnie Bruce Pratt, interview by Kelly Anderson, 2005. See also a report on a Black lesbian conference where Angela Davis, one of the keynote speakers, invoked Joan Little. Gabrielle Daniels, "First Black Lesbian Conference," *off our backs*, December 31, 1980.

18. Thompson, "Multiracial Feminism." Loretta Ross, "The Spirit of Houston: A Decade of Achievement—Women of Color, An Invisible Decade of Growth," 1987; and Ross, "International Decade for Women & Its Impact on Women of Color," box 5, LR Papers. Historically, Black women have organized against oppression in a variety of seemingly nonpolitical groups and spaces, from bridge clubs and church groups to beauty shops and juke joints. Greene, *Our Separate Ways*.

19. Minutes of the Third Meeting of the NBFO, Chicago Chapter, July 3, 1974, box 1, NBFO/NABF Papers; Taylor, *How We Get Free*.

20. In 1979, the United Nations adopted the Convention of the Elimination of All Forms of Discrimination Against Women. In 1992, a specific provision regarding violence against women—including rape, battering, murder, stalking, torture, and genital mutilation—was added under a revised convention. It required all ratifying nations to eliminate and prevent violence through legal and civil sanctions, educational campaigns, and support services for victims of violence. This was an important redefinition of human rights, which previously had demanded an end to state violence and protections for political and civil rights. Although the United States helped to draft the convention and signed it, conservatives in Congress prevented the United States from ratifying it. Bumiller, *In an Abusive State*, 133–34; Kaplan, *Crazy for Democracy*, 1, 7–14, 100.

21. Like Stephanie Gilmore, I am using the terms "alliance" and "coalition" interchangeably, though some scholars use the former for more sustained efforts and the latter for short-term, collective efforts on single issues. Gilmore, "Thinking About Feminist Coalitions," 6. Estelle Freedman argues that the greater labor force participation of white women and the civil rights achievements of Black women following World War II created greater similarities between Black and white women's experiences. Freedman, *Redefining Rape*.

22. Silliman, Ross, et al., *Undivided Rights*; Nelson, *Women of Color and the Reproductive Rights Movement*.

CHAPTER 15

1. Valk, *Radical Sisters*, 2–3, 7, 168.

2. Nkenge Touré, "Report from the First National Conference on Third World Women: An Overview of Third World Women and Violence," August 1980, box 34, LR Papers.

3. Nkenge Touré, interview by Loretta Ross, December and March 2005; Nkenge Touré, "Report from the First National Conference on Third World Women," box 3, NT Papers.

4. Nkenge Touré, interview by Loretta Ross, December and March 2005; Baxandall and Gordon, *Dear Sisters*, 199.

5. Loretta Ross, interview by Joyce Follett, 2004, 2005; Washington, D.C., Rape Crisis Center, "How to Start a Rape Crisis Center," flyer, n.d., box 17, Washington Area Women's Center Papers, Special Collections Research Center, Estelle and Melvin Gelman Library, George Washington University; "Black Women Organizing Against Rape: An Interview with Nkenge Touré and Michele Plate," in Baxandall and Gordon, *Dear Sisters*, 198, 199.

6. Some sources give 1974 and others 1975 as the date Touré joined the RCC. Touré, "Not All the Panthers Were Men," typescript, box 8, NT Papers; Valk, *Radical Sisters*, 170.

7. John Wesley Stephens later changed his name to Patrice Touré. The couple had two children and divorced in 1979. Finding Aid, NT Papers; Worthington, "Black Panther Women"; Nkenge Touré, interview by Loretta Ross, December and March 2005; Touré, "Not All the Panthers Were Men," typescript, box 8, NT Papers; Baxandall and Gordon, *Dear Sisters*, 198; Valk, *Radical Sisters*, 158–59, 170.

8. Loretta Ross, interview by Joyce Follett, 2004, 2005; Finding Guide, LR Papers; Ross, quoted in Ilana Panich-Linsman and Lauren Kelley, "When Abortions Were Illegal," *NYT*, January 23, 2022.

9. Loretta Ross, interview by Joyce Follett, 2004, 2005; Nkenge Touré, interview by Loretta Ross, December and March 2005. Local BUF chapters focused on issues that members identified as most pressing, including police brutality and housing. For conflicts over gender politics in the Black United Front, including the Black Women's United Front, see Woodard, *Nation within a Nation*; and Farmer, *Remaking Black Power*.

10. Loretta Ross, interview by Joyce Follett, 2004, 2005.

11. Matthews, *Confronting Rape*, 147.

12. "The Whitewashing of Grady Rape Crisis Center," *Great Speckled Bird*, July 1, 1974, news clipping, box 8, ALFA Archives; Press release, "Grady Memorial Hospital Counseling and Rape Victims," May 2, 1975, box 25, ALFA Archives.

13. Conference organizers defined "third world women" as those in nations "struggling to break the shackles of colonialism and neo-colonialism," both globally and in the United States. "Report from the First National Conference on Third World Women and Violence," August 1980, box 5, LR Papers.

14. "Report from the First National Conference on Third World Women and Violence." In 1976, white women at the Hartford, Connecticut, Sexual Assault Crisis Service intentionally incorporated Black and Puerto Rican women at all levels and transformed all aspects of the service's operation. Donna Landerman and Mary MacAtee, "Breaking the Racism Barrier: White Anti-racist Work," *Aegis*, Winter 1982, 16–25.

15. Several Asian American and Indigenous women were also present. Touré recalled there were eighty women present, while *off our backs* reported ninety women and ten men of color present. Nkenge Touré, interview by Loretta Ross, December and March 2005; Tracie Dejanikus, "First National Conference on Third World Women and Violence," *off our backs*, December 1980; Bevacqua, "Reconsidering Violence Against Women," 17; Valk, *Radical Sisters*, 183.

16. Marion Barry was also the first head of SNCC when it formed in 1960. Nkenge Touré, interview by Loretta Ross, December and March 2005; Dejanikus, "First National Conference"; Bevacqua, "Reconsidering Violence Against Women," 17; Valk, *Radical Sisters*, 166–70.

17. For a summary of differing viewpoints about male participation in antirape efforts, see Loretta Ross, "Working with Minority Men Committing Violence Against Women: Report from the First National Conference on Third World Women and Violence," August 1980, box 5, LR Papers; Valk, *Radical Sisters*, 175. Prisoners Against Rape was founded in 1973 by two Black male prisoners and included prisoners from Virginia and Washington, D.C., ex-sex offenders, and feminist antirape activists. The group functioned as a self-help group without support from prison officials and focused on consciousness-raising among prisoners, attitudes toward women, and the politics of rape, with the goal of eliminating rape. Members also promoted community education programs to eradicate the "rape epidemic." William Fuller and Larry Cannon, "Prisoners Against Rape, Position Paper," *Midnight Special*, February 1974, 7; Fuller and Cannon, "Prisoners Against Rape: A Message to Prisoners and Society," *Midnight Special*, March 1975, 9; Prison Research Education Project, *Instead of Prisons*, 152.

18. Loretta Ross, "Working with Minority Men Committing Violence Against Women: Report from the First National Conference on Third World Women and Violence," August 1980, box 5, LR Papers.

19. Quoted in Bevacqua, *Rape on the Public Agenda*, 120–21.

20. Loretta Ross, interview by Joyce Follett, 2004, 2005; Richie, *Compelled to Crime*; Richie, *Arrested Justice*; Moraga and Anzaldúa, *This Bridge Called My Back*.

21. Moraga cofounded Kitchen Table: Women of Color Press in 1983 with Barbara Smith and other women of color. Nkenge Touré, interview by Loretta Ross, December and March 2005; Nkenge Touré, "Report from the First National Conference on Third World Women," box 3, NT Papers; "The Second Annual National Conference on Violence Against Third World Women of Color," flyer, box 4, NT Papers; Thuma, *All Our Trials*, 149–50.

22. Nkenge Touré, "Report from the First National Conference on Third World Women: An Overview of Third World Women and Violence," August 1980, box 3, NT Papers. There is some dispute regarding who authored the Washington, D.C., Rape Crisis Center manual; some scholars claim it was authored by the white women who started the center. However, it is likely that when Black women took over much of the leadership, the manual was redone. Jacquet, *Injustices of Rape*, 88.

CHAPTER 16

1. Baxandall and Gordon, *Dear Sisters*, 132. Avery also worked with the Boston Women's Collective that produced the feminist classic *Our Bodies, Ourselves* in 1970. The Black Women's Health Project became the NBWHP in 1984 after the group's first national

conference in 1983 in Atlanta. In 1995 it moved to Washington, D.C., and was renamed the Black Women's Health Imperative (BWHI) in 2002. Finding Guide, BWHI Records.

2. Baxandall and Gordon, *Dear Sisters*, 131–32; Byllye Avery, interview by Loretta J. Ross, 2005; Reverby and Avery, "Ask a Feminist." Because of her involvement in the feminist health movement and her concern with issues affecting Black women, it is likely that Avery knew about Little's case.

3. Silliman, Ross, et al., *Undivided Rights*, 67. Legendary civil rights activist Ella Baker, who was highly critical of charismatic leadership, promoted this mode of organizing. Ransby, *Ella Baker*. Although consciousness-raising has been largely associated with white feminists, Black feminists adopted the practice too. Springer, *Living for the Revolution*.

4. Byllye Avery, interview by Loretta J. Ross, 2005; Silliman, Ross, et al., *Undivided Rights*, 69–70.

5. "2,000 Black Women at Health Conference," *Upfront: A Black Women's Newspaper* 1, no. 1 (Fall 1983): 1, box 5, LR Papers; Byllye Avery, interview by Loretta J. Ross, 2005; Silliman, Ross, et al., *Undivided Rights*, 70.

6. Avery, "What in Your Life Has Moved You to Activism?," *Between Ourselves: Women of Color Newsletter*, Winter 1985, 8–9, news clipping, box 101, MBP Papers.

7. Loretta Ross, quoted in Byllye Avery, interview by Loretta J. Ross, 2005; Silliman, Ross, et al., *Undivided Rights*, 71–72.

8. Antoinette France, "The NWHP—Meeting Black Women's Health Needs," *Radcliffe Bulletin*, 1992, box 1, Byllye Avery Papers, Sophia Smith Collection, Smith College Special Collections; Valk, *Radical Sisters*, 111, 210n3.

9. Baxandall and Gordon, *Dear Sisters*, 133.

10. Loretta Ross, interview by Joyce Follett, 2004, 2005. At one point both Avery and Lillie Allen had white women partners. Avery and Lythcott married in Massachusetts, where same-sex marriage was legal. Byllye Avery, interview by Loretta J. Ross, 2005. Ross and others claimed that the conference planners had intentionally dealt with their own internalized racism, sexism, and homophobia. Silliman, Ross, et al., *Undivided Rights*, 67. However, those sensibilities may not have fully translated to the NBWHP, especially as it spread across the country.

11. Byllye Avery, interview by Loretta J. Ross, 2005; Silliman, Ross, et al., *Undivided Rights*, 74.

12. Cooper, quoted in Giddings, *When and Where I Enter*, 82, 87–88.

13. Byllye Avery, interview by Loretta J. Ross, 2005; "Black Women's Health: A Conspiracy of Silence," *SOJOURNER: The Women's Forum*, January 1989, 15, box 1, Byllye Avery Papers, Sophia Smith Collection, Smith College Special Collections.

14. Byllye Avery, interview by Loretta J. Ross, 2005. The phrase "million-dollar blocks" was coined by Columbia University architect and professor Laura Kurgan and Eric Cadora at the Justice Mapping Center. The Million Dollar Blocks project is now part of the permanent collection of the Museum of Modern Art in New York City. Kurgan, *Close Up at a Distance*; "Million Dollar Blocks," Alternative Narratives Visualization Archives, accessed April 17, 2022, https://alternative-narratives-vis-archive.com/case_studies/million-dollar-blocks .html. See also the Columbia University Center for Spacial Research website, https://c4sr .columbia.edu/projects/million-dollar-blocks.

15. Byllye Avery, interview by Loretta J. Ross, 2005.

16. Loretta Ross, interview by Joyce Follett, 2004, 2005; Byllye Avery, interview by Loretta J. Ross, 2005.

17. "Lillie Allen Tells Her Story," *VITAL SIGNS: News from the National Black Women's Health Project* 4 (February 1987): 6–7, box 3, BWHI Records (unprocessed).

18. Silliman, Ross, et al., *Undivided Rights*, 67–69.

19. Angela Davis, "The Roots of Black Women's Oppression," *VITAL SIGNS* 4 (February 1987): 3.

20. Loretta Ross, interview by Joyce Follett, 2004, 2005.

21. Byllye Avery, interview by Loretta J. Ross, 2005. Davis, *Emancipation Circuit*.

22. Byllye Avery, interview by Loretta J. Ross, 2005; Guide, BWHI Records; Silliman, Ross, et al., *Undivided Rights*, 72.

23. See Richie's essay, "Battered Black Women," originally published in *Black Scholar* in 1985; Richie, "Black Feminist Reflection"; Richie, *Arrested Justice*; Richie, "How Anti-violence Activism Taught Me to Become a Prison Abolitionist." The wording of the heading above comes from Hull, Bell Scott, and Smith, *Some of Us Are Brave*; see also Hobson, *Are All the Women Still White?*

24. For the most recent example of their political analysis, see Davis et al., *Abolition. Feminism. Now.*

25. Beth E. Richie, podcast interview by Laura Coe, March 7, 2017; Richie, "Battered Black Women," 399. In 1992, Richie earned a PhD in sociology from the City University of New York Graduate Center.

26. Richie, "Battered Black Women," 400–401; Richie, "How Anti-violence Activism Taught Me to Become a Prison Abolitionist"; Beth E. Richie, "Task Forces: Attaining Diversity," *Aegis*, no. 41 (1986): 15; Richie, *Arrested Justice*, 1–2; Dorothy Roberts, "Drug Addicts Who Have Babies: Women of Color, Equality and the Right of Privacy," *Harvard Law Review* (1991), cited in Johnson, *Inner Lives*, 44; Beth E. Richie, podcast interview by Laura Coe, March 7, 2017.

27. Beth E. Richie, podcast interview by Laura Coe, March 7, 2017; Richie, "Black Feminist Reflection"; Richie, "Queering Anti-prison Work"; Crenshaw, "Mapping the Margins."

28. Beth E. Richie, podcast interview by Laura Coe, March 7, 2017; Crenshaw, "Mapping the Margins," 1251n35.

29. Numerous studies have confirmed that still today most women prisoners have experienced some form of violence and/or abuse. Beth E. Richie, podcast interview by Laura Coe, March 7, 2017.

30. Quoted in Crenshaw, "Mapping the Margins," 1251.

31. Quoted in Matthews, *Confronting Rape*, 140.

32. Richie, "How Anti-violence Activism Taught Me to Become a Prison Abolitionist."

33. See INCITE! and Critical Resistance, "Statement." The group changed its name to INCITE! Women, Gender Non-conforming, and Trans People of Color Against Violence, but currently uses the shorter version, INCITE! It is "a network of radical feminists of color organizing to end state violence and violence in our homes and communities." INCITE! has chapters in cities across the country. See INCITE! home page, https://incite-national.org/.

CHAPTER 17

1. Bevacqua, *Rape on the Public Agenda*.
2. Bethel, "What Chou Mean *We*, White Girl?"

3. Washington, D.C., Rape Crisis Center, Take Back the Night Flyer, September 1981; Ann Arbor Revolutionary Workers League, Take Back the Night Flyer, April 1982, box 100, MBP Papers.

4. Not all the critiques of Brownmiller centered on her racial views. Andrew Greeley, writing for the *Chicago Tribune*, called her a "heretic" and dismissed the work as "a vile, evil, vicious, sick book." Quoted in Flood, *Rape in Chicago*, 133.

5. Brownmiller, *Against Our Will*.

6. For example, in Yanceyville, North Carolina, a Black sharecropper husband and father was convicted in the 1950s of sexual assault of a white woman who was seventy-five feet away, in what came to be known as "eye rape." Greene, *Our Separate Ways*, 40.

7. Brownmiller, *Against Our Will*, 245–48, quote on 247 and 248. Despite Brownmiller's "certainty" about Till's comment, scholars have debated what if anything Till might have said. One theory is that Till's speech impediment may have been misinterpreted as a "wolf whistle." For the most recent scholarly treatment, see Tyson, *Blood of Emmett Till*.

8. Anne Moody, a young Black woman from Mississippi who was the same age as Till when he was murdered, was deeply shaken by his death and subsequently joined the civil rights movement. Moody, *Coming of Age in Mississippi*.

9. Sissy Bryant, "How to Declare a Hassle-Free Zone," *VITAL SIGNS* 3, no. 4 (October 1986), box 3, BWHI Records.

10. In addition to the Kentucky Alliance, the coalition included the local chapters of NOW and the Coalition of Labor Union Women, the Kentucky Civil Liberties Union, the Kentucky Christian Leadership Conference, and Local 557 of the Service Employees International Union. Anne Braden to Jason Williams (*Louisville Defender*), August 10, 1975, and Anne Braden, "Joan Little Case," December 22, 1975, box 132, folder 39, CAB Papers. See also Hall, "The Mind That Burns in Each Body."

11. The discovery by antiwar activists in the mid-1970s of the secret FBI COINTELPRO revealed the extent of government suppression against a range of dissenters, including civil rights, Black power, women's liberation, student, and antiwar groups. Fosl, *Subversive Southerner*, 123–24, xxvi, 95–96.

12. Braden, "Second Open Letter to Southern White Women." For another critique of Brownmiller by the Chicago-based Sojourner Truth Organization, a left-wing offshoot of the Revolutionary Youth Movement, see Edwards, *Rape, Racism and the White Women's Movement*. First published in 1976, the pamphlet includes a brief mention of the Joan Little case.

13. Braden, "Second Open Letter to Southern White Women," 51.

14. Anne Braden, "Free Thomas Wansley: A Letter to White Southern Women" (Louisville: Southern Conference Education Fund, December 1972), box 100, MBP Papers.

15. Braden, "Second Open Letter to Southern White Women."

16. Braden, 51.

17. Braden, 50; Hall, *Revolt Against Chivalry*. For white southern women's ambivalent and even racist efforts to end the lynching of Black men in the late nineteenth and early twentieth centuries, see Feimster, *Southern Horrors*.

18. *A Rush to Judgement in the Case of Willie Sanders*, pamphlet, box 142, folder 48, CAB Papers. See also Aime Sands, who wrote, "For the record, I am a white lesbian feminist." Sands, "Rape and Racism in Boston: An Open Letter to White Women," *off our backs*, January 1981; and William Worthy, "The Willie Sanders Rape Case: A Tangled Web of Deception," *Afro-American*, October 27, 1979; Boston TV News Digital Library.

19. Braden, "Second Open Letter to Southern White Women," 53. Tibbs was a former seminary student from Chicago traveling in Florida when he was arrested, tried, and convicted in two days by an all-white jury in 1974. He spent three years in prison before being exonerated and released in 1977. Florida dropped the case in 1982. His story was captured in a 2002 play, *The Exonerated*, by Jessica Blank and Erik Jensen. Bruce Weber, "Delbert Tibbs, Who Left Death Row and Fought Against It, Dies at 74," *NYT*, December 7, 2013.

20. Davis, "Joan Little," 39. For Davis's critique of white feminist antirape theorists, including Brownmiller, who perpetuated the myth of the Black male rapist, see Davis, "Rape, Racism and the Capitalist Setting," 25.

21. Segrest conceptualized what she calls "queer socialism," and Pratt joined the revolutionary socialist Workers World Party. Minnie Bruce Pratt, interview by Kelly Anderson, 2005; Segrest, *Memoir of a Race Traitor*.

22. *Feminary*, Summer 1978; Minnie Bruce Pratt, interview by Kelly Anderson, 2005; Bulkin, Pratt, and Smith, *Yours in Struggle*.

23. A twenty-fifth anniversary edition of *Memoir of a Race Traitor* was published in 2019 with a new introduction and afterward. Over the past half century, Segrest has participated in scores of social justice organizations and published nearly half a dozen books. Carter, a longtime member of the pacifist War Resisters League and an antiracist activist since 1969, is not a southerner but relocated to Durham in the 1980s. In 1990 she started Equality North Carolina and in 2003 she was a founder of the National Black Justice Coalition, which promotes LGBTQ liberation. In 2012, she coedited, with Elizabeth "Betita" Martinez and Matt Meyer, *We Have Not Been Moved: Resisting Racism and Militarism in 21st Century America*. Mab Segrest, Minnie Bruce Pratt, et al., Womanwrites Outreach Task Force on Issues of Racism and Anti-Semitism, "Womanwrites 81: Statement of Purpose," box 100, MBP Papers. Materials on Segrest's prison writing workshop can be found in box 33, Mab Segrest Papers, David M. Rubenstein Rare Book and Manuscript Library, Duke University, Durham, N.C.; Rostan, "Inside Out and Upside Down."

24. ALFA, a predominantly white southern lesbian group, pressed for an investigation into the police killing of an unarmed Black transvestite man, Tyrone Broughton, in Atlanta. "Tyrone Broughton," *ALFA Newsletter*, June 1980, box 100, MBP Papers.

25. Robin McDuff et al., Santa Cruz Women Against Rape, "Letter to the Anti-rape Movement," *off our backs*, June 30, 1977; *Women Unite, Take Back the Night*, pamphlet, October 4, 1980, box 142, folder 48, CAB Papers; Friedman, "Rape, Racism and Reality," *Feminist Alliance Against Rape (FAAR) Newsletter*, July–August 1978. An excerpt of the Santa Cruz letter was published in "Feminists Critique Anti-rape Movement," *Aegis*, June 1981, 9–11.

26. Bevacqua, "Reconsidering Violence Against Women"; Thuma, *All Our Trials*.

27. New York's corroboration law required that each aspect of a rape, including force, penetration, the rapist's identity, and other details, be supported by evidence other than the rape victim's word. Bevacqua, "Reconsidering Violence Against Women," 166–70.

28. Minutes of the Sixth Meeting of the NBFO-Chicago Chapter, July 24, 1974; Chicago NBFO Calendar of Events, 1974; Orientation Session, NBFO-Chicago, January 12, 1975, box 1, NBFO/NABF Papers; Chicago Council on Crimes Against Women, Board Meeting, June 7, 1978, box 2, NABF Papers; "Women Unite! Take Back the Night [1980], box 1, NABF Papers; Rape Action Project, Dear Sisters and Friends, June 22, 1979, Sondra

Gayle Stein Papers, Special Collections Library, Northeastern University, http://www.lib.neu/archives/voices/w-violence5.htm.

29. Touré, quoted in Baxandall and Gordon, *Dear Sisters*, 199.

30. Kathleen Cleaver, quoted in Giddings, *When and Where I Enter*, 31; Baxandall and Gordon, *Dear Sisters*, 199; *Feminary*, October 6, 1974; Randolph, "Women's Liberation or . . . Black Liberation."

31. Rostan, "Inside Out and Upside Down."

32. *Chapel Hill–Carrboro Rape Crisis Center Newsletter*, [ca. 1974], box 8, MS Papers.

33. Matthews, *Confronting Rape*, 147.

34. Roth, *Separate Roads to Feminism*, 124.

35. See, for example, Taylor, *How We Get Free*. On the Combahee River Collective's multi-issue agenda, and the importance of coalition building, especially in the South, see Jones, Eubanks, and Smith, *Ain't Gonna Let Nobody Turn Me Around*, esp. chap. 6, "Building Multi-issue Movements."

CHAPTER 18

1. Ross, quoted in Tracie Dejanikus, "First National Conference on Third World Women and Violence," *off our backs*, December 31, 1980, 13.

2. Quoted in Thuma, "Lessons in Self-Defense," 54.

3. Quoted in Thuma, 53.

4. Tracie Dejanikus, "First National Conference First National Conference on Third World Women and Violence," *off our backs*, December 31, 1980.

5. Brenda Eichelberger to Wyola Evans, African American Patrolmen's League, November 7, 1974; Eichelberger to Herman Roberts, n.d., box 1, NBFO/NABF Papers; Balto, *Occupied Territory*, 235; *Chicago Sun-Times*, July 25, 1982, news clipping, box 1, NBFO/NABF Papers.

6. See, for example, Hadden, *Slave Patrols*; Malka, *Men of Mobtown*; and Balto, *Occupied Territory*.

7. Davis, "Rape, Racism and the Capitalist Setting," 25. Davis continued to mount this critique. In her keynote address at a 2000 Color of Violence Conference in Santa Cruz, Davis linked the pitfalls of feminist antiviolence activism with tough-on-crime policies: "The major strategy relied on by the women's antiviolence movement of criminalizing violence against women will not put an end to violence against women—just as imprisonment has not put an end to 'crime' in general." Angela Y. Davis, "The Color of Violence Against Women," *Colorlines*, October 10, 2000, https://www.colorlines.com/articles/color-violence-against-women.

8. Jackie MacMillan and Fraeda Klein, editorial, *Feminist Alliance Against Rape (FAAR) Newsletter*, September–October 1974; Marlene Schmitz, untitled, *off our backs*, February 25, 1975; Deb Friedman, "Increased Convictions or Lowered Expectations," *Aegis*, June 1981; Gottschalk, *Prison and the Gallows*, 130. The FAAR newsletter was renamed *Aegis* in 1978. A 1980 special issue of the *FAAR/Aegis* newsletter again questioned whether imprisonment was the best solution to rape.

9. Quoted in Thuma, "Against the 'Prison/Psychiatric' State," 45. Thuma's research complicates scholarship by Bumiller and Gottschalk that emphasizes the mainstreaming

of feminist antiviolence as a neoliberal appropriation and incorporation into an expanding carceral state.

10. Freedman, quoted in Jacquet, *Injustices of Rape*, 58–59.

11. The last execution for nonlethal rape occurred in Missouri in 1964, when a white man was given the death penalty for the rape of an eight-year-old. In 1995, Louisiana reintroduced capital punishment for the rape of children under twelve. Jacquet, *Injustices of Rape*, 174, 202n50, 224n102. Wiseman called for capital punishment only if the victim was a child or had been mutilated. Slifkin to the Editor, *Chapel Hill Newspaper*, March 24, 1973, news clipping, box 8, MS Papers; Slifkin to Editor, *Chapel Hill Newspaper*, February 14, 1975, box 7, MS Papers; N&O, May 4, 1977, news clipping, box 9, MS Papers; Sue Bowman, "Castration for Rapists Opposed by Feminists," *Guardian*, January 18, 1984, news clipping, box 100, MBP Papers.

12. Gottschalk, *Prison and the Gallows*, 131; Freedman, quoted in Jacquet, *Injustices of Rape*, 58–59.

13. Bevacqua, *Rape on the Public Agenda*, 119.

14. Matthew Desmond's research on this phenomenon recently compelled the Milwaukee Common Council to prohibit this policy. Landlords simply devised other excuses to evict victims of domestic violence or partner abuse. Desmond, *Evicted*.

15. Cocca, "From 'Welfare Queen' to 'Exploited Teen.'"

16. "Black Women's Health: A Conspiracy of Silence," *SOJOURNER: The Women's Forum*, January 1989, box 1, Byllye Avery Papers, Sophia Smith Collection, Smith College Special Collections.

17. When Ward was mysteriously murdered in 1980, in what many believed was a political assassination, the RCC board again questioned whether the Memorial Fund and Support Committee for Ward was appropriate work for the RCC. Janis Kelly, "Yolanda Ward Murdered," *off our backs*, December 1980; Valk, *Radical Sisters*, 176; Thuma, *All Our Trials*, 150–55.

18. The idea for the program came from the International Council of African Women. The council was a network of Black women organized by Ross and Nkenge Touré to formulate a U.S. Black women's agenda in preparation for the upcoming UN Conference on Third World Women, culminating the UN Decade on Women (1975–85). The council almost collapsed after a small but vocal group opposed the lesbian rights plank. Barbara Smith called for unity among Black women, making a political argument rather than a personal appeal. Queen Mother Audley Moore, a legendary Black nationalist then in her eighties and known for her hostility to feminism, saved the council. Claiming that she failed to understand why women would have sex with other women, Moore nevertheless echoed Smith's call for unity among Black women and the plank passed. Loretta Ross, interview by Joyce Follett, 2004, 2005.

19. Ross also alluded to African liberation struggles where women were sexually abused; and violence against women, including intraracial rape, was one of the issues she and Touré hoped to address at the upcoming UN Conference on Third World Women. Loretta Ross, interview by Joyce Follett, 2004, 2005; *Upfront* 1, no. 3 (Summer 1984).

20. The effects of LEAA were uneven. For example, in Chicago LEAA funds made up only 1 percent of the police department's 1970 budget. Moreover, the department had already become "thoroughly racialized, profoundly discriminatory and deeply punitive" decades before receiving LEAA monies. Balto, *Occupied Territory*, 4–5.

21. Matthews, *Confronting Rape*, 57, 62.

22. Mary Ann Largen, "L.E.A.A. Rape Funding Review," *FAAR Newsletter*, September 1, 1974, 10–11; Jackie MacMillan, "L.E.A.A. East," *Aegis*, June 1981, 39–41. Bevacqua, *Rape on the Public Agenda*, 148.

23. Gottschalk makes this argument in *Prison and the Gallows*, 127, 128–29.

24. Gottschalk, 129. Political scientist Kristin Bumiller has called this the "therapeutic state." Bumiller, *In an Abusive State*, xii, xiv.

25. Gottschalk, *Prison and the Gallows*, 86, 77–78. Bevacqua, *Rape on the Public Agenda*, 118.

26. Matthews, *Confronting Rape*, 159.

27. Williams, quoted in Matthews, 137; Baxandall and Gordon, *Dear Sisters*, 132. Black feminist sociologist Patricia Hill Collins argues that claiming victim status for Black women has positive effects by making oppression visible and giving voice to historic silences. Collins, *Fighting Words*, 127; Bailey, *Misogynoir Transformed*.

28. Many YWCAs across the country, including those on HBCU campuses and in communities of color, offered rape crisis programs. Matthews, *Confronting Rape*, 136, 138, 141–42. Haynes, "'Sex-Ins College Style.'" "By any means necessary" was a slogan widely associated with Malcolm X.

29. When LEAA was abolished, California directed the OCJP to continue and to develop criminal justice programs. Williams, quoted in Matthews, *Confronting Rape*, 138, 139, 108–9.

30. Matthews, 160, 150–51; Bumiller, *In an Abusive State*, 146. Richie, *Arrested Justice*.

31. Quoted in Williams, *From the Bullet to the Ballot*, 95. FBI director J. Edgar Hoover understood the political potential of Panther "survival programs" as these were often targets of police raids, especially the Free Breakfast Programs. See Orleck, *Storming Caesars Palace*, for another example of how providing services for poor Black mothers also politicized them.

32. Nelson, *Body and Soul*.

33. Gottschalk claims that by the mid-1980s, about half of all RCCs surveyed reported no political work aside from lobbying. Gottschalk, *Prison and the Gallows*, 126. Tracy Matthews was one of the first historians to challenge this dichotomy and to argue for reenvisioning service provision as political. Matthews, "'No One Ever Asks What a Man's Role in the Revolution Is.'"

34. See, for example, Orleck, *Storming Caesars Palace*; Orleck and Hazirjian, *War on Poverty*; and Greene, *Our Separate Ways*.

EPILOGUE

1. Violent crime had peaked in 1991, three years prior to the 1994 Crime Bill. Although the number of welfare recipients was drastically reduced under the Personal Responsibility and Work Opportunity Act, the law had little impact on reducing poverty for very poor single mothers. Rashawn Ray and William Galston, "Did the 1994 Crime Bill Cause Mass Incarceration?," August 28, 2020, Brookings Institution Report, https://www.brookings.edu/blog/fixgov/2020/08/28/did-the-1994-crime-bill-cause-mass-incarceration/; Robert Moffitt and Stephanie Garlow, "Did Welfare Reform Increase Employment and Reduce Poverty?," *Pathways*, Winter 2018, https://inequality.stanford.edu/sites/default/files/Pathways_Winter2018_Employment-Poverty.pdf.

2. Some states have enacted their own versions of VAWA. On the myriad problems with VAWA and the legal challenge of civil rights remedies for gender violence, see Bumiller, *In an Abusive State*, 140–45. Women's Legal Defense and Education Fund, "History of the Violence Against Women Act," provides a brief legislative history of changes in the VAWA over the past twenty-five years.

3. Several historians have recently offered a cautionary note concerning the perils of selective historical memories in the wake of proposals for a new war on crime: "As we debate how to switch course, our popular understanding of the rise of 'get tough' laws should not layer selective memory atop selective hearing of the past by justifying black incarceration with trite references to black voices." Elizabeth Hinton, Julilly Kohler-Hausmann, and Vesla Weaver, "Did Blacks Really Endorse the 1994 Crime Bill?," op-ed, *NYT*, April 13, 2016. See also the statement of CBC chair Marcia Fudge, CBC press release, February 18, 2013; Rashawn Ray and William Galston, "Did the 1994 Crime Bill Cause Mass Incarceration?," August 28, 2020, Brookings Institution Report, https://www.brookings.edu/blog/fixgov/2020/08/28/did-the-1994-crime-bill-cause-mass-incarceration.

4. Gottschalk, *Prison and the Gallows*, 151–52, 327n85; Bumiller, *In an Abusive State*, 145.

5. Some opponents, like the ACLU, shifted their initial opposition to conditional support by 2005. NBWHP *Hill Briefs*, June 1995, 2, box 1, BWHI Records. The VAWA ran into partisan opposition from Republicans, far-right conservatives, and the National Rifle Association, which objected to the "boyfriend loophole" that would have denied firearms to those convicted of abusing their dating partners, to stalkers, and to abusers subjected to temporary protective orders. Sacco, "Violence Against Women Act."

6. Richie, "Black Feminist Reflection," 1136; see also Richie, *Arrested Justice*; Crenshaw, "Mapping the Margins"; Kim and Kanuha, "Restorative Justice and the Dance with the Devil." For an overview of the women's antirape movement, recent women's activism, and the scholarly debate on the VAWA and critique by women of color, see Ake and Arnold, "Brief History of Anti-violence Against Women Movements."

7. Beth E. Richie, podcast interview by Laura Coe, March 7, 2017.

8. Bumiller, *In an Abusive State*, 11, 156.

9. Quoted in Levine and Meiners, "Violence Cannot Remedy Violence."

10. Bumiller, *In an Abusive State*, 156, 159, 161, 163; Iyengar, "Does the Certainty of Arrest Reduce Domestic Violence?"

11. Gottschalk, *Prison and the Gallows*, 333n174; for a summary of feminist and critical criminology debates regarding violence against women and the pros and cons of law enforcement involvement, see 160–64.

12. Quoted in Levine and Meiners, "Violence Cannot Remedy Violence."

13. Ms. Foundation, *Safety and Justice for All*.

14. Quoted in Gottschalk, *Prison and the Gallows*, 160–61.

15. Bumiller, *In an Abusive State*, 156, 159, 161, 163; Kaba, *We Do This 'Til We Free Us*.

16. U.S. Department of Justice, *Impact of Incarceration and Mandatory Minimums on Survivors*. See also Levine and Meiners, *Feminist and the Sex Offender*. According to Bumiller, feminist cooperation did not have merely unintended consequences; instead, it was "a joining of forces with a neoliberal project of social control." Bumiller, *In an Abusive State*, 14.

17. Congressional appropriations provide grants to state, local, and tribal governments, as well as to nonprofit organizations and universities. After the VAWA expired in 2011, it was opposed by conservatives, including Concerned Women for America, who objected

to protections for same-sex partners, allowances for undocumented immigrants to claim temporary visas, and disagreements over prosecution in tribal courts of alleged non-Native men who attacked Indigenous women on reservations. The VAWA Reauthorization was signed by President Obama in February 2013 and then by President Biden in 2022. Campbell and Jacobs, "Senate Must Reauthorize Violence Against Women Act"; "Fact Sheet: Reauthorization of the Violence Against Women Act (VAWA)," March 16, 2022, https://www.whitehouse.gov/briefing-room/statements-releases/2022/03/16/fact-sheet-reauthorization-of-the-violence-against-women-act-vawa/; Richie quoted in Cheung, "Perhaps It's Time to Think Beyond the Violence Against Women Act."

18. Palacios, "Prison Rape Elimination Act"; Richie, *Arrested Justice*; Bader, "Women Prisoners Endure Rampant Sexual Violence"; Human Rights Project for Girls and Ms. Foundation, *Sexual Assault to Prison Pipeline*.

19. May, "North Carolina's Racial Justice Act."

20. Reverby and Avery, "Ask a Feminist."

21. See the Loretta J. Ross website, https://www.lorettaross.com/.

22. White, "Talking Black, Talking Feminist." For several creative expressions of Black women confronting intraracial rape, see Simmons, "State of Rage," and her documentary film, *NO! The Rape Documentary*.

23. INCITE! home page, https://incite-national.org/. See also Davis et al., *Abolition. Feminism. Now.*

24. Michaels, "If Free People Are Not Allowed to Have Unions."

25. Sturgis, "Moral Monday Movement." The North Carolina state Supreme Court reinstated the state's Racial Justice Act in June 2020. "North Carolina Supreme Court Finds Repeal of Racial Justice Act Unconstitutional," ACLU press release, June 5, 2020; Cathy Lynn Grossman, "Moral Monday Expands to a Week of Social Justice Action Across U.S.," *Washington Post*, August 19, 2021.

26. Julia Chinyere Oparah (formerly Julia Sudbury), "Beyond the Prison Industrial Complex: Women of Color Transforming Antiviolence Work," in Hobson, *Are All the Women Still White?*, 54.

27. Davis, "Race and Criminalization," 67.

28. Kaba, "Yes, Rape Survivors Do Engage in Restorative Justice Practice"; Rape, Abuse and Incest National Network (RAINN), https://www.rainn.org/about-sexual-assault.

29. See Assata's Daughters, home page, https://www.assatasdaughters.org/; Kaba, *We Do This 'til We Free Us*.

30. "'Words Matter': County Dane County Sheriff to Stop Using 'Inmate,'" ABC/WKOW Television, August 16, 2021; Emily Hamer, "Dane County Board Passes Major Criminal Justice Reform Package," *Wisconsin State Journal*, October 16, 2020.

31. Fox, "Madison School Board Votes to End Contract with Police Department"; Emilie Heidemann, "Workers at Forefront," *Wisconsin State Journal*, January 16, 2022.

32. Julia Chinyere Oparah (formerly Julia Sudbury), "Beyond the Prison Industrial Complex: Women of Color Transforming Antiviolence Work," in Hobson, *Are All the Women Still White?*, 52–53; Ryan Carter, "LA County Could Close Men's Central Jail within 2 Years, Report Says," *Los Angeles Daily*, March 30, 2021; see also "Rebel Archive" for a summary of local LA anticarceral activism, in Hernandez, *City of Inmates*, 199–220.

33. See the Amnesty International response to the U.S. Department of Justice report on sexual abuse in U.S. prisons: Amnesty International, "'Shocking Levels' of Sexual

Abuse in Prisons Cannot Continue," press release, May 16, 2013, https://www.amnestyusa.org/press-releases/shocking-levels-of-sexual-abuse-in-prisons-cannot-continue. See the regularly updated "Trends in U.S. Corrections" at the Sentencing Project website for the most recent statistics on incarceration, https://www.sentencingproject.org/publications/trends-in-u-s-corrections.

34. Hailey Fuchs, "Number of Executions by States Decline Despite Push by Trump Administration," *NYT*, December 16, 2020. Long before entering the White House, Donald Trump demonstrated his racial animus. Although as president, Trump signed the First Step Act in 2018—initiated by a bipartisan group of legislators during the Obama administration—this was a modest step toward sentencing reform, and only a fraction of federal prisoners are affected. It does however prevent the shackling of pregnant women in federal prisons, unless they are deemed a flight risk or a "threat." Many observers see Trump's support for the bill as an outlier, the result of heavy personal lobbying by his son-in-law, whose own father was imprisoned. In fact, Trump and his administration have done more to stymie criminal justice reforms and to inflame racial divisions, while pushing for harsher penal policies, and quashing Department of Justice investigations of police abuse begun under Obama.

35. Death Penalty Information Center, *Enduring Injustice*; NAACP-LDEF, *Death Row USA*; Hailey Fuchs, "U.S. Executes Lisa Montgomery for 2004 Murder," *NYT*, January 13, 2021.

36. As of October 2020, almost 150,000 incarcerated people and more than 32,000 staff tested positive, with at least 1,245 deaths among incarcerated people and 86 deaths among staff. For the class-action lawsuit filed in October 2020 against the federal prison in Butner, North Carolina, by the ACLU, the ACLU of North Carolina, and the Washington Lawyers for Civil Rights and Urban Affairs, see "Hallinan v. Scarantino," ACLU North Carolina, accessed January 2022, https://www.acluofnorthcarolina.org/en/cases/hallinan-v-scarantino.

POSTSCRIPT

1. To protect Joan Little's privacy and to shield her from possible harm, I have kept her present location ambiguous.

2. "Joan Little Paroled: Now Working in NYC," *Jet*, June 28, 1979; Mark Mooney, "Joan Little Shot," *Bilalian News*, June 12, 1981; Wolfgang Saxon, "Joan Little, Tried for Killing Jailer in 1974 Is Arrested in New Jersey," *NYT*, February 26, 1989, 34. In a 2013 interview, Little revealed a large scar and explained that the injury was the result of an accidental shooting during an argument with her boyfriend. Joan Little, interview by author, October 27, 2013.

3. W. E. B. Du Bois, *The Souls of Black Folk* (Chicago: A. C. McClurg, 1903), quoted in Alexander, *The New Jim Crow*, 212.

BIBLIOGRAPHY

MANUSCRIPT COLLECTIONS

Chicago Public Library, Carter G. Woodson Regional Library
    National Alliance of Black Feminists Papers
Duke University, David M. Rubenstein Rare Book and Manuscript Library
    Atlanta Lesbian Feminist Alliance Archives
    Joan Little Collection
    Mab Segrest Papers
    Minnie Bruce Pratt Papers
    Miriam Slifkin Papers
The Freedom Archives, Berkeley, Calif.
George Washington University, Special Collections Research
        Center, Estelle and Melvin Gelman Library
    Washington (D.C.) Area Women's Center Papers
Harvard University, Arthur and Elizabeth Schlesinger Library,
      Radcliffe Institute for Advanced Study
    National Organization for Women (NOW) Papers
New York University, Tamiment Library and Robert F. Wagner Archives, Bobst Library
    William Kunstler Papers (closed)
Northeastern University, Special Collections Library
    Sondra Gayle Stein Papers. http://www.lib.neu/archives/voices/w-violence5.htm.
Smith College Special Collections, Sophia Smith Collection
    Alliance Against Women's Oppression Papers
    Bylle Avery Papers
    Black Women's Health Imperative Records
    Loretta Ross Papers
    Nkenge Touré Papers
    Third World Women's Alliance Papers
    Voices of Feminism Oral History Project

University of Illinois at Chicago, Special Collections and
    University Archives, Richard J. Daley Library
  National Black Feminist Organization / National
    Alliance of Black Feminists Papers
University of North Carolina at Charlotte, Special Collections, J. Murrey Atkins Library
  Charlotte National Organization for Women (NOW) Papers
  T. J. Reddy Papers
University of North Carolina at Chapel Hill, Southern
    Historical Collection, Wilson Library
  Hamilton H. Hobgood Papers
  James Reston Jr. Papers
  James Reston Jr. Collection of Joan Little Trial Materials,
    1975–76, https://finding-aids.lib.unc.edu/04006/
University of North Carolina at Chapel Hill, North Carolina Collection, Wilson Library
  James B. Hunt, Governor of North Carolina, Addresses and Public Papers
Wisconsin State Historical Society, Madison
  Carl and Anne Braden Papers
  Pamphlet Collection
  Social Action Collection

NEWSPAPERS AND PERIODICALS

Action for Forgotten Women Newsletter
Aegis: Magazine on Ending Violence
    Against Women (formerly Feminist
    Alliance Against Rape (FAAR)
    Newsletter)
ALFA Newsletter
Amsterdam News (New York)
Attica News
Afro-American (Baltimore)
Between Ourselves:
    Women of Color Newsletter
Big Mama Rag
Black Panther
Carolina Times
Carolinian
Chapel Hill–Carrboro Rape Crisis Center
    Newsletter
Chicago Defender
Chicago Sun-Times
Daily Challenge (New York)
Daily Mail (London)
Durham (N.C.) Morning Herald
Fayetteville-Cumberland NOW Newsletter
Feminary
Great Speckled Bird
Guardian
Hill Briefs
Jet
Los Angeles Daily
Midnight Special
Montreal Star
Muhammad Speaks
    (later Bilalian News)
National Guardian
NCPLU (North Carolina Prisoner
    Labor Union) Newsletter
New Women's Times
New York Daily News
New York Times
North Carolina Alliance Newsletter
    (National Alliance Against Racist and
    Political Repression–N.C. Chapter)
North Carolina Political Prisoners
    Committee Newsletter
off our backs
Pathways
Plexus
Raleigh News and Observer

Raleigh Times
Radcliffe Bulletin
San Francisco Bay Guardian
San Francisco Examiner
SOJOURNER: The Women's Forum
Southern Patriot
Triple Jeopardy

Upfront: A Black Women's Newspaper
VITAL SIGNS: News from the National
   Black Women's Health Project
Washington (N.C.) Daily News
Washington Post
Washington Star
Wisconsin State Journal

PAMPHLETS

Edwards, Allison. *Rape, Racism and the White Women's Movement: An Answer to Susan Brownmiller.* Chicago: Sojourner Truth Organization, [1976, 1979] c. 1980.

National Alliance Against Racist and Political Repression, *North Carolina: Laboratory for Racism and Repression*, n.d.

North Carolina Women's Prison Project. *Break de Chains of Legalized U.$. Slavery.* Durham, N.C.: Hard Times Prison Project / Triangle Area Lesbian Feminists, 1976.

INTERVIEWS/PERSONAL COMMUNICATIONS

Archie Allen. Conversation with author, Washington, N.C., August 14, 2006.

Byllye Avery. Interview by Loretta J. Ross, 2005. Voices of Feminism Oral History Project, Sophia Smith Collection, Smith College, Northampton, Mass.

Frances Beal. Interview by Loretta J. Ross, 2005. Voices of Feminism Oral History Project, Sophia Smith Collection, Smith College, Northampton, Mass.

Karen (Galloway) Bethea-Shields. Interview by author, Durham, N.C., November 11, 2013.

Karen Bethea-Shields. Interview by David Cecelski, Durham, N.C., n.d. (transcript in author's possession).

Linda Burnham. Interview. Interview by Loretta J. Ross, 2005. Voices of Feminism Oral History Project, Sophia Smith Collection, Smith College, Northampton, Mass.

Celine Chenier. Interview by James Reston Jr., n.p., n.d. James B. Reston Jr. Joan Little Trial Materials. Southern Historical Collection. University of North Carolina at Chapel Hill (audio).

Rev. Herbert Daughtry. Conversation with author, Brooklyn, N.Y., May 1, 2012.

Thulani Davis. Conversation with author, Madison, Wisc., January 15, 2016.

Dazon Dixon Diallo. Interview by Loretta J. Ross, 2009. Sophia Smith Collection, Voices of Feminism Oral History Project, Smith College, Northampton, Mass.

Golden Frinks. Interview by Melynn Glusman, Edenton, N.C., January 1994 (tape/transcript in author's possession).

Golden Frinks. Interview by James Reston Jr., n.p., n.d. James B. Reston Jr. Joan Little Trial Materials. Southern Historical Collection. University of North Carolina at Chapel Hill (audio).

Joan Little. Interviews by author, May 1, 2012, April 8, 2013, October 27, 2013.

Joan Little. Conversations with author, notes, April 8, 2013, July 23, 2021.

Joan Little. Text message to author, April 8, 2013.

Joan Little. Telephone conversation with the author, August 15, 2015.

Marjorie Nelson. Interview by Katie Weigand, 2005. Sophia Smith Collection, Voices of Feminism Oral History Project, Smith College, Northampton, Mass.

Jerry Paul. Interview by James by James Reston Jr., n.p., n.d. James B. Reston Jr. Joan Little Trial Materials. Southern Historical Collection. University of North Carolina at Chapel Hill (audio).

Minnie Bruce Pratt. Interview by Kelly Anderson, 2005. Voices of Feminism Oral History Project, Sophia Smith Collection, Smith College, Northampton, Mass.

Louis Randolph. Interview by James Reston Jr., n.p., n.d. James B. Reston Jr. Joan Little Trial Materials. Southern Historical Collection. University of North Carolina at Chapel Hill (audio).

Beth E. Richie. Interview by Laura Coe. Podcast, *The Art of Authenticity*. March 7, 2017. https://lauracoe.com/beth-richie/.

Loretta Ross. Interview by Joyce Follett, November and December 2004, February 2005, Voices of Feminism Oral History Project, Sophia Smith Collection, Smith College, Northampton, Mass.

Christine Strudwick. Interview by Melynn Glusman, Durham, N.C., January 18, 1994 (tape/transcript in author's possession).

Dannia Sutherland. Email to author, July 1, 2004.

Nkenge Touré. Interview by Loretta Ross, December and March 2005, Voices of Feminism Oral History Project, Sophia Smith Collection, Smith College, Northampton, Mass.

Malcolm Williams. Conversations with author, May 1, 2012; July 23, 2021.

Marjorie Wright. Interview by James Reston Jr., n.p., n.d. James B. Reston Jr. Joan Little Trial Materials. Southern Historical Collection. University of North Carolina at Chapel Hill (audio).

GOVERNMENT DOCUMENTS AND MISCELLANEOUS REPORTS

Beaufort County Land Use Plan. North Carolina Department of Natural and Economic Resources, N.E. Office (May 1976). www.gpo.gov/fdsys/pkg/CZIC-HD1291 343 B43.

Beaufort County Census of Population and Housing. 1980/Summary Tape File 3a (50). www.digital.ncdcr.gov/cdm/compundobject/collection/p15012coll4/id/468/rec/160.

Bounds, V. L. *Riot at Central Prison, 1968*. Report by Commissioner of Correction. North Carolina Department of Correction, 1968. Penn State University Libraries, https://babel.hathitrust.org/cgi/pt?id=pst.000000388726&view=1up&seq=52.

Death Penalty Information Center. *Enduring Injustice: The Persistence of Racial Injustice in the U.S. Death Penalty*. September 2020. https://deathpenaltyinfo.org/.

Hunt, James B., Jr., Governor, North Carolina. "Statement on Prison System." September 22, 1977. James B. Hunt Addresses and Public Papers, vol. 1, 1977–1978, 154, North Carolina Collection, Wilson Library, University of North Carolina at Chapel Hill.

Legislative Research Commission. *Females in the Department of Correction*. Interim Report to 1977 General Assembly of North Carolina. North Carolina Collection, Wilson Library, University of North Carolina at Chapel Hill.

Marvel, Thomas, and Carlise Moody. *The Impact of Determinant Sentencing Laws on Delay, Trial Rates and Pleas Rates in Seven States*. Report prepared for the U.S. Department of Justice. Washington, D.C.: National Institute of Justice, 2000.

Ms. Foundation. *Safety and Justice for All: Examining the Relationship Between the Women's Anti-violence Movement and the Criminal Legal System* (2003), http://www.ncdsv.org/images/Ms_SafetyJusticeForAll_2003.pdf.

NAACP-LDEF (National Association for the Advancement of Colored People–Legal Defense and Educational Fund). *Death Row U.S.A., 2015.* https://www.naacpldf.org/our-thinking/death-row-usa.

North Carolina Advisory Committee to the U.S. Commission on Civil Rights. *Prisons in North Carolina, January 1976.* https://www.ojp.gov/pdffiles1/Digitization/40567NCJRS.pdf.

North Carolina Division of Prisons. "Response to *Females in the Department of Correction.*" North Carolina Collection, Wilson Library, University of North Carolina at Chapel Hill.

Prison Policy Initiative. *Following the Money of Mass Incarceration.* 2017. https://www.prisonpolicy.org/reports/money.html.

Sacco, Lisa N. "The Violence Against Women Act: Overview, Legislation, and Federal Funding." Congressional Research Service, May 26, 2015. https://fas.org/sgp/crs/misc/R42499.pdf.

U.S. Advisory Commission on Intergovernmental Relations. *Safe Streets Reconsidered: The Block Grant Experience, 1968–1975,* part B, "Case Studies." Washington, D.C., 1977.

U.S. Census Bureau. *1970 Census of the Population: General Characteristics of the Population.* Washington, D.C., June 1973. https://www.census.gov/library/publications/1973/dec/population-volume-1.html#par_list_31.

U.S. Congressional Budget Office. *Law Enforcement Assistance Administration: Options for Reauthorization.* Washington, D.C.: U.S. Congressional Budget Office, 1979.

U.S. Department of Justice. *The Impact of Incarceration and Mandatory Minimums on Survivors: Exploring the Impact of Criminalizing Policies on African American Women and Girls.* Office of Violence Against Women Report. Summary Report from the Roundtable, September 21–22, 2015. Published January 2017. https://www.justice.gov/ovw/page/file/926631/.

THESES AND UNPUBLISHED PAPERS

Davis, Thulani. "'White Gentleman Commits Rape': African American Women, Sexual Assault, and the Black Press in the Post-Reconstruction Era." New York University, April 2010. Unpublished graduate seminar paper. In author's possession.

Feulner, Megan Elizabeth. "'Women Have the Right to Fight!' The Contested Legacy of Second-Wave Feminism and Anti-rape Politics in the Trials of Inez Garcia, 1974–1977." MA thesis, City University of New York, 2014.

Gilbert, Jennifer L. "*Feminary* of Durham–Chapel Hill: Building Community Through a Feminist Press." MA thesis, Duke University, 1993.

Glusman, Melynn. "Moment of Possibility: The Joan Little Movement." Senior thesis, Duke University, 1994.

Greene, Christina. "Representations of Black Womanhood in the 1974–75 Joan Little Murder-Sexual Assault Case." Paper presented at Berkshire Conference on Women's History, Claremont, Calif., June 2005.

Harris, Caitlin A. "Shadows Behind Bars: Black Women's Activism Inside and Outside the North Carolina Correctional Institution for Women, 1956–1976." MA thesis, North Carolina Central University, 2014.
Velasco, Linda Christine. "The Incorrigible Girl: Inez Garcia and the Hudson Prison for Girls." MA thesis, San Francisco State University, August 2019.
Worthington, Leah. "Black Panther Women: Armed with Politics and Guns in the Winston-Salem, Philadelphia and Baltimore Branches." MA thesis, College of Charleston, 2016.

VIDEO AND SOUND RECORDINGS

Brown, Elaine. *Seize the Time*. Vault, 1969 (LP).
Fox, Madeline. "Madison School Board Votes to End Contract with Police Department." Wisconsin Public Radio, June 29, 2020. https://www.wpr.org/madison-school-board-votes-end-contract-police-department.
Machtinger, Evelyn, and Northern Marianas Humanities Council. "Your Humanities Half-Hour." https://www.youtube.com/watch?v=jvPTSx_Ln8U.
Olsson, Göran Hugo, dir. *The Black Power Mixtape, 1967–1975*. Louverture Films, 2011 (documentary).
Simmons, Aisha Shahidah, dir. *NO! The Rape Documentary*. AfroLez Productions, 2006.
Sweet Honey in the Rock. "Joanne Little." Flying Fish, 1976 (45 single).

MISCELLANEOUS INTERNET SOURCES

Assata's Daughters. https://www.assatasdaughters.org/.
Boston TV News Digital Library. http://www.bostonlocaltv.org/catalog.
Colorlines. https://www.colorlines.com/articles/color-violence-against-women.
Death Penalty Information Center. https://deathpenaltyinfo.org/.
The Exonerated. www.witnesstoinnocence.org/exonerees/delbert-tibbs.html.
INCITE! https://incite-national.org/.
Loretta Ross. https://www.lorettaross.com/.
Mab Segrest. https://mabsegrest.com/.
Minnie Bruce Pratt. https://minniebrucepratt.net/.
NAACP Legal Defense and Education Fund Inc. https://www.naacpldf.org/our-thinking/death-row-usa/.
Prison Policy Initiative. https://www.prisonpolicy.org/reports/money.html.
Sentencing Project. https://www.sentencingproject.org/publications/trends-in-u-s-corrections.
Southerners on New Ground. https://southernersonnewground.org/.
Women's Legal Defense and Education Fund's Legal Momentum. https://www.legalmomentum.org/history-vawa.

BOOKS, ARTICLES, AND NONGOVERNMENT REPORTS

Ake, Jami, and Gretchen Arnold. "A Brief History of Anti–Violence Against Women Movements in the United States." In *Sourcebook on Violence Against Women*, 3rd ed., edited by Claire Renzetti, Jeffrey Edleson, and Raquel Bergen, 3–25. Los Angeles: Sage, 2017.

Alexander, Michelle. *The New Jim Crow: Mass Incarceration in the Age of Colorblindness.* Rev. ed. New York: New Press, 2012.

Anderson, Carol. *Eyes off the Prize: The United Nations and the African American Struggle for Human Rights, 1944–1955.* Cambridge: Cambridge University Press, 2003.

Bader, Eleanor. "Women Prisoners Endure Rampant Sexual Violence—Current Laws Not Enough." *Truthout*, December, 21, 2012. www.truth-out.org.

Bailey, Moya. *Misogynoir Transformed: Black Women's Digital Resistance.* New York: New York University Press, 2021.

Balto, Simon. *Occupied Territory: Policing Black Chicago from Red Summer to Black Power.* Chapel Hill: University of North Carolina Press 2019.

Baxandall, Rosalind, and Linda Gordon, eds. *Dear Sisters: Dispatches from the Women's Liberation Movement.* New York: Basic Books, 2000.

Beckett, Katherine, and Theodore Sasson. *The Politics of Injustice: Crime and Punishment in America*, 2nd ed. Thousand Oaks, Calif.: Sage, 2004.

Beins, Agatha. "Radical Others: Women of Color and Revolutionary Feminism." *Feminist Studies* 41, no. 1 (2015): 150–83.

Belknap, Joanne. *The Invisible Woman: Gender, Crime and Justice.* 2nd ed. Belmont, Calif.: Wadsworth, 2001.

Bell-Scott, Patricia. *The Firebrand and the First Lady: Portrait of a Friendship, Pauli Murray, Eleanor Roosevelt and the Struggle for Social Justice.* New York: Random House /Vintage, 2016.

Berger, Dan. *Captive Nation: Black Prison Organizing in the Civil Rights Era.* Chapel Hill: University of North Carolina Press, 2014.

Berger, Dan, and Toussaint Losier. *Rethinking the American Prison Movement.* New York: Routledge, 2018.

Berry, Diana Ramey, and Kali Nicole Gross. *A Black Women's History of the United States.* Boston: Beacon, 2020.

Bethel, Lorraine. "What Chou Mean We, White Girl?" In "The Black Women's Issue," special issue, *Conditions* 5 (Autumn 1979): 86–92.

Bevacqua, Maria. *Rape on the Public Agenda: Feminism and the Politics of Sexual Assault.* Lebanon, N.H.: Northeastern University Press, 2000.

———. "Reconsidering Violence Against Women: Coalition Politics in the Anti-rape Movement." In *Feminist Coalitions*, edited by Stephanie Gilmore, 163–77. Urbana: University of Illinois Press, 2008.

Blair, Cynthia M. *I've Got to Make My Livin': Black Women's Sex Work in Turn-of-the-Century Chicago.* Chicago: University of Chicago Press, 2010.

Bloom, Joshua, and Waldo Martin Jr. *Black Against Empire: The History and Politics of the Black Panther Party.* Berkeley: University of California Press, 2016.

Bond, James E. "Plea Bargaining in North Carolina." *North Carolina Law Review* 54 (1975–76): 823–44.

Bond, Julian. "Self-Defense Against Rape: The Joan Little Case." *Black Scholar*, March 1975, 29–31.

Braden, Anne. "An Open Letter: Jerry Paul on Trial." *Southern Exposure* 6, no. 1 (1977): 38–39.

———. "Second Open Letter to Southern White Women." *Southern Exposure* 4, no. 4 (Winter 1977): 53.

Brown, Elaine. *A Taste of Power: A Black Woman's Story*. New York: Pantheon, 1992.
Brown, Elsa Barkley. "Negotiating and Transforming the Public Sphere: African American Political Life in the Transition from Slavery to Freedom." *Public Culture* 7, no. 1 (Fall 1994): 107–46.
———. "Imaging Lynching: African American Women, Communities of Struggle and Collective Memory." In *African American Women Speak Out on Anita Hill-Clarence Thomas*, edited by Geneva Smitherman, 100–124. Detroit: Wayne State University Press, 1995.
Brown, Scot. *Fighting for US: Maulana Karenga, the US Organization and Black Cultural Nationalism*. New York: New York University Press, 2003.
Browne, Angela. *When Battered Women Kill*. New York: Free Press, 1987.
Brownmiller, Susan. *Against Our Will: Men, Women and Rape*. New York: Simon and Schuster, 1975.
Bryant, Pat. "Justice vs. the Movement." *Southern Exposure* 8, no. 2 (Summer 1980): 79–87.
Bulkin, Elly, Minnie Bruce Pratt, and Barbara Smith. *Yours in Struggle: Three Feminist Perspective on Anti-Semitism and Anti-racism*. New York: Firebrand/Long Haul, 1984.
Bumiller, Kristin. *In an Abusive State: How Neoliberalism Appropriated the Feminist Movement Against Sexual Violence*. Durham, N.C.: Duke University Press, 2008.
Cade, Toni, ed. *The Black Woman*. New York: New American Library/Signet, 1970.
Campbell, Bonnie J., and Lisalyn R. Jacobs. "The Senate Must Reauthorize Violence Against Women Act." *The Hill*, June 3, 2021. https://thehill.com/opinion/civil-rights/556697-the-senate-must-reauthorize-violence-against-women-act.
Cecelski, David. *Along Freedom Road: Hyde County, North Carolina, and the Fate of Black Schools in the South*. Chapel Hill: University of North Carolina Press, 1994.
Chafe, William H. *Civilities and Civil Rights: Greensboro, North Carolina and the Black Struggle for Freedom*. New York: Oxford University Press, 1981.
Chase, Robert T. "'Slaves of the State' Revolt: Southern Prison Labor and a Prison-Made Civil Rights Movement, 1945–1980." In *Life and Labor in the New South*, edited by Robert H. Zieger, 177–213. Gainesville: University Press of Florida, 2012.
———. "We Are Not Slaves: Rethinking the Rise of the Carceral State Through the Lens of the Prisoners' Rights Movement." *Journal of American History* 102, no. 1 (June 2015): 73–86.
———. *We Are Not Slaves: State Violence, Coerced Labor, and Prisoners' Rights in Postwar America*. Chapel Hill: University of North Carolina Press, 2020.
Chavis, Benjamin. "The Wilmington Ten: Prisoners of Conscience." In *It Did Happen Here: Recollections of Political Repression in America*, edited by Budd Schultz and Ruth Schultz, 195–211. Berkeley: University of California Press, 1989.
Cheung, Kylie. "Perhaps It's Time to Think Beyond the 'Violence Against Women Act.'" *Jezebel*, January 31, 2022. https://jezebel.com/perhaps-its-time-to-think-beyond-the-violence-against-w-1848450522.
Chrisman, Robert, and Robert Allen, eds. *Court of Appeal: The Black Community Speaks Out on the Racial and Sexual Politics of Thomas vs. Hill*. New York: Black Scholar/Ballentine, 1992.
Clagget, Stephen R. "Native American Settlement of North Carolina." *Tarheel Junior Historian*, Spring 1995. https://www.ncpedia.org/history/early/native-settlement.
Cleaver, Eldridge. *Soul on Ice*. New York: McGraw Hill/Ramparts, 1968.

Cobb, Charles E., Jr. *This Non-violent Stuff Will Get You Killed: How Guns Made the Civil Rights Movement Possible*. Durham, N.C.: Duke University Press, 2015.

Cocca, Carolyn E. "From 'Welfare Queen' to 'Exploited Teen': Welfare Dependency, Statutory Rape and Moral Panic." *National Women's Studies Association Journal* 14, no. 2 (Summer 2002): 56–79.

Coffey, Michael W. "African Americans Defend Washington, N.C., 1863." North Carolina Office of Archives and History, 2016. https://www.ncdcr.gov/about/history/division-historical-resources/nc-highway-historical-marker-program.

Coker, Donna, and Lindsay C. Harrison, "The Story of *Wanrow*: The Reasonable Woman and Law of Self-Defense." In *Criminal Law Stories*, edited by Donna Coker and Robert Weisberg, 213–62. New York: Thomson Reuters Foundation, 2013. https://ssrn.com/abstract=2244312.

Colley, Zoe. *Ain't Scared of Your Jail: Arrest, Imprisonment, and the Civil Rights Movement*. Gainesville: University Press of Florida, 2012.

Collins, Patricia Hill. *Black Feminist Thought: Knowledge, Consciousness, and the Politics of Empowerment*. London: Unwin Hyman, 1990.

———. *Fighting Words: Black Women and the Search for Justice*. Minneapolis: University of Minnesota Press, 1998.

Crenshaw, Kimberlé. "Mapping the Margins: Intersectionality, Identity Politics, and Violence Against Women of Color." *Stanford Law Review* 43, no. 6 (July 1991): 1241–99.

Cummins, Eric. *The Rise and Fall of California's Radical Prison Movement*. Stanford, Calif.: Stanford University Press, 1994.

Curtin, Mary Ellen. "The 'Human World' of Black Women in Alabama Prisons, 1870–1900." In *Hidden Histories of Women in the New South*, edited by Virginia Bernhard et al., 11–30. Columbia: University of Missouri Press, 1994.

———. *Black Prisoners and Their World: Alabama, 1865–1900*. Charlottesville: University of Virginia Press, 2000.

Daley, Christine. "A Rocky Road to Posterity: The Publication of Zora Neale Hurston." www.womenwriters.net/editorials/hurston.htm.

Davis, Angela Y. *An Autobiography*. New York: Random House, 1974.

———. "Joan Little: The Dialectics of Rape." *Ms.*, June 1975, 37–40.

———. "Rape, Racism and the Capitalist Setting." *Black Scholar* 9, no. 7 (April 1978): 24–30.

———. *Women, Race and Class*. New York: Random House, 1981.

———. "From the Prison of Slavery to the Slavery of Prison: Frederick Douglass and the Convict Lease System." In *The Angela Y. Davis Reader*, edited by Joy James, 74–95. Malden, Mass.: Blackwell, 1998.

———. "Race and Criminalization: Black Americans and the Punishment Industry." In *The Angela Y. Davis Reader*, edited by Joy James, 61–73. Malden, Mass.: Blackwell, 1998.

Davis, Angela Y., ed. *If They Come in the Morning: Voices of Resistance*. New York: Third Press, 1971.

Davis, Angela Y., Gina Dent, Erica Meiners, and Beth E. Richie. *Abolition. Feminism. Now.* Chicago: Haymarket, 2022.

Davis, Thulani. *The Emancipation Circuit: Black Activism Forging a Culture of Freedom*. Durham, N.C.: Duke University Press, 2022.

Dees, Morris, with Steve Fiffer. *A Lawyer's Journey: The Morris Dees Story.* Chicago: American Bar Association, 2001, 2003.

Desmond, Matthew. *Evicted: Poverty and Profit in the American City.* New York: Penguin /Random House, 2017.

Douglas, Emory. *Black Panther: The Revolutionary Art of Emory Douglas.* New York: Rizzoli, 2007.

Earls, Anita, Emily Wynes, and LeeAnne Quatrucci. *Voting Rights in North Carolina, 1982–2006.* Report by the Renew the VRA.org, March 2006.

Eisen, Lauren-Brooke. "Breaking Down Biden's Order to Eliminate DOJ Private Prison Contracts." Brennan Center for Justice, August 21, 2021. https://www.brennancenter.org/our-work/research-reports/breaking-down-bidens-order-eliminate-doj-private-prison-contracts.

Evans, Sara. *Tidal Wave: How Women Changed America at Century's End.* New York: Free Press, 2003.

———. "Women's Liberation: Seeing the Revolution Clearly." *Feminist Studies* 41, no. 1 (2015): 138–49.

Farmer, Ashley D. *Remaking Black Power: How Black Women Transformed an Era.* Chapel Hill: University of North Carolina Press, 2017.

Feeley, Malcolm M., and Austin D. Sarat. *The Policy Dilemma: Federal Crime Policy and the Law Enforcement Assistance Administration, 1968–1978.* Minneapolis: University of Minnesota Press, 1980.

Feimster, Crystal. *Southern Horrors: Women and the Politics of Rape and Lunching.* Cambridge, Mass.: Harvard University Press, 2009.

Felber, Garrett. "'Shades of Mississippi': The Nation of Islam's Prison Organizing, the Carceral State, and the Black Freedom Struggle." *Journal of American History* 105, no. 1 (June 2018): 71–95.

———. *Those Who Know Don't Say: The Nation of Islam, the Black Freedom Movement, and the Carceral State.* Chapel Hill: University of North Carolina Press, 2019.

Fergus, Devin. "Epilogue: The Black Panther Party in the Disunited States of America: Constitutionalism, Watergate and the Closing of the Americanists' Minds." In *Liberated Territory: Untold Local Perspectives on the Black Panther Party*, edited by Yohuru Williams and Jama Lazerow, 283–86. Durham, N.C.: Duke University Press, 2008.

———. *Liberalism, Black Power and the Making of American Politics, 1965–1980.* Athens: University of Georgia Press, 2009.

Flamm, Michael. *Law and Order: Street Crime, Civil Unrest and the Crisis of Liberalism in the 1960s.* New York: Columbia University Press, 2005.

Flood, Dawn Rae. *Rape in Chicago: Race, Myth, and the Courts.* Urbana: University of Illinois Press, 2012.

Forman, James, Jr. "Racial Critiques of Mass Incarceration: Beyond the New Jim Crow." *NYU Journal of International Law and Politics* 87 (April 2012): 21–69.

———. *Locking Up Our Own: Crime and Punishment in Black America.* New York: Farrar, Straus and Giroux, 2017.

Fortner, Michael Javen. *Black Silent Majority: The Rockefeller Drug Laws and the Politics of Punishment.* Cambridge, Mass.: Harvard University Press, 2015.

Fosl, Catherine. *Subversive Southerner: Anne Braden and the Struggle for Racial Justice in the Cold War South*. New York: Palgrave/Macmillan, 2002.
Freedman, Estelle B. *Their Sisters' Keepers: Women's Prison Reform in America, 1830–1930*. Ann Arbor: University of Michigan Press, 1981.
———. *No Turning Back: The History of Feminism and the Future of Women*. New York: Ballantine, 2002.
———. *Redefining Rape: Sexual Violence in the Era of Suffrage and Segregation*. Cambridge, Mass.: Harvard University Press, 2013.
Freidman, Benjamin R. "Picking Up Where Robert F. Williams Left Off: The Winston-Salem Branch of the Black Panther Party." In *Comrades: A Local History of the Black Panther Party*, edited by Judson Jeffries, 47–88. Bloomington: Indiana University Press, 2007.
French, Lawrence. "The Incarcerated Black Female: The Case of Double Social Jeopardy." *Journal of Black Studies* 8, no. 3 (March 1978): 321–35.
Gaines, Kevin. *Uplifting the Race: Black Leadership, Politics and Culture in the Twentieth Century*. Chapel Hill: University of North Carolina Press, 1996.
Giddings, Paula. *When and Where I Enter: The Impact of Black Women on Race and Sex in America*. New York: William Morrow, 1984.
———. "The Last Taboo." In *Race-ing, Justice, En-gendering Power: Essays on Anita Hill, Clarence Thomas and the Construction of Social Reality*, edited by Toni Morrison, 441–70. New York: Pantheon, 1992.
Gilmore, Ruth Wilson. *Golden Gulag: Prisons, Surplus, Crisis, and Opposition in Globalizing California*. Berkeley: University of California Press, 2007.
Gilmore, Stephanie. "Thinking About Feminist Coalitions." In *Feminist Coalitions: Historical Perspectives on Second Wave Feminism in the United States*, edited by Stephanie Gilmore, 1–19. Urbana: University of Illinois Press, 2008.
Goffman, Alice. *On the Run: Fugitive Life in an American City*. Chicago: University of Chicago Press, 2014.
Gomez, Jewelle. "Because Silence Is Costly." In *Forty-Three Septembers: Essays*, 167–96. Ithaca, N.Y.: Firebrand, 1993.
Goodman, James. *Stories of Scottsboro*. New York: Vintage, 1995.
Gore, Dayo. *Radicalism at the Crossroads: African American Women Activists in the Cold War*. New York: New York University Press, 2011.
Gotsch, Kara, and Vinay Basti. "Capitalizing on Mass Incarceration: U.S. Growth in Private Prisons." Sentencing Project, August 2, 2018. https://www.sentencingproject.org/publications/capitalizing-on-mass-incarceration-u-s-growth-in-private-prisons.
Gottschalk, Marie. *The Prison and the Gallows: The Politics of Mass Incarceration in the United States*. Cambridge: Cambridge University Press, 2006.
Greene, Christina. *Our Separate Ways: Women and the Black Freedom Movement in Durham, North Carolina*. Chapel Hill: University of North Carolina Press, 2005.
———. "She Ain't No Rosa Parks: The Joan Little Rape-Murder Case and Jim Crow Justice in the Post–Civil Rights South." *Journal of African American History* 100, no. 3 (Summer 2015): 428–47.
———. "'I'm Gonna Get You': Black Womanhood and Jim Crow Justice in the Post–Civil Rights South." In *U.S. Women's History: Untangling the Threads of Sisterhood*,

edited by Leslie Brown et al., 98–125. New Brunswick, N.J.: Rutgers University Press, 2017.

Griffin, Farah Jasmine. "Ironies of the Saint: Malcolm X, Black Women and the Price of Protection." In *Sisters in the Struggle: African American Women in the Civil Rights–Black Power Movement*, edited by Bettye Collier and V. P. Franklin, 214–27. New York: New York University Press, 2001.

Gross, Kali N. *Colored Amazons: Crime, Violence and Black Women in the City of Brotherly Love, 1880–1910*. Durham, N.C.: Duke University Press, 2006.

———. "African American Women, Mass Incarceration, and the Politics of Protection." In "Historians and the Carceral State," special issue, *Journal of American History* 102, no. 1 (June 2015): 25–33.

Gross, Kali N., and Cheryl D. Hicks. "Introduction: Gendering the Carceral State: African American Women, History and Criminal Justice." *Journal of African American History* 100, no. 3 (Summer 2015): 357–65.

Guy-Sheftall, Beverly, ed. *Words of Fire: An Anthology of African-American Feminist Thought*. New York: New Press, 1995.

Hadden, Sally E. *Slave Patrols: Law and Violence in Virginia and the Carolinas*. Cambridge, Mass.: Harvard University Press, 2001.

Haley, Sarah. "'Like I Was a Man': Chain Gangs, Gender and the Carceral Sphere in Jim Crow Georgia." *SIGNS: Journal of Women in Culture and Society* 39, no. 1 (Autumn 2013): 53–77.

———. *No Mercy Here: Gender, Punishment and the Making of Jim Crow Modernity*. Chapel Hill: University of North Carolina Press, 2016.

Hall, Jacquelyn Dowd. *Revolt Against Chivalry: Jessie Daniel Ames and the Women's Campaign Against Lynching*. New York: Columbia University Press, 1993.

———. "'The Mind That Burns in Each Body': Women, Rape and Racial Violence." In *Powers of Desire: The Politics of Sexuality*, edited by Ann Snitow, Christine Stansell, Sharon Thompson, 328–49. New York: Monthly Review Press, 1983.

Hallett, Stephanie. "Rape Is Rape." *Ms.*, January–February 2012, 26–31.

Hames-García, Michael. *Fugitive Thought: Prison Movements, Race, and the Meaning of Justice*. Minneapolis: University of Minnesota Press, 2004.

Hannigan, Mike, Tony Platt, and Angela Davis. "Interview with Angela Davis." *Crime and Social Justice*, no. 3 (Spring–Summer 1975): 30–35.

Harris, Duchess. "From the Kennedy Commission to the Combahee River Collective: Black Feminist Organizing, 1960–80." In *Sisters in the Struggle: African American Women in the Civil Rights–Black Power Movement*, edited by Bettye Collier-Thomas and V. P. Franklin, 280–305. New York: New York University Press, 2001.

Harris-Perry, Melissa. *Sister Citizen: Shame, Stereotypes and Black Women in America*. New Haven, Conn.: Yale University Press, 2011.

Hartman, Saidiya. *Scenes of Subjection: Terror, Slavery, and Self-Making in Nineteenth-Century America*. New York: Oxford University Press, 1997.

———. *Lose Your Mother: A Journey Along the Atlantic Slave Route*. New York: Farrar, Strauss and Giroux, 2007.

Harwell, Fred. *True Deliverance: The Joan Little Case*. New York: Alfred A. Knopf, 1979.

Haynes, April. "'Sex-Ins College Style': Black Feminism and Sexual Politics in the Student YWCA, 1968–1980." In *Women's Activism and "Second Wave" Feminism:*

Transnational Histories, edited by Barbara Molony and Jennifer Nelson, 37–61. London: Bloomsbury, 2017.

Herivel, Tara, and Paul Wright, eds. *Prison Profiteers: Who Makes Money from Mass Incarceration*. New York: New Press, 2007.

Hernandez, Kelly Lytle. *City of Inmates: Conquest, Rebellion, and the Rise of Human Caging in Los Angeles, 1771–1965*. Chapel Hill: University of North Carolina Press, 2017.

Hewitt, Nancy, ed. *No Permanent Waves: Recasting Histories of U.S. Feminism*. New Brunswick, N.J.: Rutgers University Press, 2010.

Hicks, Cheryl D. *Talk with You Like a Woman: African American Women, Justice and Reform in New York, 1890–1935*. Chapel Hill: University of North Carolina Press, 2010.

Hill, Rebecca. *Men, Mobs, and Law: Anti-lynching and Labor Defense in U.S. Radical History*. Durham, N.C.: Duke University Press, 2008.

Hine, Darlene Clark. "Rape and the Inner Lives of Black Women in the Middle West." *SIGNS: Journal of Women in Culture and Society* 14, no. 4 (Summer 1989): 912–20.

Hinton, Elizabeth. "'A War Within Our Own Boundaries': Lyndon Johnson's Great Society and the Rise of the Carceral State." *Journal of American History* 102, no. 1 (June 2015): 100–12.

———. *From the War on Poverty to the War on Crime: The Making of Mass Incarceration in America*. Cambridge, Mass.: Harvard University Press, 2016.

———. *America on Fire: Police Violence and Black Rebellion Since the 1960s*. New York: Liveright, 2021.

Hobson, Janell, ed. *Are All the Women Still White? Rethinking Race, Expanding Feminisms*. Albany: State University of New York Press, 2016.

hooks, bell. *Ain't I a Woman? Black Women and Feminism*. Boston. South End, 1981.

———. *Feminist Theory from Margin to Center*. Boston: South End, 1984.

Hull, Gloria, Patricia Bell Scott, and Barbara Smith, eds. *All the Women Are White, All the Men Are Black, but Some of Us Are Brave: Black Women's Studies*. New York: Feminist Press, 1982.

Human Rights Project for Girls and Ms. Foundation for Women. *The Sexual Assault to Prison Pipeline: The Girls' Story*. Georgetown Law Center on Poverty and Inequality, 2015. www.law.georgetown.edu/go/poverty.

Hunter, Tera. *To 'Joy My Freedom: Southern Black Women's Lives and Labor After the Civil War*. Cambridge, Mass.: Harvard University Press, 1997.

INCITE! Women of Color against Violence and Critical Resistance. "Statement on Gender Violence and the Prison Industrial Complex." 2001. https://incite-national.org/incite-critical-resistance-statement.

Iyengar, Radha. "Does the Certainty of Arrest Reduce Domestic Violence? Evidence from Mandatory and Recommended Arrest Laws." Working paper 13186. Cambridge, Mass.: National Bureau of Economic Research, June 2007. http://www.nber.org/papers/w13186.

Jacquet, Catherine O. *The Injustices of Rape: How Activists Responded to Sexual Violence, 1950–1980*. Chapel Hill: University of North Carolina Press, 2019.

James, Joy. *Shadowboxing: Representations of Black Feminist Politics*. New York: St. Martin's /Palgrave, 1999, 2002.

Jewell, Sue. *From Mammy to Miss America and Beyond: Cultural Images and the Shaping of U.S. Social Policy*. New York: Routledge, 1993.

Johnson, Paula C. *Inner Lives: Voices of African American Women in Prison.* New York: New York University Press, 2003.

Jones, Alethia, Virginia Eubanks, and Barbara Smith, eds. *Ain't Gonna Let Nobody Turn Me Around: Forty Years of Movement Building with Barbara Smith.* Albany: State University of New York Press, 2014.

Joseph, Peniel. *Waiting 'til the Midnight Hour: A Narrative History of Black Power in America.* New York: Henry Holt, 2006.

Kaba, Mariame. "Yes, Rape Survivors Do Engage in Restorative Justice Practice." *Prison Culture,* May 22, 2012. http://www.usprisonculture.com/blog/2012/05/22/yes-rape-survivors-do-engage-in-restorative-justice-practice/.

———. *We Do This 'Til We Free Us: Abolitionist Organizing and Transforming Justice.* Chicago: Haymarket, 2021.

Kaplan, Temma. *Crazy for Democracy: Women in Grassroots Movements.* New York: Routledge, 1997.

Karenga, Ron (Maulana). "In Love and Struggle: Toward a Greater Togetherness." *Black Scholar* 6, no. 6 (March 1975): 16–28.

———. "In Defense of Sis. Joanne: For Ourselves and History." *Black Scholar* 6, no. 10 (July–August 1975): 37–42.

Kim, Mimi E., and Kalei Kanuha. "Restorative Justice and the Dance with the Devil." *Affilia: Feminist Inquiry in Social Work* 37, no. 2 (March 2, 2022): 189–93. https://journals.sagepub.com/doi/10.1177/08861099221084830.

Kohler-Hausmann, Julilly. "Guns and Butter: The Welfare State, the Carceral State, and the Politics of Exclusion in the Postwar United States." *Journal of American History* 102, no. 1 (June 2015): 87–99.

Korstad, Robert. *Civil Rights Unionism: Tobacco Workers and the Struggle for Democracy in the Mid-twentieth Century South.* Chapel Hill: University of North Carolina Press, 2003.

Kupenda, Angela Mae. "Law, Life, and Literature: A Critical Reflection of Life and Literature to Illuminate How Laws of Domestic Violence, Race, and Class Bind Black Women." *Howard Law Journal* 42, no. 1 (1998): 1–26.

Kunzel, Regina. *Criminal Intimacy: Prison and the Uneven History of Modern American Sexuality.* Chicago: University of Chicago Press, 2008.

Kurgan, Laura. *Close Up at a Distance: Mapping, Technology and Politics.* Princeton: Princeton University Press, 2013.

Law, Victoria. *Resistance Behind Bars: The Struggles of Incarcerated Women.* Oakland, Calif.: PM Press, 2009.

———. "Sick of the Abuse: Feminist Responses to Sexual Assault, Battering, and Self-Defense." In *The Hidden 1970s: Histories of Radicalism,* edited by Dan Berger, 39–56. New Brunswick, N.J.: Rutgers University Press, 2010.

Lawston, Jodie. *Sisters Outside: Radical Activists Working for Women Prisoners.* State University of New York Press, 2009.

Lee, Chana Kai. *For Freedom's Sake: The Life of Fannie Lou Hamer.* Urbana: University of Illinois Press, 1999.

LeFlouria, Talitha L. *Chained in Silence: Black Women and Convict Labor in the New South.* Chapel Hill: University of North Carolina Press, 2015.

Lerner, Gerda, ed. *Black Women in White America: A Documentary History*. New York: Pantheon, 1972.

Levine, Judith, and Erica R. Meiners. *The Feminist and the Sex Offender: Confronting Sexual Harm, Ending State Violence*. New York: Verso, 2020.

———. "Violence Cannot Remedy Violence." *Boston Review: A Political and Literary Forum*, August 2020. http://bostonreview.net/law-justice-gender-sexuality/judith-levine-erica-r-meiners-violence-cannot-remedy-violence.

Levine, Suzanne Braun, and Mary Thom. *Bella Abzug: How One Tough Broad from the Bronx Fought Jim Crow and Joe McCarthy, Pissed Off Jimmy Carter, Battled for the Rights of Women and Workers, and Shook Up Politics Along the Way*. New York: Farrar, Straus and Giroux, 2007.

Lichtenstein, Alex. *Twice the Work of Free Labor: The Political Economy of Convict Labor in the New South*. New York: Verso, 1995.

———. "A 'Labor History' of Mass Incarceration." *Labor Studies in Working Class History of the Americas* 8, no. 3 (Fall 2011): 5–14.

———. "Flocatex and the Fiscal Limits of Mass Incarceration: Toward a New Political Economy of the Carceral State." *Journal of American History* 102, no. 1 (June 2015): 113–25.

Lincoln, Abbey. "Who Will Revere the Black Woman?" In *The Black Woman*, edited by Toni Cade, 80–84. New York: New American Library/Signet, 1970. First published in *Negro Digest* (1966).

Little, Joan, with Rebecca Ranson. "I Am Joan." *Southern Exposure* 6, no. 1 (ca. 1978): 42–47.

Lorde, Audre. "A Litany for Survival." In Lorde, *The Black Unicorn: Poems*. 31–32. New York: W. W. Norton, 1978.

———. *Sister Outsider: Essays and Speeches*. Trumansburg, N.Y.: Crossing, 1984.

———. "The Transformation of Silence into Language and Action." In Lorde, *Sister Outsider*. 40–44.

Malka, Adam. *The Men of Mobtown: Policing Baltimore in the Age of Slavery and Emancipation*. Chapel Hill: University of North Carolina Press, 2019.

Manion, Jen. *Liberty's Prisons: Carceral Culture in Early America*. Philadelphia: University of Pennsylvania Press, 2015.

Marable, Manning. *Malcolm X: A Life of Reinvention*. New York: Viking, 2011.

Martinez, Elizabeth "Betita," Matt Meyer, and Mandy Carter. *We Have Not Been Moved: Resisting Racism and Militarism in 21st Century America*. Oakland, Calif.: PM Press, 2012.

Matthews, Donald G., and Jane Sherron De Hart. *Sex, Gender, and the Politics of ERA: A State and the Nation*. New York: Oxford University Press, 1990.

Matthews, Nancy A. *Confronting Rape: The Feminist Anti-rape Movement and the State*. New York: Routledge, 1994.

Matthews, Tracye. "'No One Ever Asks What a Man's Role in the Revolution Is': Gender Politics and Leadership in the Black Panther Party, 1966–1971." In *Sisters in the Struggle: African American Women in the Civil Rights-Black Power Movement*, edited by Bettye Collier-Thomas and V. P. Franklin, 230–56. New York: New York University Press, 2001.

May, Lyle C. "North Carolina's Racial Justice Act Can Remove Prisoners from Death Row: But Is Life Without Parole Actual Justice? Letter from Death Row." *Scalawag*, October 26, 2020. https://scalawagmagazine.org/2020/10/nc-rja-death-row-racism/.

McConahay, John, Courtney Mullin, and Jeffrey Fredrick. "The Uses of Social Science in Trials with Political and Racial Overtones: The Trial of Joan Little." *Law and Contemporary Problems* 41, no. 1 (Winter 1977): 205–29.

McDuffie, Erik. *Sojourning for Freedom: Black Women, American Communism, and the Making of Black Left Feminism*. Durham, N.C.: Duke University Press, 2011.

McGuire, Danielle L. "'It Was Like All of Us Had Been Raped': Sexual Violence, Community Mobilization and the African American Freedom Struggle." *Journal of American History* 91, no. 3 (December 2004): 906–31.

———. *At the Dark End of the Street: Black Women, Rape and Resistance—A New History of the Civil Rights Movement from Rosa Parks to the Rise of Black Power*. New York: Alfred A. Knopf, 2010.

———. "Joan Little and the Triumph of Testimony." In *Freedom Rights: New Perspectives on the Civil Rights Movement*, edited by Danielle McGuire and John Dittmer, 191–221. Lexington: University Press of Kentucky, 2011.

———. "The Maid and Mr. Charlie: Rosa Parks and the Struggle for Black Women's Bodily Integrity." In *U.S. Women's History: Untangling the Threads of Sisterhood*, edited by Leslie Brown et al., 67–82. New Brunswick, N.J.: Rutgers University Press, 2017.

McLaurin, Melton A. *Celia, a Slave: A True Story of Violence and Retribution in Missouri*. Athens: University of Georgia Press, 1991.

McNeil, Genna Rae. "'Joanne Is You and Joanne Is Me': A Consideration of African American Women and the 'Free Joan Little' Movement, 1974–1975." In *Sisters in the Struggle: African American Women in the Civil Rights–Black Power Movement*, edited by Bettye Collier-Thomas and V. P. Franklin, 259–79. New York: New York University Press, 2001.

———. "The Body, Sexuality and Self-Defense in *State vs Joan Little*, 1974–75." *Journal of African American History* 93, no. 2 (Spring 2008): 235–61.

Michaels, Jonathan. "'If Free People Are Not Allowed to Have Unions, How Are Prisoners to Have Unions?' Conversations with Organizers of North Carolina Prisoners' Labor Union." *Scalawag*, July 5, 2018. https://scalawagmagazine.org/2018/07/if-free-people-are-not-allowed-to-have-unions-how-are-prisoners-to-have-unions-conversations-with-organizers-of-the-north-carolina-prisoners-labor-union/.

Moody, Anne. *Coming of Age in Mississippi: An Autobiography*. New York: Dell, [1968] 1970.

Moraga, Cherrie, and Gloria Anzaldúa, eds. *This Bridge Called My Back: Writings by Radical Women of Color*. Watertown, Mass.: Persephone, 1981.

Morgan, Jennifer. *Laboring Women: Reproduction and Gender in New World Slavery*. Philadelphia: University of Pennsylvania Press, 2004.

———. *Reckoning with Slavery: Gender, Kinship, and Capitalism in the Early Black Atlantic*. Durham, N.C.: Duke University Press, 2021.

Morton, Patricia. *Disfigured Images: The Historical Assault on Afro-American Women*. New York: Greenwood, 1991.

Muhammad, Khalil Gibran. *The Condemnation of Blackness: Race, Crime, and the Making of Modern Urban America*. Cambridge, Mass.: Harvard University Press, 2010.

Murakawa, Naomi. *The First Civil Right: How Liberals Built Prison America*. New York: Oxford University Press, 2014.

Murch, Donna. "Crack in Los Angeles: Crisis, Militarization, and Black Response to the Late Twentieth-Century War on Drugs." *Journal of American History* 102, no. 1 (June 2015): 162–73.

NAACP-LDEF (National Association for the Advancement of Colored People–Legal Defense and Education Fund). *Death Row U.S.A., 2015*, Fall 2015, http://www.deathpenaltyinfo.org.

Nelson, Alondra. *Body and Soul: The Black Panther Party and the Fight Against Medical Discrimination*. Minneapolis: University of Minnesota Press, 2010.

Nelson, Jennifer. *Women of Color and the Reproductive Rights Movement*. New York: New York University Press, 2003.

Nichols, Susan Kelly. "Comments: Criminal Procedure—The North Carolina Fair Sentencing Act." *North Carolina Law Review* 60, no. 3 (1981): 631–55.

Ogbar, Jeffrey. *Black Power: Radical Politics and African American Identity*. Baltimore: Johns Hopkins University Press, 2004.

Olson, Lynne. *Freedom's Daughters: The Unsung Heroines of the Civil Rights Movement, 1830–1970*. New York: Scribner, 2001.

Orleck, Annelise. *Storming Caesars Palace: How Black Mothers Fought Their Own War on Poverty*. Boston: Beacon, 2005.

Orleck, Annelise, and Lisa Hazirjian, eds. *The War on Poverty: A New Grassroots History, 1964–1980*. Athens: University of Georgia Press, 2011.

Oshinsky, David. *Worse Than Slavery: Parchman Farm and the Ordeal of Jim Crow Justice*. New York, 1996.

Palacios, Lena. "The Prison Rape Elimination Act and the Limits of Liberal Reform." *Gender Policy Report*, February 17, 2017. https://genderpolicyreport.umn.edu/the-prison-rape-elimination-act-and-the-limits-of-liberal-reform.

Parenti, Christian. *Lockdown America: Police and Prisons in the Age of Crisis*. New York: Verso, 1999.

Perkinson, Robert. *Texas Tough: The Rise of America's Prison Empire*. New York: Picador, 2010.

Peskoe, Howard E. "The 1968 Safe Streets Act: Congressional Response to the Growing Crime Problem." *Columbia Human Rights Law Review* 5 (1973): 69–116.

Pinsky, Mark. "The Innocence of James Reston, Jr." *Southern Exposure* 6, no. 1 (Winter 1978): 39–41.

Plummer, Brenda Gayle. *In Search of Power: African Americans in the Era of Decolonization, 1956–1974*. Cambridge: Cambridge University Press, 2013.

Price, Pamela. Statement, *Alexander v. Yale*, December 21, 1977, https://www.clearinghouse.net/chDocs/public/ED-CT-0002-0010.pdf.

Prison Research Education Action Project. *Instead of Prisons: Handbook for Abolitionists*. Syracuse, N.Y.: Prison Research Education Action Project, 1976.

Purcell, John. "North Carolina: Corrections and Juvenile Justice in a Rural State." *Columbia Human Rights Law Review* 187 (1973): 187–206.

Rafter, Nicole Hahn. *Partial Justice: Women, Prisons and Social Control*, 2nd ed. New Brunswick, N.J.: Transaction, 1990.

Randolph, Sherrie M. "Women's Liberation or . . . Black Liberation, You're Fighting the Same Enemies: Florynce Kennedy, Black Power and Feminism." In *Want to Start a Revolution? Radical Women in the Black Freedom Struggle*, edited by Dayo F. Gore, Jeanne Theoharis, and Komozi Woodard, 223–47. New York: New York University Press, 2009.

Ransby, Barbara. *Ella Baker and the Black Freedom Movement: A Radical Democratic Vision*. Chapel Hill: University of North Carolina Press, 2005.

Ransby, Barbara, and Tracye Matthews. "Black Popular Culture and the Transcendence of Patriarchal Illusions." *Race and Class*, 1993. Reprinted in Guy-Sheftall, *Words of Fire*, 526–35.

Reagon, Bernice Johnson. "Coalition Politics: Turning the Century." In Smith, *Home Girls*, 356–68.

Reston, James, Jr. "The Innocence of Joan Little." *Southern Exposure* 6, no. 1 (1977): 36.

———. *The Innocence of Joan Little: A Southern Mystery*. New York: Times Books, 1977.

Reverby, Susan, and Byllye Avery. "Ask a Feminist: Byllye Avery Discusses the Past and Future of Reproductive Justice with Susan Reverby." *SIGNS*, July 25, 2019. www.signsjournal.org/avery/.

Richie, Beth E. "Battered Black Women: A Challenge for the Black Community." In Guy-Sheftall, *Words of Fire*, 398–404.

———. *Compelled to Crime: The Gender Entrapment of Battered Black Women*. New York: Routledge, 1996.

———. "A Black Feminist Reflection on the Antiviolence Movement." *SIGNS: Journal of Women in Culture and Society* 25, no. 4 (Summer 2000): 1133–37.

———. "Queering Anti-prison Work: African American Lesbians in the Juvenile Justice System." In *Global Lockdown: Race, Gender and Prison-Industrial Complex*, edited by Julia Sudbury, 73–85. New York: Routledge, 2005.

———. *Arrested Justice: Black Women, Violence and America's Prison Nation*. New York: New York University Press, 2012.

———. "How Anti-violence Activism Taught Me to Become a Prison Abolitionist." *Feminist Wire*, January 21, 2014.

Roberts, Dorothy. *Killing the Black Body: Race, Reproduction and the Meaning of Liberty*. New York: Vintage, 1999.

Rodrigues, Dylan. *Forced Passages: Imprisoned Radical Intellectuals and the U.S. Prison Regime*. Minneapolis: University of Minnesota Press, 2006.

Rostan, June. "Inside Out and Upside Down: An Interview with Anne Braden." *Colorlines* 4, no. 1 (Spring 2001). https://www.colorlines.com/articles/inside-out-and-upside-down-interview-anne-braden.

Roth, Benita. *Separate Roads to Feminism: Black, Chicana, and White Feminist Movements in America's Second Wave*. Cambridge: Cambridge University Press, 2003.

Schutz, J. Christopher. "The Burning of America: Race, Radicalism and the 'Charlotte Three' Trial in 1970s North Carolina." *North Carolina Historical Review* 76, no. 1 (January 1999): 43–65.

Scott, Joan. "The Evidence of Experience." *Critical Inquiry* 17, no. 4 (Summer 1991): 773–97.

Segrest, Mab. *Memoir of a Race Traitor*. Boston: South End, 1994; 25th anniversary ed., New York: New Press, 2019.

———. *Administrations of Lunacy: Racism and the Haunting of American Psychiatry at the Milledgeville Asylum*. New York: New Press, 2020.

Seigel, Micol. "Objects of Police History." *Journal of American History* 102, no. 1 (June 2015): 152–61.

Shakur, Assata. *Assata: An Autobiography*. Chicago: Lawrence Hill, 1978.

———. "Women in Prison: How We Are." *Black Scholar* 9, no. 7 (April 1978): 8–15.

Sharpe, Christina. *In the Wake: On Blackness and Being*. Durham, N.C.: Duke University Press, 2016.

Shirley, Neal, and Saralee Stafford. *Dixie Be Damned: 300 Years of Insurrection in the American South*. Oakland, Calif.: AK Press, 2015.

Showalter, Elaine. "Rethinking the Seventies: Women Writers and Violence." *Antioch Review* 74–75, no. 1–4 (Fall 2016/Winter 2017): 762–76.

Silliman, Jael, Loretta Ross, et al. *Undivided Rights: Women of Color Organize for Reproductive Justice*. Cambridge, Mass.: South End, 2004.

Simmons, Aisha Shahidah. "A State of Rage." In *Shout Out! Women of Color Respond to Violence*, edited by Maria Ochoa and Barbara K. Ige, 221–25. Emeryville, Calif.: Perseus/Seal, 2007.

Simon, Jonathan. *Governing Through Crime: How the War on Crime Transformed American Democracy and Created a Culture of Fear*. New York: Oxford University Press, 2007.

Smith, Barbara, ed. *Home Girls: A Black Feminist Anthology*. New York: Kitchen Table: Women of Color Press, 1983.

———. "Some Home Truths on the Contemporary Black Feminist Movement." In Guy-Sheftall, *Words of Fire*, 254–67.

Smitherman, Geneva. *African American Women Speak Out on Anita Hill–Clarence Thomas*. Detroit: Wayne State University Press, 1995.

Sommerville, Diane Miller. *Rape and Race in the Nineteenth-Century South*. Chapel Hill: University of North Carolina Press, 2004.

Spencer, Robyn C. "Engendering the Black Freedom Struggle: Revolutionary Black Womanhood and the Black Panther Party in the Bay Area California." *Journal of Women's History* 20, no. 1 (Spring 2008): 90–113.

———. *The Revolution Has Come: Black Power, Gender, and the Black Panther Party in Oakland*. Durham, N.C.: Duke University Press, 2016.

Springer, Kimberly. *Living for the Revolution: Black Feminist Organizations, 1968–1980*. Durham, N.C.: Duke University Press, 2005.

Stevenson, Bryan. *Just Mercy: A Story of Justice and Redemption*. New York: Spiegel and Grau, 2014.

Strum, Phillipa. "Pauli Murray's Indelible Mark on the Fight for Equal Rights." American Civil Liberties Union, June 24, 2020. https://www.aclu.org/issues/womens-rights/pauli-murrays-indelible-mark-fight-equal-rights.

Sturgis, Sue. "Moral Monday Movement Spreads Throughout the South." *Facing South: A Voice for a Changing South*, January 10, 2014.

Sweeney, Megan. *Reading Is My Window: Books and the Art of Reading in Women's Prisons*. Chapel Hill: University of North Carolina Press, 2010.

Taylor, Gregory S. *Central Prison: A History of North Carolina's State Penitentiary*. Baton Rouge: Louisiana State University Press, 2021.

Taylor, Keeanga-Yamahtta. *How We Get Free: Black Feminism and the Combahee River Collective*. Chicago: Haymarket, 2017.

Taylor, Ula. "Elijah Muhammad's Nation of Islam: Separatism, Regendering, and a Secular Approach to Black Power After Malcolm X (1965–1975)." In *Freedom North: Black Freedom Struggles Outside the South, 1940–1980*, edited by Jeanne Theoharis and Komozi Woodard, 177-198. New York: Palgrave, 2003.

———. *The Promise of Patriarchy: Women and the Nation of Islam*. Chapel Hill: University of North Carolina Press, 2017.

Theoharis, Jeanne. "I'd Rather Go to School in the South: How Boston's School Desegregation Complicates the Civil Rights Paradigm." In *Freedom North: Black Freedom Struggles Outside the South*, edited by Theoharis and Komozi Woodard, 125–51. New York: Palgrave, 2003.

———. "'They Told Us Our Kids Were Stupid': Ruth Batson and Boston's Educational Movement." In *Groundwork: Local Black Freedom Movements in America*, edited by Theoharis and Komozi Woodard, 17–44. New York: New York University Press, 2005.

———. *The Rebellious Life of Mrs. Rosa Parks*. Boston: Beacon, 2013.

Thompson, Becky. "Multiracial Feminism: Recasting the Chronology of Second Wave Feminism." *Feminist Studies* 28, no. 2 (2002): 336–60.

Thompson, Gail L. "Special Report II: African American Women and the U.S. Criminal Justice System: A Statistical Survey, 1890–2009." *Journal of African American History* 98, no. 2 (Spring 2013): 291–303.

Thompson, Heather Ann. "Blinded by a 'Barbaric' South: Prison Horrors, Inmate Abuse, and the Ironic History of American Penal Reform." In *The Myth of Southern Exceptionalism*, edited by Matthew Lassiter and Joseph Crespino, 74–51. New York: Oxford University Press, 2010.

———. "Why Mass Incarceration Matters: Rethinking Crisis, Decline, and Transformation in Postwar American History." *Journal of American History* 97, no. 3 (December 2010): 703–34.

———. "Rethinking Working-Class Struggles Through the Lens of the Carceral State: Toward a Labor History of Inmates and Guards." *Labor: Studies in Working-Class History of the Americas* 8, no. 3 (Fall 2011): 15–45.

———. *Blood in the Water: The Attica Prison Uprising of 1971 and Its Legacy*. New York: Penguin Random House, 2016.

Thuma, Emily. "Against the 'Prison/Psychiatric' State: Anti-violence Feminisms and the Politics of Confinement in the 1970s." *Feminist Formations* 26, no. 2 (Summer 2014): 26–51.

———. "Lessons in Self-Defense: Gender Violence, Racial Criminalization and Anti-carceral Feminism." *Women's Studies Quarterly* 43, no. 3/4 (Fall/Winter 2015): 52–71.

———. *All Our Trials: Prisons, Policing, and the Feminist Fight to End Violence*. Urbana: University of Illinois Press, 2019.

Tibbs, Donald. *From Black Power to Prison Power: The Making of "Jones v. North Carolina Prisoners' Labor Union."* New York: Palgrave/Macmillan, 2012.

Tyson, Timothy B. *Blood Done Sign My Name*. New York: Crown, 2004.

———. *The Blood of Emmett Till*. New York: Simon and Schuster, 2017.

———. *Radio Free Dixie: Robert F. Williams and the Roots of Black Power.* Chapel Hill: University of North Carolina Press, 2001.

Valk, Anne. *Radical Sisters: Second-Wave Feminism and Black Liberation in Washington, D.C.* Urbana: University of Illinois Press, 2008.

Van Camp, Louis. *Beaufort County, North Carolina.* Charleston, S.C.: Arcadia/Tempus, 2000, 2004.

Vera Institute of Justice. "The Price of Prisons: North Carolina, Fact Sheet." Center on Sentencing and Corrections, January 2012. www.vera.org/priceofprisons.

Wacquant, Loïc. "The Place of the Prison in the New Government of Poverty." In *After the War on Crime: Race, Democracy and a New Reconstruction,* edited by Mary Louise Frampton et al., 23–36. New York: New York University Press, 2008.

Wallace, Michele. *Black Macho and the Myth of the Superwoman.* New York: Dial, 1979.

Wandersee, Winifred. *On the Move: American Women in the 1970s.* Boston: G. K. Hall, 1988.

Welty, Jeff. "The Death Penalty in North Carolina: History and Overview." Working paper, University of North Carolina at Chapel Hill, School of Government, April 2012. http://www.deathpenaltyinfo.org.

Werner, Craig. *Higher Ground: Stevie Wonder, Aretha Franklin, Curtis Mayfield, and the Rise and Fall of American Soul.* New York: Crown, 2004.

White, Aaronette M. "Talking Black, Talking Feminist: Gendered Micromobilization Processes in a Collective Protest Against Rape." In *Still Lifting, Still Climbing: African American Women's Contemporary Activism,* edited by Kimberly Springer, 189–218. New York: New York University Press, 1999.

White, Deborah Gray. "Mining the Forgotten: Manuscript Sources for Black Women's History." *Journal of American History* 74, no. 1 (June 1987): 237–42.

———. *Too Heavy a Load: Black Women in Defense of Themselves, 1894–1994.* New York: W. W. Norton, 1999.

White, E. Frances. "Africa on My Mind: Gender, Counter Discourse and African-American Nationalism." *Journal of Women's History* 2, no. 1 (Spring 1990): 73–97.

Williams, Jacobi. *From the Bullet to the Ballot: The Illinois Chapter of the Black Panther Party and Racial Coalition Politics in Chicago.* Chapel Hill: University of North Carolina Press, 2013.

Williams, Rhonda Y. "Black Women, Urban Politics and Engendering Black Power." In *The Black Power Movement: Rethinking the Black Power–Civil Rights Era,* edited by Peniel Joseph, 79–103. New York: Routledge, 2006.

———. *Concrete Demands: The Search for Black Power in the 20th Century.* New York: Routledge, 2014.

Williams, Yohuru, and Jama Lazerow, eds. *Liberated Territory: Untold Local Perspectives on the Black Panther Party.* Durham, N.C.: Duke University Press, 2008.

Women's Legal Defense and Education Fund. "History of the Violence Against Women Act." Legal Momentum, n.d. https://www.legalmomentum.org/history-vawa.

Woodard, Komozi. *A Nation within a Nation: Amiri Baraka (LeRoi Jones) and Black Power Politics.* Chapel Hill: University of North Carolina Press, 1999.

INDEX

Page numbers in italics refer to illustrations.

Abernathy, Ralph, 34, 56–57, 268n9
abortion, 181, 187, 195, 230. *See also* reproductive justice; reproductive rights
Abzug, Bella, 39
ACLU (American Civil Liberties Union), 11, 106, 125, 233, 244; Women's Rights Project, 175
Action for Forgotten Women, 81, 107–11, *111*, 112–22, 282n18; Attica prison uprising and, 114–15; lawsuit on behalf of women prisoners, 117
Aegis / Feminist Alliance Against Rape (FAAR) newsletter, 126, 168, 170, 215, 221–22
African American singer-songwriters, prison and, 85–86
African American women. *See* Black women
African People's Socialist Party, 168, 293n50
Afro-American, 49, 71
Afro-American Patrolman's League, 220
Alderson Women's Penitentiary, 96

Allen, Lillie, 197, 199–200
Alliance Against Women's Oppression, 178
Alliance of Black Feminists, 220
allies. *See* white women; *and names of individual allies*
Alligood, Clarence: entering Little's cell, 28, 31, 69; discovery of his body, 1–2, 32–33; family of, 42, 66, 247; local praise of, 33, 263n3; sexual assault of Little, 20, 45, 64–67, 72–74, 83; various jobs of, 254n2; wife of, 66. *See also* Little, Joan, rape-murder trial of
American Civil Liberties Union. *See* ACLU
American Indian Movement (AIM), 159–61
Ames, Jessie Daniel, 212
Amnesty International, 24
Amsterdam News, 75, 98
Angela Davis Defense Committee, 294n3. *See also* Burnham, Linda; Mitchell, Charlene
antirape activism, 156, 173–74, 177, 190, 229, 213; and coalitions, 214–16;

331

antirape activism (*continued*)
  Black women and, 207; challenges of, 204, 207–8, 211, 213 (*see also* Brownmiller, Susan). *See also* Black women: antirape organizing and; coalition politics; LGBTQ+ activism
Asian Women's Health Organization, 202
Assata's Daughters, 242
Association of Southern Women for the Prevention of Lynching, 212
Atlanta Lesbian Feminist Alliance, 168, 302n24
Atlanta Socialist Feminist Women's Union, 168
Attica Brothers Defense Fund, 101
Attica News, 84, 117
Attica Prison, N.Y., 84, 278n5
Attica Prison rebellion, 75, 97–98; blamed on *Marxist* revolutionaries, 119; and fears of rebellion at Women's Prison, 111; violent suppression of, 133
Auburn Prison, N.Y., 84
Avery, Byllye, 179, 224, 238, 299n2, 299n10; Birthplace founder, 195; early life, 193–95, 197; and feminism, 193, 197–98; international work of, 202, 238; on lesbianism, 198; and sexual violence against Black women, 193, 194, 199–200, 224; on abortion rights, 195; Black women's health activism, 193–97. *See also* National Black Women's Health Project

Baker, Juanita, 109–10
Baldwin, James, 154–55
Baltimore Afro-American, 212
Baraka, Amina, 59
Baraka, Amiri, 59–60
Barber, William, II, 240
Barry, Marion, 190, 298n16
Battered Minority Women, 204
battered woman syndrome, 167
Bay Area Defense Committee for Battered Women, 171
Beal, Frances, 174

Beasley, Cheri, 237
Beaufort County, N.C., 14; grand jury in, 2, 32; sheriff of, 45
Beaufort County Jail, N.C., 1, 3, 11–12, 19–20, 28–29, 49, 56, 68–69, 72, 83, 145, 262n21
Beauvoir, Simone de, 163
Bedford Hills Prison, N.Y., 97, 106
Berger, Dan, 85–86, 90, 93–94, 96
Bernholz, Roger, 72
Bethea-Shields, Karen. *See* Galloway, Karen
Bethel, Lorraine, "What Chou Mean *We* White Girl?," 208
Bethune-Cookman College, 193, 200
Bevacqua, Maria, 207, 223
bibliotherapy, 123–25
Biden, Joseph, 232, 244, 285n13, 292n36
Black American Law Students Association, 171
"Black child-savers" movement, 87
Black feminism, 36, 88 173–78; critique of carceral policies, 228, 233, 239; critique of white feminists, 35, 173–74, 177, 208, 273n4, 294n5; influence of, 181, 217–18; on intraracial sexual violence, 172, 224; and multi-issue organizing, 173, 180–81, 188, 203, 206, 230, 242, 294n3; and National Black Women's Health Project, 101, 193, 197–98, 202; in the South, 177, 178, 179, 197; and Washington, D.C., Rape Crisis Center, 183–84, 186, 190, 192. *See also* intersectionality; "second wave" feminism; women's liberation: Black women and; *and names of individual feminists and organizations*
Black Left, 81–82; feminism of, 88
Black Liberation Army, 4, 128, 144
Black Lives Matter, 243, 247
Black men: and "Black beast rapist" myth, 59, 68, 154, 155, 191, 275n20; defense of Black women, 53, 54, 55–57, 155; disproportionate imprisonment of, 178, 191; and intraracial sexual abuse, 55, 59, 60, 62, 154, 172, 197, 203–4,

222, 224, 239. *See also* false accusations of rape; imprisonment
Black Men Against Rape, 190
Black nationalists, 33, 55, 59, 268n2. *See also* Black Power movement
Black on Vanguard, 134
Black Panther Party: assassination of Fred Hampton, 91, 276n5; and Attica prison revolt, 97; creation of, 89; Dessie X. Woods case and, 168; Free Breakfast Program, 91–92; Inez García case and, 162–63; Joan Little case and, 34, 57, 58–59, 60, 61, 83, 84, 93, 95, 139, 147; *Black Panther* newspaper, 60, 125, 168; police and FBI raids, 91, 94; prison movement and, 89–90, 93, 97, 125; survival programs, 91–92, 229, 276n7; Ten Point program, 90; in Winston-Salem, N.C., 21, 91, 92–93, 290n11; women in, 57, 58, 59–60, 61, 91, 93, 216, 229. *See also* Black Power movement; *and names of individual members*
Black Power movement, 1, 30, 33–34, 53, 81, 83, 131, 197, 268n1; and the prison movement, 89–90; government repression of, 91, 89–93, 94, 95, 275n4, 276n5; sexism in, 59–60, 187, 224; Women's Prison rhetoric of, 116, 131. *See also* Black nationalists; *and names of individual organizations*
Black Scholar, 55
Black Sisters United, 174
Black Voters Matter, 243
Black Woman's Bill of Rights (1976), 83
Black women, 44, 49; antirape organizing and, 112, 149, 155–56, 171–72, 173–74, 177–82, 203–6 (*see also* coalition politics; intersectionality; multi-issue organizing; National Black Women's Health Project; Rape Crisis Center, Washington, D.C.); accused of prostitution, 19–20 (*see also* Jezebel); imprisonment of, 5, 27, 243, 262n22; historical rape and sexual abuse of, 5, 62, 153–55; inspired by Black women's history, 201–2; intraracial sexual violence and, 154, 172, 196, 198, 199, 204, 239, 293n50, 307n22; and difficulty confronting intraracial sexual violence, 53, 59, 62, 172, 203, 222, 224, 227, 304n19; lethal self-defense and, 33, 154, 170–71; prison organizing and, 79–83, 85–88, 96–97, 100–101, 106, 108–15, *111*, 117, 124 (*see also* Action for Forgotten Women; prison activism; prison writing); support for, 154–55; trope of the "strong Black woman," 30, 31, 128, 200, 226, 227. *See also* Black feminism; *and names of individual women and organizations*
Black Women for Wages for Housework and Wages Due Lesbians, 216
Black Women Organized for Action, 35
Black Women's Health Imperative, 197, 202
Black Women's United Front, 33, 60, 175
Black Women's Wellness Center, 198
Bond, Julian, 34, 46, 56
Bounds, Lee, 99, 278n8
Braden, Anne: and antiracist organizing, 208, 210, 217; critique of Susan Brownmiller, 209–11; and Joan Little, 208, 210; and multiracial organizing, 217; and National Alliance Against Racist and Political Repression, 213, 214; "open letters" to southern white women, 211–12, 213, 222
Bradley, Mamie Till, 101
Break de Chains of Legalized U.$. Slavery, *111*, 113, 127–28, 129, 130, 131, 132–34, 137–38, *136*, 145
Brennan, William, 105
Brooks, Wayne, 100, 102
Brown, Elaine, 58–60, 62, 135
Brown, James, 85
Brown, Jerry, 165
Brownmiller, Susan, 210; African American reactions to, 208; *Against Our Will*, 208–9; Emmett Till lynching and, 209; racist stereotypes of Black men, 209–10
Brown v. Board of Education, 23
Bryant, Carolyn, 209

Index 333

Bullins, Ed, 34; *Jo Anne!*, 34
Bundy, Sarah, 171–72, 175
Burke, Yvonne Brathwaite, 36
Burnham, Linda, 174, 178, 180, 294n3
Butler, Salena Sloan, 87

California Prison Moratorium Project, 239
Calloway, Laine, 38
Camp Lejeune, 19–20
capital punishment: discriminatory use of, 87, 209, 223; in North Carolina, 82, 95, 104, 223, 255n7, 256n13, 277n16; increase under Donald Trump presidency, 243; opposition to, 95, 104, 223; and race, 223, 277n17; for rape, 59, 154, 191, 209, 223, 304n11 (*see also* false accusations of rape). *See also* Little, Joan, rape-murder trial of: and death penalty
carceral politics, 89–95. *See also* carceral solutions to sexual violence; carceral state
carceral solutions to sexual violence: dangers of, 210–11, 213, 215, 219–20, 221–22, 223–24, 225–27, 229; dilemmas for feminists and antirape activists, 220–23, 224, 226, 228; support for, 220, 223, 224, 225, 227–29. *See also* carceral politics; carceral state; prison abolition; restorative justice; Violence Against Women Act: critiques of
carceral state, 29, 231, 276n14; and Black women, 220; build-up of, 95, 232, 234, 275n3; in contrast to welfare state, 233, 234; organizing against, 237, 239–43. *See also* capital punishment; carceral politics; carceral solutions to sexual violence; imprisonment; mass incarceration; prison nation
Carey, Hugh, 4
Carmichael, Stokely, 86
Carolina Friends School, 80
Carter, Mandy, 214, 302n23
Casa Myrna Vasquez, 166
Castillo, Luis, 161, 165

Center for Constitutional Rights, 159
Center for Democratic Renewal / National Anti-Klan Network, 239
Central Prison, Raleigh, N.C., 24, 104, 108–9; protests at, 79, 99
Chalmers, Lester, 67, 69
Charlotte Three, 38, 105, 260n2
Chavis, Ben, 24
Chenier, Celine: and Action for Forgotten Women, 81, 110–12, 114, 115; and Free Joan Little campaign, 2, 79–80, 255n5, 273n2, 273n7; and Joan Little's political consciousness, 139; and prison activism, 80; and National Alliance Against Racist and Political Repression, 82
Chesimard, Joanne. *See* Shakur, Assata
Chicago Council on Crimes Against Women, 216
Chicago Defender, 34, 47, 220
Chicago Police Department, 220
Chicago Sun-Times, 220
Chisholm, Shirley, 34–36, 175, 178, 264n7, 295n6
Christmas, June Jackson, 196
Chung, Mary, 202
civility, 128, 286n16
Civil Rights Act: of 1871, 94; of 1964, 175
Civil Rights Congress, 87; "We Charge Genocide" (petition), 58
Clark, Ramsey, 85
Cleaver, Eldridge, 90, 268n7, 269n20, 269n26; rape and, 60; *Soul on Ice*, 60
Cleaver, Kathleen, 60, 216
Clinton, Bill, 232, 262n17
Coalition of Concerned Women in the War on Crime, 220
coalition politics, 35, 62, 156, 173, 178, 181, 204, 208, 210, 214, 216–17, 230, 239–40, 243, 268n1, 295n12, 296n21, 301n10, 303n35. *See also* multiracial activism; multiracial groups; *and names of individual organizations*
Coalition to Stop Institutional Violence (CSIV), 222
Coalition to Support Inez García and Joan Little, 165

Cobb, Charles, 40
Colvin, Claudette, 44
Combahee River Collective, 35, 174–75, 177, 180, 196, 214, 218, 286n19; "Statement," 177, 218
Committee for Abortion Rights and Against Sterilization Abuse, 181
Committee for a Unified Newark, 59
Communist Party, 61, 82, 273n7, 288n8; and Smith Act, 275n4
Comprehensive Employment and Training Act (CETA), 184, 192, 195
Compton YWCA Rape Crisis Center, 205, 206, 226–27
Concerned Women for Justice (CWJ), 81–82
Concerned Women for Justice for Joan Little, 21
Congressional Black Caucus, 232, 262n17, 278n6
Congress of African People, 59–60
Congress of Industrial Organizations, 81
Cooper, Anna Julia, 198–99; *A Voice from the South*, 198
Copelon, Rhonda, 291n18
Council of Southern Churchmen, 106
COVID-19, prisons and, 244, 308n36
crime, politics of: and federal anticrime legislation, 25–27; discriminatory sentencing and, 23–25; and federal funding, 25, 26–27, 28; and mass incarceration, 27, 28, 30; and prison population explosion in the South, 25, 27–28; and War on Poverty, 26. *See also* Crime Bill of 1994; Law Enforcement Assistance Act; Omnibus Crime Control and Safe Streets Act; Violence Against Women Act
Crime Bill of 1994, 232–33, 236, 305n1, 306n3; critiques of, 232–33, 236; and mass incarceration of people of color, 232, 262n17. *See also* Racial Justice Act; Violence Against Women Act
Critical Resistance, 206, 239
Crooks, Carol, 97
culture of dissemblance, 155

Dallas Women Against Rape, 170
Daughtry, Herbert, 4
Davis, Angela, 46, 87; appeal for Joan Little in *Ms.*, 61, 83, 213; Black feminism and, 175; critique of carceral solutions, 203, 206, 221–22, 239–40, 241, 274n9, 303n7; George Jackson's defense campaign and, 101; Joan Little's criticism of, 267n10, 273n7, 288n8; and National Alliance Against Racist and Political Repression, 61, 82, 213, 270n28; and National Black Women's Health Project, 201; prison as slavery, 108; sexual violence in prison and, 31, 146; support for Inez García, 163; support for Joan Little, 24, 31, 34, 61–62, 82–83, 203, 296n17; imprisonment and trial of, 90, 91, 138, 139, 267n8, 270n28. *See also* Angela Davis Defense Committee
Davis, Otis "Red," 11, 19, 73, 254n4
Davis, Sallye Bell, 87
Davis, Yvonne, 38
Davis-McCoy, Christina, 214
death penalty. *See* capital punishment
DeCrow, Karen, 36, 45, 84, 264n12
Dees, Morris, 42, 73–74, 266n26, 272n20
Delany, Sarah "Sadie," 124
Department of Correction (DOC), 27, 102, 105, 109, 118
Department of Justice, 226, 229, 236
Detroit House of Corrections, 96
Detroit Rape Crisis Center, 178
Detroit uprising of 1967, 93
Diallo, Dazon Dixon, 178–80, 196, 205, 296n15; *Sistas' Time*, 238
Division of Prisons (North Carolina), 120, 127
Dobbs Training School, 14, 109
Douglas, Emory, 135, 171
Du Bois, David, 269n17
Du Bois, W. E. B., 247, 269n17
Duke University, 14, 49, 68, 102
Dykes for the Second American Revolution, 168

Index 335

East Carolina University, 11, 45
East Los Angeles Rape Hotline, 166
Economist, 34
Edmiston, Rufus, 210
Education for Liberation, 185–86
Edwards, Ralph, 110, 116, 118
Eichelberger, Brenda, 101
Ellison, Cathy, 69, 265n17
Ellison, Ralph, 137
Emancipation, 55, 154, 202, 221, 268n10, 283n32
Emoli, Tamu Amaka. *See* Chenier, Celine
Eppinette, Charles, 102
Equal Rights Amendment, 120, 233
Ervin, Sam, 27
Evers, Medgar, 143

Fair Sentencing Act: of 1979, 24, 259n26; of 2010, 243
false accusations of rape, 59, 154, 290n10; Black men and, 208–9, 211–12, 222; Delbert Tibbs, 213, 302n19; Scottsboro Boys, 87, 101, 212, 279n15; Thomas Wansley, 211; Willie McGee, 39, 210; Willie Sanders, 212. *See also* lynching
FBI. *See* Federal Bureau of Investigation
Federal Bureau of Investigation (FBI), 91–92, 234, 276n8; Counterintelligence Program (COINTELPRO), 91, 170, 301n11; Crime Report, 25; definitions of rape and, 288n2; Most Wanted list, 46
Federal Bureau of Prisons, 125
Feminary, 126, 135–36, 146, 214
feminism, 6, 120, 175, 177, 197, 204, 217n18, 228, 234; and abolition feminism, 240; backlash against, 295n8; carceral feminism, 234; and white feminists, 35, 180–81, 203, 213; women of color and, 173, 294n3. *See also* Black feminism; Black Left: feminism of; "second wave" feminism; women's liberation; *and names of individual feminists and organizations*
Feminist Alliance Against Rape, 34, 163, 221. See also *Aegis*
Feminists Against Pornography, 208

Feminist Women's Health Network, 178
Fink, Elizabeth, 101
First National Conference on Third World Women and Violence, 172, 189, 192, 219–20
Floyd, George, 242, 274n17, 292n46
Folsom Prison, 119, 280n26
Ford, Gerald, 133
Ford, Laverne, 168
Fourteenth Amendment, 118
Freedom, Inc., 242
Free Inez García Committee, 162
Free Joan Little campaign, 2–4, 21, 31, 34–35, 44, 47, 62, 92, 161, 163, 168, 184, 247, 273n2, 273n7; antirape organizing and, 156, 229–30; and Little's prison writings, 146, 148; and Little's trial, 75, 79–80, 82–83, 85, 87, 210; national attention to, 207; white feminists and, 35, 180–81. *See also names of specific organizations*
Friedan, Betty, 163
Friedman, Deb, 215
Frinks, Golden, 2, 21, 39–40, 255n5, 265n21
Furman v. Georgia, 95

Gainesville Women's Health Center, 195
Galloway, Karen, 17, 49, 265n17, 272n20; assessment of Joan Little, 21, 47; cocounsel at Joan Little's rape-murder trial, 49–51, 50, 68, 69–70, 71; relationship with Joan Little, 267n15; on sexual abuse of incarcerated women, 115; on rape, 38–39, 65, 69
García, Inez, 33, 67, 126, 156, 162, 169–70, 215; benefit for, 164; guilty verdict, 163; lethal self-defense and, 161, 166; rape of, 161, 165–66; rape-murder trial of, 161–67, 169, 171, 219; second trial of, 165–66; supporters of, 163, 207
Garner, Eric, 242
Garry, Charles, 162
Gates, Daryl, 94
Gay Community News, 125

Georgia Alliance for Prison Alternatives, 168
Ginsberg, Ruth Bader, 175
Gonzalez, Lila, 165
Grady Hospital Rape Crisis Center, 188
Grant, Jim, 105, 121, 127, 279n21
Grasso, Ella, 45
Greensboro YWCA Public Affairs Committee, 38
Gregory, Dick, 34
Griffin, William, 64–67
Grimes, Sam, 18

Hale, Matthew, 153
Hamer, Fannie Lou, 86, 196
Hampton, Fred, 91, 276n5
Hardwick Prison, Ga., 168
Harris, Kamala, 244
Hatch, Orin, 232
Health and Hospital Workers Union (1199), 34
Hedgepath, Charsie, 82, 115
Height, Dorothy, 175
Hill, Anita, 173, 267n2
Hill, Marie, 109, 113, 126
Hobgood, Hamilton, 3, 39, 42, 51, 153
Holiday, Billie, 85; "Strange Fruit," 85
Holshouser, James, 105, 117, 120, 262n16, 262n21
Holtzman, Elizabeth, 39
Hooper, Shirley, 157–58
Hoover, J. Edgar, 91–92
Hopkins, Velma, 81–82
House Committee on Internal Security, 119
House Un-American Activities Committee, 42
Howard University, 187
Hudson, Michelle, 184
Hunt, Jim, 81, 121
Hurston, Zora Neale, 128; *Their Eyes Were Watching God*, 128, 286n17

incarceration. *See* imprisonment
"imminent danger," 167
imprisonment: of activists, 89, 93–94, 100, 105, 117, 122, 127, 128; alternatives to, 168, 221–22, 236, 239, 242 (*see also* prison abolition); Black artistic allusions to, 85–86; of women, 100, 134, 167, 219, 243; of men, 96; history of women's prison labor, 283n32; in North Carolina, 14, 25, 28, 121–22; of people of color, 219, 232, 239, 243; rape and, 148, 154, 155, 243. *See also* Black women: imprisonment of; Black men: disproportionate imprisonment of; carceral state; Crime Bill of 1994; mass incarceration
incarceration. *See* imprisonment; mass incarceration
INCITE! Women of Color Against Violence, 206, 239–40
Industrial Farm Colony for Women, 107, 280n1
Inez García Defense Committee, 165. *See also* "Viva Inez" campaign
Ingram, Rosa Lee, 87
Inmate Grievance Commission (1974), 105, 110, 118–19
In Our Own Voice, 238
International Council of African Women, 304n18
International Federation of Arab Attorneys, 34
International Tribunal on Crimes Against Women, 161
intersectionality, 83, 130, 160, 175, 177, 180, 213, 215, 230, 238–39, 286n19. *See also* multi-issue organizing

Jackson, George, 83, 90–91, 138, 143–44, 147, 267n8, 276n5; defense campaign of, 101; *Soledad Brother*, 127
Jackson, Georgia, 101
Jackson, Jesse, 98
Jalet, Frances, 101
January 6, 2021, insurrection, 244
Jet, 101
Jezebel, as sexual stereotype of Black women, 1, 20, 31, 44, 56, 58, 62, 154, 155, 158, 200
Jim Crow laws, 12, 30–31, 44, 64, 68, 133, 144, 154, 175, 231

Index   337

Jimenez, Dolores, 165
Jimenez, Miguel, 161
Joan Little Defense Committee, 255n5
Joan Little Defense Fund, 33, 38, 95
Johnson, Lyndon, 25–26, 94, 232; Great Society, 25
Jones, David, 102, 117–18
Jones, LeRoi. *See* Baraka, Amiri
Jones v. North Carolina Prisoners' Labor Union, 105, 148
Jordan, June, 196
Jordan, Susan, 161, 166

Kaba, Mariame, 75, 236, 241–42, 247
Karate for Women, 168
Karenga, Maulauna (Ron), 54–55, 57, 60, 62, 268n6
Kea, Morris, 112
Kennedy, Florence "Flo," 4, 34, 170, 216–17, 295n6
Kennedy, Robert F., 261n12
King, B. B., 85
King, Coretta Scott, 34
King, Edward, 216
King, Lourdes Miranda, 165
King, Martin Luther, Jr., 39, 137; allusions to by prisoner writers, 131, 143–44; assassination of, 57, 99; as charismatic leader, 196; Jerry Paul's invocation of, 68–69; on jail as metaphor, 86; "Letter from Birmingham Jail," 127. *See also* Southern Christian Leadership Conference
King, Yvonne, 229
Kinston Training School. *See* Dobbs Training School
KKK (Ku Klux Klan), 10, 42, 211, 214
Kunstler, William, 4, 42, 97, 159, 278n4, 291n18

Lake, I. Beverly, 23
Lambda Legal Defense Fund, 125
Largen, Mary Ann, 35, 39, 69, 225
Latinas, sexual stereotypes and, 165

Law Enforcement Assistance Act (LEAA) of 1965, 25, 27, 94, 261n14, 262n16, 262n21, 276n14, 304n20
Law Enforcement Assistance Administration (LEAA), 27–28, 178, 189, 225, 226, 228–29, 305n29
Lawson, Stanley, 162–63, 165
LEAA. *See* Law Enforcement Assistance Act; Law Enforcement Assistance Administration
Leadbelly, 85
Leadership Institute for Women, 204
League of United Latin-American Citizens, 163
lesbianism. *See* LGBTQ+ activism; LGBTQ+ issues
LGBTQ+ (lesbian, gay, bisexual, transgender, queer, plus) activism: and feminism, 174, 208; for prisoners, 84, 85, 125, 126, 287n3; in the South, 213–15. *See also* LGBTQ+ issues
LGBTQ+ issues: and censorship, 125, 244; and the International Council of African Women, 304n18; and legislation, 236, 237, and Moral Monday movement, 240; in National Black Women's Health Project, 198; as part of reproductive freedom, 181; rumors about Joan Little's sexuality, 19, 45; rumors about Nkenge Touré's sexuality, 172; vulnerability of southern Black queer people, 179, 296n17; and Washington, D.C., Rape Crisis Center, 191. *See also* coalition politics; *Feminary*; LGBTQ+ activism; multiracial activism; *and names of individuals and organizations*
Lesbian Tide, 126
Lewis, John, 232
Little, Jerome, 17, 246, 258n21, 266n25
Little, Jessie Ruth, 12–13, 18. *See also* Williams, Jessie
Little, Joan, *xiv*, 50, 71, 164, 215, 245–47, 254n1, 308n2; "committed youth offender" status denied to, 18, 27; comparisons to Rosa Parks, 5, 29,

338   Index

33, 43, 44, 49, 51, 52, 63, 68, 69, 75, 231, 247; death penalty and, 243; death threats against, 40; early life, 9, 11–15; as everywoman, 45–47; extradition to North Carolina, 4; felony theft case and, 3, 6, 16–18, 20, 23, 29–31, 75, 79, 145–46, 258nn20–21, 258n23; flight of, 19–20, 254n4; great-great-grandmother of, 80; human rights and, 54, 58; at Dobbs Training School, 109; negative public image of, 15, 19–22, 45; North Carolina Correctional Center for Women and, 3, 4, 19, 25, 79, 245, 256n11, 273n3; political consciousness of, 138, 139–46, 147–48; prison experiences of, 47, 145; prisoner protest and, 110, 117; public tours and speaking, 92, 146–47; racist stereotypes and, 221; Rikers Island jail and, 3, 84; rumors about sexuality of, 19, 45; sketch by, 142; "tough on crime" policies and, 28, writing ability, 21. *See also* Little, Joan, rape-murder trial of; Little, Joan, writings of; Free Joan Little campaign

Little, Joan, rape-murder trial of, 11, 42–43, 48, 266n27; acquittal, 3, 21, 22, 31, 59, 70, 74, 79, 117, 120, 146, 169, 273n7; and death penalty, 2, 5, 33, 42, 43, 62, 246; defense counsel, 39–43, 47, 48, 49–52, 50, 63, 65, 68–70, 71, 74, 75, 118, 271n2; Garcia case and, 33, 67, 161, 164; indictment of Little, 2, 32, 61; mishandling of evidence, 32–33, 73; lethal self-defense and, 67–68, 69, 141, 156, 188; Little's testimony at, 49, 63, 64–67, 70–71, 72, 74, 270n1; media attention to, 11, 39, 71, 95, 98, 126, 207; prosecution's use of stereotypes, 44–45; protests at, 35, 42, 37, 40, 54, 61; ramifications of, 5, 190, 219, 243, 245–46; support for Little during, 2, 33–39, 115, 174, 175, 179, 208, 210, 217; support for Little by prison activists, 80, 84–85, 104, 128; Wanrow case and, 33, 156, 158–59, 171; Woods case and, 33, 168–69, 171. *See also* Free Joan Little campaign; Galloway, Karen; Paul, Jerry

Little, Joan, writings of: "I Am Somebody," 140–41; "I Joan Little," 140; "Joan Little, from Cell 9, N.C.C.C.W.," 142, 143; "Joan—Walks with Dignity," 141; "Murder," 140, 143–44; "The Mystery of Black," 145; "Not a Poem, Just the Facts," 140; "To the People, from Lincoln's Gettysburg Address," 145

Little, Larry, 21, 92, 273n7, 276n10

Little, Malcolm. *See* Malcolm X

Little Washington, N.C. *See* Washington, N.C.

Lorde, Audre, 179

Lorton Prison, Va., 101, 112, 190, 279n16

Los Angeles Police Department, 94

Louisville Defender, 210

lynching, 61, 68, 154, 191; African American women and, 154, 290n7; Association of Southern Women for the Prevention of Lynching, 212; rape accusations and, 154, 223. *See also* Black men: and "Black beast rapist" myth; false accusations of rape; rape: Black men and

Lythcott, Ngina, 199, 299n10

Machtinger, Evelyn, 126
MacMillan, Jackie, 221
Madhubuti, Haki, 59–60
Mailman, Deborah, 102, 116
Malcolm X, 86, 90, 131, 143, 145, 227
Malcolm X Liberation University, 82
Manhattan House of Detention, N.Y., 125
March for Women's Lives (2004), 239
Marshall, Thurgood, 105
Martin, Robert, 17–18, 23–24
Martinez, Luz, 202
mass incarceration, 124, 225, 228, 232, 235; costs of, 95, 277n17 (*see also* "million-dollar blocks"); roots of, 27, 30, 93–94, 98, 263n26, 278n8; and subsidiary industries, 285n13. *See*

mass incarceration *(continued)*
    also carceral state; Crime Bill of 1994; imprisonment
Mathias, Charles, 36
Matteawan State Hospital for the Criminally Insane, 97
Mayor's Task Force on Rape (N.Y.), 178
McClellan, John, 25
McGee, Willie, 39, 210
McKinnon, Henry, 264n4
MeToo, 243, 247
Metropolitan Rape Crisis Council, 188
Midnight Special, 34, 84, 110, 116, 125, 132, 140
Milledgeville mental hospital, 169
"million-dollar blocks," 199
misogynoir, 295n9
Mitchell, Charlene, 74, 82, 273n7, 288n8
Mitchell, John, 91
Montgomery Bus Boycott, 33, 44, 86, 131
Moraga, Cherríe, 191, 298n21
Moral Mondays Movement, 240
Moreno, Dorenda, 163–64
Morgantown men's prison, 132
Morrison, Fred, 102–3, 105, 110
Moynihan, Daniel Patrick, 26
Ms., 61, 83, 128, 153, 161, 170, 213, 288n2, 288n8
Ms. Foundation, 235; "Safety and Justice for All," 235
Mueller, Robert, 288n2
multiracial activism, 230; in prisons, 97, 100, 112, 127, 136, 284n6; in the South, 214–15, 217. See also *Break de Chains of Legalized U.$. Slavery*; coalition politics; multiracial groups
multiracial groups, 140, 165, 170, 171, 178, 183, 210, 214–15, 222, 240, 275n22. *See also* coalition politics; multiracial activism; *and names of individual organizations*
multi-issue organizing: Black women and, 173, 175, 179, 180–81, 191–92, 203–5, 207, 218, 229–30, 238, 240–41, 294n3, 303n35; and needs of sexual violence survivors, 166, 183, 204, 206, 227–29. *See also* coalition politics; intersectionality; *and names of individual organizations*
Murray, Pauli, 175, 178, 295n6
My Sister's Place, 239

NAACP. *See* National Association for the Advancement of Colored People
Nairobi Third World Women's International Conference, 202
Nash, Diane, 86
National Alliance Against Racist and Political Repression, 61, 74, 82, 104, 109, 213, 270n28; Kentucky branch, 214
National Alliance of Black Feminists (NABF), 83, 101, 171, 177, 180, 216, 220–21
National Association for the Advancement of Colored People (NAACP), 10, 26, 58, 240; Legal Defense and Education Fund, 243; Legal Defense Fund, 223
National Association of Colored Women, 70; and prison activism, 87, 155, 290n11
National Black Feminist Organization (NBFO), 35, 163, 175, 177, 180, 216
National Black Justice Coalition, 302n23
National Black United Front, 4, 59, 187, 269n18; Women's Section, 187
National Black Women's Health Project (NBWHP), 179, 182, 187, 203, 238, 239; Black women's storytelling and trauma, 199–201; class issues and, 196, 198–99; creation of, 193, 197; feminism and, 193, 197–98; first national Black women's health conference and, 196–97, 198; and critique of VAWA, 233; lesbianism and, 198; "Black and Female" self-help workshops, 200–201; sexual violence and, 193, 199–202; *Vital Signs*, 201, 209
National Center for the Prevention and Control of Rape, 189, 225
National Coalition Against Domestic Violence, 204

National Committee to Defend Dessie X. Woods, 168. *See also* Woods, Dessie X.
National Committee to Free Angela Davis, 82
National Conference of Black Lawyers, 117, 245–46
National Conference of Puerto Rican Women, 163, 165
National Conference on Third World Women and Violence. *See* First National Conference on Third World Women and Violence
National Council of Churches, 4
National Council of Negro Women, 86, 175
National Crime Victimization Survey, 226
National Gay Task Force, 125
National Guard, 92
National Institute of Mental Health, 225
National Institutes of Health, 238
National Latina Health Project, 202
National Lawyers Guild, 161
National Negro Congress, 58; "We Charge Genocide" (petition), 58
National Organization for Women (NOW), 35–38, 69, 84, 161, 175, 264n12, 274n12, 295n6, 301n10; Biloxi chapter, 163; Chapel Hill chapter, 223; Charlotte chapter, 38; Criminal Justice Task Force, 35–36; Greensboro chapter, 38; Fayetteville-Cumberland chapter, 38, 179, 213–14; "Free Our Sisters: Free Ourselves," 45; Legal Defense and Education Fund, 232; Minority Women's Task Force, 35–36; North Carolina State Convention, 36–38; Northern Virginia chapter, 35; Poverty Task Force, 35–36; protests at Wake County Courthouse, 38; Raleigh chapter, 35; Rape Task Force, 35–36, 38, 225; support for Joan Little, 35–38, 45–46, 213; Women of Color programs, 187, 239. *See also* DeCrow, Karen; Largen, Mary Ann
National Prison Congress, 124

National Rifle Association, 233
National Women's Health Network, 196, 238
National Women's Political Caucus, 39, 175
Nation of Islam (NOI), 59, 90, 94, 97, 139, 288n8
Nelson, Marjorie, 36, 161
neo-Nazis, 214
Newton, Huey, 57, 59, 90, 139, 269n26, 276n4
New Women's Times, 46, 126, 168
New York Police Department, 3, 144
New York Radical Feminists, 70
New York Training School for Girls (Hudson Prison), 162
New York Women Against Rape, 178
Nixon, Richard, 26, 91, 94, 143; "law and order" campaign, 25, 30
No More Cages, 34
No More Prisons, 239
North Carolina, 2, 8, 120, 247; capital punishment in, 2, 79, 95, 104, 255n7, 256n13, 277n17; civil rights movement in, 69, 93, 213; crime rates in, 25; criminal justice system in, 14, 18, 23–25, 28, 30, 33, 75, 82, 85, 93, 95, 125, 127, 154, 237, 244, 257n15, 260n8, 285n18; and LEAA, 27, 263n16; and Moral Mondays Movement, 240; prison sexual abuse in, 36, 115; prison violence in, 96, 98–100, 113–15; "progressive mystique" of, 32, 128, 286n16; and Racial Justice Act, 237–38, 240, 256n13, 307n25; rape laws of, 69, 153. *See also* Beaufort County, N.C.; imprisonment: in North Carolina; *Jones v. North Carolina Prisoners Labor Union*; Washington, N.C.
North Carolina Agricultural and Technical College, 92
North Carolina American Federation of Labor–Congress of Industrial Organizations (AFL-CIO), 106
North Carolina Bar Association, 14, 36, 42
North Carolina Central University, 178

North Carolina Coalition Against the Death Penalty, 104
North Carolina Correctional Center for Women (NCCCW), 3, 19, 38, 79–80, 97–98, 100, *111*, 125, 127–28, 133, 139–40, 146, 213–14; strikers in yard, 38, *113*; Central Prison lawsuit, 131; class action suit against, 121; disproportionate women of color at, 281n7; prison movement in, 79; prison writing and, 123; prisoner protests at, 25, 107–12, *113*, 114–23, 126, 130, 132, 135, 146; and unpaid labor, 109, 112, 127; vocational training at, 120. *See also* Action for Forgotten Women; *Break de Chains of Legalized U.$. Slavery*; Little, Joan, writings of
North Carolina Court of Appeals, 75, 79
North Carolina General Assembly, 118; Commission on Correctional Programs, 24; Legislative Research Commission, 118, 123
North Carolina Hard Times Prison Project, 127, 283n4
North Carolina Industrial Farm Colony for Women, 107
North Carolina Prisoners' Labor Union (NCPLU): creation of, 100, 102, 260n2; crucial support of women and, 100–101, 240; labor issues and, 100, 102–5; multiracial board, 100; newsletter, 100; opposition to death penalty, 104; and prison abolition, 102. See also *Jones v. North Carolina Prisoners' Labor Union*
North Carolina State Bureau of Investigation, 48, 70
North Carolina Supreme Court, 75, 237
North Carolinians Against Racist and Religious Violence, 214
Northside Rape Crisis Intervention (Chicago), 216
NOW. *See* National Organization for Women

Obama, Barack, 243, 306n17, 308n34
Odden, Jane, 162

Odum Prison Farm, 116
Office of Criminal Justice Planning, 225, 227–28
Office of Violence Against Women, 236
off our backs, 34, 125, 140, 146, 168, 170
Omnibus Crime Control and Safe Streets Act (1968), 25, 94
Orange County Rape Crisis Center, 223
Organization of Black Liberation, 92, 276n8
Outlaw, 125
Owens, Betty Jean, 155
Owens, Paulette, 178

Parks, Rosa: legacy of, 192; support for rape victims, 33, 87, 155; Joan Little compared to, 5, 29, 33, 43, 44, 49, 51, 63, 68, 69, 75, 231, 247; Joan Little Defense Committee, 87, 231; and Montgomery Bus Boycott, 44, 49, 86, 231; politics of respectability and 49, 52, 68
Paul, Jerry, 2, 36, 48, 49–51, 50, 92, 265n17, 271n11; antiracist views of, 11; appeal of Joan Little's theft conviction, 17–19; assessment of Joan Little, 21; background of, 11, 32; and Black clients, 32,; closing summation of, 43, 68–69; contempt of court charge, 42; disparagement of legal system, 73–74, 166; invocations of Rosa Parks, 33, 49, 51, 52, 68, 69; and Jael news clipping, 73–74, 272n20; lawsuit against, 40; on Little's testimony, 63, 271n2; and the press, 39, 50, 73; on racism in the South, 20, 32; unconventional tactics of, 42–43
Payne, Ethel, 47, 220
Peachy, Willis, 33
Perdue, Bev, 24
Personal Responsibility and Work Opportunity Act, 232
Peten, Cassandra, 171
Pharr, Suzanne, 214
Phoebe, Afi, 35
Pickett, Walter, 45
Pine Ridge Reservation, S.D., 160

Poor People's Campaign, 39, 240
police shootings: of Black youth 144, 288n7, 292n46, 302n24; of Breonna Taylor, 274n17; of Fred Hampton, 91, 276n5; of George Floyd, 242, 274n17, 292n46
Pratt, Minnie Bruce, 38, 179, 213, 214, 296n17, 302n21; Womanwrites statement, 214; *Yours in Struggle*, 214
President's Commission on the Status of Women (1961), 175
Price, Amma, 171–72
Pride Inc., 190
prison, compared to slavery, 5, 83, 96, 105, 103, 108, 109, 117, 127, 128, 129, 145. See also *Break de Chains of Legalized U.$. Slavery*; Thirteenth Amendment: forced labor loophole
prison abolition, 1, 106, 111, 120, 149, 226, 233, 237, 242, 247; "abolition feminism" and, 240; movement, 83–85, 90; not central to civil rights movement, 86; NCPLU and, 102. *See also names of individual activists*
prison activism, 98, 89, 112, 213, 263n27. *See also* prisoner unions; prison movement; prison writing; protests; *and names of individual activists*
prisoners, political: Inez García as, 165; Joan Little as, 83, 85, 139, 148, 149; Joan Little's support of, 93, 147; social/common criminals and prisoners as, 6, 81, 83, 85, 130, 134. *See also names of individuals and organizations*
Prisoners Against Rape, 84, 101, 190, 298n17
Prisoners' Legal Services, 121
Prisoners' Rights Organized Defense, 117
Prisoners Solidarity Committee, 84–85
prisoner unions, 106, 280n26. *See also* North Carolina Prisoners' Labor Union
prison libraries, 123–25. *See also* prison writing
Prison Litigation Reform Act, 94–95
prison movement, 79–89, 96–106. *See also* prison abolition

prison nation, 95, 206, 277n18. *See also* carceral state
prison "parity" movement, 120
Prison Rape Elimination Act, 237
prison writing, 123, 126–27, 131, 133, 138; at Woman's Prison, 123, 126–37, 287n3. *See also* bibliotherapy; *Break de Chains of Legalized U.$. Slavery*; Little, Joan: political consciousness of; Little, Joan, writings of
protests, 54, 103; at Central Prison, Raleigh, N.C., 79, 99; at North Carolina Correctional Center for Women, 25, 84, 107–12, 109, 113, 114–23, 126, 130, 132, 135, 146; by prisoners, 79, 84, 96–98, 99, 100, 102, 107, 111–15; at trial of Joan Little, 35, 41; at Wake County Courthouse, 37, 40
Public Enemy, 85
Puerto Rican Women's Prison Project, 84
Purner, Robbie, 100, 102, 103, 240

racial insensitivity: of white antirape activists, 203, 204, 207–8, 211–13, 216, 217; of white feminists, 213. *See also* Brownmiller, Susan; racism; white supremacy; white women: and racial privilege; white women: racializing armed self-defense
Racial Justice Act, 234
racism: in Beaufort County and Little Washington, 1, 9, 11–12, 32; in criminal legal system, 22–25, 74, 94, 141, 190; Joan Little's experience of, 1, 4, 6, 140; rape as tool of, 53, 55, 62, 215; and sexism, 1, 55, 83, 117, 175, 183, 207, 215, 299n10; in Wanrow case, 160; Women's Prison protests against, 108, 117, 130–31. *See also* racial insensitivity; white supremacy
Rainey, Ma, 85
Raising Women's Voices for the Health Care We Need, 238
Raleigh Feminists Organized for Action, 35
Raleigh Women's Prison. *See* North Carolina Correctional Center for Women

Index 343

Randolph, Louis, 33, 40, 75
Ranson, Rebecca, 287n3
rape, 211, 213; abortion and, 195; Black men and, 211–12; 223; lynching and, 154, 191; in men's prisons, 275n20; in North Carolina law, 153; race and, 210–12, 215–16, 222; race and history of, 153–55. *See also* capital punishment: for rape; false accusations of rape; sexual violence
Rape Action Project, 216
Rape Crisis Center, Chapel Hill–Carrboro, N.C., 217
Rape Crisis Center, Washington, D.C. (RCC), 101, 112, 156, 163, 173, 183–92, 185, 208, 215, 220, 224, 238; antirape events, 191; origins of, 183
"rape survivor," as term, 226–27
Reagan, Ronald, 225, 262n17; War on Drugs, 25, 30
Reagon, Bernice Johnson, 34, 46, 161; lyrics to "Joanne Little," 86, 274n17
Reddick, Byllye Yvonne. *See* Avery, Byllye
Rehnquist, William, 105
Reidsville Prison, Georgia, 167
Repairers of the Breech, 240
reproductive freedom. *See* abortion; reproductive justice; reproductive rights
reproductive justice, 179, 181, 187, 238–39
reproductive rights, 181, 187, 193, 230
Reproductive Rights National Network, 181
Republic of New Afrika, 134
respectability, politics of, 5, 20, 21, 33, 44, 47, 52, 68, 86, 128, 141, 168, 267n15
restorative justice, 236
Richie, Beth, 191, 203–6, 233, 235–36, 237
Rikers Island Prison, N.Y., 3–4, 84, 117
Robinson, Ruby Doris Smith, 86
Rockefeller, Nelson, 97–98, 133; drug laws and, 98
Roe v. Wade, 195
Rogers, Julius, 14–19, 28, 72
Rosa Parks Rape Crisis Center, 205, 226–27

Ross, Loretta, 156, 183, *186*, 198, 201; achievements of, 187, 239; early life of, 187; and antirape organizing, 187–88; and Black feminism, 173, 188; critique of criminal justice system, 219; and Dessie X. Woods, 290n12; and National Black Women's Health Project, 187, 196–97, 198; National Conference on Third World Women and Violence and, 189–92, 219; on sexual abuse of Black women, 200, 219; and International Council on African Women, 304n18; on intraracial sexual violence, 224, 304n19; leader of Washington, D.C., Rape Crisis Center, 184, *186*, 187–88, 191–92; and Prisoners Against Rape, 101, 190; *We Remember* (pamphlet), 187
Royko, Mike, 71
Ruiz v. Estelle, 94

Safe Streets Act (1968), 27
Saint-Marie, Buffy, 159
Sampson County Prison, 116
Sanders, Willie, 212
San Francisco Concilio Mujeres, 163–64
San Francisco Gay Latino Alliance, 163
San Quentin Prison, Calif., 109, 119, 280n26
San Quentin Six, 130, 147
Santa Cruz Women Against Rape, 215; "Letter to the Anti-rape Movement," 215
Santa Cruz Women's Prison Project, 83
Saphire Saphos, 208
Sawyer, Sherwood, 15, 19
Say Her Name movement, 243, 247
Schlafly, Phyllis, 233
Schneider, Elizabeth, 159, 161
SCLC. *See* Southern Christian Leadership Conference
Scott, Leroy, 17, 29
Scott, Linda, 169–70
Scott-Heron, Gil, 85
Scottsboro Boys case, 87, 101, 212, 279n15

Seale, Bobby, 135; *Seize the Time*, 135, 287n33
"second wave" feminism, 81; and Black women, 88, 173–74, 230, 271n12; and critique of declension narrative, 6, 295n8; critique of "wave" paradigm, 6, 174, 230, 294n5. *See also* Black feminism; women's liberation
Segrest, Mab, 126, 213–14, 302n21; *Memoir of a Race Traitor*, 215
self-defense: against sexual violence, 37, 54, 57–58, 60, 155, 159, 167, 171, 180, 205, 244, 247; armed, 56–57, 113, 114, 170, 241, 268n1, 268n10; Black men's support of women's, 53, 55; lethal, 29, 33, 51, 126, 130, 148, 156, 159–60, 171, 231, 290n7, 290n11, 290n17, 291n22; National Organization for Women and, 35, 36, 38. *See also* García, Inez; Little, Joan, rape-murder trial of: lethal self-defense and; Wanrow, Yvonne; Woods, Dessie X
sexual assault. *See* sexual violence
sexual violence, 29; Dessie X. Woods case, 167–69, Black women and, 190, 220–21; Inez García case and, 161–67, 164, 170; incarcerated women and, 36, 83, 115, 168, 175; Yvonne Wanrow case and, 156–61, 157, 166–67. *See also* Black women: historical rape and sexual abuse of, Black women: intraracial sexual violence and; carceral solutions to sexual violence; Little, Joan, rape-murder trial of; rape
Shakur, Assata, 4, 117, 128, 130, 134, 145, 242; "To My People," 143–45
Shelton, Robert, 42
Sheridan Correctional Center for Men, Humanities Project, 101
Simone, Nina, 86; "Mississippi Goddam!," 86
Sister Love, 178–79, 238
"Sisters and Allies" (workshop series), 197
SisterSong Women of Color Reproductive Justice Collective, 238, 239
Slifkin, Miriam, 223

Sloan, Margaret, 163, 295n6
Smith, Barbara, 172, 174, 196, 294n62, 298n21, 304n18; *Yours in Struggle*, 214
Smith, Bessie, 85
Smith, Beverly, 196
Smith, Mary Louise, 44
Smith Act, 91
SNCC. *See* Student Nonviolent Coordinating Committee
Sojourners for Truth and Justice, 87–88; 275n22
Soledad Brothers, 90
Soledad Prison, 98, 101–2, 162
Southern California Rape Hotline Alliance, 206
Southern Christian Leadership Conference (SCLC), 2, 21, 39–40, 56, 91
Southern Coalition on Jails and Prisons, 85, 95
Southern Conference Education Fund, 211
Southerners Organized on New Ground, 215
Southern Exposure, 140
Southern Negro Youth Congress, 87, 294n3
Southern Organizing Committee for Economic and Social Justice, 210
Southern Patriot, 127, 210–11
Southern Poverty Law Center, 42, 57
Spain, Johnny, 147
Spelman College, 196
State University of New York (Buffalo), women's prison abolition group, 84
State vs. Wanrow, 156, 159–60
Stearns, Nancy, 159
Steinem, Gloria, 163, 170
Stender, Faye, 101
Stevens, John Wesley, 185
Stroud, Anita. *See* Touré, Nkenge
Strudwick, Christine, 21, 81
Student Nonviolent Coordinating Committee, 34, 46, 86, 174
Swan, Yvonne Wanrow. *See* Wanrow, Yvonne

SWAT teams, 94
Sweet Honey in the Rock, 86, 207, 274n17; "Joan Little," 34, 46

Take Back the Night marches, 181, 208, 214, 230; Atlanta, 197; Chicago, 216; Milwaukee, 215
Taylor, Breonna, 274n17
Taylor, Recy, 87, 275n21
Terrell, Mary Church, 87, 275n22
Texas prisoners' litigation movement, 101
Theiler, Mary Alice, 161
"Third World," as term, 294n3
Third World Women's Alliance, 35, 126, 163, 175–76; armed self-defense and, 170; West Coast branch, 174, 178
Thirteenth Amendment, 99, 129, 149; forced labor loophole, 278n8. *See also* prison, compared to slavery
Thomas, Clarence, 173, 267n2
Through the Looking Glass (newsletter), 126
Thurmon, Strom, 27
Tibbs, Delbert, 213, 302n19
Till, Emmett, 101, 143, 279n15, 301n7; lynching of, 208–9
Todd, Cheryl. *See* Woods, Dessie X.
Touré, Nkenge, 185, 187, 197; and antirape organizing, 156, 172, 187, 192; and Black Panther Party, 185; on coalitions, 216; critique of criminal justice system, 190, 220; and Dessie X. Woods case, 169, 290n12; early life, 185; on government funding for rape crisis centers, 225; housing activism and, 187, 238; *In Our Voices*, 239; inspired by Joan Little case, 156, 183, 190; leader of Washington, D.C., Rape Crisis Center, 184–86; and multi-issue organizing, 238–39, 240–41; and National Black Women's Health Project, 196–97; and National Conference on Third Women and Violence, 189–91; and U.N. Conference on Third World Women, 304nn18–19

Treadwell, Mary, 190
Triangle Area Lesbian Feminists, 82, 112, 115, 127, 214, 281n14, 284n7
Triple Jeopardy, 126
Trump, Donald, 243, 277n17, 308n34
Truth, Sojourner, 57, 134
Tubman, Harriet, 57, 134
Turner, Doris, 34
Tuskegee Veterans Hospital, 124
Tyson, Mike, 239

U.N. Conference on Third World Women, 304n18
U.N. Decade for Women, 179–80
United Church of Christ Commission for Racial Justice, 40
United Farm Workers, 163
United Nations, 58, 269n18; Convention of the Elimination of All Forms of Discrimination against Women, 296n20
United Prisoners Union, 106, 280n26
University of California, Berkeley, 90; "Tear Down the Walls" forum, 90
University of North Carolina at Chapel Hill, 11, 114, 200, 214
UpFront, 224
Us Organization. *See* Karenga, Maulauna
U.S. Civil Rights Commission, 26, 117
U.S. Congress, 26, 94, 117, 232, 235
U.S. Department of Justice, 34, 36, 114, 175
U.S. Supreme Court, 11–12, 23, 94–95, 105, 148, 195
Utter, Robert, 160

Vermont Network Against Domestic and Sexual Violence, 235
Violence Against Women Act (VAWA): amendment and expansions of, 236; critiques of, 233–37, 306n6; opposition to, 306n5, 306n17
Violent Crime Control and Law Enforcement Act, Title IV, 232
"Viva Inez" campaign, 163
Volunteers in Service to America, 184

Waddell, Joe, 93
Waddell v. North Carolina, 277n16
Walker, Alice, 177; "In Search of Zora Neale Hurston," 128
Wanrow, Yvonne (Swan), 33, 126, 157, 157, 158, 215; case of, 163; lethal self-defense and, 156–59, 161, 166, 171; reduced charges, 161; second-degree murder charge and conviction, 158, 159; self-defense trial of, 158–59, 161, 171; and son Darren, 158; stereotypes of Native Americans and, 159; support for, 161, 207; as one of first "woman's self-defense cases," 156–61
Wansley, Thomas, 211
Ward, Yolanda, 112, 187, 224, 304n17
War on Crime, 29, 232
War on Drugs, 27–29, 94, 261n13
War on Poverty, 229, 232
Warwick, Dee Dee, 34; "She Was Just One Woman," 34
Washington (D.C.) Star-News, 34
Washington, D.C., Department of Corrections, 172
Washington, D.C., Rape Crisis Center. *See* Rape Crisis Center, Washington, D.C.
Washington, Desiree, 239
Washington, N.C., 10–15, 17, 19, 21, 22, 28, 32, 33, 39, 48, 64, 72, 75, 247, 251. *See also* Beaufort County, N.C.
Washington State Supreme Court, 159
Watergate, 11, 143
Waters, Maxine, 228
Watts rebellion (1964), 124
Wells, Ida B., 87, 155, 192, 268n10
Western Correctional Institute, 115–16, 118
White, Leon, 40
White Panthers Criminal Justice Committee, 84
white supremacy, 1, 39, 55, 87, 128, 130, 144, 210, 211, 213, 215, 244, 275n22. *See also* racism
Whiteville Seventeen, 116
white women: as allies of Black women, 183–84, 187, 192, 196, 197; and anticarceral politics, 221–22; and antiracism, 180, 208, 210, 213–15, 301n18; appeal to support Joan Little by Black women, 35, 37, 217; and racial disparities in rape sentences, 205, 209; and racial privilege, 210, 212, 225; racializing armed self-defense, 171; and "second wave" feminism, 88, 173–75, 230; southern, as ladies, 51; and "whiteness," 20, 46, 57; and capital punishment, 223. *See also* coalition politics; false accusations of rape; LGBTQ+ activism, multiracial activism; racial insensitivity; women's liberation: whitewashing of; *and names of individual women*
Wilkerson, John, 42, 67, 266n25
Williams, Arthur, 13, 247
Williams, Jessie, 12, 13, 14, 40, 73
Williams, Malcolm "Mike," 245, 246, 258n23
Williams, Monica, 206, 226–27
Williams, Willis, 12–13
Wilmington Ten, 81–82, 260n2; trial of, 23
Winston-Salem (N.C.) Black Panther Party, 21, 91, 92–93. *See also* Little, Larry
Wiseman, Myrtle "Lulu Belle" Cooper, 223
womanism. *See* Black feminism
Women Against Prison, 83
Women Armed for Self-Protection (WASP), 170
Women Free Women in Prison, 84, 222
Women of All Red Nations, 161
women of color, 174, 177, 181; affected by government funding for rape crisis centers, 225–26, 228–29; and armed self-defense, 159–60, 169, 170–71; and NOW, 35, 187, 239, 264n12; organizing against sexual violence, 6, 156, 173, 184, 188–91, 192, 204, 206, 216, 219, 235, 240–41; and prison activism 83–84, 126, 240–41; and sexual harassment cases, 172; and Violence Against Women Act, 233–34, 306n6. *See also* First National Conference on

women of color (*continued*)
  Third World Women and Violence; García, Inez; intersectionality; Wanrow, Yvonne; *and names of organizations*
Women of Color Resource Center, 174, 180
Women Organized Against Rape, 178
Women's Anti-rape Coalition, 216
Women's Committee for Equal Justice, 87
Women's Equality Day March, 170
Women's International League for Peace and Freedom, 117
Women's Law Project, 288n2
women's liberation, 52, 58, 83, 231; Black women and, 6, 17, 81, 173–75, 176, 177–78, 180, 181, 192, 197; FBI surveillance of groups, 170; prison activism and, 85, 126, 128, 134, 180; southern women and, 178–79, 211–12, 215; whitewashing of, 70, 177. *See also* Black feminism; Black Left: feminism of; feminism; "second wave" feminism; *and names of individuals*
Women's Prison. *See* North Carolina Correctional Center for Women
Women's Self-Defense Project, 171; *Women in Self-Defense Cases*, 171
Women's Union, 168
Woods, Dessie X: case of, 167–69, 219; children of, 169; convicted of voluntary manslaughter, 167–68; *Aegis / Feminist Alliance Against Rape (FAAR)* newsletter and, 126, 221; lethal self-defense and, 126, 156, 157, 171, 188; killing of Ronnie Horne, 167, 171; support for, 33, 130, 168, 188, 207; Washington, D.C., Rape Crisis Center and, 290n12
Wounded Knee, 160
Wright, Marjorie, 72, 73

Yale University, 172, 294n61
Youth Against War and Fascism, 84

www.ingramcontent.com/pod-product-compliance
Lightning Source LLC
Chambersburg PA
CBHW030519230426
43665CB00010B/684